In his native land,

A Dutch host utters

these words before each meal

"Eet Smakelijk"

Meaning to eat well and with taste.

Eet Smakelijk

A COLLECTION OF RECIPES

by

MEMBERS AND FRIENDS

of

JUNIOR WELFARE LEAGUE

of

HOLLAND, MICHIGAN

OFFICIAL COOKBOOK OF HOLLAND, MICHIGAN

Proceeds to be used by the Junior Welfare League of Holland for the continuance of charitable community service projects in health, welfare and education, especially for children.

First Edition – April 1964
  Second Printing – November 1964
  Third Printing – June 1966
  Fourth Printing – June 1967
  Fifth Printing – April 1969
  Revision – September 1970
  Seventh Printing – October 1971
  Eighth Printing – September 1973
Second Edition – April 1976
  Second Printing – April 1977
  Third Printing – May 1980
  Fourth Printing – May 1982
  Fifth Printing – January 1985
  Sixth Printing – March 1989
  Seventh Printing – May 1996
  Eighth Printing – August 2001

We are grateful to:

Mrs. Thomas DePree, whose untiring efforts made the original EET SMAKELIJK possible and to Mrs. Ronald Boeve, the revision editor.

For additional copies of "Eet Smakelijk"
turn to the last page of the book for
price, mailing card and charges.

ISBN 0-9612710-0-0

HOLLAND JUNIOR WELFARE LEAGUE
P.O. Box 1633
HOLLAND, MICHIGAN 49422
www.hjwl.org

PUBLISHED BY
the
 **PRINTERY**
A Subsidiary of
Steketee-Van Huis, Inc.

Contents

Trade names of products are given only when necessary. Many recipes included in "Eet Smakelijk" without a contributor's name have been handed down through generations and have become so much a part of the city itself that it was impossible to determine contributors.

Introduction

he women of the Junior Welfare League of Holland, Michigan, are proud to present the second edition of EET SMAKELIJK.

Holland is a small community rich in traditions inherited from its earliest settlers, the Dutch. This, the second edition, represents a blend of early Dutch and modern American cuisine. Scattered among the recipes are many of the traditional Dutch favorites that have been handed down from generation to generation. You will find tempting treats like banket staven (almond roll), jan hagel (sugar cookies), marsepein (almond candy), and of course, the ever popular saucijzenbroodjes (pigs in the blanket). A special favorite is boerenjongens, a Dutch drink prepared at least three months in advance of the holiday season. Other recipes reflect the culinary expertise of cooks who are from diverse regions and ethnic backgrounds and have settled in Holland.

EET SMAKELIJK (the Dutch phrase meaning to eat well and with taste) is a uniquely successful cookbook which has traveled to the four corners of the world, and has earned the distinction of being the official cookbook of Holland. In preparation for the new cookbook the community particpated in a recipe hunt and bake off. The first and second place winners' recipes are featured along with many other exceptional entries. The cookbook contains over one thousand treasured recipes ranging from the very simple to true "haute cuisine." Uniqueness and quality were the standards of the committee during the fourteen months of testing, revising, and editing.

Whether you are a novice or an expert cook, we hope that you will find the book easy to follow, stimulating, and sometimes challenging. Our aim is to stir the imagination and to whet the appetite, and if the results please you, then our goal will have been fulfilled.

C. L. "Kim" Miller

C. L. "Kim" Miller

January, 1976

Appetizers and Beverages

NOTES

BLUE CHEESE BALL
1 ball

1 (8 oz.) pkg. cream cheese,
 softened
1 (4 oz.) pkg. blue cheese,
 softened
¼ cup margarine, softened

¼ cup ripe olives, chopped
¼ cup green pepper, chopped
1 tsp. garlic salt
⅓ cup walnuts, chopped

Blend cheeses and margarine. Add remaining ingredients, except nuts, and mix well. Shape into a ball and roll in nuts. Chill and serve with crackers.

Mrs. Ray Backus

DILL CARAWAY CHEESE BALLS
24 balls

2 (3 oz. each) pkgs. cream
 cheese, softened
¼ cup dill pickles, minced
½ tsp. caraway seeds

Salt to taste
2 hard cooked eggs, sieved
3 T. parsley, minced

Blend cheese, pickles, caraway seeds and salt. Chill. Drop from a teaspoon into mixture of eggs and parsley and roll into balls. Serve chilled.

Mrs. Althea Raffenaud

LIEDERKRANZ CHEESE BALL
2 balls

1 (8 oz.) pkg. cream cheese
½ cup butter
1 (5 oz.) pkg. imported
 Roquefort cheese

1 (4 oz.) pkg. Liederkranz
 cheese
2 (6 oz. each) rolls sharp
 cheese
½ cup nuts, chopped

Have ingredients at room temperature; mix well all ingredients, except nuts. Shape into a ball and roll in chopped nuts.

Mrs. John Tysse

RED CHEESE BALL
1 ball

½ lb. natural chedder
cheese, grated
1 (3 oz.) pkg. cream
cheese, softened
¼ cup pitted ripe olives,
coarsely chopped

3 T. sherry
½ tsp. Worcestershire sauce
Dash of onion, garlic and
celery salt
½ cup dried beef, coarsely
snipped

Combine all ingredients, except dried beef, with an electric mixer. Shape into a ball and wrap in tin foil. Refrigerate for several days. Before serving, roll ball in dried beef.

Mrs. John Workman

STUFFED CHEESE PUFFS
24 appetizers

1 (6 oz.) jar Old English
cheese, softened
¼ cup butter, softened
½ cup flour, sifted

¼ tsp. salt
½ tsp. paprika
24 stuffed olives

Use an ungreased baking sheet. Prepare 5 hrs. prior to serving time. Blend cheese with butter and stir in flour, salt, and paprika. Mix well. Wrap one teaspoon of dough around each olive, covering it completely. Place on baking sheet and refrigerate. Preheat oven to 400F. One-half hour before serving, bake for 10-15 min. Serve warm.

Variations: May be made unstuffed or rolled into strips. Substitute cocktail onions or mushrooms for olives.

Mrs. Tom Vanderkuy

FRIED MOZZARELLA CHEESE CUBES
8-12 Servings

1 lb. Mozzarella cheese
½ cup flour
½ tsp. salt

3 eggs, beaten
1 cup bread crumbs
½ cup olive oil

continued

Slice cheese into 1" cubes. Sift flour and salt together. Coat cheese cubes with flour mixture, dip into beaten eggs, then into bread crumbs, then into eggs and bread crumbs once more. Heat oil and fry cheese cubes until golden brown.

Mrs. Michael Calahan

PARMESAN RICE SQUARES

2 cups bite size rice squares
3 T. butter, melted

¼ cup grated Parmesan cheese

Preheat oven to 300F. In a shallow pan, toss rice squares in butter until well coated. Sprinkle with Parmesan cheese. Toast in oven 15 min., stirring occasionally. Cool.

Mrs. Jack Miller

HOLIDAY MEAT BALLS   *approximately 50 balls*

1¼ lbs. ground round steak
1 egg
1 tsp. salt
1 T. catsup

¼ cup water
1 slice bread, crumbled
2 T. olive oil

Sauce:
1 small onion, minced
1 clove garlic, crushed
2 T. olive oil
¼ tsp. salt
¼ tsp. oregano
1 tsp. flour

1 cube beef bouillon
1 cup water
1 tsp. dry mustard
1 dash bitters
¼ cup blended whiskey
⅛ cup sweet vermouth

Combine steak, egg, salt, catsup, water and bread. Mix thoroughly, form into tiny balls. Saute in olive oil until brown. Remove and set aside. Saute onion and garlic in olive oil until tender. Add salt, oregano and mix thoroughly. Blend flour. Add remaining ingredients, bring to a boil. Boil rapidly until sauce is reduced and thickened. Add meat balls and simmer 30 min. Serve in chafing dish.

Mrs. John R. Vande Wege

LIVERWURST MEAT BALLS

approximately 30 balls

1 egg, slightly beaten
½ lb. liverwurst
¼ lb. ground beef
¼ cup tomato soup, condensed
1 cup bread crumbs

½ tsp. salt
½ tsp. M.S.G.
½ cup flour
¼ cup butter
1 cup beef bouillon

Combine egg and liverwurst. Add the ground beef, tomato soup, bread crumbs, salt, and M.S.G. Shape into walnut size balls. Roll in flour and fry in melted butter until brown. Add bouillon and simmer for 15 min. Serve hot. Can be frozen and reheated before serving.

Mrs. Howard Davis, Jr.

SWEET-SOUR MEAT BALLS

120 balls

1 large raw potato, grated
3 egg whites
2 tsp. salt
½ tsp. pepper

3 lbs. ground beef
1 (12 oz.) jar grape jelly
2 (1 lb. each) bottles chili sauce

Preheat oven to 325F. Blend potato and egg whites in blender. Add salt and pepper. Mix into ground beef and form into balls. Brown in oven for 25 min.; drain. Heat jelly and chili sauce and bring to a boil. Add meat balls and simmer for 20 min.

Mrs. John Getz

SAUSAGE BALLS

approximately 100 balls

1 lb. lean pork sausage
3 cups Bisquick

1½ lbs. sharp cheddar cheese, grated

Preheat oven to 350F. Use an ungreased cookie sheet. Combine sausage, Bisquick, and cheese, carefully kneading with fingers until mixture sticks together and no crumbs are left. Roll into 1" balls. Bake for 30 min. Serve immediately on a hot plate. May be made ahead and frozen.

Mrs. Jack DeRoo

SAUERKRAUT BALLS
approximately 30 balls

8 oz. pork sausage, finely
   crumbled
¼ cup onion, finely chopped
1 (14 oz.) can sauerkraut,
   very well drained and
   finely chopped
2 T. dry bread crumbs
1 (3 oz.) pkg. cream cheese,
   softened
2 T. fresh parsley, chopped

1 tsp. dry mustard
¼ tsp. garlic salt
⅛ tsp. pepper
¼ cup flour
2 eggs, well beaten
¼ cup milk
¾ cup dry bread crumbs
Salad oil for deep frying

Cook sausage and onion. Drain. Add sauerkraut and 2 T. bread crumbs. Combine cream cheese, parsley, mustard, garlic salt and pepper; stir into sauerkraut mixture. Chill. Shape into ¾" balls. Coat with flour. Combine eggs and milk. Roll balls in egg mixture then in remaining bread crumbs. Allow meat balls to come to room temperature. Fry in deep fat at 375F.

Serve plain, or with nippy mustard sauce or curry dip. Balls may be made ahead, frozen and reheated at 350F.

Mrs. Herbert Eldean

NIPPY MUSTARD SAUCE
2 cups

5 T. sugar
3 T. dry mustard
   (Colemans must be used)
1 T. flour

¼ tsp. salt
½ cup vinegar
2 eggs, beaten
½ cup heavy cream

In a double boiler, combine dry ingredients; add vinegar and eggs. Mix well. Slowly add cream. Cook over boiling water, stirring constantly. Stir to desired consistency.

This sauce keeps indefinitely in refrigerator. Serve with sauerkraut balls, ham or on cold meat sandwiches.

Mrs. C.C. Andreasen
Mrs. James Pollock

CHEESE STUFFED EGGS

8 servings

4 eggs, hard boiled, sliced in
  half lengthwise, yolks
  removed
4 T. blue cheese, crumbled

1 (3 oz.) pkg. cream cheese,
  softened
2 T. fresh parsley, chopped
2 cherry tomatoes, quartered

Mix yolks, cheeses and 1 T. parsley. Stuff egg whites with mixture. Garnish with remaining parsley and tomato pieces.

Mrs. Don Disselkoen

HAM STUFFED EGGS

8 servings

4 eggs, hard boiled, sliced in
  half lengthwise, yolks
  removed
2 T. sour cream
4 T. green onion, minced
4 slices boiled ham, finely
  chopped

1 tsp. prepared mustard
Salt to taste
Pepper to taste
2 green onions, sliced

Mix yolks, sour cream, 4 T. onion, ham, mustard, salt and pepper. Stuff egg whites with mixture. Garnish with sliced onions.

Mrs. Don Disselkoen

COCKTAIL PUFFS

60 puffs

1 cup water
½ cup butter

1 cup flour, sifted
4 eggs, beaten until thick

Preheat oven to 400F. Grease a cookie sheet. Bring water quickly to a boil. Add butter; when melted, stir in flour. Continue stirring over moderate heat until dough forms a ball. Cool dough and add eggs, blend thoroughly. Drop from a tsp. onto the cookie sheet. Bake for 15 min. Cool on a rack.

When cool, may be frozen in plastic containers. When ready to use, lightly toast puffs, split and fill. Note tuna and blue cheese fillings.

Mrs. Jack H. Miller

16

BLUE CHEESE FILLING
about 40 puffs

1 (8 oz.) pkg. cream cheese
¼ lb. blue or Roquefort cheese
1 T. light cream
40 small shrimp, cooked

Blend cheeses and cream in a mixer until smooth. Fill cocktail puffs. Garnish with shrimp. May be made ahead and frozen.

Mrs. Jack H. Miller

TUNA FILLING
about 24 puffs

1 (7 oz.) can tuna
1 (3 oz.) pkg. cream cheese or
cream cheese with chives,
softened
2 T. pimento, chopped
½ tsp. smoke seasoned
salt (optional)
Dash of pepper
6 stuffed olives, sliced

Drain tuna, flake into a bowl. Blend in cream cheese, pimento, salt and pepper. Fill cocktail puffs. Garnish with olives. May be made ahead and frozen.

Mrs. Jack H. Miller

CHEESE TRIANGLES

1 (16 oz.) pkg. phyllo dough,
thawed in refrigerator
overnight
1 lb. Muenster cheese, grated
1 (8 oz.) pkg. cream cheese,
softened
¼ cup onion, minced
2 eggs
½ tsp. salt
⅛ tsp. white pepper
¾ cup butter
¾ cup margarine

Preheat oven to 350F. Use a lightly greased baking sheet. Mix cheeses, onion, eggs, salt and pepper. Set aside. Open dough and cut in 2" long strips. Stack strips and cover with a damp towel. Melt butter and margarine, brush each strip thoroughly. Place 1 tsp. cheese mixture on the end of each strip. Fold like a flag, forming a triangle, squeezing sides together. Brush top with butter. Place on baking sheet. Bake 20 min.

Mrs. William Bopf

SPINACH TRIANGLES

1 (10 oz.) pkg. frozen chopped spinach, thawed	1 tsp. dill weed
3 T. olive oil	½ tsp. salt
1 onion, finely chopped	⅛ tsp. pepper
½ lb. feta cheese	3 eggs, beaten
6 oz. pot cheese	¼ cup corn flake crumbs
¼ cup parsley, chopped	½ lb. frozen phyllo dough

Preheat oven to 400F. Use a lightly greased baking sheet. Heat oil and saute onion until limp. Add spinach, simmer until moisture evaporates. Blend cheeses, parsley, dill, salt and pepper. Add eggs, corn flake crumbs and spinach mixture. Blend thoroughly. Follow phyllo pkg. directions as for cheese triangles. Bake 20 min.

Mrs. William Bopf

MINIATURE MEAT CAKES　　　　　*approximately 32*

¾ cup margarine	1½ cups small curd cottage cheese
2½ cups flour, sifted	
½ tsp. salt	⅓ cup cold water

Filling:

1 lb. ground beef	¼ tsp. garlic salt
1½ tsp. salt	1 small onion, grated
¼ tsp. pepper	¼ cup mayonnaise
½ tsp. red pepper	

Cut margarine into flour and salt. Blend in cottage cheese. Add water. Mix and form into ball. Chill thoroughly. Roll dough on floured surface. Cut into 2¼" circles with a pastry cutter.

Preheat over to 425F. Use an ungreased cookie sheet. Mix filling ingredients. Place about 1 tsp. of filling mixture on each round. Fold over. Press edges together with a fork. Bake 15 min. or until golden. May be made ahead and frozen.

Mrs. Roger Eldean

18

BASIC STUFFED MUSHROOMS

$1^{2}/_3$ cups

1 lb. fresh mushrooms, finely chopped
2 T. butter
¾ cup onion, finely chopped
½ tsp. salt
⅛ tsp. ground black pepper
Pinch of nutmeg

Place mushrooms in a clean cloth and twist to remove all liquid. In a skillet, melt butter and saute onion; add seasonings and mushrooms. Saute; stirring until all moisture from mushroom has evaporated. Cool.

Keeps for several weeks in the refrigerator. Use with other ingredients to stuff mushrooms.

Variation No. 1
CHEDDAR MUSHROOMS

approximately 20

1 lb. large fresh mushrooms, stems removed
½ cup olive oil
¼ cup basic mushroom stuffing
dash of pepper
2 T. grated cheddar cheese
2 T. fine dry bread crumbs
2 tsp. parsley, chopped

Preheat oven to 350F. Use an ungreased 9" x 13" baking dish. Brush mushroom caps with ⅓ cup oil. Place in baking dish. Combine basic stuffing, pepper, cheese, bread crumbs and parsley. Mix and stuff in mushrooms. Drizzle remaining oil over all. Bake for 20 min.

Variation No. 2
MUSHROOMS PARMIGIANA

approximately 20

1 lb. large fresh mushrooms, stems removed
¼ cup basic mushroom stuffing
½ cup pepperoni, finely chopped
dash garlic salt
¼ tsp. oregano
¼ cup Mozzarella cheese, shredded
⅓ cup chicken broth

Preheat oven to 350F. Use an ungreased, 9" x 13" baking dish. Stuff mushrooms with a mixture of the basic stuffing, pepperoni, garlic salt and oregano. Top each mushroom with a little cheese Place in baking dish containing broth. Bake for 20 min.

Mrs. Roger Eldean

STUFFED MUSHROOMS 12

12 large fresh mushrooms,
  stems removed
3 slices of bacon, fried crisp
  drain reserving 2 T. fat
1 medium onion, finely
  chopped

¼ cup green pepper, chopped
1 cup dry bread crumbs
2 T. parsley, chopped
½ tsp. seasoned salt
¼ cup chicken stock
salt, pepper to taste

Preheat oven to 325F. Use an ungreased 9" x 13" pan. Chop mushroom stems. To bacon fat add stems, onion, green pepper and cook until tender. Then add bread crumbs, parsley, seasoned salt, stock, salt and pepper. Stuff mushroom caps. Place in baking dish with a small amount of water. Bake for 25 min.

Mrs. Ken Lakies

QUICKY STUFFED MUSHROOMS 20-25

20-25 medium mushrooms,
  stems removed
1 (4 oz.) container cream cheese
  with chives

1 T. fried bacon, crumbled,
  optional

Use an ungreased baking sheet. Generously fill each cap with cream cheese. Broil, 6" from heat, 3-5 min. or until brown and bubbling. May be made in advance. Variation: to cream cheese add bacon.

Mrs. Thomas Ambrose

STUFFED CHERRY TOMATOES 20-25 tomatoes

1 (7½ oz.) can king crabmeat
1 cup mayonnaise
¼ cup green onions, finely-
  chopped
2 T. chives, chopped
2 tsp. tarragon
1 T. parsley, chopped

1 tsp. thyme
1 T. basil
1 T. garlic, finely minced
1 hard cooked egg, sieved
salt, pepper to taste
1 lb. cherry tomatoes

Slice top off cherry tomatoes and scoop out pulp. Drain crabmeat and combine with remaining ingredients. Stuff tomatoes and chill.

Mrs. John Hartzell

SHRIMP MARINATED IN BEER
serves 8-10

2 lbs. shrimp, shelled and
  deveined
1 T. chives, chopped
1 T. parsley, chopped
2 tsps. dried basil
1 tsp. garlic, finely
  chopped

2 tsps. dry mustard
½ tsp. freshly ground
  black pepper
½ tsp. celery salt
1 tsp. salt
1 (12 oz.) can beer

Marinate shrimp in remaining ingredients, 8 hrs. or more in refrigerator. Stir frequently. Drain. Place shrimp in preheated broiler pan 3" from heat. Broil for 5 min., turning once.

Mrs. Lee Kimzey

CHEESE STUFFED SHRIMP
4-5 doz.

2 lbs. shrimp, shelled
lemon peel
1 bay leaf
a few peppercorns
1 qt. beer
¼ lb. blue cheese, softened

¼ lb. cream cheese, softened
1 tsp. prepared mustard
¼ tsp. powdered rosemary
1 tsp. horseradish
1 tsp. onion juice
1 cup parsley, finely chopped

Cook shrimp, lemon peel, bay leaf and peppercorns in beer until shrimp is pink. Drain and chill. Blend cheeses, mustard, rosemary, horseradish and onion juice. Split shrimp down the back, almost through. Stuff with cheese mixture. Dip cheese side in parsley. Chill. Serve on a bed of ice with toothpicks.

Mrs. Ken Lakies

DRIED BEEF PECAN DIP
1½ cups

1 (8 oz.) pkg. cream cheese,
  softened
2 T. milk
1 (2½ oz.) jar chipped beef,
  chopped
2 T. minced onion

¼ cup green pepper, finely
  chopped
1 tsp. ground pepper
½ cup sour cream
¼ cup whole pecans
choice of crackers

continued

Preheat oven to 325F. Use an ungreased pie plate. Mix all ingredients except pecans and crackers. Spread into pie dish and sprinkle with pecans. Bake for 15 min. Serve hot with crackers.

Mrs. William Bopf
Mrs. Robert Arkes

BRAUNSCHWEIGER SPREAD   2½ cups

1 lb. braunschweiger
½ (10½ oz.) can tomato soup
½ onion, finely chopped
Worcestershire sauce,
  to taste
1 (3 oz.) pkg. cream cheese,
  softened
1 T. milk
2-3 T. parsley, chopped
choice of crackers

Mix braunschweiger, soup, worcestershire and onion. Form into a mound in the center of a serving dish. Mix cream cheese and milk until smooth. Use cheese mixture to frost braunschweiger mound. Sprinkle with parsley. Serve with crackers.

Mrs. Anthony Garofalo

BEER CHEESE DIP   4 cups

1 lb. aged cheddar cheese,
  shredded
1 lb. mild cheese, shredded
2 cloves garlic, finely chopped
9 oz. beer
2 T. Worcestershire sauce
¼ tsp. dry mustard
½ tsp. salt
dash of Tabasco sauce
½ tsp. M.S.G.

Mix all ingredients. Beat together. Let stand in cool place for 2 hrs.

Mrs. Arthur Wyman

CHEEZY VEGETABLE DIP   1¾ cups

1 (8 oz.) jar Cheez Whiz,
  room temperature
2 (3 oz. each) cream cheese,
  softened
1 tsp. Worcestershire sauce
celery and garlic salt, to taste
cauliflower
zucchini sticks
carrot sticks
cherry tomatoes
green pepper strips

continued

Mix Cheez Whiz, cream cheese, Worcestershire sauce, garlic salt and celery salt. Whip at high speed for 5 min. until fluffy and light. Serve with vegetables.

Mrs. Jay Freriks

PARMESAN PARTY DIP   2 cups

1 (2½ oz.) jar dried beef,   **1 (8 oz.) pkg. cream cheese**
  chopped   **¼ cup Parmesan cheese, grated**
¼ cup onion, chopped   **2 T. parsley, chopped**
1 T. margarine   **½ loaf French bread, cubed,**
1 cup milk   **toasted**

Cover beef with boiling water. Drain immediately. Saute onion in margarine. Stir in beef, milk, cheeses, parsley and heat through. Serve warm with bread cubes.

Mrs. Victor Kleinheksel

ZESTY CHEESE SPREAD   3 cups

1 lb. Velveeta cheese   **9 T. mayonnaise**
¾ to 1 (5½ oz.) jar horseradish   **1 tsp. dry mustard**
7 drops Tabasco sauce   **garlic salt to taste**

Melt cheese in a double boiler then beat with other ingredients. May be served with crackers, bread sticks or vegetables.

Very similar to Win Schuler's Bar Cheese.

Mrs. Hal Thornhill
Diana Rivera

CHICKEN LIVER PATE   1 cup

½ lb. chicken livers   **1 tsp. lemon juice**
2 T. margarine, melted   **½ tsp. prepared mustard**
1 T. mayonnaise   **⅛ tsp. salt**
1 T. catsup   **⅛ tsp. pepper**
1 T. onion, grated

Cook livers in simmering water, 10 min. Drain and chop fine. Blend livers and remaining ingredients to a smooth paste. Cover and refrigerate.

Mrs. Willard Penna

HOT CLAM DIP
1¼ cups

1 (8 oz.) can minced clams
¼ cup onions, minced
2 T. butter
1 T. catsup
a few drops Tabasco sauce

1 cup sharp process American
  cheese, diced
2 T. pitted ripe olives, chopped
1 tsp. Worcestershire sauce

Drain clams, reserving 1 T. liquid. Cook onion in butter until tender; add clams, reserved liquid and remaining ingredients. Heat until cheese has melted and mixture is hot. Serve with crackers.

Mrs. Donald G. Miller

AVOCADO CRAB DIP
1¾ cups

1 large avocado, seeded,
  peeled and finely diced
1 T. lemon juice
1 T. onion, grated
1 T. Worcestershire sauce
1 (8 oz.) pkg. cream cheese,
  softened

¼ cup sour cream
¼ tsp. M.S.G.
¼ tsp. salt
1 (7½ oz.) can crab meat,
  drained and flaked
crackers

Mix well, and serve with crackers.

Mrs. Leo Jungblut

HOT CRAB DIP
4 cups

3 (8 oz. each) pkgs. cream
  cheese
2 (7½ oz. each) cans crab meat,
  drained and flaked
1 clove garlic, crushed

½ cup mayonnaise
2 tsp. dry mustard
2 tsp. confectioners' sugar
seasoned salt, to taste
¼ cup white wine, optional

Combine all ingredients. Heat in a chafing dish. Serve with crackers. May be frozen and reheated.

Mrs. Charles Bradford

LAYERED CRAB SPECIAL

8-12 servings

4 (3 oz. each) pkgs. cream
   cheese, softened
2 T. Worcestershire sauce
1 T. lemon juice
2 T. margarine
dash garlic salt

1 small onion, grated
6 oz. chili sauce
1 (7½ oz.) can crabmeat,
   drained and flaked
dried chopped parsley
sesame seed crackers

Blend together cream cheese, Worcestershire sauce, lemon juice, margarine, garlic salt and onion. Spread on a deep 8" plate. Pour chili sauce on top of mixture. Spread crabmeat on top of chili sauce. Sprinkle top generously with parsley. Cover with plastic wrap and refrigerate overnight. Serve with sesame seed crackers.

Mrs. Herbert Eldean

TEXAS CRABGRASS

2½ cups

⅓ cup butter
½ medium onion, finely-
   chopped
1 (7½ oz.) can crabmeat,
   drained

¾ cup Parmesan cheese
1 (10 oz.) pkg. frozen chopped
   spinach, cooked and
   drained
melba toast or sesame crackers

Melt butter, add onion and saute until soft. Add crab, cheese and spinach. Heat through. Serve hot with crackers.

Mrs. Roger Eldean

CURRY DIP A LA OBEROI

2 cups

2 cups mayonnaise
1 T. curry powder
dash of Tabasco
dash of garlic salt
dash of celery salt

1 tsp. A-1 sauce
1 tsp. lemon juice
1 tsp. Worcestershire sauce
1 tsp. black pepper
choice of fresh vegetables

Mix all ingredients except vegetables and chill. Serve with vegetables.

Mrs. Don Judd

DILLY DIP   2 cups

1 T. parsley, minced   fresh mushrooms
1 cup sour cream   fresh broccoli
1 cup mayonnaise   green pepper
1 T. dill weed   cucumber
1 T. beau monde   cherry tomatoes

Mix parsley, sour cream, mayonnaise, dill weed and beau monde. Chill 24 hours. Serve with vegetables. This will keep about 2 weeks.

Mrs. Alex Rivera
Mrs. James W. F. Brooks

DIPPING SAUCE FOR VEGETABLES   2½ cups

1 cup sour cream   1 T. fresh dill or dill pickle
1 cup mayonnaise   chopped
2 T. capers, chopped   1 tsp. lemon juice
3 T. chives, chopped   2 T. parsley, chopped
1 garlic clove, minced   assortment of raw vegetables
1½ tsp. garlic

Blend all ingredients, except vegetables, and chill for 2 hrs. Clean and chill vegetables; serve with dip.

Mrs. John Lomen

GUACAMOLE CON TOMATO APPETIZER   1½ cups

4 ripe avocados, peeled,   2 tsp. chili powder
   seeds removed   1 tsp. garlic powder
½ cup mayonnaise   ½ tsp. Tabasco sauce
¼ cup onion, chopped   2 medium tomatoes, peeled
1 T. salt   and chopped
3 T. lemon juice   tortillas or corn chips

Mash avocados, or puree in blender, until smooth. Mix with remaining ingredients, except tomatoes and tortillas. Chill. Garnish with tomatoes. Serve with tortillas.

Mrs. Dennis DeWitt

DEVILED HAM SPREAD

2½ cups

2 (2¼ oz. each) cans deviled
  ham
1 (8 oz.) pkg. cream cheese,
  softened
½ lb. liver sausage

1 medium sweet onion,
  finely chopped
1 large dill pickle,
  finely chopped

Mix ingredients well and refrigerate in covered jar. Spread on crackers.

Miss Althea Raffenaud

SMOKED FISH SPREAD

2 cups

¾ to 1 lb. smoked fish (salmon
  or sturgeon)
½ stalk celery, finely chopped
½ medium onion, finely
  chopped
2 eggs, hard boiled, whites
  only, finely chopped

salt and pepper, to
  taste
juice from ½ lemon
mayonnaise
crackers

Remove bone and skin from fish. Flake. Add remaining ingredients, using only enough mayonnaise to hold mixture together. Serve with crackers.

Mrs. Herbert Eldean

STEAK TARTARE

2 cups

1 lb. twice ground sirloin,
  extra lean
1 egg yolk
6 capers, rinsed, washed,
  finely chopped
1 scant T. Dijon mustard
  or Durkee's dressing

2 T. onion, finely chopped
1 tsp. salt
½ tsp. Worcestershire sauce
pepper, freshly ground
pumpernickel bread, buttered
horseradish

Mix sirloin, yolk, capers, mustard, onion salt, Worcestershire and pepper. Spread on bread. Serve with horseradish.

Mrs. William J. Lalley

TACO DIP
3 cups

¼ lb. ground beef
¼ cup onion
¼ cup chili sauce or hot catsup
1½ tsp. chili powder
½ tsp. salt

1 (8 oz.) can red kidney beans, reserving liquid
½ cup cottage cheese
½ cup sharp cheddar cheese, shredded
taco chips

Preheat oven to 350F. Use an ungreased 1½ qt. casserole. Brown beef and onion, drain. Add chili sauce, chili powder and salt. In blender combine beans, with liquid, and cottage cheese; blend until smooth. Add to ground beef mixture. Place in casserole and top with cheese. Bake 10-15 min., until cheese bubbles. Serve hot with taco chips. May be made ahead and frozen.

Mrs. Don Disselkoen

CHEESE AND MUSHROOM CANAPES
32 appetizers

1 (8 oz.) pkg. cream cheese, softened
2 egg yolks
¼ tsp garlic salt

9 slices thin bread
½ lb. fresh mushrooms
⅓ cup butter

With electric mixer, combine cream cheese, yolks and garlic salt. Clean and slice mushrooms; saute in butter. Remove crust from bread and cut into design of your choice. Spread cheese mixture on bread, covering to edges. Add mushroom slices and cover with more cheese mixture. Broil until slightly brown.

Hint: After adding mushrooms, freeze until firm. Add top layer of cheese. Refreeze. Heat in 325F oven for 10 min., then broil until brown.

Mrs. Herbert Eldean

MUFFIN CANAPES

48 appetizers

6 green onions and tops,
  thinly sliced
1½ cups cheddar cheese,
  grated
¼ tsp. garlic salt
1¼ cups mayonnaise
1 (12 oz.) pkg. English muffins,
  split and quartered

Combine onions, cheese and mayonnaise. Spread mixture on muffins and broil until bubbly.

Mrs. Jack Faber

PARMESAN SQUARES

36 appetizers

9 slices sandwich bread
1 cup mayonnaise
¼ cup onion, chopped
3 T. parmesan cheese, grated
garlic salt, to taste

Remove bread crusts; cut each slice into 4 squares. Spread each square generously with mayonnaise. Sprinkle each with onion, cheese and garlic salt. Broil until edges turn brown. Serve warm.

Mrs. Philip Fredrickson

CRAB MEAT HORS D'OEUVRES

48 appetizers

1 (7½ oz.) can crab meat,
  drained
1 (5 oz.) jar Kraft English
  cheese
½ cup butter, softened
2 T. mayonnaise
½ tsp. garlic salt
½ tsp. seasoned salt
1 (12 oz.) pkg. English muffins,
  split and quartered

Blend all ingredients, except muffins. Spread mixture on muffins. Broil for 8 min. or until hot and bubbly. Serve immediately.

Mrs. Ken Etterbeek

HAM PINWHEELS

64 appetizers

2 (4½ oz. each) cans deviled
   ham
1 (3-4 oz.) can mushrooms,
   chopped
½ cup dill pickle, minced

2 T. parsley, chopped
1 T. mustard
2 (8 oz. each) pkgs.
   refrigerated crescent rolls

Preheat oven to 375F. Use an ungreased cookie sheet. Blend ham, mushrooms, pickle, parsley and mustard. Separate 1 pkg. of rolls into 4 rectangles, pinching dough at markings to seal. Spread each with 3 T. ham mixture. Starting at short end, roll up. Seal. Cut into 8 slices. Repeat with remaining rolls. Bake 15 min. Serve hot or cold.

Mrs. Delwyn VanDyke

BABY PIZZAS

12 appetizers

6 English muffins, toasted
   and split
½ cup chili sauce
12 slices Mozzarella cheese

1 (1 lb.) pkg. brown and serve
   sausage, broiled, drained
   and sliced
garlic, to taste
¼ cup Parmesan cheese, grated

Spread muffins with chili sauce, cover with Mozzarella cheese. Dot with sausage, sprinkle with garlic and Parmesan cheese. Broil 2-3 min. or until cheese is bubbly.

Mrs. Kenneth Elhart

CHEEZY ARTICHOKE BAKE

80

½ cup onion, chopped
½ cup water
3 eggs, well beaten
¼ cup fine, dry bread
   crumbs
2-3 drops hot pepper sauce
⅛ tsp. oregano, crushed

2 cups natural cheddar cheese,
   shredded
2 (6 oz. each) jars marinated
   artichoke hearts, drained,
   chopped
½ tsp. salt
⅛ tsp. pepper
1 (2 oz.) jar pimento strips

continued

Preheat oven to 350F. Grease an 11" x 7½" x 1½" baking dish. Cook onion in water until tender, about 5 min., drain. In a bowl, combine eggs, crumbs, hot pepper, oregano, salt and pepper. Stir in onion, cheese and artichokes. Spread in baking dish and bake 20-25 min. Remove from oven, wait 5-10 min., cut into 1" squares. Garnish with pimento strips. Serve hot.

Mrs. Don Disselkoen

PICKLED ARTICHOKES AND MUSHROOMS

4 servings

⅓ cup vinegar
⅓ cup salad oil
⅓ cup water
1 clove garlic, crushed
2 T. sugar
1½ tsp. salt

2 T. parsley
¼ tsp. whole black
  peppercorns
dash hot sauce
1 (14 oz.) can artichoke hearts,
  drained
1 cup fresh mushrooms, sliced

Combine vinegar, oil, water, garlic, sugar, salt, parsley, peppercorns, and hot sauce. Pour marinade over artichokes and mushrooms. Cover and refrigerate 8 hrs. or overnight, stirring frequently. Drain before serving.

Mrs. Herbert Eldean

BACON CRISPS

Club Crackers, separated
bacon

garlic salt

Preheat oven to 200F. Use an ungreased jelly roll pan. Cut bacon in half, wrap around each cracker lengthwise and sprinkle with garlic salt. Bake for 2 hrs. Serve warm. Can be prepared the day before and reheated.

Mrs. Jay Freriks

EGG ROLLS WITH MUSTARD SAUCE

1 ½ cups flour
3 eggs
1 ¼ cup water

dash of salt
oil for frying

Filling:

1 cup shrimp, chicken or
   pork pieces
1 (16 oz.) can bean sprouts,
   drained
1 (6 oz.) can water chestnuts,
   drained, sliced
1 (4 ¼ oz.) can mushroom stems
   and pieces

1 (16 oz.) can chinese
   vegetables, drained
1 T. sugar
1 tsp. salt
2 cups celery, sliced,
   cooked in a small
   amount of water
   until just crunchy
oil for frying

Sauce:

½ cup prepared mustard
¼ cup water

3 T. vinegar
1 cup brown sugar

Mix flour, eggs, water and salt. Beat in mixer 15 min. In a 6 - 8" frying pan heat 1 tsp. oil. Pour a scant ¼ cup batter into pan and cook until edges are dry. Slide wrapper out onto a napkin. Before each additional wrapper add ¼ tsp. oil to pan. Continue stacking wrappers on napkins.

Mix all filling ingredients. Place 1 heaping T. on wrapper and fold. Hint: Fold in sides first. Then begin at the bottom and roll up. Fry until brown.

Mix sauce ingredients. Boil 5 min. Will be syrupy. Serve warm or cold over egg rolls.

Mrs. Lyle Sprik

MAPLY APPETIZERS

2 (8 oz. each) pkgs. brown and
serve sausage links
1 (13½ oz.) can pineapple
chunks, drained, reserve juice
4 tsp. cornstarch
½ tsp. salt
½ cup maple syrup

⅓ cup water
⅓ cup vinegar
1 large green pepper, cut in
¾" squares
½ cup maraschino cherries,
drained

Cut sausage in thirds crosswise; brown in skillet. Blend pineapple juice, cornstarch, salt, syrup, water and vinegar. Heat to boiling stirring constantly. Add sausage, pineapple, green pepper and cherries. Cook 5 min.; green pepper should be crunchy. Serve warm in chafing dish. May be prepared ahead, adding sausage, pineapple, green pepper and cherries just before serving.

Mrs. Jay Freriks

RAMAKI

chicken livers, cut in half
soy sauce
water chestnuts, sliced in half

bacon, cut in half, fried and
drained, reserving
drippings

Batter:
¾ cup flour
¾ tsp. salt
¾ tsp. baking powder

¾ cup milk
1 egg
oil for deep frying

Sauce:
1 (5 oz.) bottle A-1 sauce
1 T. brown sugar
garlic powder, to taste

1 T. onion salt
1 T. parsley flakes
3 T. bacon drippings

Marinate livers in soy sauce for several hours. Drain. Wrap 1 piece of liver and water chestnut in bacon. Secure with toothpick. Dip in batter and deep fry.

Combine ingredients for sauce. Heat and simmer. Keep sauce hot in chafing dish. Serve hot ramaki with sauce.

Mrs. John Lomen
Mrs. Jay Freriks

SEAFOOD BACON ROLLS
2 doz.

½ cup tomato juice
1 egg
½ cup fine dry bread crumbs
¼ tsp. salt
1 tsp. parsley
1 cup cooked rice

1½ T. minced onion
1 (7½ oz.) can crabmeat,
  drained
12 slices of bacon, cut
  in half

Mix juice, egg, crumbs, salt, parsley, rice, onion and crabmeat. Shape into finger size rolls and wrap in bacon. Secure with a toothpick. Broil 10-12 min. May be prepared ahead and frozen.

Mrs. James Nelson

ORIENTAL SPARERIBS
15-20

3 lbs. spareribs, cut into
  single ribs
⅔ cup soy sauce

2 tsp. sugar
½ tsp. garlic powder
⅓ cup water

Use a 9" x 13" baking pan. Place ribs into pan. Combine remaining ingredients, pour over ribs. Marinate, turning once, about 1 hr. Preheat oven to 350F. Pour off marinade, reserve. Bake ribs 1 hr. and 45 min., basting with marinade several times and turning twice. Serve warm.

Mrs. Jack DeRoo

ANNIVERSARY PUNCH
approximately 2 gal.

1 (46 oz.) can pineapple juice
1 (46 oz.) can orange juice
1 (46 oz.) can apricot nectar
1 (46 oz.) can grapefruit-orange
  juice
¼ cup lemon juice
red food coloring, enough to
  make mixture pink

½ cup sugar
2 (32 oz. each) bottles 7-Up
1 pt. raspberry sherbet
1 (16 oz.) pkg. frozen
  strawberries, separated and
  water added to make an
  ice ring

Mix all the juices, food coloring and sugar. Add 7-Up, sherbet and ice ring just before serving.

Mrs. Fred Laninga
Mrs. Claude Cantrell

BOERENJONGENS COCKTAIL
1¾ qts.

Served especially during the Christmas season in Dutch homes.

1 lb. raisins	*2 cups sugar*
2 cups water	*2 cups whiskey or*
1 cinnamon stick	*brandy*

Cook raisins, water and cinnamon about 20 mins. Add sugar and whiskey and cook until dissolved. Place mixture in sterilized container. Seal. Let stand 3 months.

BOERENMEISJES COCKTAIL
2 qts.

This cocktail, being sweeter than the boerenjongens cocktail, is often served to the Dutch women while the men drink boerenjongens.

¾ lb. dried apricots	*3 cups sugar*
lemon peel	*3 cups whiskey or*
2 cups water	*brandy*

Wash apricots. Soak apricots and lemon in water 24 hrs. Cook 20 mins. until soft. Add sugar and whiskey, stirring until dissolved. Place in a sterilized container. Seal. Let stand 3 months.

BUMBLE BEE
16 servings

1 fifth gin	*1 (6 oz.) can frozen lemon*
1 cup honey	*concentrate*
	7-Up

Mix gin, honey and lemon. For each serving use ⅓ gin mixture to ⅔ 7-Up. Pour over ice and serve.

Mrs. Burt Jones

BURGUNDY PUNCH
2¾ qts.

2 cups port wine
½ cup lemon juice
1 (6 oz.) can frozen
   orange juice concentrate

1 cup sugar
1 (⅘ qt.) bottle Burgundy
1 qt. club soda

In punch bowl combine port, juices and sugar. Stir until orange juice is completely thawed and sugar dissolved. Pour in Burgundy and soda. Add ice.

Mrs. Loren Meengs

CHAMPAGNE PUNCH
20 glasses

1 cup brandy
½ cup rum
½ cup Cointreau

2 cups strong tea
1 gal. champagne

Mix all ingredients except champagne. When ready to serve pour mixture over ice and add champagne

Mrs. Jack E. Faber

COFFEE LIQUEUR
2 fifths

1 (2 oz.) jar instant coffee
4 cups sugar
2 cups boiling water

1 pt. brandy
1 whole vanilla bean

Combine coffee, sugar and boiling water; cool. Add brandy and pour into 2 fifth containers. Add ½ vanilla bean to each.

Let stand 6 weeks before serving.

Mrs. Jay Freriks

DAIQUIRI PUNCH
20 cups

2 (6 oz. each) cans frozen
daiquiri concentrate
1 fifth white rum

1 (16 oz.) jar maraschino
cherries
cherry syrup, to taste
1 qt. soda, chilled

Combine daiquiri mix, rum, cherries and syrup. Stir and chill 2 hrs. or more. Before serving add soda. Serve in a punch bowl with a block of ice.

Mrs. Ted DeLong

SUMMER SLUSH
3-4 servings

Frozen Daiquiri

1 (6 oz.) can frozen
lemon juice concentrate
6 oz. rum

dash of red food
coloring — a must
ice cubes

Place juice, rum and food coloring in blender. Fill to top with ice cubes. Blend until ice becomes slush.

Mrs. James Pollock

ADVOCAAT
6-8 servings

Eggnog

3 eggs, beaten
3 tsp. sugar

2 cups milk
½ cup whiskey or brandy

Add ingredients in order given. Beat. Excellent for parties.

Mrs. Kenneth Kleis

EGG NOG

1¼ qts.

1 (3 oz.) pkg. egg custard
2 T. sugar
3 cups milk
⅛ tsp. nutmeg
1 tsp. rum extract

1 cup prepared whipped
    topping
rum (optional)
dash of nutmeg

Combine custard, sugar and 1 cup of milk. Stir over medium heat until boiling. Remove from heat. Stir in remaining milk. Chill. Before serving beat in nutmeg, extract and topping. Add rum if desired. Sprinkle with nutmeg.

Mrs. Don Disselkoen

FRAMBROSIA

1 qt.

1 fifth brandy
1 qt. fresh or frozen red
    raspberries

1 cup water
1 cup sugar
¼ lemon peel

Mix all ingredients. Place in tightly sealed jar. Let stand 8 days; remove lemon peel. Continue to stand until berries turn white. Remove berries and strain through a cloth.

Mrs. Claude Cantrell

FRUIT SOUR PUNCH

2⅓ qts.

1 (6 oz.) can frozen
    orange juice concentrate
1 (6 oz.) can frozen
    lemon juice concentrate
2 T. sugar
1 (8 oz.) bottle maraschino
    cherries

1 (9 oz.) can pineapple tidbits
1 pt. whiskey, chilled
1 (26 oz.) bottle club
    soda
1 orange, sliced
1 lemon, sliced
ice

continued

Four hrs. before serving combine juices, sugar and cherry juice. With toothpicks, spear cherries and pineapple. Cover and chill. Thirty mins. before serving chill punch bowl. Combine juice mixture with whiskey and soda. Add oranges, lemons and ice. Place cherries and pineapple in each individual serving.

Mrs. Jerry Steinpres

HOLIDAY PUNCH   3 qts.

*1 qt. cranberry juice cocktail,
 chilled
2 cups orange juice, chilled
1 (32 oz.) bottle lemon-lime,
 carbonated beverage, chilled*

*orange slices
fresh cranberries*

In a punch bowl place a cake of ice. Add fruit juices and stir. Pour carbonated beverage down side of bowl. Garnish with orange slices and cranberries.

Miss Althea Raffenaud

ORANGE BREAKFAST NOG   3-4 servings

*½ (6 oz.) can frozen orange
 juice concentrate, thawed
1 cup vanilla ice cream,
 slightly-softened*

*1 cup milk
2 eggs
1 T. sugar
mint leaves*

Place all ingredients, except mint, in a blender. Blend at low speed until just combined, then at medium high speed until foamy, about 30 sec. Pour into glasses. Garnish with mint.

Mrs. L. C. Miller

ORANGE FREEZE

3-4 servings

1 cup gin
1 cup orange juice
2 packets instant
daiquiri mix

1 cup water
8 to 10 ice cubes

Combine all ingredients. In blender, blend half of the mixture, then blend remaining mixture. It should be the consistency of a frozen drink.

Mrs. Jack Carter

PIÑATA PUNCH

1 gal.

6 oz. pineapple juice
1 pt. orange juice
6 lemons, juiced
¾ cup confectioners'
sugar

6 oz. Cointreau
1 qt. vodka
2 (28 oz. each) bottles
ginger ale
block of ice

Combine ingredients, except ginger ale. Pour over ice block. Add ginger ale. Stir.

Mrs. Michael Calahan

SANGRIA

1 gal.

1 cup water
⅔ cup sugar
2 oranges, peeled,
sliced
2 lemons or limes,
peeled, sliced

½ gal. dry red wine
1 cup brandy
1 qt. club soda
ice
oranges, sliced
maraschino cherries

Heat water and sugar until dissolved. Add orange and lemon slices. Let stand 4 hrs. Add wine and brandy. Just before serving add soda. Serve over ice. Garnish with oranges and cherries.

Mrs. Herbert Eldean

TANGERINE COOLER

6 servings

1 pt. lemon sherbet
1 (6 oz.) can frozen tangerine
    concentrate, thawed

4 (7 oz. each) bottles
    club soda,
    well chilled

In each of 6 tall, chilled glasses place a scoop of sherbet. Mix concentrate and 3 bottles of soda. Fill glasses ⅔ full. Just before serving, fill remainder of glasses with soda. Serve with straws.

BRAZILIAN MOCHA

4-6 servings

5 T. cocoa
5 T. sugar
½ cup cold water
pinch of salt

1 cup water, boiling
1½ cups strong coffee
1½ cups evaporated
    milk

Combine cocoa, sugar, cold water and salt. Cook over low heat 2 to 3 mins. Add boiling water, coffee and milk. Bring to a boil, remove. Beat, with beater, until frothy.

Mrs. Fred Leaske

GLÖGG

2 qts.

A traditional Swedish holiday drink

1 (⅘ qt.) bottle claret
1 (⅘ qt.) bottle port
½ (⅘ qt.) bottle brandy
10 Cardamom seeds, peeled
    crushed
18 whole cloves

3 cinnamon sticks,
    broken
orange peel, a twist
½ cup sugar
golden raisins
blanched almonds

In saucepan combine claret, port and brandy. Tie Cardamom seeds, cloves, cinnamon and orange into a cheese cloth bag. Add to wine mixture. Bring to a boil. Simmer, on low heat, 15 mins. Add sugar, stir until dissolved. Serve hot, placing a raisin and almond in each cup.

Mrs. James D. Van Putten, Jr.

HOT CRANBERRY PUNCH
10-12 servings

2 T. whole cloves
1 T. whole allspice
12" stick cinnamon,
  broken
¼ cup brown sugar
4 cups water
¼ tsp. salt
4 cups pineapple juice,
  unsweetened

2 (1 lb. each) cans jellied
  cranberry sauce, mashed
few drops red food
  coloring
few dots of butter
orange slices, halved
cloves
cinnamon sticks

Place 2 T. cloves and allspice in a cheesecloth bag. In saucepan place bag, cinnamon, sugar, 1 cup water and salt. Bring slowly to a boil. Add pineapple juice, 3 cups water and cranberry sauce. Bring to a boil, simmering 5 mins. Remove spices. Add food coloring. Pour into heated bowl. Dot with butter. Garnish with clove-studded oranges. Serve in mugs with cinnamon sticks.

Miss Althea Raffenaud
Mrs. Michael Doyle

HOT MULLED CIDER
10 servings

½ cup brown sugar
¼ tsp. salt
2 qts. cider
1 tsp. whole allspice

1 tsp. whole cloves
3" stick cinnamon
2 oranges, sliced
cloves

Combine brown sugar, salt and cider. Place spices in a cheesecloth bag. Add to cider mixture. Bring slowly to a boil. Cover and simmer 20 mins. Remove spices. Serve hot. Garnish with clove-studded orange slices.

Miss Althea Raffenaud
Mrs. James D. Van Putten, Jr.

HOT PUNCH
1 gal.

½ gal. cider or apple juice
1 (32 oz.) can apricot juice
2 (6 oz. each) cans frozen
    orange juice concentrate
1 (6 oz. can) frozen
    lemon juice concentrate
1 qt. hot tea
½ cup sugar

¼ tsp. salt
1 tsp. nutmeg
4 tsp. allspice
2 tsp. ground cloves
8 sticks cinnamon
2 oranges, sliced
whole cloves

In large saucepan combine juices, tea, sugar, salt and cheesecloth bag containing spices. Heat, do not boil, 20 mins. Stir often. Remove spices. Float oranges and cloves in punch and simmer 20 more mins. Serve hot.

Variation: Delicious with rum or brandy, to taste.

Mrs. Theodore B. Bosch

IRISH COFFEE
1 serving

1 tsp. sugar
1½ oz. Irish whiskey

5 oz. strong hot coffee
1 T. whipped cream

Rinse an 8 oz. goblet with very hot water. Shake dry. Place sugar in glass. Add whiskey and coffee, stirring to dissolve sugar. Top with whipped cream.

Mrs. Michael Calahan

NOTES

Soups and Sandwiches

NOTES

BEEF BARLEY SOUP
8 servings

2 lbs. beef short ribs
2 T. cooking oil
5 cups water
1 (16 oz.) can tomatoes, cut up
1 large onion, sliced
1 T. salt

1 cup carrot, sliced
1 cup celery, sliced
¾ cup green pepper, chopped
⅔ cup quick cooking barley
¼ cup parsley, chopped

In Dutch oven brown beef ribs in hot oil. Drain. Add water, tomatoes, onion and salt. Simmer, covered, 1½ hrs. Add carrot, celery, green pepper, barley and parsley. Simmer, covered, 45 mins. more. Remove from heat. Cut meat from short ribs; cut into small pieces, discarding bones. Skim excess fat from soup. Return meat to soup, heat through. Extra water may be added, testing for seasoning.

Mrs. Robert Hampson

SCOTCH BARLEY SOUP
6 servings

1 lb. lamb, diced
⅓ cup barley
1 tsp. salt
¼ tsp. pepper

6 cups water
½ cup each: carrot, onion,
    turnip and celery, diced
2 T. minced parsley

In large pan cook lamb, barley, salt and pepper in water. Cover and simmer 1 hr. or until tender. Skim fat. Add vegetables, simmer 30 mins. longer. Serve sprinkled with parsley.

Mrs. Arnold Dood

BEEF 'N BEAN SOUP
(2nd Place Bake Off)

10-12 servings

1 cup dried navy beans	2 onions, diced
2 qts. water	¼ cup raw rice
1 (1 lb.) can tomatoes	2 beef bouillon cubes
2 cups celery, diced	1 T. salt
4 potatoes, cubed	1 lb. ground chuck, browned

Wash beans and soak overnight. Cover with water, cook 1 hr. or until tender. Remove from heat. Let stand 1 hr. Add remaining ingredients, except beef. Cook to boiling, add beef and simmer covered 1 hr.

Mrs. Harold J. Mouw

CUBAN BLACK BEAN SOUP

10 servings

1 lb. black beans	1½ tsp. cumin
8 cups water	3 cloves garlic, crushed
2 T. salt	1½ tsp. oregano
½ cup olive oil	3 T. white vinegar
2 cups onion, finely chopped	1 cup white rice, boiled
2 cups green pepper, finely chopped	1 cup onion, chopped
	1 cup ham, chopped

Wash beans well. Drain. Soak overnight in 8 cups water. Add salt to water. Boil beans until soft, about 2 hrs. Heat oil in pan, add onions and peppers; brown slightly. Add crushed cumin, garlic and oregano, frying slowly for 5 mins. Add vinegar and cook 1 min. longer. Drain or add 1 cup water to beans as desired. Add ingredients from fry pan, cooking slowly ½ hr. longer. Pass the white rice, chopped onion and chopped ham as condiments to be put on top of soup if desired.

Mrs. William Bopf

MO'S COUNTRY BEAN AND CABBAGE SOUP
It's a feast!

10 servings

1 lb. dry pea beans
2 lb. smoked picnic ham or
  ham shank
1 stalk celery, sliced
2 carrots, sliced
2 bay leaves
5 parsley sprigs, chopped
2 onions, sliced
1 whole onion
2 whole cloves

3 cloves garlic, crushed
½ tsp. thyme
1 tsp. salt
½ tsp. pepper
1 (2 lb.) can tomatoes
1 (6 oz.) can tomato paste
1 (2 lbs.) cabbage, finely
  chopped
1 T. sugar, optional

Rinse beans and place in 8 qt. container and cover with water. Let stand overnight. Drain. Rinse ham, add to pot, cover with cold water; bring to boil. Simmer 15 mins., skimming off all foam that rises to top. Add celery, carrots, bay leaves, onions (2 sliced, one whole with 2 whole cloves pressed into it) garlic, thyme, salt, pepper and cabbage. Cover and simmer all day on low.

Mrs. Mary G. Smith

HEARTY BEEF NOODLE SOUP

12 servings

4 lbs. beef shank with bones
3 qts. water
2 carrots, cut in thirds
2 medium onions, quartered
2 stalks celery with leaves
1 bay leaf
2 garlic cloves, whole

4 cloves, whole
6 peppercorns
½ tsp. dried thyme
2 tsp. salt
2 beef bouillon cubes
1 (6 oz.) pkg. noodles

Simmer all ingredients together except bouillon cubes and noodles in a large kettle for 4 hrs. Strain stock and cool. Chill overnight. Skim off fat from top. Cut up meat, add to stock with cooked carrots, celery, onion, bouillon cubes and noodles. Cook until noodles are done.

Mrs. Clyde Line

COLD BEET SOUP

4 servings

For a hot summer lunch.

1 (1 lb.) can beets, chopped,
   include juice
2 T. vinegar or lemon juice
2 T. sugar

salt and M.S.G. to taste
dash of ground cloves
1 cucumber, diced
sour cream

Mix first five ingredients and chill well. Add cucumber and serve in chilled bowls. Top with dollop of sour cream.

Mrs. Kenneth Leggett

BORSCH

8 servings

3 lb. meaty soup bone
1 small cabbage,
   finely chopped
1 cup onion, sliced
4 beef bouillon cubes
1 (1 lb.) can shoestring beets,
   diced, undrained

1 (10½ oz.) can tomato soup
salt and pepper to taste
sour cream
parsley, sweet basil or
   dill, chopped

In large container, generously cover soup bone with water. Simmer until meat is done. Remove meat, cut up and set aside. Add cabbage, onion and bouillon cubes, simmering until cabbage is done. Add beets, tomato soup, cut up meat, salt and pepper. Serve with dollop of sour cream and parsley, sweet basil or dill. Use your imagination!

Mrs. Richard Taylor

CARROT SOUP   *4 servings*

2 slices bacon, diced
¼ cup onion, chopped
1 clove garlic, crushed
2 (13¾ ozs. each) cans
  condensed chicken broth
2 cups carrots, chopped

1 cup potatoes, diced
1 medium tomato, chopped
1 tsp. salt
dash white pepper
sour cream
parsley

In large saucepan, cook bacon, onion and garlic, until bacon is crisp, stirring constantly. Stir in next six ingredients. Heat to boiling, reduce heat. Simmer uncovered until vegetables are tender; 20-25 mins. Pour mixture into electric blender. Cover, blend on high until smooth. Garnish with a dollop of sour cream and snipped parsley.

Mrs. Roger Eldean

CORN CHOWDER   *4-6 servings*

2 strips bacon, diced
1 medium onion, chopped
1 cup water
1 potato, diced

2 cups creamed corn
salt and pepper
1 (13 oz.) can evaporated milk
2 T. butter

Cook bacon and onion until tender, not brown. Add water, potato and corn. Cook slowly until potato is tender. Add salt and pepper. Just before serving add evaporated milk and butter.

Mrs. John H. Jones

MANHATTAN CLAM CHOWDER   *8 servings*

2 (10¾ oz. each) cans
  Manhattan clam chowder
4 (10¾ oz. each) cans cream of
  celery soup
2 (8 oz. each) cans minced clams,
  drained
2 soup cans water

½ cup butter, melted
1 small onion, minced
4 cups milk
1 (1 lb.) pkg. frozen hash
  brown potatoes
1 tsp. M.S.G.
2 T. parsley flakes

Combine all ingredients and simmer slowly until potatoes are tender. *Do not boil.* Season to taste.

Mrs. Lorenzo Meengs

NEW ENGLAND CLAM CHOWDER
8 servings

2 T. butter
2 slices bacon
½ cup onion, coarsely chopped
1 cup carrots, thinly sliced
1 cup water
1 tsp. salt
1 tsp. seasoned salt
⅛ tsp. pepper

2 cups milk
1 cup light cream
3 T. flour
1 cup potatoes, cooked,
  peeled, diced
2 (8 oz. each) cans clams,
  minced
1 T. parsley, chopped

Sauté bacon in butter until crisp. Remove bacon and set aside. Add onion and carrots and sauté until onion is tender. Add water, salt and pepper. Cover; cook until vegetables are tender, 10-15 mins. Combine milk, cream and whisk in flour. Add to vegetables; cook, stirring until thickened. Add potatoes, clams with liquid, parsley and bacon, crumbled. Heat to serving temperature.

Mrs. Donald G. Miller

SAUSAGE BEAN CHOWDER
6-8 servings

1½ lbs. pork sausage
2 (16 oz. each) cans kidney
  beans, undrained
1 (1 lb. 13 oz.) can tomatoes
1 qt. water
1 large onion, chopped
1 bay leaf

1½ tsp. seasoning salt
½ tsp. garlic salt
½ tsp. thyme
⅛ tsp. pepper
2 cups potatoes, diced
1 green pepper, chopped

Brown sausage; drain. In a large kettle combine remaining ingredients except potatoes and green pepper. Add sausage. Simmer covered 1 hr. Add potatoes and green pepper and cook 20-25 mins. longer. Remove bay leaf.

Mrs. Tom Brown

KERRY SOEP
Curry Soup

8 servings

4 cups beef stock or
    4 cups water and 4 or 5
      bouillon cubes
2 cloves
1 bay leaf
1 small red pepper
1 tsp. curry

4 T. flour
2½ T. butter
1 large onion, chopped
1 egg, beaten
croutons, meat balls or
    hard-boiled eggs, chopped

Boil beef stock, cloves, bay leaf and red pepper. Strain. Fry onion and curry in butter, add flour and slowly add stock, stirring constantly. Boil 10 mins., remove from heat, add beaten egg carefully. Strain if desired. Croutons, small meatballs or chopped hard-boiled eggs are served with this soup.

CREAM OF CUCUMBER SOUP
(1st Place Bake-Off)

6 servings

2 cups peeled and coarsely
    chopped cucumbers
1 cup chicken broth
1 cup light cream
¼ cup chives, chopped

¼ cup celery leaves, chopped
3 sprigs of parsley
3 T. butter
2 T. flour
salt and pepper to taste

In the container of a blender combine the above ingredients and blend until smooth.

Serve either hot or cold. If served hot, garnish with a small amount of dill weed. If served cold, garnish with finely chopped cucumber and a bit of grated lemon rind.

Mrs. Donald K. Williams

FIN KUE

12 servings

Chinese Dumpling Soup

Broth:
3 qts. chicken broth
1 large onion, sliced
1 tsp. coriander seed, crushed

2 slices ginger root or 1 tsp.
* ground ginger*
2 lbs. bony chicken parts

Simmer 1½-2 hrs. Pour soup through strainer, discarding residue and bones. Return to pan; add dumplings, simmering in broth.

Pork dumpling mixture:
1 lb. lean pork, ground
½ cup mushrooms, diced
⅓ cup green onions, minced
¼ cup celery, minced
¼ cup water chestnuts,
* minced*
¼ cup bean sprouts or
* bamboo shoots*

2 tsp. Chinese parsley, minced
* or ½ tsp. ground coriander*
¼ tsp. ground ginger or 1 tsp.
* grated fresh ginger root*
3 T. soy sauce
1½ T. cornstarch
1 egg white

Blend thoroughly, divide into 48 equal size balls. Wrap balls in dumpling dough.

Dumpling dough:
½ cup boiling water

1 cup flour

Knead for 10 mins., until smooth and velvety. Roll onto lightly floured board. Cut dough into 3" circles, put pork ball in middle, wrap dough around. Drop into chicken broth above.

Mrs. Lyle Sprik

FRIENDSHIP CUP

6-8 servings

1 (10½ oz.) can tomato soup
1 (10½ oz.) can consomme
2 cans water
¼ tsp. marjoram

¼ tsp. thyme
1 T. butter
6-8 lemon slices

Combine soups and water; add marjoram, thyme, and butter. Simmer until seasonings mix well. Pour into cups and float a thin slice of lemon on top.

Mrs. John Workman

54

SWEDISH FRUIT SOUP
10-12 servings

½ cup dried apricots
½ cup dried prunes
½ cup dried pears
½ cup dried peaches
2½ cups pineapple juice
2 or 3 sticks of cinnamon

½ cup water
½ cup currant jelly
½ cup tapioca
½ cup sugar
1 lemon, sliced
1 orange, sliced

Soak dried fruit 2 or 3 hrs. in enough water to cover in a 4 qt. pan. Cook slowly for 1 hr., add juice, cinnamon, water, jelly, tapioca, sugar and stir until thickened. Add lemon and orange slices, cooking 10 mins. longer. Remove cinnamon sticks. Store in refrigerator at least overnight. Keeps well up to 3 or 4 weeks. Serve warm as soup or chilled for appetizer or dessert. If desired add orange or pineapple juice to make a thinner mixture.

Mrs. John H. Van Dyke

GAZPACHO
8 servings

Liquid Salad From Spain

½ loaf round dark
   pumpernickel bread
⅓ cup salad oil
¾ cup vinegar
½ cup each: celery, green
   pepper, radishes, green onion,
   cucumber and parsley, chopped

salt and pepper to taste
2 (24 oz.) cans tomato juice
1 (24 oz.) can V-8 juice
2 garlic cloves

Discard crusts and break bread into bite size pieces. Place bread in large bowl, adding oil and vinegar. Toss well, adding chopped vegetables and seasonings. Add juices and garlic cloves; chill at least 24 hrs. Remove garlic cloves (an inserted toothpick in each makes them easy to find) and serve. Especially refreshing on hot days.

Mrs. Hal Thornhill

GEZONDHEID'S BRIJ
Health Soup

10 servings

½ cup barley
3 qts. water
1½ cups raisins

⅓ cup brown sugar, packed
½ cup currant juice
½ (3 oz.) pkg. strawberry jello

Cook barley in water for ½ hr., covered. Add raisins and sugar and simmer for 2½ hrs. Add currant juice and bring to a boil. Remove from heat and add jello. Stir thoroughly. Allow to cool and refrigerate. Serve cold.

Mrs. Mathilda Jacobs

MINNIE CATHERINE'S
HAMBURGER TOMATO SOUP

8 servings

1 lb. ground beef
2 onions, chopped
¼ head cabbage, chopped
2 potatoes, chopped
4 carrots, chopped
1 green pepper, chopped
½ lb. fresh mushrooms, sliced

1 (16 oz.) can green
  beans, drained
3 stalks celery, sliced
1 (46 oz.) can tomato juice
2 tsp. sugar
1 tsp. celery seed
salt and pepper to taste

In a Dutch oven brown beef with onions; drain. Add remaining ingredients and simmer covered until vegetables are tender.

Elizabeth Barton

HARDY HODGEPODGE

8-10 servings

6 slices bacon
1 medium onion, sliced
1 lb. beef shank
¾ lb. ham hock
6 cups water
2 tsp. salt
2 (15 oz. each) cans
   garbanzo beans

3 cups potato, diced
1 clove garlic, minced
4 oz. Polish link sausage,
   thinly sliced
toasted and buttered
   French bread

In Dutch oven cook bacon until crisp; drain, crumble and set aside. Add sliced onion to drippings and cook until tender but not brown. Add beef, ham, water and salt. Cover and simmer 1½ hrs. Remove meat from shank (both beef and ham) and dice. Carefully skim off fat. Return meat to soup, add undrained beans, potatoes and garlic. Simmer, covered 30 mins. Add sausage slices and crumbled bacon. Continue to simmer 15 mins. more. Serve with French bread.

Mrs. John Whittle

KNIFE AND FORK SOUP

8-10 servings

1½ lbs. roasted sausage,
   thinly sliced
1 cup each: carrots and celery,
   thinly sliced
1 pkg. dry onion
   soup mix
2 T. sugar
1 tsp. salt

6 cups boiling water
1 (28 oz.) can whole tomatoes
1 (5.5 oz.) pkg. dehydrated
   hash brown potatoes
1 (10 oz.) pkg. frozen sliced
   green beans
¼ tsp. oregano

In Dutch oven combine sausage, carrots, celery, onion soup mix, sugar and salt. Add boiling water, stir, heat to boiling; reduce heat and simmer covered 10 mins. Mix in tomatoes, break up with large spoon; add potatoes, beans and oregano. Heat to boiling, reduce heat and simmer covered 1 hr. Stir twice during cooking.

Mrs. Len Lemmen

LENTIL AND MEATBALL SOUP

10-12 servings

1 lb. lentils, rinsed and drained	½ tsp. marjoram
2 tsp. salt	½ tsp. salt
1 bay leaf	⅛ tsp. pepper
2½ qts. water	1 (1 lb.) can stewed tomatoes
1 cup onion, chopped	1 cup carrots, sliced
⅓ cup bacon drippings	1 cup celery, sliced

Meatballs:

1 lb. ground beef	1 garlic clove, minced
½ cup dry breadcrumbs	¾ tsp. salt
2 eggs, beaten	½ tsp. marjoram
¼ cup milk	⅛ tsp. pepper
2 T. onion, finely chopped	¼ cup oil
2 T. parsley, finely chopped	

Combine lentils, salt, bay leaf and water in a 6 qt. container. Bring to a boil; reduce heat and simmer, covered 45 mins. Do not drain. Meanwhile prepare meatballs by combining all ingredients, mix lightly and shape into walnut-sized meatballs. Brown in hot oil. Drain and set aside. Sauté onion in bacon drippings. Stir in tomatoes, marjoram, salt and pepper. Bring to a boil. Combine with cooked lentils, meatballs, carrots and celery. Return to a boil. Cover. Simmer 30 mins.

Mrs. Ernest Penna

UIENSOEP

4 servings

Easy Onion Soup

12 medium onions, thinly sliced	butter
1 qt. beef stock	salt and pepper
2 T. flour	toast

Fry onions in butter until limp. Add beef stock and cook, thicken with flour, adding salt and pepper to taste. Toast slices of bread and pour soup over.

SOUPE A LA OIGNON
French Onion Soup

8 servings

4 T. butter
2 T. oil
2 lbs. (7 cups) onions,
  thinly-sliced

1 tsp. salt
3 T. flour
2 qts. College Inn
  Beef Broth

Croûtes:
8-12 slices French bread,
  ½" thick
2 tsp. oil

garlic powder
1 cup Swiss cheese, grated
½ cup Parmesan cheese

Melt butter with oil in Dutch oven. Add onions and salt; cook uncovered over low heat, stirring occasionally for 20-30 mins. Sprinkle flour over onions, cook, stirring for 2-3 mins. Remove from heat. In saucepan, bring stock to simmer; stir stock into onions. Return soup to low heat, correct seasonings and simmer partially covered 30-40 mins.

While soup simmers, make croûtes. Preheat oven to 325F. Place bread on baking sheet, bake for 15 mins. Brush both sides with oil. Turn slices over, sprinkle lightly with garlic powder and bake another 15 mins. or until bread is completely dry.

Ladle hot soup into individual oven-proof bowls, top with croûtes, sprinkle 2 T. grated Swiss cheese and 1 T. Parmesan cheese over each. (Croûte should be large enough to cover top of soup.) Place bowls on large baking sheet and slip under hot broiler until cheese is melted. Serve immediately!

Mrs. Ray Backus

ERWTENSOEP
Dutch Pea Soup

8-10 servings

1 lb. peas
1 medium pig hock, shoulder
    pork or metworst
3 qts. water
salt and pepper to taste
1½ cups celery, diced

3 medium onions, chopped
3 potatoes, diced
2 carrots, diced
parsley
1 cup milk

Soak peas overnight completely covered with cold water. Drain. Cook meat, peas and water for 2 hrs. Add next 5 ingredients; cooking 1 hr. Add parsley and milk. Cook 10 mins. more.

Mrs. Ken Kleis

GOURMET POTATO SOUP

4-6 servings

4-5 medium potatoes, diced
1 large onion, diced
2 carrots, diced
2 celery stalks, diced
3 strips bacon, chopped
4 cups water

milk or light cream
butter
salt and pepper
¼ cup bacon, fried, crumbled
¼ cup cheddar cheese,
    shredded

Place first six ingredients in Dutch oven and boil uncovered until the vegetables are well cooked and water has been reduced. Put soup in blender and puree. Add milk or light cream to desired consistency and return to Dutch oven. Add butter, salt and pepper to taste. Do not boil! Garnish with crumbled bacon and shredded cheddar cheese.

Mrs. Wm. G. Beebe

AARDAPPEL SOEP
Potato Soup

6 servings

6 medium potatoes	2 cups milk
1 T. salt	½ cup vinegar
1 T. butter, melted	12 slices bacon, fried,
2 T. flour	drained, crumbled
1 egg	¼ cup parsley, chopped

Pare and cut each potato in 6 pieces. Cook in salted water to cover until tender; do not drain. Blend butter, flour, egg and milk. Add gradually to hot potatoes and potato water. Heat again to boiling, remove from heat, add vinegar. Serve in soup plates containing chopped fried bacon. Garnish with parsley.

CREAM OF SPINACH SOUP

4-6 servings

2 T. butter	1 cup fresh spinach,
2 T. flour	finely chopped
2 cups milk	dash pepper
½ tsp. salt	dash onion salt or 1 tsp.
	grated onion

Melt butter; stir in flour and salt. Add milk; cook until bubbly and slightly thick, stirring constantly. Add spinach and seasonings to taste. Simmer 10 mins.

Variation: 1 cup cooked asparagus, finely chopped, may be used.

Mrs. David Linn

KANSAS CITY STEAK SOUP   *8 servings*

1 lb. ground round steak
2 cups water
½ cup each: celery, onion,
  carrot and potatoes,
  chopped
1 (10 oz.) pkg. frozen mixed
  vegetables
4 cups beef broth
½ cup margarine

¾ cup flour
1 (1 lb.) can whole tomatoes,
  chopped
1 tsp. each: salt, M.S.G., and
  seasoning salt
1½ tsp. Kitchen Bouquet
½ tsp. freshly ground
  pepper

Brown meat, drain. Parboil vegetables; covered, in 2 cups water, including frozen vegetables. In 4 qt. Dutch oven, melt margarine, whisk in flour, blending well. Add 4 cups beef broth, cooking until thickened. Add chopped tomatoes, including juice, parboiled vegetables, including liquid, meat and remaining seasonings. Simmer 30 mins.

Mrs. Michael Calahan

BACON BURGER TURNOVERS   *40 finger sandwiches*
(1st Place Bake-Off)

3¾ cups flour
1½ tsp. salt

1½ cups shortening
¾ cup cold water

Filling:
¾ cup onion, chopped
1 T. margarine
6 strips bacon, fried and
  crumbled
1½ lbs. ground chuck
1½ tsp. salt

¼ tsp. pepper
2 T. flour
1 (10¾ oz.) can cream of
  mushroom soup
1 cup sour cream
½ cup margarine, melted

continued

62

Preheat oven to 425F. Use ungreased cookie sheets. Prepare dough for crusts by combining flour and salt, cut in shortening and stir in water. Roll thin, cut out circles with a 1 lb. plastic coffee can lid.

Sauté onions in margarine; add crumbled bacon, set aside. Brown beef, add salt, pepper and flour. Add onion mixture and soup. Stir, cover and simmer for 20 mins. Add sour cream, simmer 5 mins. longer. Do not boil.

Fill half of each crust circle with a rounded tsp. of meat filling. Fold crust over and brush with margarine. Seal edge and prick with fork. Bake 15 to 20 mins. Can be frozen.

Mrs. Donald W. Schipper

BARBECUED GROUND BEEF
8 servings

1 lb. ground beef
½ cup onion, chopped
½ cup celery, finely diced
¼ cup green pepper,
  finely chopped
¼ cup chili sauce
¼ cup catsup
1 cup water
1 tsp. salt

dash pepper
1 tsp. Worcestershire sauce
2 T. vinegar
2 tsp. brown sugar
1 tsp. dry mustard
½ tsp. paprika
½ tsp. chili powder
1 T. parsley, chopped

Brown meat, onions and celery. Combine remaining ingredients, mix and simmer 30 mins. Thicken with flour if necessary.

Mrs. Norman Kalkman

QUICK 'N EASY BAR-B-Q
18 servings

2 lbs. ground beef
1 medium onion, chopped
½ tsp. celery seed

½ tsp. mustard seed
¼ cup vinegar
1 pt. chili sauce

Brown onions and ground beef. Add remaining ingredients and simmer 30 mins.

Mrs. Myron Van Ark

BATTER FRANKS

8-10 servings

1 egg
½ cup milk
1 cup Bisquick
2 T. yellow corn meal
¼ tsp. paprika

⅛ tsp. cayenne pepper
½ tsp. dry mustard
1 lb. frankfurters (8-10)
wooden skewers

Heat deep fat to 375F. Blend egg and milk. Stir in dry ingredients. Dip franks into batter. Fry 2-3 mins. on each side, until brown. Drain on paper toweling. Insert a wooden skewer in the end of each frank. Great for birthday party treats.

Mrs. James Pollock

BAKED CORNED BEEF BURGERS

6 servings

1 (12 oz.) can corned beef,
  finely chopped
½ cup green pepper, chopped
½ cup onion, chopped
½ cup mayonnaise
dash of pepper
1 egg, beaten
¾ cup fine dry bread crumbs

¼ cup margarine
3 slices American cheese,
  halved diagonally
1 (10¾ oz.) can cream of
  vegetable soup, undiluted
⅓ cup milk
6 English muffin halves,
  toasted

Preheat oven to 350F. Use a 9" x 13" baking dish. Combine first 5 ingredients and shape into 6 patties. Dip patties into egg, then into crumbs. Brown lightly in margarine. Arrange in baking dish. Place a cheese triangle on each. Combine soup and milk; heat. Pour around patties and bake uncovered 15 mins. or until heated through. Serve on muffin halves.

Mrs. Helena Lemmen

HOT CORNED BEEF SANDWICHES

6-8 servings

½ cup corned beef, shredded
½ cup American cheese,
  shredded
¼ cup catsup

2 T. onion, chopped
1 T. Worcestershire sauce
⅓ cup green olives, chopped
6-8 hamburger buns

continued

Preheat oven to 325F. Combine all ingredients; spread on buns. Wrap individually in foil and bake 20 mins.

Mrs. Hal Thornhill

HOT CORNED BEEF SQUARES
8 servings

2 cups Bisquick
2 (12 oz. each) cans corned
  beef
2 T. mustard
2 T. salad dressing
1 sweet medium onion,
  sliced
½ cup ripe olives, finely
  chopped or ½ cup
  mushrooms, chopped
sliced tomatoes
American or Swiss cheese
slices
½ cup green pepper, chopped

Preheat oven to 425F. Use an ungreased cookie sheet. Make Bisquick recipe as directed on box and roll to approximately 12" x 7". Transfer dough to cookie sheet. Slice corned beef and lay on dough. Mix mustard and salad dressing and spread over corned beef. Top with onion and ripe olives and bake 15 mins. Remove and top with tomato, green pepper and cheese slices. Return to oven, bake 5 mins. longer or until cheese bubbles. Cut into squares.

Mrs. Arthur Hills

CHEESE-RIPE OLIVE SANDWICH
12 servings

1½ cups processed American
  cheese, shredded
½ cup mayonnaise or salad
  dressing
1 cup ripe olives, sliced
½ cup green onions,
  thinly sliced
½ tsp. curry powder, optional
6 buns or English muffins,
  split and toasted

Combine ingredients and spread on buns. Broil 4"-6" from flame 2-3 mins.

Mrs. Hal Thornhill

CHICKEN MUFFWICHES
6 servings

3 large halved chicken breasts,
   skinned and boned
2 T. butter
1 tsp. seasoned salt
3 English muffins
1 cup mayonnaise

2 green onions, chopped
1 tsp. dill weed
1 (1 lb. 4 oz.) can sliced
   pineapple, drained
½ cup cheddar cheese,
   shredded

Flatten each chicken breast half. In medium skillet melt butter. Saute chicken until golden on both sides. Cover and simmer for 15 mins. Sprinkle with seasoned salt. Split and toast muffins. In small bowl combine mayonnaise, onion and dill weed. Spread two-thirds of mixture over muffin halves. Place one piece of chicken on each half. Top each with pineapple slice. Spread remaining mayonnaise mixture over top. Sprinkle with cheese. Broil about 4" from heat for 3-4 mins., or until bubbly and browned.

Mrs. Donald G. Miller

CHICKEN SWISSWICHES
4 servings

1½ cups chicken, cooked
   and diced
⅓ cup mayonnaise
¼ cup celery, diced
¼ cup Swiss cheese, diced
8 slices bread

1 (14½ oz.) can asparagus
   spears, drained
½ cup butter
1 (2⅜ oz.) pkg. seasoned
   coating mix for chicken

Combine chicken, mayonnaise, celery, and cheese. Spread on 4 slices of bread, using about ¼ cup mixture on each. Arrange asparagus spears atop filling, then top with remaining bread. Melt butter; brush on both sides of bread. Coat sandwiches with seasoned coating mix; brown on both sides in remaining butter on griddle.

HAMBURGER-CHEESE LOAF

6-8 servings

1 lb. ground beef
1 tsp. salt
¼ tsp. pepper
1 T. Worcestershire sauce
¼ cup catsup or chili sauce

¼ cup onion, chopped
½ cup corn flake crumbs
½ cup evaporated milk
Swiss cheese
2 loaves French bread

Preheat oven to 350F. Mix all ingredients except cheese and spread on French bread loaves cut lengthwise. Bake 25 mins. Top with Swiss cheese, return to oven until cheese melts.

Mrs. David Kempker

HONEY'S CRAB SANDWICH

8 servings

(2nd Place Bake-Off)

8 Holland Rusks or
    English muffins
8 slices sharp process cheese
8 slices salted tomatoes
1 (7½ oz.) can crabmeat,
    drained
1 (8 oz.) pkg. cream cheese

2 T. mayonnaise
1 T. lemon juice
½ tsp. Worcestershire
1 T. onion, grated
dash of Tabasco
    sauce

Preheat oven 300F. On each rusk place a slice of cheese, then a slice of tomato. Combine crabmeat, cream cheese, mayonnaise, lemon juice, Worcestershire, onion and Tabasco. Pile crabmeat mixture on top of each sandwich at least 1'' high. Bake 30-40 mins. Crabmeat mixture may be made the day before serving.

Mrs. Clarence Becker

HOT CHEESE SURPRISES

8 servings

8 slices rye bread
1 cup cheddar cheese,
    grated
8 thin slices boiled
    ham

8 thin slices turkey
1 (4 oz.) can sliced
    mushrooms, drained
8 slices Monterey
    Jack cheese

continued

Toast bread under broiler on one side. On untoasted side of each slice place about 2 T. cheddar cheese, top with a ham slice, turkey slice, mushrooms and sliced cheese. Place under broiler for 5 mins., or until cheese is melted and bubbly.

Variation: Use summer sausage and olives in place of turkey and mushrooms.

Janice Van Faasen

LUNCHEON SANDWICHES   6 servings

2 cups ham, cooked and
  ground
¼ cup onion, finely chopped
¼ cup dill pickle,
  finely chopped
½ cup salad dressing or
  mayonnaise

1 T. horseradish mustard
3 English muffins, split
  and toasted
6 slices pimento cheese
6 thin slices tomato

Combine ham, onion, pickle, mayonnaise and mustard. Spread on muffin halves and broil 4 mins. Put a slice of cheese on each sandwich and broil 2 mins. more. Top with tomato slices and broil long enough to heat through, about 3 mins.

Miss Althea Raffenaud

OPEN FACE CHEESE SANDWICH   6 servings

8 slices of bacon, diced
1 lb. sharp cheese, shredded
1 small onion, diced

mayonnaise
6 hamburger buns or
  English muffins

Fry bacon until crisp, drain. Mix bacon, cheese and onion. Add enough mayonnaise to moisten and spoon onto open buns. Broil until cheese melts.

Mrs. Gerald Boeve

OPEN FACE SANDWICH SUPREME
4 servings

*½ cup mayonnaise or salad
   dressing*
½ cup catsup
¼ cup pickle relish
2 T. prepared mustard
1 T. milk
4 slices rye bread
margarine

leaf lettuce
4 oz. brick or Provolone cheese
*8 thin slices roast beef,
   cooked rare*
tomato slices
2 hard cooked eggs, sliced
bacon curls

Combine mayonnaise, catsup, pickle relish, mustard and milk. Spread bread with margarine. Top with lettuce, cheese, roast beef and tomato slices. Spoon ¼ cup mayonnaise mixture over each. Garnish with egg slices and bacon curls. Pass any additional dressing.

Mrs. Herbert Eldean

SAUCIJZENBROODJES
30-36 servings

Pig In The Blankets

2¾ - 3 lbs. sausage
3 cups flour
3 T. baking powder

1 tsp. salt
1 cup margarine
1 cup milk

Meat:
Divide sausage, forming 30-36 "pigs". Do not roll in hands, form carefully with finger tips or fork.

Dough:
Sift together flour, baking powder and salt. Cut in margarine as for pie dough. Mix in milk. Form into smooth ball. Roll dough to ¼" thickness, cut into strips about 3½" wide. Wrap "pig" loosely in dough, over-lapping on the bottom. Do not pinch ends shut. Prick top of each "pig" with a fork. Place on ungreased cookie sheets, bake 15 mins. at 400F. then 15 mins. at 350F. till brown. May be frozen up to 4 months.

Mrs. Harvey Kronemeyer

PIZZA BUNS
18 servings

1 (4½ oz.) can deviled ham
1 (8 oz.) can tomato sauce
1 T. onion, minced
½ tsp. oregano

2 T. Parmesan cheese
1 cup medium cheddar or
   American cheese, grated
9 English muffins

Blend all ingredients except grated cheddar cheese. Spread on split muffins; top with cheese, approximately 1 T. per bun. Place under broiler until cheese is bubbly and slightly browned.

Mrs. John Schmidt

PIZZA-BURGERS
6 servings

1 lb. ground beef
¼ cup onion, chopped
½ tsp. pepper
1 tsp. salt

1 tsp. oregano
1 tsp. basil
1 cup tomato paste or sauce
grated pizza cheese
3 hamburger buns, split

Lightly brown ground beef and onion. Add remaining ingredients. Place on buns and top with cheese. Broil until cheese is bubbly.

Mrs. Norman Kalkman

REUBEN ROLL-UPS
8 servings

1 cup sauerkraut, well drained
1 tsp. caraway seeds
1 (4 oz.) pkg. corned beef,
   thinly sliced

4 slices Swiss cheese,
   cut in half
1 (8 oz.) can crescent rolls,
   rye or plain

Preheat oven to 375F. Use an ungreased cookie sheet. Combine sauerkraut and caraway seeds. Place about 2 T. on each of the 8 slices of corned beef; top with a half slice of cheese. Roll up to make 8 rolls. Separate dough into triangles. Place meat rolls on wide end of triangle; roll up. Bake 15-20 mins. or until golden brown.

Mrs. John Whittle

STUFFED BUNS
6 servings

6 hard rolls
¼ cup butter, melted
garlic salt to taste
¼ cup onion, chopped
¼ cup green pepper, chopped
1 T. butter

½ (10¾ oz.) can tomato soup
1 egg, slightly beaten
½ tsp. pepper
1 tsp. salt
¾ lb. ground beef

Preheat oven to 350F. Use a greased 9" x 13" pan. Cut tops off rolls, hollow out, save crumbs. Spread hollowed rolls with melted butter and garlic salt. Sauté onion and green pepper in 1 T. butter. Add remaining ingredients and crumbs and mix well. Fill rolls with mixture. Bake 30 mins.

Mrs. Arthur Hills

SWISS AVOCADO SANDWICHES
4 servings

2 avocados
8 slices pumpernickel bread
½ tsp. salt
2 tsp. fresh lemon juice

2 tomatoes, peeled
  and chopped
8 slices Swiss cheese

Cut avocados in half lengthwise, remove pit and peel. Cut in crosswise slices and arrange on bread. Sprinkle with salt and lemon juice. Spoon chopped tomato over avocados and place a slice of Swiss cheese over each sandwich. Place sandwich on baking sheet. Broil 6 inches from heat for 5 mins. or until cheese is melted. Serve immediately.

Mrs. Charles VandeKerck

"TANGY" MEAT FOR BUNS
4-6 servings

1 (12 oz.) can corned beef
1 cup celery, chopped
1 T. prepared mustard
2 T. onion, chopped
6 slices pickle, chopped

2 hard boiled eggs, chopped
salt and pepper to taste
1 T. salad dressing
1 cup sour cream
hamburger buns

Preheat oven to 250F. Combine ingredients, spread on buns, wrap in foil and bake 30 mins.

Barb Zoet

TOMATO-HAM SUBS   *2 servings*

2 medium tomatoes, fully ripe   ⅛ tsp. salt
⅓ cup mayonnaise   ⅛ tsp. ground black pepper
3 T. celery, finely chopped   1½ cups cooked ham, diced
2 T. green onions,   2 individual
  thinly sliced   submarine rolls

Dice one tomato; slice remaining tomato; set aside. Combine
mayonnaise, celery, green onions, salt, pepper and diced tomato.
Fold in ham. Split rolls lengthwise. Spoon mixture onto bottom of
each roll. Arrange sliced tomato over ham mixture. Cover with top
half of roll.

Mrs. Robert Hampson

TUNA PUFFS   *6 servings*

1 (6½ oz.) can tuna   ¾ cup mayonnaise
1 T. green pepper, chopped   6 tomato slices
1 tsp. onion, chopped   3 hamburger buns, split
1 tsp. Worcestershire sauce   ½ cup American cheese,
½ tsp. mustard   shredded

Mix tuna, green pepper, onion, Worcestershire sauce, mustard
and ¼ cup mayonnaise together. Spread on half of bun. Place
tomato slices on top of each bun. Mix together ½ cup mayonnaise
and ½ cup shredded American cheese and top each tomato slice
with mixture. Broil until slightly brown.

Mrs. Clyde Line

NOTES

NOTES

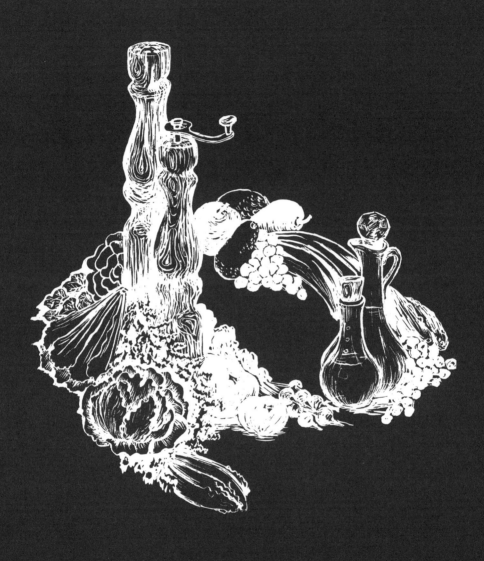

Salads and their Dressings

NOTES

APPLE-GEL SALAD

12-15 servings

1 (3 oz.) pkg. orange
   flavored gelatin
1 (3 oz.) pkg. lemon
   flavored gelatin
2 cups boiling water

Topping:
2 eggs
juice of 1 lemon
¾ cup sugar

3 or 4 Delicious
   apples, diced
1 (20 oz.) can crushed
   pineapple, undrained
3 T. vinegar

⅛ tsp. salt
1 cup heavy cream, whipped
chopped nuts, optional

Use a 9" x 13" pan. Add boiling water to gelatin and stir until dissolved. Add remaining ingredients and chill until set.

Beat eggs thoroughly; mix in lemon juice, sugar and salt. Cook in double boiler until thickened. Cool. Fold in whipped cream and spread over chilled gelatin. Garnish with nuts.

Mrs. Walter Kimberley

7-UP APPLESAUCE SALAD

9 servings

2 (3 oz. each) pkgs. raspberry
   flavored gelatin
2 cups hot applesauce
1 (9 oz.) can crushed
   pineapple, undrained

juice and grated rind of
   2 small oranges
1 (10 oz.) bottle 7-Up

Dissolve gelatin in applesauce. Add pineapple, juice, rind and 7-Up. Pour into 8" x 8" pan. Chill and serve.

Mrs. Bill Seyboldt
Mrs. Michael Calahan

APRICOT-CHEESE DELIGHT
12 servings

1 (29 oz.) can apricots, drained and cut

1 (20 oz.) can crushed pineapple, drained

1 (6 oz.) pkg. orange flavored gelatin

2 cups boiling water

1 cup combined apricot and pineapple juice

¾ cup miniature marshmallows

Topping:

½ cup sugar

3 T. flour

1 egg, slightly beaten

1 cup combined apricot and pineapple juice

2 T. butter

1 cup heavy cream, whipped

¾ cup cheddar cheese, grated

Drain and chill fruit. Reserve juice. Dissolve gelatin in boiling water. Add 1 cup fruit juice (reserving remaining juice for topping). Chill until slightly congealed. Fold in fruit and marshmallows. Pour into 9" x 13" pan. Chill until firm. Spread with Fruit-Cheese Topping.

Combine sugar and flour, blend in egg. Gradually stir in juices. Cook over low heat until thickened, stirring constantly. Remove from heat. Stir in butter. Cool. Fold in whipped cream and spread over gelatin layer. Sprinkle top with grated cheese. Chill.

Mrs. Vern Schipper

APRICOT SALAD WITH LEMON DRESSING

9 servings

2 cups apricot nectar
1 (3 oz.) pkg. orange
    flavored gelatin
2 (3 oz. each) pkgs. cream
    cheese

1 cup crushed pineapple,
    drained
1 cup mandarin oranges,
    drained
½ cup walnuts, chopped

Dressing:
2 eggs
1 cup sugar
4 T. vinegar

grated rind of 2 lemons
1 cup heavy cream, whipped

Use an 8" x 8" pan. Heat nectar to boiling. Add gelatin and refrigerate until it starts to congeal. Whip the cream cheese and then add to gelatin, beating in. Fold in fruits and nuts; pour into pan and refrigerate until firm.

Bring to a boil all dressing ingredients except whipped cream. Stir constantly so it does not stick. Cool thoroughly and fold in whipped cream. This is a good dressing on any fruit salad and it keeps indefinitely in the refrigerator.

Mrs. William Keizer, Jr.

MOLDED BLUEBERRY SALAD

9 servings

1 envelope unflavored gelatin
1 (12 oz.) can apricot nectar
1 tsp. lemon juice
pinch salt

1 (3 oz.) pkg. cream cheese,
    softened
¼ cup sour cream
1½ cups fresh blueberries

Sprinkle gelatin into ¼ cup nectar to soften. Heat remaining nectar and dissolve gelatin in it. Stir in lemon juice and salt. Cool until slightly thickened. Blend cream cheese into sour cream. Blend in cooled gelatin gradually. Fold blueberries into gelatin mixture. Turn into mold and chill until firm.

Mrs. Robert Fitzsimmons

RUSSIAN BLUEBERRY SALAD   *9-12 servings*

1 cup light cream   *¼ cup boiling water*
1 cup sugar   *2 cups sour cream*
1 envelope unflavored gelatin   *1 tsp. vanilla*

Topping:
1 (3 oz.) pkg. raspberry   *1 (15 oz.) can blueberries,*
*   flavored gelatin*   *   plus juice*
1 cup boiling water

Mix cream and sugar, heat just to boiling, remove from heat. Dissolve gelatin in water. Add to hot cream mixture. Stir in sour cream and vanilla. Pour into 9" x 13" pan, refrigerate until firm.

Dissolve raspberry gelatin in water, add blueberries. Pour over cream layer; refrigerate until firm.

Mrs. Jay Freriks

CHRISTMAS CRANBERRY SALAD   *10-12 servings*

1 lb. fresh cranberries   *1 cup nut meats*
1 small orange   *1 cup miniature marshmallows*
2 cups sugar   *1 cup celery, chopped*
1 (3 oz.) pkg. lemon or lime   *1 cup apples, chopped*
*   flavored gelatin*   *1 (9 oz.) can pineapple,*
2 cups boiling water   *   drained, optional*

Grind cranberries and orange, add sugar, mix and let stand over night. Dissolve gelatin in water; when partially set, add to first mixture. Add nuts, marshmallows, celery, apples and pineapple. Pour into mold and refrigerate. If desired, salad dressing or whipped topping may be used as a garnish.

Mrs. Ben Kroeze

FROZEN CRANBERRY CREAM CHEESE MOLDS

6-8 servings

6-8 (5 oz.) paper cups
1 (1 lb.) can jellied
  cranberry sauce
2-3 T. lemon juice
1 (3 oz.) pkg. cream cheese,
  softened

¼ cup mayonnaise
¼ cup confectioners' sugar,
  sifted
1 cup walnuts, chopped
1 cup heavy cream, whipped
lettuce

Crush cranberry sauce with fork. Add lemon juice and mix. Pour into paper cups. Combine cream cheese, mayonnaise and sugar. Blend well. Add walnuts. Fold in whipped cream and spread over cranberry mixture. Freeze. Unmold onto lettuce. The red layer will then be on top. Excellent to serve on Christmas or Valentines Day.

Mrs. John Marquis

CRANBERRY PINK FREEZE

8-10 servings

Good with poultry or ham — or pass with cookies for dessert.

2 (3 oz. each) pkgs. cream
  cheese, softened
2 T. mayonnaise
2 T. sugar
1 (1 lb.) can whole cranberry
  sauce

1 (9 oz.) can crushed
  pineapple, drained
½ cup walnuts, chopped
1 cup heavy cream,
  whipped

Blend cream cheese, mayonnaise and sugar. Add fruits and nuts. Fold in whipped cream. Pour into 8" x 4" x 3" loaf pan. Freeze firm for 6 hrs. or overnight. Let stand at room temperature about 15 mins., then slice.

Mrs. Ken Lakies

CONGEALED FRUIT SALAD

9 servings

1 (3 oz.) pkg. apricot or orange
    flavored gelatin
1 (9 oz.) can crushed pineapple,
    reserve juice

1 banana, sliced
1 cup miniature marshmallows
¼ cup pecans, chopped

Topping:
¼ cup pineapple juice
⅓ cup sugar
1 egg, beaten
1 T. flour

½ (3 oz.) pkg. cream cheese,
    softened
1 cup heavy cream, whipped

Prepare jello as directed, adding pineapple, banana, marsh-mallows and pecans. Pour into 9" x 9" pan, congeal for about three hrs.

Cook pineapple juice, sugar, egg and flour until thickened. Cool. Blend cream cheese with cooled mixture, fold in whipped cream. Spread over congealed gelatin. Refrigerate.

Mrs. Hoyt Hackney

FROZEN FRUIT SALAD

9 servings

1 envelope unflavored gelatin
½ cup pineapple juice
1 cup boiling pineapple juice
1 T. lemon juice
1 cup mayonnaise
1 cup heavy cream, whipped

2 T. confectioners' sugar
¼ tsp. salt
2 cups fruit (pineapple
    chunks, grapes, Bing
    cherries, or any fruit
    combination)

Sprinkle gelatin in cold juice. Add hot juice, dissolve and add lemon juice. Cool. Add mayonnaise to cream slowly, then add to gelatin mixture. Add salt, sugar and fruits. Pour into 8" x 8" pan and freeze.

Mrs. John Winter

82

MOLDED GARDEN SALAD   9 servings

1 (3 oz.) pkg. lime flavored
  gelatin
1 cup boiling water
1 cup cottage cheese, small
  curd
1 cup salad dressing

2 T. onion, finely chopped
3 T. carrot, finely chopped
2 T. green pepper,
  finely chopped
3 T. cucumber, finely chopped
1 cup heavy cream, whipped

Dissolve gelatin in water, cool. Add remaining ingredients, fold whipped cream in last. Pour into 8" x 8" pan. Chill until firm.

Mrs. Tom Vander Kuy

MOLDED ORANGE SALAD   12 servings

4 (3 oz. each) pkgs. orange
  flavored gelatin
1½ cups boiling water

3 cups orange juice
1 (11 oz.) can mandarin
  oranges, drained

Lemon dressing:
1 egg
½ cup sugar

juice and rind from 1 lemon
1 cup heavy cream, whipped

Dissolve gelatin in water. Add orange juice. Place orange sections in molds or 9" x 13" pan. Add gelatin mixture. Refrigerate until firm. When set, top with lemon dressing.

Beat egg in saucepan, add sugar, lemon rind and juice. Stir. Cook until transparent over moderate heat, about 5 mins. Cool. Fold in whipped cream.

Miss Joan Tanis

ORANGE ORIENTAL SALAD   *9 servings*

1 (3 oz.) pkg. orange flavored
   gelatin
1 cup hot black tea
1 cup juice from oranges
   and pineapple

1 (11 oz.) can mandarin
   oranges, drained
1 (9 oz.) can crushed
   pineapple, drained
½ cup water chestnuts, sliced

Garnish:
1 envelope whipped topping
   mix, whipped
¼ cup salad dressing

2 T. chopped ginger or a
   dash of mace

Dissolve gelatin in tea. Add juices. Stir in fruits and water chestnuts. Pour into individual molds or 8" x 8" pan. Chill until firm.

Mix salad dressing and ginger into whipped topping mix and use as garnish for salad.

Mrs. John Whittle

ORANGE SOUFFLE GELATIN   *12 servings*

2 (3 oz. each) pkgs. orange
   flavored gelatin
2 cups boiling water
1 cup combined pineapple
   orange juice
1 pint orange sherbet

1 (9 oz.) can crushed
   pineapple, drained
1 (11 oz.) can mandarin
   oranges, drained
½ cup crushed nuts, optional

Mix together gelatin and water; stir in juice and sherbet and allow to partially set. Then fold in remaining ingredients. Pour into 9" x 13" pan. Refrigerate until firm.

GRAND MARNIER PEAR SALAD   12 servings

1 (20 oz.) can pears, drained
2 cups liquid, pear juice
   plus water
1 (6 oz.) pkg. orange flavored
   gelatin
1 (8 oz.) pkg. cream cheese

⅓ cup Grand Marnier
2 pkgs. whipped topping mix
   (to make 2 cups each)
1 cup light cream
mandarin oranges and
   cherries for garnish

Heat liquid to boiling, add gelatin. Chill until slightly thickened. Combine pears and cream cheese in blender. Add gelatin mixture and blend. Add Grand Marnier and chill. Beat whipped topping mix with cream. When gelatin mixture begins to thicken, fold in whipped cream, mixing until smooth. Pour into 9" x 13" pan, chill until set. Garnish with mandarin oranges and cherries.

Mrs. Jay Freriks

WHIPPED PEAR SALAD   9 servings

1 (3 oz.) pkg. lime flavored
   gelatin
2 (3 oz. each) pkgs. cream
   cheese, softened
2 T. light cream

1 (29 oz.) can pears, drain and
   reserve juice
½ cup each: mandarin
   oranges, pineapple and nuts
1 cup heavy cream, whipped

Heat 1 cup pear juice to boiling, pour over gelatin. Stir until dissolved. Cool. Mix cheese and light cream until smooth. Add gelatin and beat until smooth. Chill until partially set. Fold in pears, oranges, pineapple, nuts and whipped cream. Pour into 9" x 9" pan. Chill until set.

Mrs. Wm. Seyboldt
Mrs. Fred Leaske

PINEAPPLE CREAM SALAD
8-9 servings

2 (3 oz. each) pkgs. lemon or
   lime flavored gelatin
½ cup boiling water
2 cups crushed
   pineapple and juice
¾ cup sugar

juice of one lemon
¾ cup American cheese,
   grated
1 cup heavy cream, whipped
½ cup pecans, chopped

Dissolve gelatin in water. Add pineapple and juice, sugar and lemon juice. Chill. When slightly thickened, fold in grated cheese, nuts and whipped cream. Turn into mold. Chill until firm.

Mrs. Jack Topp

HEAVENLY RASPBERRY SALAD
12 servings

½ cup water
½ cup pineapple juice
1 (3 oz.) pkg. lemon flavored
   gelatin
1½ cups miniature
   marshmallows

1 (8 oz.) pkg. cream cheese,
   softened
1 cup salad dressing
1 cup heavy cream, whipped
1 (20 oz.) can crushed
   pineapple, drained, reserve
   juice

Topping:
2 cups boiling water
2 (3 oz. each) pkgs. raspberry
   flavored gelatin

1 (1 lb.) pkg. frozen raspberries, thawed

Heat water and juice to boiling. Pour over gelatin, marshmallows and cream cheese. Blend with rotary beater and cool. Add salad dressing and whipped cream. Fold in crushed pineapple, pour into 9" x 13" pan and allow to set. Dissolve raspberry gelatin in water. Add berries; cool. Spoon over first layer, refrigerate.

Mrs. Richard Forwood

RASPBERRY SALAD

12 servings

2 (3 oz. each) pkgs. raspberry
  flavored gelatin
2 cups boiling water
2 cups vanilla ice cream
6 T. orange juice

1 (16 oz.) pkg. frozen
  raspberries, drained
2 bananas, diced
1 cup nuts

Dissolve gelatin in water; add ice cream and stir until melted. Add remaining ingredients, pour into a 9" x 13" pan. Refrigerate. Delicious served as a salad or dessert.

Mrs. George A. Lievense

RUBY RED RASPBERRY SALAD

12 servings

1 (3 oz.) pkg. raspberry
  flavored gelatin
1 cup boiling water
1 (10 oz.) pkg. frozen
  raspberries
2 cups sour cream
1 (3 oz.) pkg. cherry flavored
  gelatin

1 cup boiling water
1 (20 oz.) can crushed
  pineapple, drained
1 (1 lb.) can whole cranberry
  sauce
mayonnaise or whipped
  cream for garnish

Dissolve raspberry gelatin in water, add berries together in 9" x 13" pan; refrigerate until set. Spread with sour cream. Mix remaining ingredients together and let set until they can be spooned on sour cream layer. Refrigerate until firm. Serve with mayonnaise or whipped cream as garnish.

Mrs. Martin Japinga

MOLDED SPRING SALAD
25 servings

2 (6 oz. each) pkgs. lime
   flavored gelatin
3 cups boiling water
3 cups cottage cheese
2 cups blanched almonds

3 cups cucumbers, chopped
½ cup lemon juice
1 medium onion, grated
3 cups mayonnaise
Mayonnaise for garnish

Dissolve gelatin in water, cool. When partially congealed add ingredients in order. Chill in two 9" x 13" pans until firm. Garnish with additional mayonnaise.

Mrs. Arnold Dood

STRAWBERRY HOLIDAY SALAD
12 servings

2 (3 oz. each) pkgs. strawberry
   flavored gelatin
1 cup boiling water
1 (1 lb.) can whole cranberry
   sauce

1 (1 lb.) pkg. frozen
   strawberries
1 (20 oz.) can crushed
   pineapple, drained

Topping:
1 cup heavy cream, *whipped*
½ tsp. sugar

2 T. salad dressing

Dissolve gelatin in water. Add cranberry sauce, frozen strawberries and pineapple. Chill in 9" x 13" pan. Spread gelatin salad with topping mixture.

Mrs. Blaine Timmer
Mrs. Norm Japinga

MOLDED WALDORF SALAD
6 servings

1 (3 oz.) pkg. lemon flavored
   gelatin
1 cup boiling water
⅛ tsp. salt
½ cup mayonnaise

1 cup celery, diced
1½ cups red apples, diced
½ cup nuts, chopped
½ cup heavy cream, *whipped*
salad greens

continued

88

Dissolve gelatin in water. Chill until slightly thickened, add salt and blend in mayonnaise. Fold in remaining ingredients, except greens. Turn into a 1 qt. mold and chill. Unmold on greens.

Mrs. Ronald Dalman

CANTALOUPE SALAD   *8 servings*

1 large handful fresh parsley
1 clove garlic, mashed or ⅛ tsp.
  garlic powder
⅔ cup olive oil
⅓ cup wine vinegar

1 tsp. salt
1 tsp. pepper
4 medium tomatoes, diced
2 large cantaloupes, made
  into balls

Mix first six ingredients in blender. Place tomatoes and melon balls in wooden bowl. Add prepared dressing, marinate in refrigerator at least six hours, stirring occasionally. To serve spoon melon balls, tomatoes and some of the dressing into empty cantaloupe shells or small bowls. May also be drained and used on a relish tray.

Mrs. James E. Bultman

CRANBERRY SALAD   *8 servings*

1 cup raw cranberries, ground
1 cup sugar
1 (8¾ oz.) can light sweet
  cherries
½ cup walnuts, chopped

1 cup orange segments
1 cup heavy cream, whipped
1 cup miniature
  marshmallows

Combine cranberries and sugar, let stand in refrigerator overnight. Drain off liquid. Add cherries, nuts and oranges. Fold in whipped cream and marshmallows.

Mrs. Paul Elzinga

CREME DE MENTHE PEAR SALAD   *6 servings*

6 canned pear halves
1 (3 oz.) pkg. cream cheese,
  softened
¼ cup nutmeats
cinnamon

1 cup crushed pineapple,
  drained
½ cup Creme de Menthe
maraschino cherries
lettuce

Combine cream cheese and nuts; fill center of pears. Sprinkle cinnamon lightly over top and chill. Mix pineapple and Creme de Menthe and use as dressing over pears. Serve on lettuce leaf and top with cherries.

HOT CURRIED FRUIT CASSEROLE   *8 servings*

1 (16 oz.) can pear halves
1 (16 oz.) can peach halves
1 (16 oz.) can apricots
1 (16 oz.) can pineapple chunks
1 (3 oz.) jar maraschino cherries

¼ cup brown sugar
¼ cup butter, melted
½ tsp. curry powder
1 T. cornstarch

Preheat oven to 350F. Use an ungreased 9" x 13" baking dish. Drain fruit and arrange hollow side up in baking dish. Mix remaining ingredients; pour over top. Bake for 1 hr. Best made a day ahead and reheated at 350F. for ½ hour. Any fruits may be substituted.

Mrs. John Van Dyke

FRUIT SALAD PLATE   *4-5 servings*

2 bananas, sliced
2 T. lemon juice
1 (1 lb.) can pitted dark
  sweet cherries
1 (11 oz.) can mandarin oranges

1 (20 oz.) can sliced pineapple
lettuce
½ cup mayonnaise
½ cup heavy cream, whipped

Chill and thoroughly drain canned fruit. Sprinkle bananas with lemon juice. Combine bananas, cherries and oranges. For each serving, overlap two pineapple slices on lettuce lined plate. Top with a serving of mixed fruit. Fold mayonnaise into whipped cream and serve with fruit.

Mrs. Robert Hampson

WINTER FRUIT BOWL
8 servings

1 (1 lb.) can pitted dark
  sweet cherries
1 (13½ oz.) can pineapple
  tidbits
1 (11 oz.) can mandarin oranges

1 (8¾ oz.) can seedless green
  grapes
1 tart apple

Sour Cream Honey Dressing:
  ½ cup sour cream
  1 T. honey

1 T. orange juice
1 T. Cointreau

Chill all fruit. Just before serving, drain canned fruit thoroughly, place in large bowl. Cut unpared apple into thin wedges; add to bowl. Pour dressing over fruit and toss until well coated.

Mrs. Leo Jungblut

BARB'S CAESAR SALAD
8 servings

1 clove garlic
⅓ cup olive oil
2 T. fresh lemon juice
1 T. Worcestershire sauce
1 egg, slightly beaten
4 anchovy fillets, mashed

¼ tsp. pepper, freshly ground
1 cup bread cubes
¼ cup oil
1 clove garlic, minced
⅓ cup Parmesan cheese
1 large head Romaine, torn
  in pieces
blue cheese

Rub large salad bowl with clove of garlic. Combine olive oil, lemon juice, Worcestershire sauce, egg, anchovy fillets and pepper in small bowl. Let stand several hours or overnight to blend flavors. Toast bread cubes in oil and minced garlic. Put greens in salad bowl, add bread cubes and Parmesan cheese. Pour dressing over all and toss. Sprinkle with blue cheese to taste.

Mrs. William Boyer

POOR MAN'S CAESAR SALAD
6-8 servings

1 clove garlic, crushed
1 tsp. salt
2 tsp. sugar
½ tsp. black pepper, freshly-
    ground
½ tsp. dry mustard
½ cup oil

¼ cup fresh lemon juice
1 head lettuce
1 medium onion, sliced in rings
¼ cup dry roasted peanuts,
    halved, optional
grated Parmesan cheese

Place garlic, salt, sugar, pepper, mustard, oil and lemon juice in jar. Shake well and chill. Wash lettuce and tear into bite size pieces. Combine lettuce and onion rings in salad bowl. Sprinkle peanuts and cheese over salad. Toss with dressing.

Mrs. Herbert Eldean

GRECIAN SALAD
6 servings

1 small head iceberg lettuce,
    chilled
½ cup radishes, thinly-sliced
    and chilled
½ cup green onion,
    thinly-sliced and chilled
3 T. olive oil
2 T. salad oil
2 T. lemon juice

2 tsp. sugar
½ tsp. salt
cracked black pepper
4 oz. Feta or Romano cheese
1 (2 oz.) can flat anchovy fillets,
    drained
⅔ cup Greek olives or pitted
    ripe olives
cooked potato or beets, optional
oregano leaves

Break lettuce into bite size pieces. Toss in large bowl with radishes and onion. Combine olive oil, salad oil, lemon juice, sugar, salt and cracked pepper to taste and mix well. Pour over lettuce mixture and toss gently. Crumble cheese coarsely and sprinkle over salad. Wrap anchovies around olives and arrange over cheese. Sprinkle with oregano. Serve immediately.

Mrs. Anthony Garofalo

LAYERED SALAD MEDLEY
12 servings

1 large head lettuce, shredded
⅓ cup green onion, finely chopped
⅓ cup celery, sliced
1 (6 oz.) can water chestnuts, sliced
1 (10 oz.) pkg. frozen peas, not thawed

2 cups mayonnaise
1½ T. sugar
¾ lb. bacon, fried and crumbled
3-4 hard cooked eggs, sliced
3 tomatoes, sliced
Parmesan and Romano cheese

Place lettuce in 9" x 13" casserole. Sprinkle next three ingredients on top in layers. Break peas apart and sprinkle on top while frozen. Spread mayonnaise over top like frosting; sprinkle with sugar. Cover and refrigerate overnight. Before serving, add layers of bacon, egg slices and tomato slices. Sprinkle with grated cheeses. Do not toss this salad. Cut into squares. Each serving should go to the bottom of the dish to get the effect of the layers.

Mrs. Donald G. Miller

FRESH GERMAN SPINACH SALAD
4 servings

1 lb. fresh spinach
½ cup mayonnaise
½ cup sour cream
6 anchovies, minced
1½ T. green onion tops, chopped

1½ T. parsley, minced
1½ T. cider vinegar
1½ T. fresh lemon juice
½ clove garlic, minced
cheddar cheese cubes and garlic croutons

Wash and dry spinach. Blend remaining ingredients except cheese and croutons in blender. Pour over spinach, toss lightly; garnish with cheese and croutons.

Mrs. Michael Calahan

KOREAN SPINACH SALAD   8 servings

Dressing:
½ cup brown sugar, packed
1 cup salad oil
1 T. Worcestershire sauce

1 medium onion, quartered
¼ cup vinegar
⅓ cup catsup

Salad:
1 lb. fresh spinach, washed,
   torn into pieces
2 hard cooked eggs, chopped
8 strips bacon, fried crisp and
   crumbled

1 (8 oz.) can water chestnuts,
   sliced
1 (1 lb.) can bean sprouts,
   drained
½ lb. fresh mushrooms,
   cleaned and sliced, optional

Puree dressing ingredients in blender. Store in refrigerator. Just before serving, toss salad ingredients. Pour dressing over top, toss and serve immediately.

Eet Smakelijk's Best

SPINACH SALAD   6 servings

⅔ cup salad oil
3 T. tarragon vinegar
¼ cup red wine vinegar
2 T. bacon grease
2 cloves garlic, crushed
1 tsp. Worcestershire sauce
¼ tsp. pepper
1 tsp. salt

4-5 slices white bread or
   packaged croutons
butter
garlic salt, Parmesan cheese
1 lb. fresh spinach, washed,
   torn into pieces
1 lb. bacon, fried crisp,
   crumbled

Preheat oven to 250F. Combine first eight ingredients in jar and set aside to blend flavors. Slice edges off white bread. Butter both sides and sprinkle one side slightly with garlic salt. Cut into cubes. Place on cookie sheet in oven for 2-3 hrs. Toss so they are toasted on both sides. Sprinkle with Parmesan cheese.

In large salad bowl, combine spinach, bacon and desired amount of croutons. Toss with dressing and serve.

Mrs. Anthony Garofalo

94

MANDARIN AND BLUE CHEESE TOSSED SALAD

8-10 servings

1 head endive lettuce
1 head romaine lettuce
1 head leaf lettuce
1 (11 oz.) can mandarin oranges
1 (2-4 oz.) pkg. blue cheese,
 depending on taste
12 pieces bacon, fried and
 crumbled
1 (0.6 oz.) pkg. Good Seasons
 Blue Cheese Dressing mix

Make Blue Cheese Dressing according to package directions. Clean and tear lettuce. Drain oranges. Crumble blue cheese. Add all together in large bowl and toss with dressing. Serve immediately.

Mrs. George Daily

ORANGE AVOCADO TOSSED SALAD

6 servings

1 medium head lettuce, torn
 in bite size pieces
1 small cucumber, thinly sliced
1 (11 oz.) can mandarin
 oranges, drained
2 T. green onion, sliced
1 avocado, peeled and
 sliced

Dressing:
½ tsp. orange peel, grated
¼ cup orange juice
½ cup salad oil
2 T. sugar
2 T. red wine vinegar
1 T. lemon juice
¼ tsp. salt

Combine ingredients for dressing in jar. Cover and shake well. Just before serving pour over salad and toss.

Mrs. Paul Elzinga

ISLAND TOSSED SALAD

6 servings

Salad:

6 cups leaf lettuce, torn in
  pieces
1 (11 oz.) can mandarin
  oranges, chilled and drained
1 cup fresh mushrooms, sliced

1 small red onion, sliced in
  rings
1 green pepper, sliced in rings
½ avocado, sliced

Dressing:

½ cup mayonnaise
½ cup sour cream
¼ cup dill pickle juice
½ avocado, peeled and
  mashed

1 T. parsley, snipped
2 tsp. chives, snipped
½ tsp. seasoned salt
1 tsp. dill weed, dried

Mix all ingredients for dressing; refrigerate to blend flavors.
Place lettuce in bowl; arrange vegetables and oranges atop lettuce. Toss with desired amount of dressing.

Mrs. Roger Eldean

MAKE-AHEAD TOSSED SALAD

6 servings

2 cups torn head lettuce
2 cups torn curly endive
2 cups torn romaine leaves
6 T. mayonnaise
1 medium red or white onion,
  thinly sliced

salt and pepper
1½ cups cooked peas, drained
1 cup Swiss cheese strips
6 slices bacon, cooked and
  crumbled

Place ⅓ of greens in large bowl. Dot with ⅓ of mayonnaise. Top
with ⅓ of onion slices. Sprinkle with salt and pepper. Add ⅓ of
the peas and cheese. Repeat layers, seasoning each. Do not toss.
Cover, chill for 2 hours. Just before serving, top with bacon and
toss.

Mrs. Vernon Kraai

OREGANO TOSSED SALAD

6-8 servings

2 cloves garlic, mashed
½ T. olive oil
2 tomatoes, cut up
2 stalks celery, chopped
¼ cup salad oil
¼ cup wine vinegar

sliced ripe olives
head of lettuce
salt and pepper
⅛ cup Romano cheese, grated
1 T. oregano
2 oz. blue cheese

Mix garlic with olive oil in wooden bowl and let stand. Transfer to another bowl; add tomatoes, celery, salad oil, vinegar and olives and let stand for at least 30 mins. In large salad bowl tear lettuce, season with salt and pepper, add Romano cheese and oregano. Toss with oil mixture and top with crumbled blue cheese.

Mrs. Arthur Hills

RAINBOW TOSSED SALAD

8-12 servings

Salad:
1 cup cabbage, shredded
1 cup carrots, grated
1 cup celery, sliced
1 cup tomato, chopped
½ cup cucumber, chopped
½ cup red bell peppers, chopped
1 cup fresh green beans, optional

1 cup green pepper, chopped
1 cup English peas, cooked
1 cup lettuce, chopped
½ - 1 cup American cheese, grated
½ cup onion, sliced in rings
1 (4 oz.) jar pimento, chopped
1 cup raw cauliflower

Dressing:
1 tsp. sugar
⅛ tsp. pepper

½ tsp. salt
½ cup vinegar

Combine salad ingredients. Mix dressing ingredients well. Pour over salad, toss lightly. Chill well.

Mrs. Donald Wassink

PENNSYLVANIA DUTCH WILTED LETTUCE

6 servings

1 medium head lettuce
6 slices bacon
⅔ cup green onion, sliced
⅓ cup vinegar
¾ tsp. sugar

1 beef bouillon cube
½ cup water
⅛ tsp. pepper
2 hard boiled eggs, optional

Reserve outer lettuce leaves to line salad bowl and tear remaining lettuce in bite size pieces. Cook bacon until crisp, crumble and drain on absorbent paper. Add green onions, vinegar, sugar, bouillon cube, water and pepper to bacon drippings in pan; bring to a boil and toss with lettuce and bacon. Sliced hard boiled eggs may be used as a garnish.

Mrs. George Vander Wal

SLA STAMPPOT

4 servings

A popular Dutch Lettuce dish of the 1890's.

1 lb. potatoes, peeled
1 lb. leaf lettuce
1 cup radish slices
1 cup celery, chopped
½ cup cucumber, diced
1 small onion, minced

2 T. butter
¼ cup vinegar
¼ cup potato water
½ lb. bacon and bacon fat
3 eggs

Cook potatoes in salted water. Cut lettuce into small pieces. Put lettuce, radish slices, chopped celery, cucumber and minced onion into large salad bowl. Put butter and vinegar into small pan. Cut bacon into small pieces and fry. Pour fried bacon and bacon fat over butter and vinegar. Save enough fat in pan to fry eggs. Fry eggs until hard, then cut fine. Steam potatoes and mash enough to break into fine pieces. Before draining potatoes, add ¼ cup potato water to butter and vinegar mixture. Add hot eggs, hot potatoes and butter mixture to lettuce mixture. Mix thoroughly and serve immediately.

GOURMET ASPARAGUS SALAD 4 servings

1 (10 oz.) pkg. frozen asparagus
  spears, or ¾-1 lb. fresh
  asparagus
1 (15 oz.) can artichoke hearts,
  halved and drained
⅓ cup olive oil
¼ cup lemon juice
¼ tsp. oregano, crushed
1 clove garlic, crushed
½ tsp. seasoned salt
¼ tsp. freshly ground pepper
dash hot sauce
¼ cup ripe olives, sliced
4 lettuce cups

Cook asparagus and mix with artichokes. Combine remaining ingredients except lettuce and olives. Pour over vegetables and marinate overnight. Drain. Arrange on lettuce cups. Top with olive slices.

Mrs. Herbert Eldean

GARBANZO BEAN SALAD 4-6 servings

Dressing:
¼ cup salad oil
¼ cup vinegar
¼ tsp. marjoram
1 T. sugar
1 tsp. salt
¼ tsp. paprika
¼ tsp. pepper

Salad:
1 (1 lb.) can garbanzo beans,
  drained
⅔ cup Parmesan or cheddar
  cheese, grated
1 green pepper, chopped
½ cup sweet pickle, chopped
½ cup carrot, shredded
1 T. onion, minced

Combine dressing ingredients and set aside. Combine salad ingredients and toss with dressing. Chill for at least 2 hrs. before serving.

Mrs. Herbert Eldean

KIDNEY BEAN SALAD

6-8 servings

1 (1 lb.) can kidney beans,
  drained
1½ cups celery, chopped
½ cup sweet pickle, chopped
¼ cup salad oil
1 T. onion, chopped

2 hard boiled eggs, chopped
2 T. vinegar
1 T. salt
1½ tsp. prepared mustard
hard boiled eggs, sliced, used
  for garnish

Combine all ingredients. Toss lightly. Garnish with egg slices if desired.

Mrs. Richard Forwood

SUMMER BEAN SALAD

8-10 servings

¾ cup sugar
½ cup vinegar
½ cup salad oil
salt and pepper
1 onion, sliced
1 green pepper, chopped

1 (1 lb.) can cut green beans,
  drained
1 (1 lb.) can cut yellow beans,
  drained
1 (1 lb.) can red kidney beans,
  drained

Combine sugar, vinegar, oil, salt and pepper. Mix until sugar is dissolved. Pour over onion, green pepper and beans. Let stand in refrigerator for a day before serving.

Mrs. Jack I. Dykstra
Mrs. Donald Kuipers

HEALTHFUL BEET SALAD

4 servings

1 cup beets, grated
1 cup apples, grated

⅓ cup nuts, chopped
⅓ cup raisins

Mix ingredients together and let stand several hrs. so the flavors combine. Excellent blood builder.

Dorothy Koeman

BROCCOLI 'N CELERY SALAD
(2nd Place, Bake-Off)

4 servings

1 large bunch fresh broccoli
1 cup celery, sliced
1 T. onion, minced
2 T. pimento, diced
1 T. celery seed

1 T. lemon juice
½ cup mayonnaise
2 T. sour cream
freshly-ground pepper

Cut broccoli into 1" pieces. Cook in small amount of boiling salted water about 5-8 mins. until tender-crisp. Drain and cool. Add next 5 ingredients and mix well. Combine mayonnaise and sour cream and pour over broccoli mixture. Add pepper and toss gently. Refrigerate 4-6 hrs. prior to serving.

Mrs. Paul Van Kolken

CAULIFLOWER SENSATION

3-4 servings

2 cups cauliflower, thinly-
*   sliced*
½ cup pitted ripe olives,
*   chopped*
⅓ cup green pepper, finely-
*   chopped*
¼ cup pimento, finely-
*   chopped*

3 T. onion, chopped
4½ T. salad oil
1½ T. lemon juice
½ T. wine vinegar
1 T. sugar
1 tsp. salt
dash of pepper

In medium bowl combine cauliflower, olives, green pepper, pimento and onion. In a small bowl mix the oil, lemon juice, vinegar, sugar, salt and pepper with a rotary beater. Pour over vegetables. Mix and refrigerate at least 1 hr.

CUCUMBERS IN SOUR CREAM   *6 servings*

2 medium cucumbers, peeled
    and thinly-sliced
1 medium onion, thinly-sliced
    in rings
1 tsp. salt

1 T. vinegar
1 cup sour cream
1 T. sugar
⅛ tsp. paprika
1 T. parsley flakes

Sprinkle cucumbers and onion with small amount of salt, refrigerate. Combine remaining ingredients and chill. Just before serving drain cucumbers and onion, add dressing and mix lightly.

Mrs. William Hakken Jr.

MARINATED CARROTS   *6 servings*

2 lbs. carrots, sliced
2 medium onions, chopped
1 green pepper, chopped
1 (10¾ oz.) can tomato soup
½ cup salad oil

¾ cup vinegar
¾ cup sugar
1 tsp. each: prepared mustard,
    Worcestershire sauce, salt
    and pepper

Cook carrots 5-8 mins. until tender-crisp. Cool and drain. Add to onion and green pepper. Blend remaining ingredients and pour over vegetables. Refrigerate. Use as a side dish or salad.

Mrs. Alex Rivera

MARINATED VEGETABLES
15 servings

1 (1 lb.) can mixed Chinese
vegetables
1 (1 lb.) can French-style green
beans
1 (1 lb.) can small peas
1 (6 oz.) can water chestnuts,
sliced
2 stalks celery, cut diagonally

1 medium onion, sliced
in rings
¾ cup sugar
½ cup white vinegar
2 T. tarragon vinegar
¾ tsp. salt
½ tsp. black pepper

Drain canned vegetables. Mix with celery, water chestnuts, and onion rings. Mix sugar, vinegars, salt and pepper; pour over vegetables. Cover; refrigerate overnight. This recipe will keep in a covered container in the refrigerator at least a week.

Mrs. Donald Wassink

MARINATED ZUCCHINI SALAD
6 servings

1 (16 oz.) can tiny carrots,
whole, drained
2 small zucchini, thinly-
sliced
1 (14 oz.) can hearts of palm,
drained and cut in
thick slices
⅔ cup salad oil
¼ cup vinegar

1 tsp. sugar
1 small clove garlic, crushed
¾ tsp. salt
¾ tsp. dry mustard
dash freshly ground pepper
lettuce leaves
1 (2 oz.) pkg. blue cheese,
crumbled

In shallow dish, combine carrots, zucchini and hearts of palm. In screw top jar, combine oil, vinegar, garlic, sugar, salt, mustard and pepper. Cover and shake well. Pour over vegetables. Chill several hrs. or overnight. To serve, drain marinade. Arrange vegetables on lettuce, top with cheese.

Variation: ¼ lb. sliced fresh mushrooms can be added to the marinade 2-3 hrs. before serving.

Mrs. Herbert Eldean

SAUERKRAUT SALAD   20 servings

2 (1 lb. each) cans sauerkraut,   ½ cup salad oil
   chopped   ¾ cup vinegar
1 cup celery, diced   1¼ cups sugar
1 green pepper, diced   ½ cup water
1 onion, chopped   dash of Worcestershire sauce
1 (4 oz.) jar pimento, chopped   celery seed, optional

Combine first 5 ingredients in large bowl. Mix remaining ingredients; pour over vegetables. Marinate several hrs. or over night. Drain when ready to serve.

Mrs. Donald Wassink

UNEN RINGEN   4-6 servings
Dutch Onion Rings

2 large onions   ¼ tsp. salt
boiling water   ½ tsp. celery salt or seed
¼ cup sour cream   1 tsp. lemon juice

Slice onions ¼" thick and separate into rings. Place in bowl; cover with boiling water. Let stand for 2 mins. Pour off liquid and chill. Combine sour cream, salt, celery seed or salt and lemon juice. Toss with onions just before serving.

Mrs. R. A. Boersma, Jr.

WEDGEWOOD INN WINTER SALAD I   8 servings
Salad:

1 (1 lb.) can cut green beans   4 stalks celery, chopped
1 (1 lb.) can tiny green peas   1 green pepper, chopped
1 small onion, cut into rings   1 (4 oz.) jar pimento, chopped

continued

Dressing:

½ cup vinegar	1 tsp. salt
½ cup salad oil	1 tsp. paprika
⅓ - ½ cup sugar	½ cup water

Drain canned vegetables, combine with fresh vegetables. Marinate overnight or at least 10 hrs. in dressing mixture. Drain well and serve.

Mrs. Arnold Dood

WEDGEWOOD INN WINTER SALAD II   *30 servings*

Salad:

1 (10 oz.) pkg. frozen chopped broccoli	1 (16 oz.) can chick-peas
1 (10 oz.) pkg. frozen cauliflower	1 (15 oz.) can artichoke hearts
1 (10 oz.) pkg. frozen cut green beans	1 lb. fresh mushrooms, *whole*
1 (16 oz.) can fingerling carrots, *whole*	1 lb. cherry tomatoes, *whole*
1 (16 oz.) can *whole pitted ripe olives*	1 large onion, *sliced into rings*

Dressing:

2½ cups vinegar	5 tsp. salt
2½ cups salad oil	1 T. paprika
2 cups sugar	2½ cups water

Drain canned vegetables, combine with uncooked, thawed, frozen vegetables and washed fresh vegetables. Marinate overnight in dressing mixture. Drain well and serve. This salad keeps well in refrigerator for 2-3 weeks.

Mrs. James Brooks

FRENCH POTATO SALAD
8-12 servings

8 - 10 medium potatoes
4 T. dry white wine
2 T. stock or bouillon
2 T. wine vinegar, or 1 T.
   wine vinegar and 1 T.
   lemon juice

1 tsp. prepared mustard
¼ tsp. salt
6 T. olive oil or salad oil
pepper
2 T. green onion, minced
2 T. parsley, chopped

Boil, peel and slice potatoes. Place in large bowl. Pour wine and bouillon over the warm potato slices and toss very gently. Set aside a few mins. until potatoes have absorbed liquids. With a wire whip, beat vinegar, mustard and salt in a small bowl. Beat in oil by droplets. Season to taste and stir in onions. Pour dressing over potatoes and toss gently to blend. Serve while still warm or chill. Garnish with parsley.

Mrs. David Vander Leek

HOT DUTCH POTATO SALAD
6 servings

1 lb. leaf lettuce, shredded
1 small onion, chopped
salt and pepper to taste
6 slices bacon
¼ cup vinegar
2 T. sugar
½ cup water

2 T. flour
1 T. mustard
1 egg
4 medium potatoes, cooked,
   mashed
2 eggs, hard cooked, sliced

In a large bowl combine lettuce, onion, salt and pepper. Dice bacon and fry. Reserve 3 T. bacon drippings. Blend vinegar, sugar, water, flour, mustard and egg together; add to bacon drippings and cook until thickened. Add hot mashed potatoes to lettuce and pour over hot dressing. Add hard cooked eggs and toss. Diced ham or chicken may be added.

Cornelia Van Voorst

HOT GERMAN POTATO SALAD   *8 servings*

6 potatoes	½ cup vinegar
½ lb. bacon	1 cup water
4 T. bacon grease	½ cup green pepper, chopped
3 T. flour	⅓ cup onion, chopped
½ cup sugar	1 (2 oz.) jar pimentos, chopped

Boil potatoes, drain, peel and slice. Fry bacon crisp, drain and crumble. Return 4 T. bacon grease to pan, add flour, sugar, vinegar and water; cook until thickened. Pour over warm potato slices, add green pepper, onion and pimento; toss gently. Place potato mixture in greased 2 qt. oven proof dish, add crumbled bacon. Chill in refrigerator 8 hrs. Bake at 350F. for ½ hr. or until hot and bubbly.

Mrs. Bruce Williams

HOT POTATO SALAD DELUXE   *12 servings*

10 boiled potatoes, diced	1 (2 oz.) can pimento, chopped
½ lb. cheddar cheese, cubed	4 slices bread, cubed
parsley flakes	1 cup butter, melted
1 large onion, chopped	¾ cup milk
1 large green pepper, chopped	

Mix first seven ingredients together, put in casserole and pour melted butter and milk over top. Bake at 350F. for 45 mins. or until bubbly.

Mrs. David Credo

PENNSYLVANIA DUTCH POTATO SALAD

8-10 servings

8 potatoes
1 stalk celery, diced
2 hard cooked eggs, chopped
1 onion, minced
4 slices bacon
2 eggs, well-beaten

1 cup sugar
½ cup vinegar diluted with ½
  cup cold water
¼ tsp. dry mustard
½ tsp. salt
¼ tsp. pepper
1 T. parsley, minced

Boil potatoes in their jackets; cool, peel and dice. Add celery, eggs and onion. Fry bacon until crisp, reserving grease. Mix together remaining ingredients and pour into hot bacon grease; cook, stirring until thickened (about 10 mins.). Pour over potatoes and mix. Serve warm or cold. Garnish with crumbled bacon.

Mrs. John Hutchinson

SOUR CREAM POTATO SALAD

8-10 servings

7 medium potatoes
⅓ cup French dressing
¾ cup celery, finely-diced
½ cup onion, finely-diced
5 hard boiled eggs, diced

1 cup mayonnaise
½ cup sour cream
1 T. mustard
salt, pepper and celery seed
  to taste

Dice and cook potatoes in salted water. Drain, pour dressing over potatoes and chill 2 hrs. Add remaining ingredients and toss gently.

Mrs. Jason Krikke

CREAMY CABBAGE SLAW
6-8 servings

1 medium head cabbage,
    finely shredded
¼ cup green onion, sliced
1 cup mayonnaise or
    salad dressing

2 T. sugar
2 T. vinegar
2 tsp. celery seed
1 tsp. salt

In small bowl, combine mayonnaise, sugar, vinegar, celery seed and salt; stir until sugar is dissolved and ingredients are well blended. In serving dish combine cabbage and green onions. Drizzle mayonnaise mixture over cabbage and toss.

Mrs. Herbert Eldean

METHODIST COLE SLAW
6-8 servings

1 large head cabbage
salt
1 T. mustard seed

1 medium sweet pepper, grated
1 cup sugar
½ cup cider vinegar

Grate and salt cabbage, let stand several hrs. until liquid forms. Drain well, add mustard seed and chopped pepper; pack tightly in jar or crock. Bring sugar and vinegar to boil, cover cabbage. Store in refrigerator for several days before using.

Mrs. Dale Anthonsen

SWEET-SOUR CABBAGE
6 servings

An old-fashioned hot slaw flecked with parsley

4 slices bacon
¼ cup vinegar
1 T. brown sugar
1 tsp. salt

1 T. onion, chopped
4 cups cabbage, shredded
½ cup parsley, chopped

Cook bacon until crisp, remove from skillet and crumble. Add vinegar, sugar, salt and onion to bacon grease in pan. Add crumbled bacon, heat thoroughly. Remove from heat, toss cabbage and parsley in hot dressing.

Mrs. James Chamness

BLENDER BLUE CHEESE DRESSING   *5 cups*

2 T. white vinegar
1 cup salad oil
1 clove garlic, minced, or
    ⅛ tsp. garlic salt
¼ tsp. salt
dash pepper
dash onion salt

1 T. dried parsley flakes
1 (8 oz.) pkg. cream cheese,
    softened
1 cup salad dressing
1 (4 oz.) pkg. blue cheese,
    crumbled
1½ - 2 cups sour cream

Blend above ingredients, except sour cream, at medium speed in blender until smooth. Add sour cream, blending a few seconds or until just blended. If too thick after refrigerating, add small amount of sour cream or water.

Mrs. Theodore B. Bosch

BLENDER MAYONNAISE   *1⅓ cups*

1 egg
2 T. vinegar or lemon juice
½ tsp. dry mustard

¼ tsp. salt
1 cup salad oil

Put egg, vinegar or lemon juice, mustard, salt and ¼ cup of salad oil in blender. Cover and blend for 15 seconds on medium speed. Immediately remove inner cap and pour in remaining oil quickly while blender is still going. Blend 3 seconds more on highest speed.

Mrs. Albert Wesseldyk

BOILED SALAD DRESSING

2 tsp. sugar or honey
1 tsp. salt
2 T. flour
1 egg, well beaten
2 T. melted butter
¼ cup mild vinegar

¾ cup water
1 tsp. prepared mustard
few grains cayenne
heavy cream or evaporated
    milk, whipped

continued

110

Combine sugar, salt and flour, add egg and mix thoroughly. Add butter, vinegar, mustard, cayenne and water, mixing well. Cook over hot water, stirring constantly, until thick and smooth. Cool. Thin with whipped cream or whipped evaporated milk before using. If desired, more sugar may be added.

Miss Margaret Van Vyven

EGG DRESSING

1 cup oil	1 tsp. sugar
½ cup white vinegar	1 tsp. salt
2 T. dry mustard	3 drops Tabasco sauce
1 T. onion, finely-chopped	¼ cup lemon juice
1 T. chives	2 hard cooked eggs, finely-chopped
1 clove garlic, crushed	

Shake the above ingredients together well and serve on your favorite salad greens.

Mrs. John Hutchinson

FRENCH DRESSING I
1 quart

1 cup sugar	1 tsp. paprika
1 cup catsup	1 small onion, grated
½ cup salad oil	¼ cup lemon juice
¾ cup vinegar	garlic, celery seed and
2 tsp. salt	parsley, optional
½ tsp. celery salt	

Blend above ingredients in blender or shake together in quart jar.

Mrs. David Linn
Mrs. Robert Slocum

FRENCH DRESSING II

1 cup Wesson oil
¾ cup sugar
½ cup vinegar
1 (10¾ oz.) can tomato soup

1 T. dill weed
1 small garlic clove, minced
salt and pepper to taste

Blend above ingredients in blender.

Mrs. Alex Rivera

FRUIT DRESSING

1 (6 oz.) can frozen orange
  juice
1 (6 oz.) can frozen pineapple
  juice
pinch salt

1 T. maraschino cherry juice
3 T. honey
1 T. cornstarch
¼ tsp. dried parsley
¼ tsp. celery seed

Blend all ingredients together except celery seed. Cook over hot water until thick. Add celery seed. Chill.

Mrs. Jack Miller

FRUIT SALAD DRESSING   1 quart

½ cup pineapple or orange
  juice
¼ cup lemon juice
¼ cup sugar
2 eggs

1 tsp. orange peel, optional
½ tsp. nutmeg
⅛ tsp. salt
1 cup heavy cream, whipped

Beat eggs slightly, add remaining ingredients except heavy cream. Cook approximately 5 mins. over medium heat, stirring until thickened. Cool. Add to whipped cream. Serve on any type of fruit salad.

Mrs. J. H. Van Dyke

GREEN GODDESS DRESSING

1 cup mayonnaise
½ cup sour cream
3 T. vinegar
1 T. lemon juice
⅓ cup fresh parsley, chopped
3 T. onion, minced

1 (2 oz.) tube anchovy paste
1 T. chives, chopped
1 clove garlic, crushed
⅛ tsp. salt
⅛ tsp. pepper
2 tsp. capers, optional

Combine all ingredients in blender. Chill at least 2 hrs. before serving on tossed lettuce salad. If sour cream is fresh, dressing will keep 2 weeks.

Mrs. Herbert Eldean

HERB DRESSING

½ cup olive oil
2 T. vinegar
1 tsp. salt
½ tsp. pepper
1 tsp. marjoram

1 T. parsley, chopped
1 tsp. lemon juice
few drops Worcestershire
   sauce

Combine all ingredients and chill.

Mrs. William G. Winter

POTATO SALAD DRESSING

2 eggs, beaten
3 T. sugar
2 T. flour
2 T. butter
scant tsp. dry mustard
1 tsp. prepared mustard

1 tsp. salt
3 T. milk
pepper to taste
½ cup water
½ cup vinegar

Mix first 9 ingredients. Add to water and vinegar in a double boiler. Cook until thickened, stirring frequently. Chill. Shake well before pouring over potato salad.

Mrs. Roger Baar

PRETTY TOMATO DRESSING

3 whole green onions, minced	*1 tsp. paprika*
3 sprigs parsley, chopped	*1½ tsp. salt*
2 large tomatoes, diced	*1 T. vinegar*
¼ cup Parmesan cheese	*1 cup sour cream*

Mix and chill above ingredients well. Pour over salad greens.

Mrs. Philip K. Cyrocki

RUSSIAN DRESSING

¼ cup sugar	*3 T. water*
1 cup salad oil	*½ cup catsup*
1 T. lemon juice	*1 T. Worcestershire sauce*
1 tsp. salt	*¼ cup grated onion*
½ tsp. paprika	*garlic to taste*
1½ tsp. celery salt	*1 T. vinegar*

Blend all ingredients in blender.

Mrs. Charles Leach

SOUR CREAM DRESSING   *1¼ cups*

1 cup sour cream	*dash Tabasco sauce*
2 T. mayonnaise	*½ tsp. Worcestershire sauce*
¼ cup light cream	*¼ tsp. horseradish*
¼ tsp. curry powder	*½ tsp. dry mustard*
dash salt	*1 small clove garlic, minced*

Mix and serve over tossed green salad.

Mrs. Donald Kuipers

SWEDISH SALAD DRESSING

1 cup vinegar	*1 large onion, finely-chopped*
1 cup sugar	*2 stalks celery,*
1 cup salad oil	*finely-chopped*
2 tsp. paprika	*1 green pepper,*
1½ tsp. salt	*finely-chopped*

Stir and let stand — the longer the better. A sweet dressing to serve with shredded cabbage or tart fruit.

Mrs. Paul Klomparens

THOUSAND ISLAND DRESSING

1 cup mayonnaise	*dash of salt*
½ cup chili sauce	*2 hard cooked eggs, chopped*
⅓ cup pickle relish, drained	*onion, optional*

Combine ingredients and chill.

Mrs. Richard Forwood
Mrs. David Paulson

ZERO SALAD DRESSING
Low Calorie

½ cup tomato juice	*1 T. onion, finely-chopped*
2 T. lemon juice or vinegar	*salt and pepper*

Chopped parsley, green pepper, horseradish, mustard or any salad herb may be added. Combine ingredients, cover and mix well before serving.

Mrs. James Brown

NOTES

Fish, Fowl, and Game

NOTES

GOLDEN-FRY BATTER FOR LAKE PERCH OR SMELT

3-4 servings

cooking oil
½ cup sifted flour
1 egg
¾ cup milk

12-15 perch fillets or
25-30 smelt
salt

Fill large electric frying pan about one half full of oil. Heat to 400-420F. Blend ¼ cup oil with flour. Add egg and milk. Beat with rotary beater until smooth. Batter will be thin. Dry fish thoroughly. Coat with flour and dip into batter until completely covered. Place fish into hot oil and fry until golden brown. Fry only 5 perch or 10 smelt at one time; otherwise, the oil will cool down, and the fish will become tough from frying too long. Drain on paper towels; place on hot platter in warm oven until all fish are fried. Season with salt and serve.

Mrs. John R. Marquis

JAMBALAYA
(1st Place, Bake-Off)

6 servings

½ cup green onion, chopped
½ cup white onion, chopped
1 large green pepper,
*   cut in strips*
½ cup celery with a few
*   leaves, chopped*
1 garlic clove, minced
⅓ cup butter
1½ lb. raw shrimp, peeled
*   and cleaned*

1 cup raw oysters or 1 cup
*   cooked ham, cubed*
1 (1 lb.) can tomatoes
1 cup chicken broth
½ tsp. salt
¼ tsp. cayenne
1 cup raw rice

In a large pan, saute onions, green pepper, celery and garlic in butter until tender, but not browned. Add shrimp and oysters and cook 5 mins. (If ham is used add when rice is added.) Add the tomatoes, chicken broth, salt, cayenne and rice, stir and cover. Cook 25 to 30 mins. over low heat or until rice is done. If mixture becomes too dry, add tomato juice. Taste for seasoning.

Mrs. Donald K. Williams

LOBSTER NEWBURG

4 *servings*

1 lb. lobster, fresh, frozen
   or canned
3 T. butter
1 T. flour
½ tsp. salt
⅛ tsp. paprika
⅛ tsp. cayenne pepper

1 tsp. onion, chopped
½ cup mushrooms,
   sliced
¼ cup cognac
¼ cup sherry
1 cup light cream
3 egg yolks

Cut lobster into bite size pieces. Melt butter, blend in flour; add salt, paprika, pepper, onion and mushrooms. Add lobster, cognac and sherry and stir well. Beat cream with egg yolks and add to lobster mixture. Stir gently until thickened and hot. Serve over toast points.

Mrs. Michael Calahan

STUFFED LOBSTER TAIL

8 *servings*

8 frozen lobster tails
½ cup butter
2 tsp. onion, minced
½ cup flour, scant
1 tsp. salt
½ tsp. pepper
1½ cups milk

½ cup light cream
1 lb. shrimp, cooked and
   diced
1 cup clams (optional),
   drained
1 cup buttered bread
   crumbs

Cook lobster according to package directions. Cool, remove meat, leaving trimmed shells intact. Cut lobster into bite size pieces. Melt butter, add onion and cook 5 mins. over low heat. Blend in flour, salt and pepper. Combine milk and cream stirring until thickened and smooth. Add lobster, shrimp and clams to sauce. Refill lobster shells, sprinkle with crumbs and broil until brown.

Mrs. R. A. Boersma

LOBSTER TAILS THERMIDORE   *4-6 servings*

4-6 frozen lobster tails
¼ cup butter
¼ cup flour
1 tsp. salt
½ tsp. dry mustard
1½ cups milk

½ cup light cream
1 (3 or 4 oz.) can
  mushrooms, drained
3 T. Parmesan cheese,
  grated
paprika

Place frozen tails in boiling salt water to cover (1 tsp. salt to 1 qt. water). When water reboils, lower heat and cook tails 9 mins. (If tails are thawed cook only 7 mins.) Cool under running water. Cut through under shell on both sides with scissors. Remove shell covering. Pull meat loose from shell covering, chill and dice. Set shells aside. Melt butter, add flour, salt and mustard, stirring until smooth. Add milk and cream and cook over low heat until thickened, stirring constantly. Add lobster and mushrooms. Heat through. Refill shells and sprinkle with cheese and paprika. Brown lightly under broiler.

Mrs. F. K. Macdonald

BAKED COHO SALMON SURPRISE   *6 servings*

2 lbs. Coho Salmon or
  other fish fillets
½ cup thick French
  dressing
2 T. lemon juice

¼ tsp. salt
1 (3½ oz.) can French fried
  onion rings, crushed
¼ cup Parmesan
  cheese, grated

Preheat oven to 350F. Use a well greased 12" x 8" x 2" baking dish. Thaw fillets and cut into serving pieces. Combine dressing, lemon juice, and salt. Pour sauce over fish and marinate 30 mins., turning once. Remove fish and place in baking dish. Combine onions and cheese and mix thoroughly. Sprinkle onion mixture over fish and bake 25-30 mins. or until fish flakes easily. Do not over cook. Thickness of fish determines length of cooking time.

Mrs. Karl Siebers

SALMON LOAF SUPREME

4 servings

1 egg, beaten
½ cup salad dressing
1 cup cream of celery soup,
*   undiluted*
½ cup onion, chopped
¼ cup green pepper, chopped

1 T. lemon juice
1 tsp. salt
2 cups flaked salmon
1 cup fine bread
*   crumbs*

Preheat oven to 350F. Use a greased 8" x 4" x 2½" loaf pan. Combine egg, salad dressing, soup, onion, green pepper, lemon juice and salt and mix thoroughly. Add salmon and bread crumbs and mix gently. Pour into pan and bake 60 mins.

Mrs. Lee Beyer

SHRIMP DEL PRADO

6 servings

1 onion, finely-chopped
1 tart apple, finely-chopped
2 T. butter
2 T. curry powder
2 cups coconut milk
2 T. coconut

2 T. cornstarch
2 tsp. salt
2 lbs. shrimp, cooked
2 T. sherry
3 T. butter, melted
¼ cup heavy cream

Brown onion and apple in the butter. Blend in curry powder, coconut milk, coconut, cornstarch and salt. Cook until thickened. Add remaining ingredients and stir until well blended. Serve over rice.

Mrs. William T. Hakken, Jr.

SHRIMP EGG FU YUNG

4 servings

½ cup onion, chopped
1 clove garlic, minced
3 T. oil
1 cup canned shrimp

6 eggs, lightly-beaten
½ tsp. salt
⅛ tsp. pepper

continued

Sauté onion and garlic in 1 T. oil; add shrimp and cook until lightly browned. Remove from heat and cool. Combine eggs, salt and pepper and add to cooled shrimp mixture. Heat 2 T. oil in heavy skillet and pour in egg-shrimp mixture. Cover and cook slowly until eggs are set, about 10 mins. Fold over in center. Place on hot platter and serve with Brown Sauce.

Chinese Brown Sauce:

3 tsp. margarine	1 cup hot water
3 tsp. flour	2 T. soy sauce
2 tsp. sugar	1 cup bean sprouts,
½ tsp. salt	drained

Melt margarine and add flour, sugar and salt. Blend well. Add water and soy sauce and cook over low heat until thickened; stirring constantly. Add bean sprouts and serve hot.

Mrs. John Jones

SHRIMP SUPREME
6-8 servings

¼ cup butter	1 T. Worcestershire sauce
½ lb. fresh mushrooms, sliced	¼ cup sherry
1 medium onion, finely-chopped	½ tsp. salt
	¼ tsp. pepper
2 tomatoes, canned or fresh, finely-chopped	¼ tsp. paprika
	3 lbs. cooked shrimp
½ cup light cream	½ cup dry
2 T. flour	bread crumbs

Preheat oven to 350F. Use a large baking dish. Sauté mushrooms in 2 T. butter; add onions and tomatoes. Cook 10 mins. Mix cream with flour to make a paste and add to mushrooms. Season with Worcestershire sauce, sherry, salt, pepper and paprika and cook, stirring until blended. Add shrimp and pour into baking dish. Melt remaining butter, mix with crumbs and pour over top. Bake 20 mins. Scallops can be used with shrimp if desired.

Mrs. Robert Hall

ORIENTAL SHRIMP
IN VEGETABLE RICE RING

6 servings

1 (10 oz.) pkg. frozen Japanese
    style vegetables

4 cups hot cooked medium
    grain rice
2 T. margarine

Filling:
1 chicken bouillon cube
1 cup boiling water
1 (1 lb.) pkg. frozen shrimp,
    shelled
1 (6 oz.) pkg. frozen Chinese
    pea pods (or sugar peas)
½ cup sliced water chestnuts

¼ cup green onion, sliced
2 T. soy sauce
¼ tsp. salt
3 T. cornstarch
⅓ cup cold water
2 medium tomatoes,
    cut in eighths

Use a greased 5½" cup mold. Prepare vegetables according to pkg. directions. Cut up large pieces of vegetables. Do not drain off liquid. Combine vegetables, hot rice, and margarine. Press the rice mixture lightly into mold. Unmold onto serving platter at once. Keep rice ring warm.

In large skillet, dissolve bouillon cube in hot water. Add next 6 ingredients. Return mixture to boiling. Cook, uncovered, for 2-3 mins., stirring occasionally. Blend cornstarch and cold water; stir into shrimp mixture. Stir constantly until mixture thickens and bubbles. Add tomato wedges and heat through. Spoon shrimp mixture into center of rice ring.

Mrs. John Whittle

SHERRIED FILLET OF
SOLE ALMONDINE

4 servings

4 large fillets of sole,
    about ¾" thick
2 green onions, including
    tops, chopped
½ cup fresh mushrooms,
    cleaned and chopped

¼ tsp. salt
pinch dried rosemary
½ cup dry sherry
¾ cup heavy cream
2 T. butter
½ cup slivered almonds

continued

Combine fish, onions, mushrooms, salt, rosemary and sherry in frying pan. Simmer over low heat 10 mins. Place fillets in shallow baking dish. Reduce liquid remaining in pan by half, over high heat. Lower heat; add cream and butter; bring to boiling. Pour over fish, distributing onions and mushrooms evenly. Sprinkle almonds over top. Broil about 10 mins., watching carefully to avoid burning.

Mrs. Michael Calahan

STUFFED FILLET OF DOVER SOLE   *4 servings*
8 Dover sole fillets

Dressing:

12 oz. frozen peeled and deveined shrimp	*2 tsp. horseradish, drained*
	2 tsp. chopped chives
12 oz. frozen, cooked Alaskan king crabmeat	*2 tsp. fresh parsley, chopped and washed*
10 saltine crackers, coarsely broken	*1 egg, lightly-beaten*
½ cup heavy mayonnaise	*pinch grated lemon rind*
2 tsp. dry white wine	

Topping:

¼ cup white wine	*2 T. lemon juice*

Preheat oven to 450F. Use a large shallow baking dish. Cook and cool shrimp, thaw and squeeze most of the liquid from crabmeat. Cut shrimp and crabmeat into large pieces and mix lightly by hand with balance of ingredients for dressing. Place fillets, smooth side down, and mound dressing on top of each fillet the entire length of it. Roll up lengthwise and skewer with toothpicks. Place in dish one inch apart with ends turned down. Add small amounts of butter and water. Sprinkle with additional fine cracker crumbs and paprika. Bake approximately 25 mins. Remove from oven and drizzle with topping.

Mr. Richard Den Uyl

FILLET OF SOLE IN WHITE WINE
4 servings

4 fillets of sole	1 T. parsley, chopped
1 ¼ tsp. salt	½ tsp. thyme
½ tsp. white pepper	2 bay leaves, crushed
2 green onions, chopped	1 T. butter
¼ cup butter, melted	1 ½ tsp. flour
½ cup dry white wine	2 T. heavy cream

Preheat oven to 375F. Use a greased 9" x 13" covered baking dish. Season fillets with salt and pepper; arrange in baking dish. Sprinkle with green onions, butter, wine, parsley, thyme and bay leaves. Cover with greased wax paper facing down, then cover dish and bake for 20 mins. Carefully remove fillets from baking dish. Strain pan juices into a small saucepan, add butter, blend in flour, add cream and cook 4 mins. Pour over fillets and serve.

Mrs. J. P. Bailey

BAKED TROUT SUPREME

trout (any amount)	2 thin lemon slices
salt	⅛ tsp. dill or rosemary
freshly ground pepper	2-4 T. white wine
2 T. butter	or sherry

Preheat oven to 400F. Place each trout in center of large sheet of foil; cup foil up around fish. Sprinkle with salt and pepper; top with 2 T. butter and 2 lemon slices. Sprinkle dill or rosemary over top. Pour 2-4 T. (depending on size of fish) wine over each fish. Pull foil edges together; seal well, leaving small air space inside. Bake 30 mins.

Variation: Fresh salmon can also be used by adding a bay leaf along with other above ingredients. Trout and salmon can also be grilled over hot barbecue coals for 30-40 mins.

Mrs. Kenneth Bell

FRENCH BAKED TROUT
6 servings

6 trout fillets, cut in halves,
   or 3 lbs. lake trout, cut
   into 6-8 pieces
4 slices bacon
1 cup onions, chopped
1 cup carrots, grated
1 cup fresh mushrooms,
   chopped
½ cup celery, chopped

½ cup cooked ham,
   diced
2 tsp. salt
½ tsp. dried thyme
½ tsp. pepper
1 cup dry white wine
3 T. butter

Preheat oven to 375F. Use a shallow casserole dish. Fry bacon until half done, drain well and cut into small pieces. Place in casserole. Mix all vegetables, ham and seasonings. Spread half of mixture over bacon. Add fish and remaining vegetable mixture. Pour on wine and dot with butter. Bake 45-50 mins.

Mrs. Robert J. Westerhof

VISKOEKJES
4 servings
Dutch Fish Cakes

1 lb. fish
3-4 T. parsley
3 T. butter
1 med. onion, chopped
2 eggs

5 Dutch rusks, crushed
½ cup milk
⅛ tsp. each: salt, pepper,
   nutmeg and allspice

Clean fish well and boil until tender. Separate fish from bones and place in a large bowl. Fry parsley in butter and add to fish with onion, eggs, rusk and milk. Add spices and mix well. Shape into round cakes and fry in margarine in a hot skillet until brown on both sides. Cakes can be eaten either hot or cold and served with fried potatoes and salad or as a sandwich for lunch.

Viskoekjes or fish cakes are an important item in the Dutch national diet. They are made from both left-over and fresh fish. The best fish to use is one with firm meat and few bones.

CHICKEN BREASTS WITH ARTICHOKE HEARTS

6 servings

3 whole chicken breasts, split and boned	2 chicken bouillon cubes
flour	2 T. brandy
2 T. salad oil	2 T. lemon juice
2 T. butter	1 cup sour cream
1 tsp. salt	2 (9 oz.) pkgs. frozen
paprika	artichoke hearts, thawed and well drained

Coat chicken with flour. Brown in hot oil on both sides. Place chicken in a 9" x 12" baking dish. Set aside.

Preheat oven to 350F. Melt butter in a saucepan. Stir in 2 T. flour with salt and paprika until smooth. Gradually stir in 1½ cups water, chicken bouillon cubes, brandy and lemon juice; cook, stirring constantly, until thickened and smooth. Gradually blend in sour cream with a wire whisk. Do not boil. Pour mixture over chicken. Cover tightly with foil and bake 35-40 mins. Remove foil and add artichoke hearts. Cover and return to oven for 15 mins. longer or until chicken and artichoke hearts are tender.

Mrs. Michael Calahan

OVEN BARBECUED CHICKEN

4-6 servings

8-10 chicken pieces	1 T. Worcestershire sauce
½ cup flour	3 T. sugar
1 tsp. paprika	½ tsp. salt
butter	½ cup vinegar
⅓ cup Heinz 57 steak sauce	¼ cup water

Preheat oven to 300F. Use a covered greased 9" x 13" baking dish. Coat chicken in flour and paprika. Place in baking dish and dot each piece with butter. Combine remaining ingredients for sauce and pour over top. Cover dish and bake 2 hrs., basting often; remove cover the last ½ hour to brown.

Mrs. Ronald Dalman

128

CHINESE FRIED TOFU
Soybean Curd

2 T. cooking oil
2 cups pork or chicken, diced
4 water chestnuts, chopped
3 green onions, sliced
1 T. soy sauce

1 cup bean sprouts, drained
1 egg, slightly-beaten
½ pkg. Tofu, diced
salt and pepper to taste

Sauce:
2 cups chicken broth
2 tsp. soy sauce

1 T. cornstarch

Heat oil in skillet. In a large bowl combine next 8 ingredients. Drop by large spoonfuls into hot oil and form into small cakes. Fry until lightly browned.

Heat chicken broth, soy sauce and cornstarch until thickened. Pour mixture over cakes and serve.

Mrs. Lyle Sprik

CHICKEN CACCIATORE   4 servings

3½ lb. fryer, disjointed
¼ cup flour
1 tsp. salt
1 tsp. seasoned salt
½ tsp. freshly ground pepper
¼ cup olive oil
1 garlic clove, minced
1 small onion, finely-chopped

½ cup dry white wine
1 (1 lb.) can tomatoes, chopped
¼ tsp. oregano
¼ tsp. basil
2 T. minced parsley
½ lb. fresh mushrooms,
   sliced
2 T. butter

Rub chicken with a mixture of flour, salts and pepper. Heat oil in a heavy skillet; brown the chicken. Drain. Add garlic, onion, wine, tomatoes and seasonings. Cover and cook over low heat 40 mins., or until chicken is tender. Sauté mushrooms in butter while chicken is cooking. Drain and add to chicken just before serving.

Mrs. Landis Zylman

CHICKEN CHINESE STYLE   *4-5 servings*

1 clove garlic, crushed   *3 T. dark corn syrup*
1 T. sugar   *3 T. soy sauce*
¼ cup brandy, bourbon,   *3 lbs. fryer chicken*
   or dry sherry   *cut in pieces*
2 T. honey   *melted butter*

Combine above ingredients and brush on chicken, marinate 4-6
hrs. Brush melted butter on one side of chicken and broil, turn
and repeat. Broil only to brown chicken, then bake at 325F. for 30
mins.

Mrs. Howard Poll

BREAST OF CHICKEN DELUXE   *12 servings*

6 whole chicken breasts,   *2 (10¾ oz. each) cans cream of*
   halved, skinned and boned   *chicken soup*
pepper   *2 cups sour cream*
12 bacon slices   *1 (3 oz.) pkg. cream cheese,*
2 (4 oz. each) pkgs. dried beef   *softened*
½ lb. fresh mushrooms,   *6 cups hot cooked*
   sliced   *rice*

Preheat oven to 325F. Use a 9" x 13" baking dish. Cook bacon to
limp stage; drain. Sprinkle chicken breasts with pepper and wrap
a slice of bacon around each breast. Place a layer of dried beef in
bottom of baking dish. Arrange chicken breasts on beef. Cover
with mushrooms. Cover all with a mixture of soup, sour cream
and cream cheese. Cover dish tightly with foil. Bake 2 hrs. The last
15 mins. of baking remove foil and let brown slightly. Serve over
hot rice.

Mrs. Stafford Keegin

CHICKEN WITH DUMPLINGS   6 servings

4-5 lbs. stewing chicken, cut
   into pieces
5 cups water
1 tsp. salt

4 carrots, chopped
1 large onion stuck
   with 1 clove
2 stalks celery, chopped

Sauce:
¼ cup butter
⅓ cup flour

1¼ cups milk

Dumplings:
2 cups flour
3 tsp. baking powder
½ tsp. salt

¼ cup parsley, finely-
   chopped
⅔ cup milk

Bring water to a boil, add chicken, salt and vegetables. Bring to a boil again. Skim; reduce heat and simmer gently for 1 hr. or until tender. Remove cooked chicken and vegetables from stock. Skim fat from stock, reserving 6 T. for dumplings. Strain stock and reserve.

Melt butter, stir in flour until smooth; add milk and cook, stirring constantly, until sauce is smooth and creamy. Bring 3 cups chicken stock to a boil and add cream mixture, stirring constantly, return to boil and simmer 5 mins. Add chicken pieces (skin and bones removed) to sauce. Correct seasonings.

Sift flour, baking powder and salt into mixing bowl. Stir in 6 T. reserved melted chicken fat and parsley. Add milk in small amounts, stirring with fork, until mixture is dampened. Drop by tablespoonfuls onto chicken pieces in gently bubbling sauce. Cover and cook 25 mins.

Mrs. Donald G. Miller

CHICKEN BREASTS WITH GRAPE SAUCE

6 servings

3 whole chicken breasts,
   boned and split
2½ T. flour
½ tsp. salt
¼ tsp. white pepper
1 tsp. paprika
¼ cup butter

½ tsp. curry powder
⅓ cup flour
1 cup chicken broth
1 cup light cream
1½ cups seedless white grapes

Rub chicken with a mixture of flour, salt, pepper and paprika. In large skillet heat butter, add chicken and brown. Cook over low heat, turning occasionally until tender; 20-30 mins. Remove to serving dish and keep warm. To skillet drippings blend in curry powder and flour over low heat. Gradually stir in chicken broth and cream. Stir until thickened and smooth. Add grapes; spoon over chicken and serve.

Mrs. Roy J. Kee, Jr.

OVEN LEMON CHICKEN

6 servings

2½-3 lbs. fryer chicken,
   cut in pieces
1 cup flour

2 tsp. salt
1 tsp. paprika
6 T. butter, melted

Marinade Sauce:
¼ cup lemon juice
1 T. salad oil

½ tsp. each: salt, pepper,
   thyme, garlic and onion

Marinate chicken 3-4 hrs. in sauce. Preheat oven to 375F. Use a 9" x 13" baking dish. Coat chicken pieces in flour, salt and paprika. Arrange in a single layer and pour butter over top. Bake 30 mins. Turn chicken pieces and pour marinade over top. Continue baking 30 mins. more or until chicken is brown and tender.

Mrs. Roger Prins

CHICKEN LOAF
8-10 servings

3 cups diced, cooked
   chicken
2 cups soft bread crumbs
½ cup cooked celery, chopped
4 eggs, beaten
2 cups milk

2 T. parsley flakes
1 tsp. salt
½ tsp. paprika
4 T. pimento, finely-chopped
4 T. butter, melted
sage to taste

Preheat oven to 350F. Use a well greased mold or large loaf pan. Mix all ingredients together well. Pour into pan and bake 35 mins. or until firm. Remove from oven and allow to stand covered about 10 mins. before serving. Thinned mushroom soup may be served over top as a sauce.

Mrs. Bill Flaherty

CHICKEN PAPRIKASH
6 servings

3 lbs. frying chicken,
   cut up or chicken breasts
½ cup margarine, melted
¾ cup flour
2 T. paprika
1 T. seasoned salt

¼ tsp. pepper
1 small onion, finely-diced
½ cup chicken broth
½ cup water
1 cup sour cream

Preheat oven to 400F. Use an ungreased 9" x 13" baking dish. Dip chicken pieces in margarine and coat with a mixture of flour, paprika, seasoned salt and pepper. Arrange in dish and pour over remaining margarine. Bake uncovered 1 hr. Remove to platter and keep warm. Put 2 T. drippings in a sauce pan, blend in 2 T. seasoned flour and add onion; stir in broth and water. Cook until thickened and smooth; boil 1 min. Blend in sour cream, but do not bring to a boil. Pour over chicken or serve as a sauce on the side.

Mrs. Fred De Wilde

PINEAPPLE CHICKEN
4-6 servings

2 lbs. chicken breasts
¼ cup flour
1½ tsp. salt
½ tsp. pepper
¼ tsp. thyme
5 T. butter

1 cup sharp cheddar
 cheese, shredded
½ lb. cooked ham,
 cut in strips
1 (4 oz.) can sliced mushrooms
1 (14 oz.) can pineapple tidbits

Preheat oven to 350F. Use a covered 2 qt. baking dish. Coat chicken in a mixture of flour, salt, pepper and thyme. Brown in butter on all sides. Place in baking dish and sprinkle with cheese and ham. Add mushrooms and liquid. Add pineapple and ¼ cup juice. Cover and bake 30 mins.; remove cover and bake 10 mins. longer.

Mrs. Don Bryant

CHICKEN POT ROAST
3-4 servings

3½ lb. whole chicken
3 T. butter
1 carrot, sliced
1 stalk celery, sliced
2 bay leaves

1 tsp. crushed rosemary
1 large onion, chopped
½ cup white wine
salt and pepper

Preheat oven to 300F. Brown chicken in butter, breast side first. Add remaining ingredients and bring to a boil. Remove pot to oven, cover and roast 2 hrs. Prior to serving, cornstarch may be added to gravy for thickening.

Mrs. L. L. Jones

CHICKEN ROYALE
4 servings

4 whole chicken breasts,
  skinned and boned
¼ cup flour
½ tsp. salt

¼ tsp. paprika
dash pepper
2 cups stuffing (your favorite)
⅓ cup butter, melted

Sour Cream Mushroom Sauce:
½ lb. fresh mushrooms,
  sliced
¼ cup onion, minced
2 T. butter
2 T. flour

½ cup heavy cream
½ cup sour cream
½ tsp. salt
¼ tsp. pepper

Preheat oven to 325F. Use a 9" x 13" baking dish. Combine flour and seasonings in paper bag, add chicken and shake. Fill cavity of chicken breasts with stuffing. Skewer closed with toothpicks. Dip chicken in melted butter, place in baking dish. Drizzle remaining butter over chicken. Bake 45 mins. turn and bake an additional 45 mins. or until tender. Serve with mushroom sauce.

Cook mushrooms and onions lightly in butter until tender but not brown; cover and cook 10 mins. over low heat. Push mushrooms to one side and stir flour into butter. Add cream, sour cream, and seasonings. Heat slowly, stirring constantly, until well blended. Do not boil. Makes about 1½ cups.

Mrs. Kenneth Kooiker

SHERRIED CHICKEN   4 servings

3½ - 4 lb. frying chicken,   ¾ cup sherry
  cut in pieces   1 (10¾ oz.) can cream
½ cup flour   of mushroom soup
2 tsp. salt   1 small onion,
¼ tsp. pepper   chopped
¼ tsp. paprika   ½ cup celery, chopped
¾ cup butter

Preheat oven to 350F. Use a 9" x 13" covered baking dish. Coat chicken in flour seasoned with salt, pepper and paprika. Brown on all sides in butter. Arrange in baking dish. Combine sherry, soup, onion and celery and heat. Pour over chicken. Cover and bake about 1 hr.

Mrs. Robert Bernecker

SHERRIED SUPREMES   6-8 servings

4 whole chicken breasts,   2 T. chicken stock
  halved, boned and skinned   ¼ cup dry sherry
½ cup all-purpose flour   8 thin slices boiled
2½ tsp. salt   or smoked ham
1 tsp. paprika   8 thin slices Swiss cheese
¼ cup butter   Parmesan cheese

Preheat oven to 350F. Use a 9" x 13" baking dish. Combine flour, salt and paprika and coat chicken lightly. Melt butter in a large skillet and brown chicken on both sides. Add chicken stock and sherry, simmer covered 20 mins. or until tender. Arrange chicken breasts in baking dish. Place a slice of ham (about size of chicken breast) on each chicken breast; repeat with cheese slices, then sprinkle Parmesan cheese over all. Drizzle with remaining juices from skillet. Bake uncovered 20 mins. or until cheese is bubbly and lightly browned.

Mrs. Dennis Brewer

WINE-ROASTED TURKEY

6 servings

1 (10-14 lb.) turkey
1½ tsp. salt
½ tsp. pepper
dressing (your favorite)

softened butter
½ cup Mogan David
  Rosé Wine
½ cup chicken broth

Preheat oven to 350F. Use a shallow roasting pan with a rack. Rub inside of turkey with salt and pepper. Stuff with your favorite dressing, packing loosely. Truss. Rub entire bird with softened butter. Place in pan. Mix together Rosé Wine and chicken broth and pour over bird. Cover turkey breast with aluminum foil. Do not tuck foil under bird. Place in oven and roast 3½ - 4 hrs. basting frequently with pan drippings. If more basting liquid is needed, mix Rosé and chicken stock in same proportions.

Mrs. John Hill

CORN BREAD, SAUSAGE AND WATER CHESTNUT STUFFING

3 quarts

1½ cups celery, chopped
1½ cups onion, chopped
1 cup margarine, melted
1 lb. sausage, cooked,
  crumbled and drained
2 qts. stale white bread,
  cubed
1¼ qts. stale cornbread,
  crumbled

1 (8 oz.) can water chestnuts,
  sliced
2 tsp. sage
1 tsp. thyme
1 tsp. salt
½ tsp. pepper
½ cup parsley, chopped
2 eggs, slightly beaten
½ cup chicken broth

Sauté celery and onion in margarine until tender. Combine with sausage, breads, water chestnuts and seasonings. Add parsley, eggs and broth.

Mrs. Bernice Miller

CURRANT FRENCH BREAD STUFFING
10-12 lb. turkey

½ cup dried currants
10 cups French bread cubes
1¼ cups coarse cracker
   crumbs (20 soda crackers)
¼ tsp. ground nutmeg
¼ tsp. ground allspice
⅛ tsp. pepper

½ cup onion, chopped
½ cup celery, chopped
½ cup butter, melted
1 (10¾ oz.) can condensed
   cream of chicken soup,
   undiluted
2 beaten eggs

Cook currants in water to cover until tender. Drain. Combine remaining ingredients, mixing thoroughly. Fill turkey cavity loosely.

Mrs. Robert Hampson

GIBLET GRAVY
2 cups

giblet and neck
   from turkey
1 onion, quartered
2 stalks celery and leaves
2 carrots
1 tsp. salt

⅛ tsp. pepper
3 cups water
⅓ cup turkey drippings
⅓ cup flour
2 cups giblet broth

In saucepan combine turkey giblets and neck, onion, celery, carrots, salt, pepper and water. Bring to a boil; reduce heat and simmer covered 1 hr., or until giblets are fork-tender. Drain, discard vegetables, reserve broth. Chop giblets finely.

Blend turkey drippings and flour until smooth. Gradually add broth. Heat to boiling, stirring constantly. Correct seasonings. Add giblets.

Mrs. Bernice Miller

BEAVER PAR EXCELLENCE

2 medium beaver legs, cubed
    or other parts of beaver
salt and pepper
1 cup butter
2 lbs. small onions
1 (6 oz.) can tomato paste
⅓ cup red wine

2 T. red wine vinegar
1 T. brown sugar
1 tsp. garlic salt
1 bay leaf
1 small cinnamon stick
½ tsp. whole cloves
2 T. raisins

Remove all fat from beaver. Season with salt and pepper. Melt butter in a large covered pot; add meat but do not brown. Arrange onions over meat. Mix tomato paste, wine, vinegar, sugar, and garlic salt and pour over meat and onions. Add bay leaf, cinnamon stick, cloves and raisins. Cover onions with a heavy plate to hold them intact. Cover pot and simmer 3 hrs. or until meat is tender. Do not stir sauce. Dish out meat and onions and pour sauce over top.

Mrs. Ernest H. Phillips

ROCK CORNISH GAME HENS WITH WILD RICE STUFFING AND CHERRY SAUCE

4 servings

4 Rock Cornish Game Hens
2 T. butter

2 T. Rosé Wine

Wild Rice Stuffing:
¼ cup celery, chopped
¼ cup onion, chopped
3 T. butter
½ cup wild rice or long
    grain, washed and drained
½ tsp. salt

⅛ tsp. sage
¼ cup mushrooms, chopped
1 cup chicken broth
2 T. fine dry bread
    crumbs

Rosé-Cherry Sauce:
1 (10 oz.) jar cherry preserves
¼ cup Rosé Wine

1 tsp. cinnamon
½ tsp. nutmeg

continued

Sauté celery and onion in butter until tender. Add rice, salt, sage, mushrooms and broth. Cover. Simmer over low heat 35 mins. Stir in bread crumbs. Fill cavities loosely with stuffing. Truss and place in roasting pan. Preheat oven to 450F. Melt butter and wine together. Brush on hens and place in oven for 30 mins. Reduce heat to 350F. and roast, basting often, for another 20 mins. Remove from oven, transfer to platter and serve with Rosé-Cherry sauce.

Sauce: Heat all ingredients together until preserves are melted. Serve warm.

Mrs. Donald G. Miller

ROAST DUCK IN SOUR CREAM   *4-5 servings*

2 wild ducks, dressed	parsley and fennel
2 onions	salt and pepper
2 cups hot chicken	nutmeg
broth or water	2 cups sour cream
3 garlic cloves	2 T. sugar
4 bay leaves	2 T. lemon juice
1 tsp. thyme	

Preheat oven to 350F. Use a covered roasting pan. Place onions in ducks and truss for roasting. Place in roaster with hot chicken broth or water. Tie the following in a cheese cloth: garlic cloves, bay leaves, thyme, a little parsley and fennel and place in broth. Salt and pepper birds and sprinkle with nutmeg. Cover and roast 1 hr. adding more liquid if necessary. Remove bag of spices and onions. Remove birds and skim off fat. Blend sour cream, sugar and lemon juice and add to broth in pan. Boil rapidly until thickened, stirring vigorously, adding more liquid if necessary. Return birds to pan and roast at 250F. for 15 to 20 mins.

Mrs. Ernest H. Phillips

140

ROAST DUCK A LA ORANGE

4 servings

5 lb. duck
1 tsp. salt
¼ tsp. pepper
⅛ tsp. marjoram
⅛ tsp. thyme
2 T. olive oil
2 oranges, peeled
  and sliced

1 cup dry white wine
2 T. chopped parsley
1 bay leaf
1 small garlic clove, crushed
grated rind and juice
  of 1 orange
2 T. cornstarch
1 cup chicken broth

Preheat oven to 450F. Rinse duck and wipe with a damp cloth. Combine salt, pepper, marjoram and thyme and rub duck inside and out with mixture. Brush with olive oil. Fill with orange slices and truss. Roast duck in white wine with herbs and garlic for 10 mins., reduce heat to 350F. and cook for 1 hr., basting every 10 mins. with wine in pan. Remove excess fat now and then. When finished roasting, remove duck to a warm platter. To pan drippings, add orange rind and thicken with cornstarch. Stir in broth gradually. Bring to a boil and add orange juice. Correct seasonings, strain and serve.

Mrs. Robert Hampson

SMOTHERED PHEASANT, RABBIT OR SQUIRREL

3-4 servings

2-3 pheasants, cut up
3 T. flour
½ tsp. salt

¼ tsp. pepper
½ cup butter
½-1 pt. light cream

Preheat oven to 350F. Use an ungreased roasting pan. Shake pheasant pieces in a bag containing flour, salt and pepper. Brown in butter. Pour cream over top and bake 1 hr. or until tender. Use pan drippings for delicious gravy.

Mrs. William J. Lalley

PHEASANT WITH MUSHROOMS   *6 servings*

3 pheasants
½ cup butter
2 cups fresh mushrooms,
*   washed and sliced*
¾ cup white wine

2 T. lemon juice
½ cup green onions,
*   chopped*
1 tsp. salt
¼ tsp. freshly ground pepper

Soak pheasants in salted water several hrs. or overnight. Cut into pieces and drain. Sauté pheasant in butter over moderate heat 10 mins. Remove pheasant; sauté mushrooms in remaining butter for 10 mins. or until golden brown. Return pheasant to skillet; add wine, lemon juice, green onions, salt and pepper. Cover; simmer 1 hr. or until tender. Serve with rice.

Mrs. Michael Calahan

ROAST RABBIT   *3-4 servings*

1 rabbit
oil
salt and pepper

floured strips
*   of bacon*

Preheat oven to 350F. Use a covered roasting pan. Cut rabbit in serving pieces. Brown slightly in hot oil. Place in roaster and sprinkle lightly with salt and pepper. Lay floured strips of bacon over top of meat. Roast 30 mins. per pound. Bacon will eliminate game taste.

Mrs. John DuMez

VENISON CHOPS   *4-5 servings*

3 lbs. venison chops
5 T. flour
1 tsp. each: salt and pepper
¼ cup each: olive oil and
*   butter or margarine*

2-3 garlic cloves,
*   crushed*
¼ tsp. sage
1 cup Burgundy wine
1 shot of brandy

continued

142

Remove all fat from chops, coat with flour seasoned with salt and pepper. In a large heavy skillet, brown meat in hot olive oil, butter and garlic. Sprinkle with sage and pour over wine. Simmer covered over low heat for 45-50 mins. or until tender. Just before serving pour over shot of brandy. Venison steaks can also be used.

Mrs. Dennis Brewer

SAVORY VENISON ROAST
6-8 servings

1 (5½ lb.) venison roast
1 clove garlic, minced
1 tsp. salt
½ tsp. pepper
1 bay leaf, crushed
½ tsp. ginger
½ tsp. thyme
½ tsp. sage
½ tsp. marjoram
1 T. salad
   oil or butter

Preheat oven to 500F. Use a covered roasting pan. Cut small gashes ½" long all over roast. Combine all ingredients except oil. Rub well into roast and then coat with oil. Roast for 15-20 mins. Reduce heat to 350F. for remainder of roasting time, 20-25 mins. per pound.

Mrs. Holmes Linn

SWISS VENISON STEAK
8 servings

2 or 3 venison round steaks
flour
salt and pepper
oil
1 (10¾ oz.) can cream
   of mushroom soup
½ cup water

Cut steaks into serving pieces and coat with flour. Season with salt and pepper. Brown in oil in a pressure cooker. Add soup and water, cover and cook under pressure for 20 mins. Remove from stove and allow pressure to return to normal before removing lid. The result is a delicious tender meat with a savory gravy.

Mrs. Edward L. Herrinton

NOTES

Meats

NOTES

BOEUF BOURGUIGNONNE

8 servings

16 (about 1 lb.) small white
    onions
6 strips lean bacon, diced
¼ cup butter
4 lbs. beef chuck, cut
    in 1½" cubes
¼ cup brandy
1½ tsp. salt
¼ tsp. pepper, freshly-ground
2 cups Burgundy or other
    dry table wine
2 whole cloves garlic

2 cups fresh mushrooms,
    whole or sliced
1½ cups water
1 or 2 sprigs parsley
1 celery top
1 carrot, quartered
1 bay leaf
1 tsp. dried thyme
6 T. flour
½ cup cold water
wild rice, cooked

Brown onions with bacon and butter in a Dutch oven; remove onions and bacon with a slotted spoon, set aside. Add meat to pan, brown on all sides. Pour brandy over beef and set aflame, tilting pan to keep flame going as long as possible. Sprinkle meat with salt and pepper. Add Burgundy, garlic, mushrooms, 1½ cups water, onions and bacon. Make a bouquet garni by placing parsley, celery top, carrot, bay leaf and thyme in a piece of cheese cloth tied with a long string. Add bouquet garni. Cover and simmer about 1½ hrs. or until tender. Remove beef, onions and mushrooms. Arrange in a covered 3 qt. casserole. Strain the liquid through a sieve, discarding bouquet garni, garlic and bacon. Mix flour and ½ cup water to a smooth paste. Stir into meat stock, and cook, stirring, until sauce is thick and smooth. Pour sauce over meat; serve with wild rice.

May be refrigerated and reheated in a covered casserole at 350F. for 35 mins. or until hot.

Mrs. Donald G. Miller

BEEF CROQUETTES   4 servings

½ cup butter	1 lb. beef chuck, cooked and
1 cup onions, chopped	chopped or ground
3 T. flour	1 egg, beaten
1 cup beef broth	dry bread crumbs
salt and pepper to taste	fat for deep frying

Melt butter, sauté onions. Add flour making a smooth paste. Add broth slowly, stirring until smooth. Add salt and pepper. Add beef, mix thoroughly. Refrigerate mixture until completely cool.

To form croquettes, take mixture and form into small balls. Roll in egg then crumbs. Repeat until well coated. Deep fry until golden brown.

Mrs. Roger Eldean

BEEF WITH SAUERKRAUT   6-8 servings

2 T. oil	1 tsp. paprika
3 lbs. beef chuck, cut into	3 cups sauerkraut, rinsed
2" cubes	and drained
1½ cups onion, sliced	bay leaf
1½ tsp. salt	1½ cups canned, chopped
½ tsp. pepper	tomatoes

In a Dutch oven heat oil. Add meat and onions, brown. Sprinkle with salt, pepper and paprika. Cover, cook over low heat 20 min. Add water only to prevent burning. Add sauerkraut, cook 10 min. Add bay leaf and tomatoes. Cover, continue cooking 1½ hrs. Discard bay leaf.

Mrs. Sheldon Wettack

SHERRIED BEEF A LA MODE
6 servings

2 lbs. beef chuck roast, cubed,
fat removed
1 (10¾ oz.) can cream of mushroom soup, undiluted
1 envelope dry onion soup mix

¾ cup dry sherry
½ lb. fresh mushrooms
2 T. margarine
rice or noodles, cooked
1 cup sour cream

Preheat oven to 325F. Use an ungreased 2 qt. casserole. Place meat
in casserole. Combine soups and sherry, spoon over meat. Cover,
bake for 3 hrs. or until meat is fork tender. Saute mushrooms in
margarine over low heat until tender. Drain mushrooms and add
to meat when removed from oven. Serve over rice or noodles with
a dollop of sour cream on each serving.

Mrs. James W. Cook

ITALIAN CUBE STEAKS
4 servings

4 cube steaks
oil for browning
1 (16 oz.) can tomato sauce
¼ cup Burgundy
½ tsp. each oregano, basil,
garlic salt, pepper, seasoned salt

2 T. parsley, chopped
1½ cups Mozzarella cheese,
shredded
Parmesan cheese

Brown cube steaks in a small amount of oil. In a small bowl combine tomato sauce, Burgundy, seasonings and parsley. Spread
mixture evenly over steaks. Cover and cook 10-15 min. or until
tender. Sprinkle each steak with Mozzarella cheese and
Parmesan over all. Cover and cook 2-3 min. until cheese is melted.

Mrs. Don Bryant

STUFFED BEEF

4-6 servings

1 flank steak
2 slices white bread
½ cup water
¼ lb. chicken livers, diced
¾ cup onion, chopped
¼ cup celery, chopped
¼ cup parsley, minced
¼ cup Parmesan cheese, grated

¼ lb. cooked ham, cut julienne
1 egg, beaten
2½ tsp. salt
¾ tsp. freshly ground pepper
¾ tsp. oregano
3 T. olive oil
2 cups water

Pound steak very thin. Soak bread in water 10 min.; drain and mash smooth. Combine with livers, onion, celery, parsley, cheese, ham, egg, 1 tsp. salt, ¼ tsp. pepper and ¼ tsp. oregano. Spread over steak; roll and tie with string. Heat oil in a heavy skillet or Dutch oven; brown the roll. Sprinkle with remaining salt, pepper and oregano; add water. Cover and cook over low heat 2 hrs. or until tender. Meat should stand at room temperature 20 min. for easier slicing.

Mrs. Don Bryant

STUFFED FLANK STEAK

4-6 servings

1¾ to 2 lb. flank steak
2 garlic cloves
2 T. soy sauce
¼ tsp. pepper
¼ cup butter
½ cup onion, chopped
1 clove garlic, crushed
1½ cups cooked rice
½ cup fresh parsley, chopped

½ cup grated Parmesan
  cheese
½ tsp. salt
¼ tsp. pepper
2 T. butter
½ cup condensed broth
½ cup water
1 T. crystallized ginger or ¾
  tsp. powdered ginger

Wipe steak with a damp towel. Score both sides of steak lightly into diamonds. Rub both sides with 2 garlic cloves. Brush with soy sauce and pepper. Marinate overnight.

continued

Preheat oven to 350F. Use a shallow roasting pan. Saute onion and crushed garlic in butter. Remove from heat and add rice, parsley, cheese, salt and pepper. Spread steak with 1 T. butter. Place rice mixture over steak, keeping 1½" from edges. Roll up steaks, fasten ends with skewers. Spread 1 T. butter on top of roll. Combine broth and water; pour over roast. Sprinkle with ginger. Roast 1 hr. for rare meat. Baste occasionally with pan juices.

Mrs. Herbert Eldean

SOUR CREAM PORCUPINES
4-6 servings

1½ lbs. lean ground beef
⅓ cup Minute Rice, uncooked
1 tsp. paprika

1 tsp. salt
¼ cup onions, diced

Sauce:
½ cup hot water
1 bouillon cube
1 (10¾ oz.) can cream of mushroom soup, undiluted

1 tsp. Worcestershire
½ cup sour cream

Use an ungreased 2 qt. casserole. Mix ingredients for porcupines. Shape into 16-20 balls. Place in casserole.

Blend ingredients for sauce; pour over balls. Cover. Chill 4 hrs. or overnight. Prior to serving preheat oven to 350F. Bake for 1 hr.

Mrs. Brian Ward

MEAT BALLS
4-6 servings

2 lbs. ground beef
1 cup corn flakes, crumbled
1 small onion, chopped
1½ tsp. salt
⅛ tsp. pepper

¼ tsp. garlic salt
1 egg, beaten
½ cup applesauce
1 (8 oz.) can tomato sauce
1 T. brown sugar, optional

Preheat oven to 325F. Use an ungreased 9" x 13" pan. Mix ingredients together in order given, except tomato sauce and sugar. Roll into balls. Mix tomato sauce and sugar; pour over balls. Bake 1 hr.

Mrs. John Suby

SAUCEPOT MEAT BALLS

3-4 servings

1 envelope dry onion soup mix	**½ tsp. garlic salt**
1¼ cups water	**½ tsp. thyme**
2 (8 oz. each) cans	**¼ tsp. pepper**
tomato sauce	**½ tsp. parsley, chopped**
1 lb. ground beef	**noodles or rice**

Mix soup, water and tomato sauce; bring to a boil. Simmer covered for 10 min. Combine meat and seasonings. Shape into 16 meat balls and brown. Drain and add to soup mixture. Simmer uncovered for 25 min. Serve over hot buttered noodles or rice.

Mrs. Gregory Burhans
Mrs. Fred Leaske

SWEDISH MEAT BALLS

5-6 servings

1 lb. ground beef	**⅛ tsp. allspice**
½ lb. ground pork	**¼ tsp. pepper**
½ cup soft bread crumbs	**1¼ tsp. salt**
½ cup sour cream	**butter for browning**
1 egg, slightly-beaten	**2 beef bouillon cubes**
2 T. onion, grated	**2 cups hot water**

Sauce:

½ cup sour cream	**dash allspice**
2 T. flour	**½ tsp. onion salt**

Combine beef, pork, crumbs, sour cream, egg, onion and spices. Shape teaspoons of meat into balls. Brown in butter. Dissolve bouillon in hot water and pour over meat balls. Cover and simmer 30 min. Remove balls, set aside.

Mix sauce ingredients. Briskly stir into hot bouillon. Cook over moderate heat, stirring constantly until thickened. Add meat balls. Heat through.

Mrs. William Buis

152

SWEDISH MEAT BALLS IN SOUR CREAM SAUCE

6 servings

1½ lbs. ground beef
2 cups bread crumbs, soaked
   in ½ cup milk
1 small onion, chopped, sauteed
   in 2 T. margarine
2½ tsp. salt
2 tsp. nutmeg

2 tsp. paprika
1 tsp. dried mixed herbs
1 tsp. dry mustard
¼ tsp. pepper
¼ tsp. garlic salt
3 eggs, beaten
3 to 4 T. margarine

Sauce:
¼ cup flour
2 T. tomato paste
2 cups boiling water

5 tsp. instant beef bouillon
1 cup sour cream
noodles, cooked

Combine all meatball ingredients except 3 to 4 T. margarine. Chill. Form into small balls. Brown in margarine. Blend in sauce ingredients except sour cream and noodles. Stir over low heat until thickened. Just before serving add sour cream. Blend well, heat through. Serve over buttered noodles. May be frozen.

Mrs. James Chamness
Mrs. Theodore B. Bosch

PINWHEEL MEAT ROLL

6 servings

1 lb. ground beef
½ tsp. salt
¼ tsp. pepper
⅓ cup bread cubes

2 T. milk
2 T. minced onion
1 egg, beaten

Filling:
2 T. margarine
¼ cup onion, chopped

1½ cups carrots, cooked,
   chopped
½ tsp. salt

Combine all ingredients except filling. On waxed paper pat into rectangle about ½" thick.

continued

Preheat oven to 350F. Use an ungreased roasting pan with rack. Brown onions in margarine, add carrots and salt. Spread carrot mixture over meat and roll as for jelly roll. Place roll in pan. Bake for 45 min.

Mrs. Ward Perry

ITALIAN SPAGHETTI SAUCE   3½ pts.

¼ cup olive oil
½ cup onions, chopped
2 garlic cloves, minced
¾ lb. ground beef
¼ lb. ground pork
2 (16 oz. each) cans tomatoes
2 (6 oz. each) cans tomato
    paste

½ cup water
1 T. salt
1 tsp. sugar
¼ tsp. pepper
2 T. chopped parsley
pinch of sweet basil
any macaroni product,
    cooked as directed

Heat oil, add onions and garlic. Cook until soft, about 5 min. Add beef and pork, brown. Add remaining ingredients except macaroni. Simmer several hrs. until sauce thickens. Serve over macaroni product.

Hint: Any left over steak or roast enhances the flavor of spaghetti sauce when simmered in it. It also makes a delicious piece of meat to serve with spaghetti.

Mrs. William Gargano

PRIZE SPAGHETTI SAUCE   3 pts.

2 T. olive oil
⅓ lb. ground beef
⅓ lb. ground pork
⅓ lb. ground veal
½ tsp. allspice
1 tsp. mace
2 (6 oz. each) cans tomato
    paste
dash celery salt

2½ cups tomato juice
½ lb. fresh mushrooms,
    cleaned, stems removed
1 T. Worcestershire
½ cup onion, chopped
½ celery stalk, chopped
1 T. green pepper, chopped
2 garlic cloves, chopped
water, as needed

continued

In a large skillet heat oil. Add meat and brown. Add remaining ingredients except water and simmer slowly for several hrs. Check occasionally to add water to maintain desired consistency of sauce.

Mrs. F. K. MacDonald

SPAGHETTI SAUCE WITH MEAT BALLS   2½ pts.

½ lb. ground beef
½ lb. ground pork
1 cup cracker or bread
  crumbs
2 garlic cloves, minced
1 medium onion, finely-
  chopped
2 eggs
salt and pepper, to taste

oregano and basil, to taste
olive oil, for frying
1 (6 oz.) can tomato paste
3 cups water or tomato
  juice
scant tsp. sugar
whole allspice
spaghetti, cooked
Parmesan cheese

Combine beef and pork, mix well. Add crumbs, garlic, onion, eggs, salt, pepper, oregano and basil. Form into small balls. In a skillet, heat oil and brown meat balls. Add tomato paste, water and sugar. Place allspice in a cheese cloth bag and float in mixture. Cook for 1 hr. Remove allspice, continue cooking 30 min. Add more water or juice if needed.

For thicker sauce, mash some of the meat balls. Serve on spaghetti with parmesan cheese.

Variation: To thickened sauce add fresh mushrooms, sliced, and chicken livers, fried and chopped.

Mrs. Ward Hansen

HAMBURGER STROGANOFF   4-6 servings

½ cup onions, minced
¼ cup margarine
1 lb. ground beef
2 T. flour
1 garlic clove, minced
2 tsp. salt
¼ tsp. MSG
¼ tsp. pepper

¼ tsp. paprika
1 lb. fresh mushrooms, sliced
1 (10¾ oz.) can cream of
  chicken soup, undiluted
1 cup sour cream
snipped parsley, chives, fresh
  dill or ripe olives (optional)
noodles, rice, mashed
  potatoes or toast

continued

Sauté onions in margarine. Add beef, flour, spices and mushrooms. Sauté 5 min. Add soup, simmer uncovered 10 min. Stir in sour cream, heat through. Garnish with parsley, chives, dill or olives. Serve on noodles, rice, hot mashed potatoes or toast.

Mrs. R. D. DeBruyn
Mrs. Don Cochran

MEAT LOAF
6-8 servings

2 lbs. ground beef
1 lb. ground pork
2 garlic cloves, finely-chopped
1 large onion, finely-chopped
1 tsp. salt
1 tsp. ground *black pepper*

1 bay leaf, crumbled
½ tsp. thyme
1 tsp. green pepper, chopped
1½ cups dry bread crumbs
2 eggs
bacon

Preheat oven to 325F. Use an ungreased 9" x 5" x 3" pan. Mix all ingredients, except bacon. Knead until thoroughly blended. Arrange enough slices of bacon in the bottom of the pan to hold meat loaf. Press meat mixture firmly into pan. Cross 2 to 4 additional slices of bacon over the top of the meat loaf. Bake 1½ - 1¾ hrs. or until cooked through, basting occasionally with meat juices.

Constant basting will make a moister loaf. Before serving, let stand on a hot platter, allowing juices to settle. Great the following day for sandwiches.

Mrs. Paul Elzinga

MEAT LOAF WITH MUSHROOM SAUCE   *4 servings*

¾ lb. ground beef
¼ lb. ground pork
1 egg, beaten
½ cup cracker crumbs
1 small onion, chopped
1 T. horseradish

⅛ cup catsup
1 tsp. Worcestershire
¾ cup milk
1 tsp. salt
1 tsp. sugar

continued

156

Sauce:

1 lb. fresh mushrooms
3 T. butter
1 T. Worcestershire
½ cup catsup

1 cup light cream
2 T. flour
salt and pepper, to taste

Preheat oven to 350F. Use an ungreased 9" x 5" x 3" pan. Combine all meat loaf ingredients. Mix well and place in pan. Bake for 1 hr.

In a large skillet sauté mushrooms in butter. Combine Worcestershire, catsup, cream, flour, salt and pepper; pour over mushrooms. Cook 5 min., stirring constantly. Serve with meat loaf.

Mrs. Jack Marquis

MEAT LOAF WELLINGTON   10-12 servings

1 egg, beaten
½ cup milk
1 cup tomato, skinned and
   diced
3 slices white bread, crusts
   removed, bread broken
   into ¼" pieces
¾ cup onion, chopped

1 cup celery, chopped
1 tsp. poultry seasoning
2 tsp. salt
¼ tsp. pepper
1½ lbs. ground beef
½ cup pine nuts (chopped
   blanched almonds
   may be substituted)

Topping:

2 (10 oz. each) pkgs. frozen
   patty shell pastry, thawed
½ cup mushrooms, sliced,
   cooked
¼ cup green onions, chopped

1 cup American cheese,
   shredded
1 egg, beaten with
   2 T. water

Preheat oven to 375F. Grease an 8½" x 4½" x 2½" loaf pan. Combine egg, milk and tomato. Add bread cubes, onion, celery, seasonings, beef and nuts. Place in pan. Bake 1 hr. and 15 min. Cool and remove from pan. Freeze, if desired, before ready to use, but thaw before preparing for Wellington.

Preheat oven to 400F. Use an ungreased baking sheet. Let pastry stand at room temperature about 15 min. Form into ball. Combine mushrooms, onions, cheese and spread on top of loaf. Roll out pastry 18" x 12". Wrap meat loaf. Use egg to seal loaf, also brush top and sides. Place on baking sheet and bake for 30-40 min. Let stand 10 min. before carving.

Mrs. Herbert Eldean

MEAT BALL STROGANOFF
6 servings

1½ lbs. ground chuck
¾ cup milk
¾ cup dried bread crumbs
1½ tsp. salt
¼ tsp. pepper
3 T. parsley flakes
¼ cup margarine
¾ cup onions, chopped
½ lb. mushrooms, sliced
¾ tsp. paprika

2 T. flour
1 (10¾ oz.) can beef
    bouillon, undiluted
¾ tsp. salt
⅛ tsp. pepper
½ tsp. Worcestershire
½ cup sour cream
hot, fluffy cooked rice
snipped fresh dill

Combine meat, milk, crumbs, salt, pepper and parsley. Shape into walnut size balls. Brown in 2 T. margarine. Remove. Add 2 T. more margarine and saute onions and mushrooms with paprika until tender. Sprinkle flour over mixture. Stir, slowly adding bouillon, salt and pepper. Return meat balls to sauce. Cover, simmer 10 min. Just before serving add Worcestershire and sour cream. Heat through. Serve over rice; garnish with dill.

Mrs. William J. Hakken, Jr.

BEEF LIVER
For Tender, Delicious Liver

water, boiling
liver, purchase an ample
    amount because there
    is ⅓ waste

salt and pepper, to taste
flour
oil or bacon drippings
onions, sliced

Pour boiling water over the liver; let stand 3 min. Drain. Peel off all membrane from outside of liver and the gristly part spaced throughout. Sprinkle liver with salt and pepper; roll in flour. In a skillet, fry onions in oil for 15 min.; push to one side. Add liver. Fry over medium heat until a golden crust forms on both sides. Serve onions over liver.

Mrs. Thomas DePree

HUNGARIAN GOULASH

6-8 servings

1 ½ lbs. stewing meat,
  (blade roast) cubed
¼ cup flour
2 T. shortening
1 cup water
2 strips bacon, chopped

1 large onion, chopped
3 T. paprika
1 T. salt
1 (16 oz.) can tomatoes
1 cup raw rice

Sprinkle meat with flour. In a skillet, brown meat in shortening. Place meat into a deep kettle. Rinse skillet with water, adding this juice to meat. Cover, cook slowly 1 hr. Cook bacon and onion until bacon is crisp. Add paprika and salt. Add this mixture and tomatoes to meat. Continue cooking 1 hr. 30 min. Prepare rice. Arrange rice on a heated plater, top with beef and gravy.

Mrs. Larry Den Uyl

POT ROAST HUNGARIAN

8-10 servings

¼ cup flour
1 T. salt
¼ tsp. pepper
1 (3 to 4 lb.) arm or blade
  pot roast
3 T. oil or drippings
1 clove garlic, minced
1 large onion, sliced

½ cup celery, coarsely diced
¼ cup water or sherry
1 (8 oz.) can tomato sauce
2 T. flour
½ cup sour cream
3 T. parsley, chopped
noodles, cooked

Combine flour, salt and pepper; dredge meat on both sides. Brown meat in hot oil, drain. Add garlic, onion, celery, water and tomato sauce. Cover tightly. Cook slowly for 3½ hrs. or until tender. Remove meat to hot serving platter. Thicken liquid with flour; stir until smooth. Add sour cream and parsley, heat through. Serve sauce over meat, with noodles.

Mrs. Robert Hall

SAVORY POT ROAST   *6 servings*

1 (3 lb.) blade pot roast
oil for frying
salt
¼ cup wine vinegar
¼ cup oil
¼ cup catsup

2 T. soy sauce
2 T. Worcestershire
1 tsp. dried crushed rosemary
½ tsp. garlic powder
½ tsp. dry mustard

In skillet brown meat in a small amount of oil. Sprinkle meat with a little salt. Combine remaining ingredients; pour over meat. Cover tightly, simmer 2 hrs. or until tender. Remove meat to heated platter. Skim excess fat from sauce. Spoon sauce over meat.

Mrs. Herbert Eldean

SAUERBRATEN   *8-10 servings*

1 (4 to 5 lb.) rump roast
1 ¾ cup water
¾ cup vinegar
2 tsp. salt
3 T. brown sugar
⅛ tsp. ground cloves
⅛ tsp. allspice

1 tsp. MSG
1 tsp. ground ginger
1 bay leaf
½ to ¾ tsp. coarsely ground
   pepper
¾ cup onion, chopped
flour, to make gravy

In a heavy kettle brown meat; drain off fat. Add ¾ cup water. Cover, simmer 1 hr. Remove meat, cut into ½" thick slices; return to kettle. Combine 1 cup water and remaining ingredients, except flour. Pour over meat. Cover and simmer 1½ hrs. or until tender. Strain, if desired, and use flour to thicken gravy. Delicious served with noodles or potato pancakes.

Mrs. Robert Hampson

RHEIMISCHER SAUERBRATEN
8-10 servings
Rhemish Sauerbraten

2 cups vinegar
2 cups water
4 onions, sliced
1 stalk of celery, chopped
1 carrot, chopped
2 bay leaves
8 peppercorns, crushed
8 whole cloves
¼ tsp. mustard seed
1 (4 to 5 lb.) rump roast
1 tsp. salt
¼ tsp. pepper
¼ cup salad oil
¼ cup flour
½ cup seedless raisins
½ cup sour cream

Combine vinegar, water, onions, celery, carrot, bay leaves, peppercorns, cloves and mustard seed in saucepan. Bring to a boil, cool. Place in refrigerator; marinate meat in mixture 2 to 3 days, turning often. Remove meat from marinade, dry well. Sprinkle meat with salt and pepper. Heat oil in Dutch oven. Brown meat well on all sides. Add 2 cups of marinade. Cover, simmer 2 to 3 hrs. or until tender. Remove meat, keep warm.

Strain sauce, skim off fat. Measure liquid, add water or marinade to make 2 cups. Stir in flour. Return to pan. Cook over low heat, stirring and scraping brown bits until thickened. Stir in raisins and sour cream, blend well. Serve with meat. Delicious with hot curried fruit and dumplings.

Mrs. Leo Jungblut

LEFTOVER CURRIED ROAST

1 to 2 tsp. curry powder
small amount of oil or
   butter
1 cup onion, chopped
leftover roast, cubed
1 (10½ oz.) can beef bouillon
   or thinned gravy
avocados, peeled, pit removed
parsley or chives, chopped

Sauté curry in oil for 1 to 2 min. Add onion, cook until just tender. Add roast and bouillon. Simmer uncovered 20 to 30 min. to blend flavors and reduce liquid. Spoon mixture into avocado halves, garnish with parsley or chives.

Mrs. Tom Carey

SAUCE FOR LEFTOVER ROAST   1½ cups

2 T. butter
1 large onion, chopped
¼ tsp. nutmeg
1 bay leaf
½ tsp. chili powder

2 T. flour
2 T. vinegar
1½ cups beef or chicken broth
salt to taste

In a saucepan melt butter, saute onion until light brown. Add remaining ingredients. Stir until sauce bubbles. Strain. Serve hot or cold over leftover roast.

Mrs. W. A. Butler

BEEF CURRY   8-10 servings

4 lbs. round steak, cut
  in cubes
½ cup butter
2 T. flour
2 onions, chopped
3 bay leaves

1 to 2 tsp. curry, to taste
1 T. lemon juice
1 tsp. paprika
salt and pepper, to taste
3 whole cloves or dash
  of ground cloves

Sauce:
2 T. butter
3 T. flour
1 T. Bovril or
  B-V soup and gravy base
1 cup hot water
2 beef bouillon cubes

2 cups hot water
2 apples, peeled,
  finely-diced
½ cup currants
½ tsp. curry
salt and pepper, to taste

Relishes:
Spanish peanuts
India relish
French fried onion rings
chutney

shredded coconut
raisins or currants
hard boiled eggs, chopped

Brown meat in butter, slowly. Stir in flour. Add onions, bay leaves and curry. Cover, simmer 1 hr. Add lemon juice, paprika, salt and pepper. Continue simmering until tender. Add cloves.

continued

Melt butter, add flour and mix thoroughly. Dissolve Bovril in 1 cup water. Add slowly to flour mixture, stirring constantly. Add bouillon and 2 cups of water. Bring to a boil, slowly. Add remaining sauce ingredients. Simmer 30 min. Add sauce mixture to cooked meat. Let stand. When ready to serve, heat to piping hot. Remove bay leaves and cloves. Serve with a choice of curry relishes.

Mrs. Allen Butler

COUNTRY STEAK
6 servings

2 lbs. round steak
seasoned flour
½ cup margarine
2 onions, sliced
½ lb. fresh mushrooms
½ cup water or red wine

2 T. Parmesan cheese
1 tsp. salt
⅛ tsp. pepper
¼ tsp. paprika
½ cup sour cream

Cut steak in serving pieces and dredge in flour. Melt ¼ cup margarine in large skillet. Add onions and mushrooms and cook until lightly browned, remove; add remaining margarine and brown steak. Add onions and mushrooms to steak; combine remaining ingredients and pour over steak. Cover and cook over low heat until tender (approximately 1½ hrs.).

Mrs. Jos. Scharf

15 MINUTE BEEF STROGANOFF
4 servings

1 lb. round steak, ¼" to ½" thick
2 T. margarine
⅔ cup water
1 (3 oz.) can sliced mushrooms, with liquid

1 envelope dry onion soup mix
1 cup sour cream
2 T. flour
buttered fine noodles or rice

Have meat cut diagonally across grain in strips ¼" wide. Heat margarine, add meat. Brown quickly. Add water and mushrooms, with liquid. Stir in soup, heat to boiling. Mix sour cream with flour and add to soup mixture. Cook, stirring until slightly thick. Serve over hot noodles or rice. May be frozen.

Mrs. Vernon Ten Cate

163

ITALIAN BRACIOLE
4 servings
Rolled Round Steak

1 round steak, ¼" to ½" thick,
    cut in 2" x 4" strips
garlic
salt and pepper
1 T. parsley
2 T. butter

½ cup Mozzarella cheese,
    shredded
2 T. oil
1 (15½ oz.) can spaghetti sauce
cooked noodles

Rub steak with garlic, sprinkle with salt and pepper. Add parsley, dot with butter, sprinkle with cheese. Roll up and secure with toothpicks. Brown in hot oil, drain. Add sauce and continue cooking 1 hr. or until tender. Serve over noodles.

Mrs. William Gargano

PEPPER BEEF CANTONESE
8 servings
(2nd Place Bake-Off)

3 lbs. round steak,
    ¼" thick
1 lb. mushrooms, sliced
2 green peppers, diced
2 onions, chopped
½-¾ lb. brown sugar
1 cup cooking sherry
½ tsp. soy sauce

½ tsp. salt
½ tsp. Worcestershire sauce
½ tsp. crushed black pepper
½ tsp. garlic powder
1 tsp. vinegar
2 cups water
cornstarch
sliced garlic bread

Cut steak in serving size pieces. In a Dutch oven brown meat. Add mushrooms, green peppers and onions. Mix sugar, sherry, seasonings and water; pour over meat and vegetables. Stir well, cover and simmer over low heat for 2 hrs. Thicken slightly with cornstarch before serving. Serve over hot garlic bread slices.

Mr. Kars Petersen

SWISS STEAK   *6-8 servings*

3 lbs. round steak, 1" thick   3 T. butter
¾ cup flour   1 (12 oz.) can beer
2 tsp. salt   2 T. tomato paste
½ tsp. pepper   1 bay leaf (optional)

Cut steak into 6 or 8 serving size pieces. Combine flour, salt and pepper. Pound into meat with a mallet. In a Dutch oven heat butter and brown meat well on both sides. Add remaining ingredients. Cover, cook over low heat 1 hr. Discard bay leaf before serving.

Mrs. Roger Prins

FAMILY STYLE SWISS STEAK   *6 servings*

1 cup onions, sliced   2 T. margarine
water, enough to cover   1 (16 oz.) can stewed
½ cup flour   tomatoes
2 tsp. salt   1 cup sharp cheddar
½ tsp. pepper   cheese, grated
2 lbs. round steak, 1" thick, cut
   into serving pieces

In a skillet place onions and water. Simmer on very low heat until water is absorbed, 30 min. to 1 hr. Combine flour, salt and pepper. Dredge meat in flour mixture. Brown meat in hot margarine. Preheat oven to 325F. Use an ungreased 9" x 13" pan. Layer meat and onions in pan. Pour tomatoes over and bake, covered, 3 to 4 hrs. or until tender; uncover the last ½ hr. to brown. Sprinkle with cheese, broil until cheese is melted.

Mrs. William Mendenhall

SWISS STEAK WITH MUSHROOM SAUCE

4-6 servings

½ cup flour
2 tsp. salt
½ tsp. pepper
2 lbs. round steak, cut into
   serving pieces
2 T. oil

1 medium onion, sliced
1 (10¾ oz.) can mushroom
   soup, undiluted
½ medium green pepper,
   chopped
⅓ cup dry sherry

Mix flour, salt and pepper. Pound into meat. Brown meat in oil. Add onion, soup, green pepper and sherry. Simmer, covered, for 1 hr.

Mrs. Gene Grotenhuis

OLD FASHIONED SWISS STEAK

8 servings

1 cup flour
¾ T. dry mustard
3 lbs. round steak
¾ cup onion, chopped
6 T. margarine
1 (16 oz.) can stewed tomatoes

3 carrots, diced
1 (4½ oz.) can mushrooms
1 beef bouillon cube
1½ cups hot water
3 T. brown sugar
1 T. Worcestershire

Preheat oven to 350F. Use a large ungreased baking dish. Combine flour and mustard and pound into meat. Brown onion in margarine. Add meat and brown. Place meat in a baking dish. Top with tomatoes, carrots, mushrooms and browned onions. Combine bouillon, water, sugar and Worcestershire. Pour over meat. Bake 2 to 2½ hrs.

Mrs. Harold Lampen

166

SPICY SHORT RIBS

6 servings

3 lbs. short ribs, cut up
1 cup catsup
1 cup water
1 T. sugar
4½ tsp. horseradish
2 to 3 bay leaves
4½ tsp. prepared mustard

few drops of Tabasco
1 T. vinegar
¼ tsp. pepper
1 tsp. salt
1 T. Worcestershire
2 medium onions, sliced

Place ribs in large bowl. Blend all remaining ingredients and pour over ribs. Refrigerate overnight. Place ribs with mixture in a large skillet. Simmer, covered, 1½ hrs. or until tender. Cool, then refrigerate.

When ready to use, skim off fat. Reheat. Dumplings are delicious added to the short rib stew and cooked, covered, 15 to 20 min. Serve at once.

Mrs. Ronald Dalman

BEEF ORIENTAL

6 servings

1½ lbs. beef sirloin,
  ½"-¾" thick
1 clove garlic, minced
½ cup water
⅓ cup soy sauce
¼ cup oil
1 green pepper, thinly-sliced,
  lengthwise
1 cup celery, thinly-sliced

2 medium onions, thinly-sliced
1 (6 oz.) can water chestnuts,
  drained and thinly-sliced
2 (4 oz. each) cans sliced
  mushrooms, drained
1½ T. cornstarch
1 cup tomato juice
rice, cooked

Cut meat across the grain into very thin (⅛") slices; place meat in bowl. Combine garlic, water and soy sauce; pour over meat and mix. Cover; refrigerate 1 hr. Drain meat; save marinade. Pat meat dry. Heat oil in large skillet. Brown meat quickly, stirring constantly. Add next 5 ingredients; stir fry just until vegetables are tender, yet crisp. Combine cornstarch, remaining marinade and tomato juice; stir until smooth and add to vegetables. Cook until mixture thickens. Serve with rice.

Mrs. Donald Brewer

BEEF STROGANOFF

4 servings

1 lb. sirloin steak, ¼" thick
1 clove garlic, peeled and cut
3 T. flour
1½ tsp. salt
¼ tsp. pepper
1 tsp. paprika
¼ cup margarine
½ cup onion, chopped
1 (10¾ oz.) can beef consomme
½ cup water or red wine
1 lb. fresh mushrooms, sliced
½ cup sour cream
2 T. chives, finely-chopped
wide boiled noodles or
　　mashed potatoes

Rub both sides of meat with garlic. Cut meat into strips 1½" x 1". Mix flour, salt, pepper and paprika. Add meat and toss lightly until strips are well coated. Reserve remaining mixture. In heavy skillet, heat margarine, add meat and brown well. Add onions, cook until transparent. Add remaining flour mixture, consomme, water and mushrooms. Cover, cook slowly about 1½ hrs. or until meat is tender. Stir occasionally. Remove cover and continue cooking until sauce is slightly thickened. Before serving add sour cream and chives. Blend and heat through. Serve with wide boiled noodles or mashed potatoes.

Mrs. William Gargano

RUNDERLAPPEN

4 servings

Marinated Beef

1½ lbs. lean beef, cut in
　　4 steaks
salt and pepper
6 T. butter or bacon drippings
1 large onion, sliced
¼ cup water
1½ T. vinegar
1 tsp. mustard
1 bay leaf
5 whole cloves
5 peppercorns
rice or mashed
　　potatoes

Scrape meat and rub with salt and pepper. In a Dutch oven heat fat very hot, thoroughly brown meat. Add onions, brown lightly. Add water, vinegar, mustard and spices. Cover. Simmer 2-3 hrs. or until very soft, turning every 30 min. Serve meat on a heated platter in a ring of rice or potatoes. Strain sauce and pour over meat. Red cabbage is a favorite complement to this dish.

LOBSTER STUFFED TENDERLOIN   *8 servings*

1 (3 to 4 lb.) whole tenderloin
2 (4 oz. each) frozen lobster
   tails
water, enough to cover
1/8 tsp. garlic salt
1 T. butter, melted

1 1/2 tsp. lemon juice
6 slices of bacon
1/2 cup green onion, sliced
1/2 cup butter
1/2 cup dry white wine

Preheat oven to 425F. Use a shallow roasting pan with a rack. Cut beef lengthwise to within 1/2" of bottom, to butterfly. Place frozen lobster tails in boiling water with garlic salt. Return to boiling, reduce heat and simmer 5 min., drain. Carefully remove lobster from shells. Cut in half lengthwise. Place lobster, end to end, inside beef. Combine 1 T. butter and juice, drizzle over lobster. Close meat around lobster, tie meat together with string at 1" intervals. Place on rack in pan and bake 40 to 50 min. for rare meat. Lay bacon on top, return to oven 5 more min.

In a saucepan cook green onion in remaining butter over low heat until tender. Add wine. Slice roast, spoon on wine sauce.

Mrs. Jack Dozeman

STIR-FRY CHINESE BEEF   *4 servings*

1 lb. beef tenderloin or sirloin
   tip, sliced very thin in narrow
   strips, across the grain
2 T. peanut oil
1 green pepper, cut in strips
1 clove garlic, minced
1 cup green onions, including
   tops, sliced
1/2 medium cauliflower, cut into
   flowerets, sliced thin

1 T. soy sauce
1 (10 3/4 oz.) can beef broth,
   undiluted
2 T. cornstarch
1/2 tsp. sugar
1/4 cup soy sauce
1/4 cup cold water
cooked rice

continued

In electric skillet or heavy fry pan, stir-fry half the beef in 1 T. hot oil for 1 min. Remove beef and set aside. Stir fry remaining beef. Remove. Add 1 T. oil to pan and quickly stir-fry vegetables. Add 1 T. soy sauce and ½ the can of broth. Simmer, covered 5 min.

Combine cornstarch, sugar, ¼ cup soy sauce, cold water and remaining broth. Stir into vegetable mixture, cook until thickened. Add beef and heat through. Serve over hot rice.

Variation: Add 1 small bunch of broccoli, cut into thin slices, to vegetables used.

Mrs. Graham Duryee

ARTICHOKE AND HAM SUPREME   *6 servings*

¼ cup margarine
¼ cup flour
2 cups warm milk
dash of salt, white pepper
¼ tsp. nutmeg
½ tsp. paprika
⅔ cup shredded Swiss and
  Parmesan cheese, mixed
¼ cup sherry

2 (1 lb. each) cans artichoke
  hearts, drained
12 thin slices boiled or
  baked ham (rectangular
  Polish ham is best)
½ cup buttered corn flake
  crumbs
⅔ cup Swiss and Parmesan
  cheese, mixed

Preheat oven to 350F. Use a greased 9" x 11" casserole. Melt margarine, blend in flour and remove from heat. Stir in milk; when smooth return to heat stirring until thickened. Add seasonings and cheeses stirring until cheeses melt. Remove from heat; add sherry. Wrap 2 artichoke hearts in each ham slice. Arrange in a casserole, sides touching. Pour cheese mixture over all. Combine crumbs, cheeses and sprinkle on top. Bake 25 to 30 mins. This dish may be made 12 to 24 hrs. ahead and refrigerated.

Mrs. Leo Jungblut

HAM HAWAIIAN

3-4 servings

¼ cup margarine
½ cup green pepper, chopped
2 cups slivered cooked ham
1 (9 oz.) can pineapple tidbits
  or chunks, drained, juice
  reserved
2 T. brown sugar

1½ T. cornstarch
1½ T. vinegar
1½ tsp. prepared mustard
⅛ tsp. pepper
¾ cup cold water
rice, cooked

Melt margarine in a skillet. Add green pepper and ham. Cook 5 min. Mix pineapple juice with remaining ingredients except rice. Stir into ham mixture. Cook, stirring until thickened. Add pineapple, heat through. Serve over hot rice.

Mrs. Loren Meengs

CRANBERRY-BURGUNDY GLAZED HAM

18-22 servings

1 (10 to 14 lb.) bone-in fully
  cooked ham
15 to 20 whole cloves
1 (16 oz.) can whole cranberry
  sauce

1 cup brown sugar
½ cup Burgundy
2 tsp. prepared mustard

Preheat oven to 325F. Use a shallow roasting pan. Place ham, fat side up, in pan. Score fat in diamond pattern; stud with cloves. Bake 2½ to 3 hrs. In a saucepan combine remaining ingredients, simmer uncovered 5 min. During last 30 min. spoon half of cranberry glaze over ham. Serve remaining glaze as a sauce.

Mrs. Herbert Eldean

HAM BAKED IN RASPBERRY GRAND MARNIER SAUCE

8-10 servings

Sauce:

½ orange, unpeeled, diced
½ cup dark brown sugar, firmly-packed
1 cup raspberry preserves or jam

1 T. prepared mustard
1½ tsp. Worcestershire
½ cup cream sherry
¼ cup Grand Marnier liqueur

½ fully cooked bone in ham, shank or butt (about 6 lbs.)
whole cloves
½ cup prepared mustard

1 cup dark brown sugar, firmly-packed
1 cup cream sherry

Prepare sauce. Combine all sauce ingredients; puree in blender, chill. Pour sauce back into blender, blend again. Let stand at room temperature.

Preheat oven to 325F. Use a shallow roasting pan. To prepare ham, score fat, stud with cloves. Combine mustard and brown sugar, spread over ham. Place ham in pan, add sherry to pan. Bake for 1½ to 2 hrs. During last 30 mins., pour sauce over, basting often. To serve, slice ham and pour sauce over slices.

Mrs. Lee Kimzey

HAM LOAF WITH SAUCE

8 servings

1 lb. ground cured ham
1½ lbs. ground pork steak
⅛ tsp. pepper

2 eggs, beaten
1 cup milk
1 cup cracker crumbs

Sauce:

1½ cups brown sugar
1 T. dry mustard

½ cup vinegar
½ cup water

Preheat oven to 350F. Use an ungreased 9" x 5" x 3" pan. Combine all ingredients for meat loaf. Shape into a loaf, place in pan. Bake for 2 hrs. Combine ingredients for sauce, baste loaf often.

May also be made into balls and baked 1 hr.

Mrs. Clayton Ter Haar
Mrs. Bruce G. Van Leuwen

172

MARINATED ONE POUND PORK CHOPS   6 servings

2 cups soy sauce

1 cup water

½ cup brown sugar

1 T. dark molasses

1 tsp. salt

6 (1 lb. each) pork chops

Red Sauce:

1 T. dry mustard

½ cup brown sugar

⅓ cup water

1 (14 oz.) bottle catsup

1 (12 oz.) bottle chili sauce

Mix soy sauce, water, ½ cup brown sugar, molasses and salt. Bring to a boil. Cool. Place chops in a pan, bone side up; pour mixture over chops. Let stand overnight in refrigerator.

Preheat oven to 375F. Use an ungreased 9" x 11" baking pan. Remove chops from sauce, place in pan. Cover tightly with foil. Bake until tender, 1½ to 2 hrs.

For red sauce, dilute dry mustard and sugar with water. Add remaining ingredients, bring to a slight boil. Dip chops in sauce and return to baking pan. Bake at 350F for 30 min. more or until slightly glazed.

Mrs. James W. F. Brooks
Mrs. Don Judd

LEMON BRAISED PORK CHOPS   4 servings

4 pork chops, cut 1" to 1½"

thick

salt, pepper to taste

1 T. oil

1 medium onion, sliced

1 lemon, sliced

1 cup beef bouillon

dill weed, to taste

Season chops with salt and pepper. Brown chops in oil. Drain. Place onion and lemon on top of chops. Add bouillon and dill. Cover, simmer 1 to 1½ hrs. Strain sauce and serve over chops.

Mrs. Gregory Burhans

STUFFED PORK CHOPS   *4 servings*

¼ cup butter, melted   ¼ cup onion, chopped
¾ cup water   ¼ tsp. poultry seasoning
½ (8 oz.) pkg. prepared   salt, pepper to taste
   stuffing   4 pork chops, 1¾" thick with
1 egg, beaten   pockets cut in them

Preheat oven to 300F. Use an ungreased 9" x 11" pan. Combine butter, water and pour over stuffing; mix lightly. Add egg, onion and seasonings. Stuff chops, seal with toothpicks. Brown on top of stove. Place in pan, bake 2 hrs.

Mrs. Don Hillebrands

SWEET-SOUR PORK CHOPS   *6-8 servings*

6 to 8 loin pork chops   ½ tsp. soy sauce
1 (13½ oz.) can pineapple   2 tsp. cornstarch
   chunks, drained, reserving 2 tsp. cold water
   syrup   ½ green pepper, chopped
½ cup light molasses   1 (11 oz.) can mandarin
½ cup vinegar   oranges, drained
½ tsp. salt   6 maraschino cherries
¼ tsp. ginger

Preheat oven to 325F. In an ungreased 9" x 11" baking pan, bake chops 1 hr. In a saucepan, combine ½ cup syrup, molasses and vinegar. Add salt, ginger and soy sauce. Blend cornstarch and water until smooth; add to saucepan. Add peppers. Over medium heat, bring to a boil. Simmer, stirring constantly 5 min. Add pineapple, oranges, cherries. Simmer 2 min. more. Pour fruit mixture over chops. Continue baking 15 to 20 min.

Mrs. Don Judd

BURRITOS

leftover pork
leftover gravy, thickened
1 green pepper, chopped,
  cooked

2 hot peppers, chopped,
  cooked (optional)
flour tortillas
oil

To pork and gravy add cooked peppers. Dip tortillas in a pan of warm oil, coat well. Remove to plate, put meat mixture in the center of each tortilla. Fold tortillas up to center from the bottom, then roll from one side to the other. Place under broiler, turning until evenly browned. Serve with taco sauce.

Mrs. Lyle Sprik

TACO SAUCE
1½ cups

¼ cup margarine
1 small onion, minced
½ tsp. garlic salt
1½ tsp. mustard

2 T. chili powder
1 cup catsup
¼ cup vinegar
1 T. Worcestershire sauce

Combine ingredients in a saucepan. Bring to a boil. Simmer. Serve hot or cold over burritos or tacos.

Mrs. Forest Hamilton

SWEET-SOUR PORK
6 servings

1½ lbs. lean pork shoulder,
  cut in 2" x ½" strips
oil for frying
½ cup water
1 (20 oz.) can pineapple
  chunks, drained, liquid
  reserved
¼ cup brown sugar
2 T. cornstarch

¼ cup vinegar
2 to 3 T. soy sauce
½ tsp. salt
1 small green pepper,
  cut in strips
¼ cup onion, thinly-
  sliced
cooked rice

continued

175

Brown pork in a small amount of fat. Add water; cover and simmer until tender, about 1 hr. Do not boil. Combine sugar and cornstarch, add pineapple liquid, vinegar, soy sauce and salt. Add to pork, stirring until thick. Add pineapple, green pepper and onion. Cook 2 to 3 min. Serve over hot rice.

Mrs. Myron Van Ark

HAWAIIAN PORK
3-4 servings

1 lb. lean pork, cut into
  ½" thick chunks
1 T. wine or sherry
1 T. soy sauce
1 T. cornstarch
1 egg, slightly-beaten
3 T. flour
oil for deep frying

3 T. oil
1 small onion, quartered
2 green peppers, quartered,
  seeded
1 garlic clove, crushed
3 slices canned pineapple,
  quartered
rice, cooked

Sauce:
⅓ cup sugar
¼ cup catsup or Chinese
  crabapple sauce
1 T. wine

2 T. vinegar
1 T. cornstarch
¼ cup soy sauce
⅓ cup water

Mix pork with wine, soy sauce, cornstarch, egg and flour. Remove pork, reserving mixture. In a frying pan, heat oil for frying. Add pork and fry until well done. Remove to hot platter. Heat 3 T. oil, sauté onions, peppers and garlic over high heat, 2 min. Mix sauce ingredients, add to vegetable mixture and bring to a boil. Thicken with reserved cornstarch mixture, stirring constantly. Add pork and pineapple. Mix well. Serve hot over rice. May be prepared ahead and frozen.

Mrs. Don Judd

SPANISH PORK
4-6 servings

1½ lbs. pork steak, diced
1 medium onion, sliced
1½ cups cooked tomatoes
¼ cup green pepper, chopped
½ cup celery, chopped
1 T. Worcestershire sauce
(optional)
1 tsp. salt

Preheat oven to 350F. Use an ungreased 2½ qt. casserole. Brown pork and onion. Combine remaining ingredients, add to pork. Place mixture in casserole. Cover and bake 1 hr. or until tender.

Mrs. Barbara Reif
Mrs. Clyde Line

OVEN BARBECUED SPARERIBS
6 servings

3 lbs. spareribs
1 cup catsup
¼ cup Worcestershire sauce
¼ cup vinegar
¼ cup brown sugar
2 tsp. salt
1 tsp. celery seed

Preheat oven to 350F. Place spareribs in pan, cover and bake 30 min. Drain. Combine remaining ingredients. Baste ribs with ½ the mixture. Continue baking 1 hr., uncovered. Turn ribs, baste with remaining sauce. Bake 30 to 45 min. more or until tender.

Mrs. Robert Van Wieren

SWEET-SOUR SPARERIBS
6-8 servings

4-5 lbs. spareribs
2 cups bottled lemon juice
1 (14 oz.) bottle catsup
½ cup light corn syrup
½ cup red wine vinegar
¼ tsp. Tabasco sauce
1 tsp. Worcestershire sauce
½ tsp. garlic salt
¼ tsp. pepper

Cut ribs in serving size pieces and marinate in lemon juice for 4 hrs.; drain. Preheat oven to 375F. Combine remaining ingredients and pour over ribs. Bake, covered, 2 hrs. and, uncovered, 30 min.

Mrs. James Highstreet

SPARERIBS/KRAUT AND STUFFING BALLS

6-8 servings

3 lbs. ribs
1 (1 lb. 11 oz.) can sauerkraut
1 apple, sliced
1½ cups tomato juice
2 T. brown sugar

1½ cups water
½ cup margarine
1 (8 oz.) pkg. herb seasoned
  stuffing mix
2 eggs, beaten

In a Dutch oven, brown ribs. Combine sauerkraut, apple, juice and sugar. Spoon over ribs. Simmer covered 1-1½ hrs. Heat water and margarine; pour over stuffing mix, stir. Add eggs mixing well. Shape into balls. Place on sauerkraut. Cover, continue cooking 20 min. more.

Mrs. Jack Dozeman

BLINDE VINKEN
(1st Place, Bake-Off)

6-8 servings

1 whole pork tenderloin
¾ lb. unseasoned pork
  sausage
¾ lb. ground chuck
¼ tsp. each salt and pepper
1 tsp. Kitchen Bouquet
2 eggs, slightly beaten

¼ cup rusk crumbs
¼ cup light cream
8 slices bacon
¼ cup margarine
½ lb. fresh mushrooms, sliced
¼ cup onions, chopped
2 T. margarine

Split pork tenderloin horizontally almost all the way through. Pound gently to a thickness of ¼". Cut flattened tenderloin into rectangular 3" x 5" pieces.

Combine sausage, chuck, salt, pepper, Kitchen Bouquet, eggs, crumbs and cream; shape into rolls 1" x 3". Roll into tenderloin pieces; wrap the tenderloin rolls with bacon strips and fasten with toothpicks. Brown evenly in margarine. Add 2 T. water and fry gently for about 30 min., turning often. Remove to platter.

In a small skillet, sauté mushrooms and onions in margarine until tender. Serve over tenderloin rolls.

Mrs. Miriam J. Van Eyl

POLISH PORK AND POTATO DUMPLINGS

6-8 servings

1 (3 to 5 lb.) pork loin
6 medium onions, sliced
water
5 small potatoes, unpared
1 egg

1 tsp. salt
¾ cup flour
2 qts. water, boiling
8 oz. sauerkraut, drained

Preheat oven to 300F. Use an ungreased roasting pan. Place pork and onions in roaster, add enough water to cover bottom of pan. Bake 1½ to 2 hrs. Add more water if onions begin to look dry. Boil potatoes for 20 min. or until tender. Peel cooked potatoes. Rice or grate potatoes, let cool. Twenty min. before pork is done add egg, salt and flour to potatoes. Blend. Dough should not be too dry, but should slip off fingers easily. Roll dough into sausage shaped dumplings. Place dumplings, a few at a time, into boiling water. When dumplings float to the top, continue to simmer 2 min. Remove from water, slice. Place in an ungreased 9" x 11" baking dish, cover with sauerkraut. Bake 10 min. Just before serving cover with juice from pork roast.

Mrs. Ralph Hensley

VEAL CORDON BLEU

4 servings

1 lb. veal cutlets, sliced thin
slices of ham
slices of Swiss cheese
1 egg, beaten

2 T. red wine
⅓ cup cheese, grated
oil and butter for frying
2 T. wine

Pound veal until very thin. Cut in even slices and put together like a sandwich with ham and cheese in between. Combine egg and wine. Dip veal in egg mixture, then in cheese. Let stand 20 min. Sauté veal in mixture of oil and butter 20 min.

Mrs. Arnold Dood

VEAL PARMIGIANO   *6-8 servings*

12 veal cutlets, pounded
  very thin
2 eggs, beaten
½ tsp. pepper
¾ tsp. salt
1½ cups fine bread crumbs
½ cup Parmesan cheese

½ cup butter
2 (8 oz. each) cans
  tomato sauce
1 (6 oz.) pkg. Mozzarella
  cheese, sliced or shredded
Parmesan cheese

Dip veal in a mixture of egg, salt and pepper. Mix crumbs and ½ cup Parmesan cheese; roll veal in mixture. Refrigerate 30 min. or more. Preheat oven to 350F. Use an ungreased 9" x 11" baking dish. Saute veal in butter, until brown. Place in baking dish. Pour tomato sauce over all and top with remaining cheese. If 2 layers of veal are necessary, repeat all layers. Bake for 30 min.

VEAL ROULADES FLORENTINE   *6 servings*

½ cup onion, finely-chopped
1 clove garlic, finely-chopped
1 T. butter
1 cup Croutettes stuffing
½ lb. sausage
1 (10 oz.) pkg. frozen chopped
  spinach, cooked, drained
1 egg
¼ tsp. oregano
salt, pepper, to taste

12 veal cutlets, sliced thin
2 T. butter
½ cup onion, finely-chopped
½ cup whole mushrooms
1 cup dry white wine
1 T. flour
1 T. butter
noodles, cooked
parsley, chopped

Sauté onion and garlic in 1 T. butter until soft. Add Croutettes and sausage cooking until sausage is browned. Stir in spinach, egg and seasonings. Blend well and heat through. Place 2 heaping T. on each veal slice. Roll, secure with a toothpick. Brown veal in 2 T. butter with additional onions and mushrooms. Add wine. Cover, simmer 30 min.

continued

Strain sauce through a sieve into a saucepan. Mix flour with a small amount of water until smooth. Add flour mixture and 1 T. butter to sauce in pan. Cook over low heat, stirring until blended. Serve roulades on a bed of buttered noodles, covered with sauce and sprinkled with parsley.

Mrs. John Hutchinson

VEAL BIRDS   *4 servings*

2 T. butter	dash of paprika
1/3 cup onion, chopped	water
3/4 cup celery, finely-chopped	4 ground veal patties
4 slices dry bread,	2 large potatoes, peeled,
broken into 1/2" cubes	cut into 2" cubes
1 egg, beaten	1 (10 3/4 oz.) can mushroom
1/2 tsp. poultry seasoning	soup, undiluted
salt, to taste	

Preheat oven to 350F. Use an ungreased 7" x 11" flat glass baking dish. In a small skillet, melt butter and sauté onion and celery. When tender, add to bread cubes. Add egg and seasonings. If dressing appears dry add a small amount of water. Divide each veal patty in 1/2, flatten to make 2 thin patties. Place 1/2 cup dressing on patty, top with second patty. Seal edges, place 1 filled patty in each corner of baking dish.

Boil potatoes in salted water about 3 min. Drain. Arrange potatoes in the center of baking dish. Spoon soup evenly over all. Cover tightly, bake 35 to 40 min.

Mary Jane Bougie

BAKED VEAL AND HAM ROLLS   *8 servings*

8 slices (approx. 2 lbs.) veal
  round, ¼" thick, tenderized
8 slices boiled ham
8 slices Swiss cheese
1 egg, beaten
2 T. milk
⅔ cup corn flake crumbs
1 (10¾ oz.) can cream of
  mushroom soup, undiluted
½ cup light cream
2 T. sauterne wine

Preheat oven to 350F. Use an ungreased 9" x 13" baking dish. Top each veal slice with a slice of ham. Cut each cheese slice into 4 strips and stack on ham. Loosely roll veal around cheese, secure with toothpicks. Combine egg and milk, brush on veal rolls. Roll in crumbs. Place seam side down in dish. In a saucepan, combine soup, cream and wine. Heat to bubbling; pour over veal. Cover tightly; bake 50 min. or until tender. Uncover; bake 10 min. longer.

Mrs. G. S. MacKenzie

VEAL SCALLOPINI WITH MUSHROOMS   *4 servings*

1 lb. veal round steak, cut
  ½" thick
½ cup flour
½ tsp. salt
⅛ tsp. black pepper
¼ cup olive oil
½ clove garlic, minced
¼ cup butter
½ lb. fresh mushrooms,
  cleaned, sliced lengthwise
  through stems and caps
1 medium onion, sliced
1¾ cups tomatoes,
  sieved
1 tsp. salt
⅛ tsp. black pepper
¼ tsp. parsley, chopped
¼ tsp. oregano
¼ cup capers, optional
noodles or rice, cooked

Pound veal and cut into 1" pieces. Coat with a mixture of flour, salt and pepper. In a large skillet, heat oil and garlic. Add veal, brown. In another skillet heat butter; add mushrooms, onions. Brown lightly. Add to veal mixture. Add remaining ingredients except noodles. Cover and simmer 25 min. or until veal is tender, stirring occasionally. Serve over noodles or rice.

Mrs. William J. Lalley

182

Casseroles That Please

NOTES

AU GRATIN BEEF AND SPINACH CASSEROLE

6-8 servings

2 lbs. ground beef
2 medium onions, chopped
2 (10 oz. each) pkgs. frozen chopped spinach, thawed
2 cups sharp cheese, grated
1 tsp. seasoning salt

1 tsp. salt
¼ tsp. pepper
2½ tsp. Worcestershire sauce
¾ cup corn flake crumbs
2 T. margarine, melted

Preheat oven to 350F. Use a greased 2 qt. casserole. Brown beef and onion. Squeeze water from spinach and add spinach to beef mixture. Blend in cheese, and seasonings. Turn into casserole. Combine crumbs and butter; sprinkle over top. Bake uncovered 30 mins.

Mrs. George Becker

BEEF PASTIES
(1st Place, Bake-Off)

6 servings

3 cups flour
1 cup lard
1 tsp. salt

1 egg
4 T. water
1 T. vinegar

Filling:
5 medium potatoes, finely diced
4 carrots, finely diced
2 medium onions, finely diced

½ small rutabaga, finely diced
1½ lbs. ground chuck (very important)
salt & pepper
butter

Preheat oven to 350F. Bake on ungreased cookie sheets. Blend flour, lard, and salt. Combine egg, water and vinegar and add to flour mixture. Mix lightly. Divide dough into 6 equal parts. Roll each section of dough to about 7" in diameter.

Assemble the pasties in the following manner. On half of each section place in layers a portion of the potatoes, carrots, onions, rutabaga and ground chuck. Sprinkle with salt and pepper, dot with butter. Fold other half of crust over filling; seal and flute the edge. Bake for 1 hr. Serve hot with catsup.

The pasties can be frozen before or after baking.

Mrs. Don Housenga

BUSY DAY CASSEROLE
serves 4-6

1 lb. beef, 1" cubes	1 (10¾ oz.) can chicken soup
1 lb. pork, 1" cubes	1 (10¾ oz.) can mushroom soup
2 small onions, chopped	1 soup can water
3 stalks celery, chopped	¾ cup Minute Rice

Preheat oven to 350F. Use a 3 qt. ungreased casserole. Brown beef, pork, onions and celery together. Combine with remaining ingredients. Pour into casserole and bake uncovered for 1 hr. or until done.

Mrs. Chandler Oakes

CABBAGE ROLLS WITH CREOLE SAUCE
4-6 servings

1 cup raw rice	¼ tsp. pepper
1 lb. ground beef	2 T. onions, minced
¾ tsp. salt	cabbage

Sauce:

1 onion, chopped	¾ tsp. salt
2 T. margarine	⅛ tsp. pepper
2 T. flour	1 cup vegetable liquid
2 cups tomatoes	dash Worcestershire sauce
1 T. brown sugar	dash of sage

Preheat oven 350F. Grease a 9" x 13" casserole. Combine rice, ground beef, salt, pepper and onion. Cook 12 cabbage leaves in boiling water for 5 mins. until leaves are pliable. Wrap a leaf of cabbage around 2 T. meat mixture. Place rolls seam side down in casserole. Top with Creole sauce.

For sauce sauté onions in margarine until golden. Blend in flour and stir in remaining ingredients. Pour over cabbage rolls and bake covered 1 hr.

Mrs. Harold VanderBie

MOCK STUFFED CABBAGE CASSEROLE 6-8 servings

1 small head cabbage,
  shredded
6 slices bacon
¾ cup onion, chopped
1 cup raw rice
1½ lb. ground beef

1 tsp. salt
⅛ tsp. pepper
1 (15½ oz.) jar spaghetti
  sauce with mushrooms
3 cups water

Preheat oven to 400F. Use a buttered 9" x 13" casserole. Spread half of shredded cabbage in bottom of casserole. Sauté bacon to limp stage. Set aside. To bacon drippings add onion and rice. Cook, stirring constantly, until onion is soft and rice is lightly browned. Spoon over cabbage in casserole. Brown meat and spoon over rice mixture. Sprinkle with seasonings. Top with remaining cabbage. Heat spaghetti sauce and water in pan in which onion and rice were sautéed. Pour over cabbage. Top with bacon slices. Cover. Bake 50 mins., uncover and bake 10 mins. longer.

Mrs. Paul Terpstra

STUFFED CABBAGE serves 4
True Italian style

12 cabbage leaves
1¼ lbs. ground beef
1 cup cooked rice
1 small onion
1 egg
½ tsp. poultry seasoning

2 T. oil
2 (8 oz. each) cans
  tomato sauce
1 T. brown sugar
¼ cup water
1 T. lemon juice or
  vinegar

Preheat oven to 325F. Use an ungreased 9" x 13" casserole. Boil cabbage leaves in water until leaves are pliable, about 5 mins. Mix beef, rice, onion, egg and seasonings together. Divide mixture and wrap in cabbage leaves. Blend oil, tomato sauce, sugar, water and lemon juice; pour over cabbage leaves. Cook covered for 2 hrs.

Mrs. Robert Olesen

CHASEN'S CHILI
makes 4 quarts

½ lb. pinto beans
5 cups canned tomatoes
1 lb. green peppers, chopped
1½ T. oil
1½ lbs. onions, chopped
2 garlic cloves, crushed
½ cup parsley, chopped
½ cup butter

3½ lbs. ground beef or
1½ lbs. ground beef and
  1½ lbs. ground pork
⅓ cup chili powder
2 T. salt
1½ tsp. pepper
1½ tsp. cumin seed
1½ tsp. M.S.G.

Wash beans, soak overnight in water 2" above beans. Simmer covered in same water until tender, about 2 hrs. Add tomatoes and simmer 5 mins. Sauté green pepper in oil 5 mins.; add onion and cook until tender, stirring often. Add garlic and parsley. Sauté meat in butter for 15 mins. Combine this mixture with beans, add spices. Simmer, covered 1 hr.; uncover and cook additional 30 mins. Cool and skim fat from top. Freezes well.

Mrs. Jack Faber

CHINESE BEEF CASSEROLE
6 servings

2 lbs. ground beef
2 (10 oz. each) pkgs. frozen
  peas, thawed
2 cups celery, sliced
1 (10¾ oz.) can cream of mushroom soup, undiluted

¼ cup light cream
1 tsp. seasoning salt
½ tsp. salt
¼ tsp. pepper
1 onion, chopped
1 cup crushed potato chips

Preheat oven to 375F. Use an ungreased 1½ qt. casserole. Brown beef; drain. Turn into casserole. Add peas, then celery. Combine remaining ingredients and pour over all. Sprinkle chips on top. Bake uncovered for 30 mins.

Mrs. Alvin Crooks

COUNTRY CALICO BEANS

10-12 servings

½ lb. bacon
1 lb. ground beef
1 cup onion, chopped
¾ cup brown sugar
1 tsp. salt
1 tsp. dry mustard
1 T. vinegar
½ cup catsup

1 (15 oz.) can butter beans,
  partially drained
1 (15 oz.) can kidney beans,
  partially drained
2 (16 oz. each) cans pork and
  beans, partially drained

Preheat oven to 350F. Use an ungreased 3 qt. casserole. Fry bacon until crisp. Crumble. In bacon fat, sauté onion and ground beef. Drain. Combine the bacon bits, onions, and ground beef with remaining ingredients, and bake uncovered for 40 mins.

Mrs. Herbert Eldean

EASY MOUSSAKA

serves 8-10

3 medium size eggplants
1 cup butter
3 large onions, finely chopped
2 lbs. ground beef
3 T. tomato paste
½ cup dry wine
½ cup parsley, chopped
¼ tsp. cinnamon
salt and pepper to taste

6 T. flour
1 qt. milk, heated
4 eggs, beaten until
  frothy
nutmeg to taste
2 cups ricotta cheese
1 cup fine bread crumbs
1 cup Parmesan cheese

Preheat oven to 375F. Use a greased 11" x 6" x 2½" pan. Peel eggplants and slice ½" thick. Brown slices quickly in large, heavy skillet in ¼ cup butter (more as needed). Set aside. Heat ¼ cup butter in same skillet. Cook onions until lightly browned. Add ground meat. Cook 10 mins. Combine tomato paste with wine, parsley, cinnamon, salt, pepper. Stir into meat; simmer, stirring frequently, until all liquid has absorbed. Remove from heat.

continued

Melt ½ cup butter in saucepan; blend in flour. Gradually add hot milk, stirring constantly until thickened and smooth. Cool slightly; stir in eggs, nutmeg and ricotta cheese. Sprinkle bottom of casserole lightly with bread crumbs. Arrange alternate layers of egg plant and meat. Sprinkle each layer with Parmesan cheese and bread crumbs. Pour cheese sauce over top. Bake 1 hr. or until golden. Cool slightly before cutting into squares.

Mrs. John Marquis

FIESTA CASSEROLE   *12 servings*

2 lbs. ground beef
2 large onions, chopped
3 T. chili powder
1 tsp. salt
¼ tsp. pepper
2 garlic cloves, crushed
¼ tsp. Tabasco
1½ cups yellow corn meal

½ cup milk
1 (1 lb. 12 oz.) can tomatoes
1 (16 oz.) can corn, drained
1 (dr. wt. 6 oz.) can whole pitted
   ripe olives, drained
1-2 cups cheddar cheese,
   grated

Preheat oven to 350F. Use a 3 qt. greased casserole. Brown beef and onions; add chili powder, salt, pepper, garlic, and Tabasco sauce; simmer for 2 mins. In a saucepan combine corn meal, milk and tomatoes; cook until thickened. Add more milk if necessary.Combine meat mixture, tomato mixture, corn and olives; pour into casserole and top with grated cheese. Bake uncovered for 30 mins.

Mrs. Herbert Eldeon

190

HAMBURGER DELIGHT CASSEROLE — *10-12 servings*
Best refrigerated overnight before baking.

1 (8 oz.) pkg. shell macaroni	1 (4 oz.) can mushrooms,
½ cup margarine	drained
3 medium onions, chopped	½ cup dry sherry
1 green pepper, chopped	1 T. Worcestershire sauce
3 cloves garlic, minced	1 T. chili powder
2 lbs. ground chuck	1 T. brown sugar
2 (15 oz. each) cans tomato	2 tsp. salt
sauce	¼ tsp. pepper
1 (12 oz.) can whole kernel	½ tsp. oregano
corn	1 cup cheddar cheese, grated

Use an ungreased 3 qt. casserole. Cook macaroni as directed on pkg., drain. Melt margarine, add onions, green pepper and garlic; sauté until onions are transparent. Add meat and brown until no pink shows. Place meat mixture and macaroni in casserole. Combine tomato sauce, corn, mushrooms, sherry, and seasonings. Pour over meat mixture and mix well. Sprinkle cheese over top. Cover and refrigerate overnight. Preheat oven to 350F. and bake covered 2 hrs., or until bubbling.

Mrs. Philip Boyer

ITALIAN MEAT PIE — *4-6 servings*

1 (12¾ oz.) can crescent rolls	1 (6 oz.) can tomato paste
1 lb. ground beef	salt and pepper to taste
⅓ cup onion, chopped	1 cup Mozzarella
½ tsp. Italian seasoning	cheese, shredded
½ tsp. dill weed	

Sauce:

1 (6 oz.) can tomato paste	¾ cup water
½ cup margarine	½ tsp. Italian seasoning

Preheat oven to 375F. Spread rolls in a 9" pie plate to form a crust. Brown beef with onions; add seasonings and tomato paste and blend well. Pour beef mixture into pie crust. Sprinkle with cheese. Bake for 25 mins. Combine sauce ingredients and simmer 15 mins. Serve sauce over individual pie wedges.

Mrs. Linda Anderson

ITALIAN-STYLE MANICOTTI 12 servings

2 onions, chopped
1 garlic clove, minced
2 T. olive oil
1½ lbs. ground chuck
½ lb. sausage, Italian or regular
1 cup Mozzarella cheese, shredded
1 cup soft bread crumbs, soaked in ½ cup milk
1 egg, slightly beaten
½ cup mushrooms, chopped
1½ tsp. salt
¼ tsp. pepper
½ tsp. oregano
2 (3 oz. each) pkgs. spaghetti sauce mix
2 (6 oz. each) cans tomato paste
6 cups canned tomatoes
24 manicotti noodles
2 (6 oz. each) pkgs. Mozzarella cheese, sliced
Parmesan cheese

Preheat oven 300F. Use 2 - 9" x 13" baking pans. Saute onions and garlic in oil. Add meats and cook until browned; drain. Add cheese, soaked bread crumbs, egg, mushrooms, and seasonings. Set aside. Combine sauce mix with tomato paste and tomatoes; simmer until thickened. Cook noodles according to pkg. directions. Stuff noodles with meat mixture and arrange in baking dishes. Top with Mozzarella cheese and pour over sauce. Sprinkle with Parmesan cheese; cover and bake 45 mins.

Mrs. Ken Michmerhuizen

LASAGNE 12 servings

1 lb. ground round
½ lb. Italian sausage
2 onions, chopped
1 (6 oz.) can tomato paste
no-salt 2 (8 oz. each) cans tomato sauce
1 (10½ oz.) can tomato puree
1 cup red wine

Cheese Mixture:
1 lb. ricotta or cottage cheese
½ cup Parmesan cheese, grated
1 T. parsley flakes
1 egg, beaten

1½ tsp dried parsley
1½ tsp. oregano
1½ tsp. basil
2 bay leaves
2 garlic cloves, minced
1½ tsp. salt
8-10 lasagne noodles
pepper to taste

1 tsp. sugar
1½ tsp. salt
¼ tsp. pepper
1 lb. Mozzarella cheese, sliced

continued

192

Brown meats and onions; drain. In a large saucepan combine the tomato paste, sauce, puree, wine, and seasonings. Add meat mixture and simmer uncovered for 45 mins. Cook noodles according to pkg. directions. Combine all ingredients in cheese mixture, except the Mozzarella cheese.

Preheat oven to 375F. Use an ungreased 9" x 13" x 2" pan. Place half the noodles in pan. Cover with half the cheese mixture and half the Mozzarella cheese and half the meat sauce. Repeat. Sprinkle top generously with additional Parmesan cheese if desired. Bake uncovered for 30 mins. If refrigerated before cooking, bake 15-20 mins. longer or until bubbling. Let set 10 mins. before cutting.

Mrs. Lee Kimzey
Mrs. Lorenzo Meengs

LASAGNE

8-10 servings

1 lb. ground chuck
½ lb. seasoned or Italian
   sausage
1 T. olive oil
2 large onions, chopped
2 cloves garlic, minced
½ cup celery, chopped
½ cup green pepper, chopped
2 cups tomatoes, chopped
2 cups tomato sauce

1 (6 oz.) can tomato paste
1 (4 oz.) can mushrooms,
   drained
½ cup water or red wine
1 T. parsley, chopped
1 T. oregano
2 tsp. salt
1½ tsp. sweet basil
¼ tsp. thyme
lasagne noodles

Cheese Mixture:
1 pt. cottage or ricotta cheese
2 eggs, slightly beaten
1 tsp. salt
dash pepper

1 T. parsley
½ cup Parmesan cheese
12 oz. Mozzarella cheese, sliced

continued

Lightly brown meats in oil; drain. Combine remaining ingredients, except noodles, and add to meat. Simmer 2-3 hrs.

Preheat oven to 350F. Grease a 9" x 13" casserole. Prepare noodles according to pkg. directions. Combine all ingredients for cheese mixture except Mozzarella cheese. Place 3 noodles on bottom of casserole; cover with half of meat mixture, then with half of cheese mixture. Repeat layers and top with Mozzarella. Bake for 30 mins.

Mrs. Keith Lankheet

MEXICALLY PIE   6 servings

1 cup flour	⅓ cup bacon drippings
2 T. corn meal	3-4 T. cold water

Filling:

1 lb. ground round	¼ cup onion
½ tsp. oregano	1 cup drained corn
½ tsp. chili powder	1 (8 oz.) can tomato sauce
¼ cup corn meal	

Topping:

1 egg, beaten	1½ cups cheddar cheese,
¼ cup milk	grated
1 tsp. mustard	6 olives, sliced
½ tsp. salt	6 slices bacon, fried

Preheat oven to 425F. Combine flour and corn meal. Stir in drippings and water; blend well. Roll out and pat in a 9" pie plate. Fry ground round and combine with remaining filling ingredients. Simmer 5 min. Pour into crust and bake 25 mins.

Prepare topping by mixing all the ingredients together except the bacon. Sprinkle over top of pie and arrange bacon in a spoke wheel fashion on top. Return pie to oven and bake an additional 5-8 min.

Mrs. Ron Bergman

POTATO POT CASSEROLE

serves 8-10

2 lbs. boneless beef or veal,
  thinly sliced, and cut into
  1" squares
5-6 large onions, sliced
5 large potatoes, thinly sliced

salt and pepper
8 strips lean bacon
8 tomatoes, sliced
½ cup red wine
1 cup water

Preheat oven to 300F. Use a greased 4 qt. casserole. Arrange squares of beef in a layer on bottom of casserole. Layer the onions and potatoes. Repeat until all 3 ingredients are used. Season each layer to taste. Arrange bacon strips into a spoked wheel shape, with a slice of tomato in the center and between each strip on the outside. Pour the wine and water mixture over top. Cover and bake for 1½ hrs. Remove cover; bake until bacon is crisp.

Mrs. Katie Worbois

SPAGHETTI AMORE

serves 4

1 lb. ground beef
2 T. shortening
½ cup onions, chopped
¼ cup green pepper, chopped
1 (10¾ oz.) can cream
  mushroom soup

1 (10¾ oz.) can tomato soup
1 soup can water
1 garlic clove, minced
1 cup sharp process cheese,
  grated
¼ lb. spaghetti, cooked

Preheat oven to 350F. Use an ungreased 3 qt. casserole. Lightly brown meat, onion, green pepper in shortening. Add soups, water and garlic, heat. Blend with ½ cup cheese and cooked spaghetti. Top with remaining cheese. Bake uncovered for 30 mins.

Mrs. Richard Forwood

SPANISH NOODLES
serves 8

2 lbs. ground round steak
4 strips bacon, diced
1 (8 oz.) pkg. wide noodles
3 medium onions, sliced
2 green peppers, chopped
1 (16 oz.) can corn,
   drained

1 (4 oz.) can mushrooms,
   drained
2 (10¾ oz. each) cans tomato
   soup, undiluted
1 (dr. wt. 6 oz.) can pitted
   ripe olives, chopped
½ lb. cheese, grated

Preheat oven to 350F. Use a 3 qt. greased casserole. Fry beef and bacon together. Cook noodles according to package directions. Combine all ingredients in casserole; top with cheese. Bake 1 hr.

BEEF STEW
serves 6

2 lbs. chuck meat, cubed
4 carrots, chopped
2 medium onions, sliced
2-3 stalks celery, chopped
1 green pepper, chopped
3 potatoes, chopped
1 cup tomato juice
1 T. sugar

2 T. instant tapioca
1 tsp. seasoned salt
1 tsp. salt
¼ tsp. pepper
dash Worcestershire sauce
¼ cup Burgundy
1 (10 oz.) pkg. frozen peas
chopped parsley

Preheat oven to 250F. Combine all ingredients, except peas and parsley, in a Dutch oven. Cover and cook 4-5 hrs. Remove lid last ½ hr. if gravy has not thickened. The last 15 mins. add peas and parsley.

Mrs. John Shepherd

FIVE HOUR STEW
serves 4

2 lbs. stew meat
3-4 potatoes, halved
carrots, as desired, chopped
1 medium onion, chopped

1 (1¼ oz.) pkg. dry onion
   soup mix
2½ cups water
3 T. tapioca

Preheat oven to 300F. Combine all ingredients together in a Dutch oven and bake covered for 5 hrs. Stir occasionally.

Mrs. Jack Dozeman

ITALIAN BEEF STEW

8 servings

2 lbs. stew beef, cubed
¼ cup oil
⅔ cup onions, chopped
⅔ cup green pepper, chopped
⅔ cup celery, sliced
1 (10½ oz.) can condensed
  beef broth
½ cup water

1 (8 oz.) can tomato sauce
1 (.6 oz.) pkg. dry Italian salad
  dressing mix
4 small potatoes, halved
6 medium carrots, chopped
4 small whole onions
1 T. flour
2 T. water

Brown beef cubes in oil in a Dutch oven. Remove browned beef and add onions, green pepper, and celery and sauté 5 mins. or until tender. Return beef to pan. Add broth, water, tomato sauce and salad dressing mix. Bring to a boil. Reduce heat, cover and simmer 1¼ hrs., stirring occasionally. Add vegetables; simmer 1 hr. longer, or until meat and vegetables are tender.

Remove from heat; skim off excess fat. Blend flour with water and stir into hot stew. Cover and simmer 10 mins., or until thickened.

Mrs. Ernest Penna

NO PEEK STEW

6-8 servings

2 lbs. stew meat
1 cup celery, sliced
1 cup carrots, sliced
1 cup onion, sliced
1 cup fresh mushrooms,
  sliced
salt and pepper

1 (21 oz.) jar Ragu cooking
  sauce
2½ T. tapioca
1 T. each A1 sauce and
  Worcestershire sauce
1½ T. sugar
½ cup red wine

Preheat oven to 325F. Use an ungreased large flat baking dish. Place meat in center of baking dish and surround meat with vegetables. Combine remaining ingredients and pour over meat and vegetables. Cover dish with foil and seal tightly. Bake for 2½ hrs. No Peek.

Mrs. Robert Hampson

SAUERKRAUT-CORNED BEEF CASSEROLE *serves 4*

1 (16 oz.) can sauerkraut,
  drained and rinsed
1 (16 oz.) can corned beef
  hash, chopped
1 onion, finely chopped

2 cups tomato juice
2 tsp. horseradish
4 tsp. brown sugar
6-8 strips bacon,
  fat slightly trimmed

Preheat oven to 350F. Use a 9" x 13" ungreased casserole. Place sauerkraut in casserole. Add the hash; sprinkle with onions. Combine tomato juice, horseradish, and brown sugar. Pour over ingredients in casserole. Add 6-8 bacon strips. Bake uncovered 1 hr.

Mrs. Frank Harbin

TAGLIARINI *serves 10-12*

1 lb. ground beef
1 lb. country sausage
1 cup catsup, or barbecue
  sauce
1 tsp. sage
1 tsp. chili powder
salt and pepper to taste

1 large green pepper, chopped
1 (16 oz.) can corn, drained
1 (16 oz.) can tomatoes
1 (4 oz.) can mushrooms,
  drained
1 (7 oz.) jar green olives,
  drained, halved
1 (8 oz.) pkg. flat noodles
1 ½ cups mild cheese, shredded

Preheat oven to 300F. Use an ungreased 9" x 13" casserole. Brown beef and sausage together; drain. Add catsup, sage, chili powder, salt and pepper. Mix well. Add green pepper, corn, tomatoes, mushrooms and olives. Cook for 10 mins. Cook noodles according to pkg. directions; drain. Combine with meat mixture. Pour into casserole; top with cheese. Bake uncovered for 1 hr. Can be made ahead and frozen. Serve with garlic bread and tossed salad.

Mrs. William Boyer

VEGETARIAN SEVEN LAYER CASSEROLE

2-4 servings

½ cup celery, chopped
½ cup onions, chopped
2 cups potatoes, diced
1½ cups carrots, chopped

½ cup raw rice
1 (15 oz.) can lima beans, drained
1 (10¾ oz.) can tomato soup

Preheat oven to 350F. Use an ungreased 2 qt. casserole. Place vegetables in layers in order given. Pour soup, diluted with equal amount of water over vegetables. Bake covered 1 hr. 15 mins., removing cover after 45 mins.

Mrs. H. Vander Bie

CURRIED LAMB CASSEROLE

8 servings

2 lbs. lamb breast or
   shoulder, cubed
2 T. fat
salt and pepper
1 bay leaf
6 whole black
   peppercorns

2 small onions, sliced
1 tsp. parsley, chopped
¼ cup flour
1 tsp. curry powder
2 T. cold water
6 apples, peeled, sliced
rice with raisins

Brown meat in hot fat. Cover with boiling water, add seasonings, onions and parsley. Cover and cook slowly for about 2 hrs. Strain and reserve 2 cups of broth. Mix flour and curry powder, add cold water and blend. Stir into stock, cook until thick. Add apples and meat; cook additional 30 min. Serve with fluffy rice with raisins. May pass coconut, sweet relish, or chopped cashew nuts with curry.

Mrs. Wm. Vandenberg, Jr.

CHEESE CORN RING WITH HAM AND MUSHROOMS

6 servings

2 T. butter
2 T. flour
¾ cup milk
2 cups cream style corn
2 T. onion, chopped
1 pimento, chopped
8 oz. process American
   cheese, grated
1½ cups soft bread crumbs

salt and pepper
4 eggs, beaten
¼ cup butter
6 T. flour
2 cups milk
2 cups cooked ham, diced
1 (4 oz.) can sliced
   mushrooms, drained

Preheat oven to 350F. Use a well greased 1 qt. ring mold. Add flour to melted butter, blend, and add milk. Cook to smooth sauce. Add next 7 ingredients and mix well. Pour mixture into mold and bake 50-60 min. uncovered until firm. Melt butter, stir in flour; gradually add milk; stirring constantly. Cook until thickened. Unmold cheese corn ring and fill center with combination of sauce, ham and mushrooms.

Mrs. Russell A. Klaasen

CREAMY HAM CASSEROLE

6 servings

1 medium head cauliflower
¼ cup butter
⅓ cup flour
1 cup milk
1 cup sharp cheddar cheese,
   cubed

½ cup sour cream
2 cups cooked ham, cubed
1 (3 oz.) can sliced
   mushrooms, drained
buttered bread crumbs

Preheat oven to 350F. Use an ungreased 2 qt. casserole. Break cauliflower into buds, about 4 cups. Cook, covered, in boiling salted water till tender, 10-20 min. Drain. Melt butter; stir in flour. Add milk and cook, stirring until mixture thickens. Add cheese and sour cream to sauce; stir till cheese melts. Combine with cauliflower, ham and mushrooms. Turn into casserole. Sprinkle on bread crumbs. Bake uncovered 40 min.

Mrs. Herbert Eldean

HAM AND RICE CHANTILLY

serves 6

2 cups cooked ham, diced
3 cups cooked rice
1 cup green peas, cooked
1 cup cheddar cheese, grated

1 tsp. salt
¼ tsp. pepper
dash cayenne
1 cup heavy cream, whipped

Preheat oven to 350F. Use a 2 qt. greased casserole. Combine ham, rice, peas, ½ cup cheese, salt, pepper and cayenne. Spoon into casserole dish and add remaining cheese to the whipped cream. Spread over top of rice mixture. Bake uncovered for 30 min.

Mrs. Herbert Eldean

HAM STUFFED MANICOTTI
WITH CHEESE SAUCE

4 servings

1 (4 oz.) pkg. manicotti shells,
(8 shells)
¼ cup onions, chopped
2 T. oil
3 cups ground cooked ham
1 (6 oz.) can mushrooms,
drained, chopped
3 T. Parmesan cheese

¼ cup green pepper,
chopped
3 T. margarine
3 T. flour
2 cups milk
1 cup Swiss cheese,
shredded

Preheat oven 350F. Use a greased 11¾" x 7½" x 1¾" baking dish. Cook manicotti according to pkg. directions. In small skillet, cook onions in oil until tender. Add ham and mushrooms; cool. Stir in Parmesan; set aside. In small saucepan, cook green pepper in margarine till tender; blend in flour. Add milk at once. Cook and stir till thickened and bubbly. Stir in Swiss cheese till melted. Mix ¼ cup cheese sauce with ham and mushrooms. Fill each tube with ⅓ cup ham filling. Arrange tubes in baking dish. Pour remaining cheese sauce over stuffed manicotti. Sprinkle with paprika. Bake covered for 30 mins. or till heated through.

Mrs. Tom Brown

MACARONI HAM LOAF

6 servings

1 cup ham, diced
1 cup cooked macaroni
1 cup bread crumbs, soft
1 cup medium cheese,
   shredded
1 large onion, chopped
1 T. green pepper, chopped
1 tsp. parsley

1 cup light cream
⅓ cup butter, melted
3 eggs, well beaten
1 (10¾ oz.) can mushroom
   soup
1 (4 oz.) can sliced
   mushrooms, drained
½ cup light cream

Preheat oven to 350F. Use an ungreased loaf pan. Combine first 10 ingredients, pour into pan. Bake uncovered in a pan of water for 1 hr. Make a sauce by heating together the soup, mushrooms and cream. Serve with macaroni loaf.

Mrs. Fred Pickel

CHOP SUEY CASSEROLE

6 servings

2 lbs. chop suey meat
1 cup onions, chopped
1 cup celery, chopped
1 (10¾ oz.) can cream of
   mushroom soup
1 (10¾ oz.) can cream of
   chicken soup
2 soup cans of water
1 cup raw rice

1 (3 oz.) can mushrooms,
   drained
1 cup bean sprouts,
   drained
sugar to taste
1 tsp. Worcestershire sauce
1 (9 oz.) can chow mein
   noodles

Brown meat; add onion, celery and cook 2-3 mins. Add soups, water and rice. Cover and simmer for 30 mins. Add mushrooms, bean sprouts, sugar, and Worcestershire sauce. Mix well. Sprinkle noodles on top.

"Eet Smakelijk's Best"

HUTSPOT

serves 4

3 lbs. pork roast
1 small cabbage, cut in
* 4-6 pieces*

8 potatoes, cut in half
1 large onion, cubed
salt and pepper, to taste

Preheat oven to 350F. Put roast in Dutch oven, adding enough water so that 1" of roast is exposed. Bake for 1½ to 2 hrs. Cool and remove bones. Return boned pork to the pan of broth and add vegetables. Boil ½ hr. Add more water if needed. When vegetables are tender, drain juice, then mash all together. Serve with butter, salt and pepper. It's delicious!

Mrs. Alvern Kapenga

SURPRISE CASSEROLE

8 servings

1 lb. veal, cut in 1" cubes
1 lb. lean pork, cut in 1" cubes
3 T. drippings
½ tsp. salt
¼ tsp. pepper
1 (10¾ oz.) can cream of
* chicken soup, undiluted*
1 (16 oz.) can bean sprouts,
* drained, reserve liquid*

1 (8 oz.) pkg. noodles, cooked
½ lb. fresh mushrooms, sliced
* and sautéed*
½ green pepper, diced
1 (2½ oz.) jar pimentos,
* diced*
8 oz. sharp cheese, grated

Preheat oven to 350F. Use an ungreased 2 qt. casserole. Brown meat in drippings. Add salt, pepper, soup and bean sprout liquid. Bring to a boil and simmer for 45 mins. Add remaining ingredients and mix thoroughly. Place in casserole and bake uncovered for 30 mins.

Mrs. Roger Baar

WILD RICE CASSEROLE

6-8 servings

1 cup wild rice
½ lb. pork, cubed
1½ lb. veal, cubed
½ cup Spanish onion, chopped
1½ cup celery, diced

½ cup green pepper, chopped
1 (10¾ oz.) can cream of mushroom soup, undiluted
1 (10¾ oz.) can cream of
   chicken soup, undiluted

Soak rice overnight. Next day, drain rice. Preheat oven to 300F.
Use an ungreased 2 qt. casserole. Brown meat and onion. Combine all ingredients together and place in casserole. Bake covered
for 2 hrs. Serve with a mushroom sauce using canned mushroom
soup if desired.

Mrs. Vern Schipper

CHEESY FRANKFURTER CASSEROLE

serves 4-6

¾ cup macaroni
6 frankfurters
⅓ cup onion, chopped
⅓ cup green pepper, chopped
2 T. butter
3 T. flour

1 tsp. Worcestershire sauce
1 tsp. prepared mustard
¼ tsp. salt
dash pepper
1 cup milk
1½ cups cottage cheese

Preheat oven to 350F. Use an ungreased 1½ qt. casserole. Cook
macaroni according to directions; drain. Cut 4 franks into thin
slices. Set aside. Sauté onions and pepper in butter until tender.
Blend in flour, Worcestershire sauce, mustard, salt, pepper. Add
milk. Cook until thickened. Stir in sliced franks, macaroni and
cottage cheese. Mix well. Turn into casserole; bake uncovered
20 mins., stirring once. Slice remaining franks and arrange in cart-
wheel pattern on top of casserole. Bake 15 mins. more

Mrs. Herbert Eldean

SCALLOPED VEGETABLES WITH FRANKS

4-6 servings

*2 cups carrots,
  coarsely shredded
4 cups potatoes,
  coarsely shredded
1 (10 oz.) pkg. frozen
  cut green beans
2 medium onions, chopped*

*¼ cup flour
2 tsp. salt
½ tsp. pepper
3 cups milk
1 lb. frankfurters or
  (sausage, sliced and
  sauteed.)*

Preheat oven to 375F. Use a 2½ qt. casserole. Combine vegetables in casserole. Mix flour, salt and pepper, whisk in milk; pour over vegetables. Add frankfurters. Bake covered 1 hr.

Mrs. William T. Hakken Jr.

KNACKWURST WITH RED CABBAGE

6 servings

*6 slices bacon, diced
2 cups onion, chopped
1 small head red cabbage,
  cored and shredded
1½ tsp. salt
dash of pepper*

*¼ cup red wine vinegar
2 T. brown sugar
3 medium tart apples,
  pared, cored, sliced
2 lbs. Knackwurst
boiled potatoes*

Saute bacon until crisp; remove. Add onion to bacon grease and cook 5 mins. Add cabbage, salt, pepper and vinegar; mix well, cover and cook 30 mins. over low heat. Add sugar, apples and bacon. Stir gently into cabbage. Arrange sausage over cabbage; cook till heated through. Serve with potatoes.

Mrs. H. Wise

DUTCH KALE 'N METWURST MOUSSE

serves 6-8

*2 (10 oz. each) pkgs. frozen
  kale, chopped
1 Metwurst, skimmed
  and cubed
⅓ cup quick barley*

*2 cups water
2 ½ cups water
1 cup milk
1 tsp. salt
4 cups potato buds*

continued

Bring kale, Metwurst and barley to a boil in 2 cups water, lower heat and simmer for 1 hr., stirring occasionally. In Dutch oven bring to boil 2½ cups water, milk and salt. Remove from heat, add potato buds and stir. Cover, and let stand for 5 min. Add kale-Metwurst mixture and mix thoroughly.

Mr. Barney Sheaffer

BAVARIAN BEANS AND SAUSAGE — 6 *servings*

½ lb. Idaho Great Northern beans
6 cups water
2 tsp. salt
1 (16 oz.) jar sauerkraut, drained
¼ cup onion, minced
1 cup beer
1 T. prepared mustard
1 T. brown sugar
¼ tsp. celery seed
½ tsp. caraway seed
1½ lbs. Bratwurst or frankfurters, lightly browned in butter

Soak beans in water overnight. (For quick soak method, combine beans and water, bring to a boil and boil 2 mins. Cover and let stand 1 hr.). Add salt to soaking water and simmer beans 1 to 1½ hr. or until tender. Drain beans and combine with sauerkraut, onion, beer, mustard, brown sugar, celery seed and caraway seeds in 2 qt. casserole. Cover and bake at 325F. for 1 hr. 15 mins. Uncover. Top with lightly browned Bratwurst and bake an additional 20 mins.

Mrs. Robert Hampson

BEAN-SAUSAGE CASSEROLE — 6 *servings*

2 (20 oz. each) cans cannelline (white kidney beans)
½ lb. pork sausage
1 medium onion, chopped
1 garlic clove, crushed
1 lb. ground chuck
½ tsp. thyme
1 tsp. salt
¼ tsp. pepper
1 T. parsley flakes
1 cup white wine
1 (8 oz.) can tomato sauce

continued

Preheat oven to 350F. Use an ungreased 3 qt. casserole dish. Drain beans; reserve 1 cup liquid. Brown sausage. Add onion and garlic. Cook 2-3 mins. Pour off fat; add chuck and brown. Add seasonings and parsley. Alternate layers of beans and meat mixture, beginning with ½ of beans. Combine reserved liquid, wine and tomato sauce. Bring to a boil. Pour over ingredients in casserole. Bake uncovered for 1 hr.

Mrs. Eleanor Van Dyke

SAUSAGE-LIMA BARBECUE   *6 servings*

1 (1 lb.) pkg. pork sausage links   *½ cup chopped onions*
4 cups cooked lima beans   *1 cup catsup*
1 T. horseradish   *1 tsp. Worcestershire sauce*

Preheat oven to 375F. Use a 1½ qt. casserole. Brown sausages; drain. Combine remaining ingredients. Place one half of bean mixture in casserole; top with one half of sausages. Repeat. Bake uncovered 20 mins.

Mrs. Helena Lemmen

CHICKEN A LA CAN CAN   *6 servings*

2 (5 oz. each) cans chicken   *salt and pepper to taste*
or turkey   *1 (3 oz.) can evaporated*
1 (10¾ oz.) can chicken rice   *milk*
soup, undiluted   *1 small onion, diced*
1 (10¾ oz.) can cream mush-   *1 (9 oz.) can chow mein*
room soup, undiluted   *noodles*
1 cup celery, chopped, cooked

Preheat oven to 350F. Grease a 1½ qt. casserole. Combine all ingredients except noodles. Pour into casserole. Top with noodles. Bake uncovered 35 to 45 mins.

CHICKEN DIVINE
8 servings

3 (10¾ oz. each) cans chicken
   or mushroom soup, undiluted
1 ⅓ cups mayonnaise
1 T. lemon juice
3 whole large chicken breasts,
   cooked and diced

2 (10 oz. each) pkg. frozen
   broccoli or asparagus,
   cooked
1 cup cheese, grated
buttered bread crumbs

Preheat oven to 350F. Use an ungreased 9" x 13" pan. Mix soup, mayonnaise and lemon juice together. Layer in pan ½ each of soup mixture, then chicken, broccoli and cheese. Repeat. Top with bread crumbs and bake uncovered 30-40 mins. or until bubbly.

Mrs. Dirk Den Hartog

CHICKEN AND SAUERKRAUT
4 servings

2½-3 lbs. frying chicken, cut up
   or chicken breasts
½ cup margarine
1 garlic clove, crushed

8 small red skinned potatoes,
   peeled around center
1 qt. jar sauerkraut, drained,
   reserve juice
sour cream

Preheat oven to 350F. Use a 9" x 13" casserole. Brown chicken in margarine and garlic. Place chicken in casserole with potatoes and sauerkraut juice. Saute sauerkraut in margarine, add to casserole. Cover and bake for 1½ hr. basting occasionally or until potatoes are tender. Serve with sour cream.

Mrs. Anthony Garofalo

CHOW YUK
8 servings

1 (10 oz.) box frozen pea pods
½ lb. mushrooms, sliced
1 cup celery, sliced
½ cup Chinese (celery) cabbage, sliced
2 thin carrots, sliced
10 green onions, cut into 1" pieces
1 (6 oz.) can water chestnuts, drained and sliced
1 (16 oz.) can bamboo shoots, drained and cut half

1 chicken breast, boned and skinned
16 shrimp, cut in half lengthwise
½ lb. sirloin tip, sliced
½ lb. pork, fat removed, sliced
oil
hot rice

Sauce:
2 cups chicken broth
½ tsp. salt
½ tsp. pepper
1 T. sugar

1 T. Worcestershire sauce
2 T. soy sauce
cornstarch to thicken

Prepare all vegetables, meats, and sauce before beginning to cook. Cut all meat in strips to match the size of shrimp. Combine sauce ingredients and cook until thickened.

To stir fry, heat about 2 T. oil in wok or a heavy skillet. Stir fry each ingredient; remove each vegetable as it reaches its brightest color, meat as it loses its color. Place in large bowl after foods are all cooked. Add the hot thickened sauce. Serve with hot rice.

Mrs. Wm. Orr

GOURMET CHICKEN BAKE
6 servings

1 cup wild rice
1 lb. bulk pork sausage
1 (10¾ oz.) can mushroom soup, undiluted
1 (10¾) can cream of chicken soup, undiluted

1 (4 oz.) can sliced mushrooms, drained
½ tsp. Worcestershire sauce
2 cups chicken or turkey, cubed
1 cup buttered bread crumbs

continued

Preheat oven to 350F. Use a 2 qt. casserole. Cook rice as directed on pkg. Sauté sausage until brown, pour off fat and break into bits. Add soups, mushrooms and Worcestershire sauce. Toss mixture lightly with rice, spoon half of mixture into casserole, add fowl and rest of mixture. Top with buttered bread crumbs. Bake uncovered for 40 mins.

Mrs. Roger Prins

HOT CHICKEN CRUNCH   *6-8 servings*

3 cups chicken, diced, cooked
1 (10¾ oz.) can cream of
    chicken soup
2 cups celery, chopped
½ cup almonds, chopped
¼ cup pimento, chopped
¾ cup mayonnaise
2 T. lemon juice

3 T. onions, chopped
1 tsp. salt
¼ tsp. pepper
3 hard boiled eggs, sliced
½ cup American cheese,
    grated
2 cups potato chips, crushed

Preheat oven to 450F. Use an ungreased 9" x 12" casserole. Combine all ingredients except eggs, cheese and potato chips. Pour into casserole. Top with last 3 ingredients, bake uncovered for 15 mins. Reduce heat to 350F. and bake 25 mins. longer.

Mrs. Ken Louis

SWISS CHICKEN CASSEROLE   *8 servings*

4 cups cooked chicken, diced
2 cups celery, sliced
2 cups toasted bread cubes
1 cup salad dressing
½ cup milk
1 tsp. salt

⅛ tsp. pepper
¼ cup onion, chopped
8 oz. Swiss cheese,
    shredded
¼ cup toasted slivered
    almonds

Preheat oven to 350F. Lightly butter a 2 qt. casserole. Combine chicken, celery and bread cubes. Blend well salad dressing, milk, salt, and pepper; mix in onion and cheese. Pour over chicken mixture and toss until well blended. Spoon into casserole. Sprinkle with almonds. Bake uncovered for 25 mins.

Mrs. Billy J. Boes

TASTY CHICKEN CASSEROLE
4 servings

1 cup cooked narrow noodles
1 (5 oz.) can boned chicken
1 cup celery, diced
½ cup slivered almonds
2 tsp. onions, chopped
½ cup mayonnaise

1 (10¾ oz.) can cream of
  chicken soup
3 T. milk or cream
salt and pepper to taste
2 cups potato chips,
  crushed

Preheat oven to 425F. Use an ungreased 1½ qt. casserole. Mix all ingredients except potato chips. Place in casserole, top with potato chips and bake uncovered for 20 mins. or until bubbly.

Mrs. Walter Kimberley

TURKEY BUFFET CASSEROLE
6 servings

2 T. butter
2 T. flour
1 tsp. salt
¼ tsp. prepared mustard
¼ tsp. pepper
2 cups milk
1 cup grated American
  cheese

1 (10 oz.) pkg. frozen broccoli
  spears, cooked
½ (8 oz.) pkg. wide noodles,
  cooked
3 cups chicken or turkey,
  cooked and diced
⅓ cup toasted slivered
  almonds

Preheat oven to 350F. Use a greased 2 qt. casserole. Melt butter, stir in flour, salt, mustard, pepper, and milk; cook, stirring constantly until thickened. Remove from heat. Stir in cheese until melted. Dice broccoli stems; leave flowerets whole. Arrange noodles, broccoli stems and chicken in casserole. Pour cheese sauce over all. Arrange flowerets on top. Sprinkle with almonds. Bake uncovered 20 mins.

Mrs. Don Cochran

TURKEY 'N DRESSING BAKE
serves 6

2 cups stuffing mix
1 cup water
3 T. butter
½ cup celery, chopped
½ cup onion, chopped
3 T. flour
1 (13 oz.) can evaporated milk

1 (6 oz.) can water chestnuts
   drained, sliced
3 cups turkey, cooked
   diced
1 tsp. salt
⅛ tsp. pepper
1 tsp. Worcestershire sauce

Preheat oven to 400F. Use a well greased shallow 2 qt. casserole. Combine stuffing mix with water. Mix well. Reserve ½ cup for topping. Press remaining into casserole to form a crust. Bake for 10 mins. Melt butter. Add celery and onion and saute until onion is transparent, stirring frequently. Push vegetables to one side and blend in flour. Add milk, mixing well. Cook until sauce is smooth and thickened. Stir in remaining ingredients; lower oven temperature to 350F. Pour mixture in crust, sprinkle remaining stuffing mixture over top and bake uncovered for 30 mins.

Mrs. Allen Butler

CIOPPINO
6-8 servings

1 large onion, chopped
1 medium green pepper,
   chopped
1 clove garlic, minced
2 T. olive oil
1 (28 oz.) can tomatoes,
   chopped, undrained
½ cup white wine
¼ cup parsley, chopped
1 T. salt

¼ tsp. basil
1½ lbs. Dungeness crab or 2
   (12 oz. ea.) pkgs. frozen
   Alaska King Crab legs, split,
   thawed, cut into chunks
1½ doz. hard-shelled clams
1½ lbs. striped bass fillets, cut
   into serving pieces
1 lb. shrimp, shelled and
   deveined

In Dutch oven over medium heat, cook onion, green pepper, and garlic in hot oil until tender. Add tomatoes and liquid, wine, parsley, salt and basil; reduce to low heat, cover and simmer 15 mins. Increase heat to med-high; add crab and clams, cook 10 mins., stirring occasionally. Add fillet pieces and shrimp, cooking 5 mins. more or until fish flakes easily and shrimp are tender. Serve immediately.

Mrs. Thomas Brown

PANVIS
Dutch Fish Casserole

½ lb. dried cod
1 lb. rice, cooked
1 lb. potatoes, boiled and
   diced
1 large onion, chopped
   and sauteed

salt, pepper, and nutmeg
   to taste
prepared mustard to taste
bread crumbs
3 T. butter

Preheat oven to 350F. Use a deep 2 qt. casserole dish. Boil, clean and shred fish. Mix with rice, potatoes, onion, salt, pepper, nutmeg, and mustard. Place in casserole. Sprinkle generously with bread crumbs and dot with butter. Bake uncovered for 30 mins. or until nicely browned. Serve with a salad. Hollanders like this dish to be quite snappy.

SHRIMP CASSEROLE

8-10 servings

1 cup butter
½ lb. fresh mushrooms, sliced
1 medium onion, chopped
2 T. parsley, chopped
¾ cup flour
6 cups milk
4 eggs, beaten
4 tsp. dry mustard
2 tsp. Worcestershire sauce

½ cup sherry
dash of salt and pepper
2 cups sharp cheddar
   cheese, shredded
1 (2½ oz.) jar pimentos,
   chopped
2 lbs. shrimp, cooked
paprika
patty shells, rice, or toast

Preheat oven to 325F. Use a 2 qt. casserole. Melt butter; add mushrooms, onions and parsley and saute until tender. Stir in flour and slowly add milk, stirring until smooth. Combine eggs, mustard, Worcestershire, sherry, salt and pepper. Add to sauce. Blend in cheese, pimentos and shrimp. Pour into casserole and bake uncovered for 30 mins. Sprinkle with paprika and serve over patty shells, rice or toast.

Mrs. Henry Mass

CAPTAIN'S CASSEROLE

6 servings

1 (10¾ oz.) can cream of mushroom soup, undiluted
½ cup milk
⅔ cup cheese, grated
1½ cups Minute Rice
¼ tsp. each salt and pepper
½ tsp. oregano

1 (16 oz.) can tomatoes
1 cup water
½ cup onion, minced
2 (7 oz. each) cans tuna,
 drained
⅓ cup stuffed olives
½ cup potato chips, crushed

Preheat oven to 375F. Use a 2 qt. casserole. Combine soup, milk and cheese; heat until cheese melts. Set aside. Combine rice, salt and pepper, and oregano. Measure ½ cup juice of tomatoes. Stir juice and water into rice. Slice tomatoes. Add tomatoes, onion, tuna and olives to rice. Pour into casserole. Pour on cheese sauce and top with potato chips. Bake uncovered for 25 mins.

Mrs. Fred Leaske

MAI-KAI

4 servings

1 (7 oz.) can water packed
 tuna, drained
1 (10¾ oz.) can cream of
 chicken soup
¼ cup water
1½ cups celery, diced
1 green pepper, chopped
1 large onion, chopped

1 cup canned mushrooms,
 drained
½ tsp. M.S.G.
¼ cup almonds, slivered
½ tsp. salt
1 (9 oz.) can chow mein
 noodles

Preheat oven to 325F. Grease a 1½ qt. casserole. Combine all ingredients except noodles; pour into casserole. Top with noodles and bake uncovered for 1 hr.

Mrs. Robert Bernecker

TUNA CASHEW CASSEROLE

4 servings

1 (7 oz.) can tuna, drained
1 (10¾ oz.) can mushroom soup,
  undiluted
¼ cup water
1 cup celery, chopped

¼ cup onion, chopped
½ cup cashew nuts
1 (9 oz.) can chow mein
  noodles

Preheat oven to 350F. Grease a 1½ qt. casserole. Combine all ingredients using only ½ can of chow mein noodles. Pour into casserole. Top with remaining noodles. Bake uncovered for 1 hr.

Mrs. Norm Japinga

NOTES

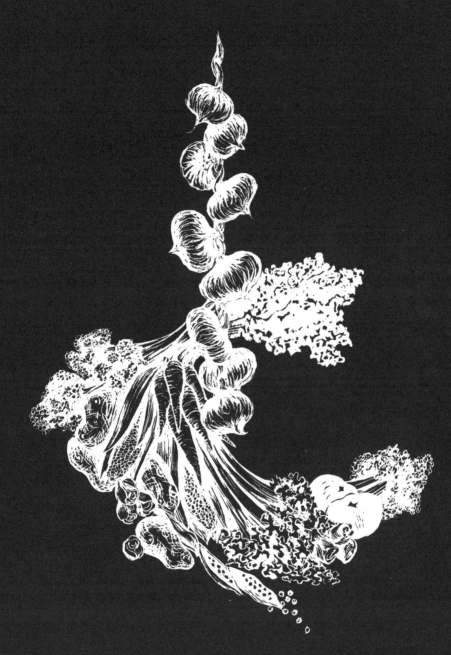

Vegetables and Accompaniments

NOTES

ASPARAGUS A LA PARMESAN   *8 servings*

2 (10 oz. each) pkgs.
  frozen asparagus, chopped
¼ cup margarine
1 large clove garlic,
  minced
½ lb. mushrooms,
  sliced
1 (6 oz.) can tomato paste

asparagus liquid plus water
  to make 1½ cups liquid
¼ cup flour
1 tsp. nutmeg
salt and pepper
  to taste
¼ cup Parmesan cheese,
  grated

Preheat oven 350F. Grease a 10" pie plate. Cook asparagus according to package directions; drain, reserving liquid. Arrange asparagus in pie plate. In saucepan, melt margarine, add garlic and saute several minutes. Add mushrooms, cook about 5 mins. turning often. Add tomato paste, asparagus liquid and water; whisk in flour. Season with nutmeg, salt, pepper, and cheese. Cook about 15 mins. Pour sauce over asparagus, sprinkle with additional cheese. Bake uncovered for 30 mins.

Mrs. Gerald Boeve

ASPARAGUS AU GRATIN   *6-8 servings*
(1st Place Bake-Off)

1 lb. fresh mushrooms
3 T. margarine
5 eggs, hard cooked, sliced

2 lbs. fresh asparagus,
  cooked to tender-crisp
  stage

Sauce:
3 T. margarine
3 T. flour
1½ cups milk or light cream
1 cup cheddar cheese, grated

1 tsp. Worcestershire sauce
¼ tsp. pepper
1 tsp. salt
bread crumbs and paprika

Preheat oven to 350F. Grease a 2 qt. casserole. Brown mushrooms in margarine until tender; drain. Carefully combine mushrooms, cooked asparagus (which has been cut in ½" pieces) and eggs. Place in casserole.
Melt margarine, add flour and gradually stir in milk. Add next 4 ingredients and heat slowly until cheese melts. Pour over asparagus mixture. Edge the casserole with bread crumbs and sprinkle the center generously with paprika. Bake 20 mins. or until bubbly.

Mrs. Walter Kimberley

ASPARAGUS DOLORES   6 servings

3 eggs, beaten
1 cup cracker crumbs
1 cup milk
1 (2 oz.) jar
  red pimento, chopped
½ tsp. salt

2 (10 oz. each) pkgs.
  frozen chopped
  asparagus, cooked and
  drained
¼ cup butter, melted

Preheat oven to 350F. Lightly grease a 2 qt. casserole. Combine all ingredients except butter. Pour into casserole. Bake uncovered 25 mins. Pour melted butter over top and bake 20 mins. longer.

Mrs. William G. Beebe

ITALIAN BAKED ASPARAGUS   4-6 servings

3-6 T. butter
1 lb. asparagus spears
3 T. onion, finely chopped
3 T. celery, finely
  chopped
1 T. Parmesan cheese,
  grated

1 T. bread crumbs
4 canned Italian
  peeled tomatoes, diced
salt and pepper,
  freshly-ground
pinch of oregano
pinch of thyme

Preheat oven to 375F. Melt butter in an 8" x 12" baking dish. Line bottom with asparagus spears; sprinkle over with onion, celery, cheese, bread crumbs and tomatoes. Season to taste with salt, pepper, oregano and thyme. Cover dish and bake for 45 mins. or until tender.

Mrs. Lee Kimzey

BAKED BEANS SUPREME

8 servings

½ lb. bacon, diced
2 medium onions,
  chopped
2 (20 oz. each) cans
  pork and beans

1½ tsp. dry mustard
1 (9 oz.) can crushed
  pineapple
¼ cup chili sauce
¼ tsp. salt

Preheat oven to 300F. Use an ungreased 1½ qt. casserole. Saute bacon and onions slowly until onions are tender; drain off fat. Combine bacon and onions with remaining ingredients. Place in a casserole or bean pot. Cover and bake for 2 hours.

Mrs. Don Bryant

CALICO BAKED BEANS

12-15 servings

1 (16 oz.) can lima
  beans, drained
1 (16 oz.) can kidney
  beans, drained
1 (16 oz.) can butter
  beans, drained
2 (16 oz. each) cans
  pork and beans
½ cup tomato soup

2 T. vinegar
¼ cup brown sugar
¼ cup white sugar
2 T. white corn syrup
2 T. prepared mustard
1 medium onion,
  chopped
¼ lb. bacon, diced

Preheat oven to 350F. Use an ungreased 3 qt. casserole. Combine all ingredients and bake uncovered 1½ hrs.

Mrs. Tom Buis

221

HELEN'S GOURMET BAKED BEANS
serves 8

1 cup evaporated milk
1 T. cider vinegar
⅓ cup brown sugar,
  firmly-packed
¼ cup flour, sifted
1 tsp. dry mustard
½ tsp. salt
1 T. molasses

¼ tsp. Worcestershire
  sauce
2 drops Tabasco
2 (16 oz. each) cans
  molasses style
  baked beans
bacon
onion rings (optional)

Preheat oven to 350F. Grease a 1½ qt. casserole. Combine evaporated milk and vinegar in a small bowl. In large bowl mix brown sugar, flour, dry mustard, salt; add milk mixture, blending thoroughly. Blend in molasses, Worcestershire and Tabasco. Add beans, mix well. Pour into casserole and top with slices of bacon. Bake uncovered 40 mins. Garnish with onion rings if desired.

Mrs. Albert De Groot

GREEN BEANS NAPOLI
serves 4

1 T. butter
¼ cup dry bread crumbs
½ tsp. paprika
2 to 4 T. grated
  Parmesan cheese

1 (16 oz.) can green beans
1 T. olive oil or
  salad oil
garlic salt to taste

Melt butter, add crumbs and stir over moderate heat until crumbs are golden. Add paprika. Remove from heat, add Parmesan cheese; toss lightly. Heat beans and drain. Add oil and garlic salt to beans. Place in serving dish and top with crumb mixture.

Mrs. Leonard Johnston

GREEN BEANS WITH SOUR CREAM
serves 6-8

2 (10 oz. each) French style
  frozen beans or 2 lbs.
  fresh beans
¼ lb. sharp cheddar
  cheese, cubed

1 cup sour cream
½ tsp. salt
⅛ tsp. pepper
2 T. onion, grated

Preheat oven to 350F. Grease a 1½ qt. casserole. Cook frozen beans until heated through. If fresh beans are used, cook until just tender. Drain beans; add cheese, sour cream, seasonings and onion. Mix lightly and place in an uncovered casserole for 40-45 mins.

Mrs. Frank Conley

LIMA BEANS PROVENCAL
serves 4

1 (10 oz.) box frozen
  lima beans
½ cup light cream
2 sprigs parsley
1 clove
3 thin slices onion

1 bay leaf
nutmeg to taste
pepper to taste
¼ tsp. salt
2 T. butter

Cook lima beans until tender; drain. Simmer cream with parsley and seasonings; strain cream and pour over lima beans. Reheat and serve.

Mrs. Bruce G. Van Leuwen

GOURMET LIMA BEANS
4 servings

1 (10 oz.) pkg. lima beans,
  cooked, drained
salt and pepper, to taste
4 slices bacon, diced,
  partially fried, and drained

4 canned pear halves
¼ cup butter, melted
2 slices bacon, halved,
  partially fried

Preheat oven to 375F. Grease a 1½ qt. casserole. Season lima beans with salt and pepper; toss with diced bacon. Pour into casserole. Arrange pears on top of beans, drizzle butter over top. Place a half slice of bacon on top of each pear half. Bake 30 mins.

Mrs. Charles Bauer

BEETS WITH RAISINS
4 servings

1 (16 oz.) can
  sliced beets
⅓ cup dark raisins
⅓ cup sugar

1 tsp. cornstarch
3 T. lemon juice
2 T. margarine
twist of lemon, optional

Drain beets saving ⅓ cup liquid. In medium saucepan, combine reserved beet liquid and raisins. Cover, simmer 5 mins. until raisins are plump. Combine sugar and cornstarch; add to raisins stirring to blend. Add lemon juice and margarine; cook and stir over medium heat until slightly thickened. Stir in beets and simmer until heated through, about 5 mins. Pour into serving dish and garnish with lemon twist.

Mrs. Robert King

BEETS RUSSE
6-8 servings

2 cups cooked beets,
  cubed
½ cup French dressing

¼ cup sour cream
¼ cup green onion,
  minced

Combine beets and French dressing and heat until bubbly. Pour into serving dish and spoon sour cream on top. Sprinkle with green onion. Serve while warm.

Mrs. John Whittle

BOUNTIFUL BROCCOLI

12 servings

3 (10 oz. each) pkg. frozen,
  chopped broccoli
2 (6 oz. each) jars
  Cheez Whiz
2 cups cooked rice
1 cup celery, chopped

1 cup onion, chopped
1 tsp. salt
2 (10¾ oz. each) cans
  cream of mushroom
  soup, undiluted

Preheat oven to 325F. Use a 3 qt. casserole or 12 inch au gratin pan. Thaw broccoli and drain well. Combine all ingredients and pour into baking dish. Bake 45 mins.

This recipe can easily be cut in half, or make 2 smaller casseroles and freeze one for later use.

Mrs. Michael Gerrie
Mrs. John Schmidt

BROCCOLI IN SHRIMP SAUCE

serves 6

1 (3 oz.) pkg. cream
  cheese with chives
¼ cup milk
1 (10¾ oz.) can cream of
  shrimp soup, undiluted

2 tsp. lemon juice
2 (10 oz. each) pkgs.
  frozen broccoli spears,
  cooked, drained

Heat cream cheese and milk in top of double boiler until cheese is melted. Add soup and heat thoroughly. Add lemon juice. Pour shrimp sauce over broccoli and serve.

This can be served in a casserole and garnished with slivered almonds.

Mrs. Henry Mass

BROCCOLI WITH
MUSHROOM-WINE SAUCE
6 servings

½ lb. fresh mushrooms, sliced	1 tsp. salt
¼ cup margarine, melted	¼ tsp. nutmeg
1 small clove garlic, minced	¼ tsp. allspice
	¼ cup Parmesan cheese
1 (6 oz.) can tomato paste	2 T. dry sherry
1 cup liquid, either broccoli or mushroom liquid or bouillon	2 (10 oz. each) pkgs. frozen broccoli, cooked, drained
	Parmesan cheese

Saute mushrooms in margarine, about 5 mins. Drain. Add garlic, tomato paste and liquid. Season with salt, nutmeg and allspice. Add cheese. Cook slowly for 30 mins. in covered saucepan. Mixture should be thick. Finally stir in sherry. Serve over broccoli and sprinkle with Parmesan cheese.

Mrs. Roger Eldean

FANCY BROCCOLI
4-6 servings

2 (10 oz. each) pkgs. frozen broccoli	⅔ cup evaporated milk
2 (2 oz. each) cans grated process American cheese	1 (3 oz.) can French fried onion rings
1 (10¾ oz.) can cream of mushroom soup, undiluted	

Preheat oven to 350F. Grease a 2 qt. casserole. Cook broccoli 4 mins., drain. Place in casserole, sprinkle with cheese. Combine soup and milk, pour over broccoli. Bake 25 mins. Top with onion rings and bake additional 8-10 mins. or until onions are crisp.

Mrs. J.C. Petter, Jr.

226

SAVORY BROCCOLI
8 servings

2 (10 oz. each) pkgs. frozen
   broccoli spears, thawed
1 (10¾ oz.) can cream of mushroom soup, undiluted
1 cup sour cream

¼ tsp. summer savory
¼ tsp. onion salt
1 (3½ oz.) can French
   onion rings

Preheat oven to 350F. Use an ungreased 1½ qt. shallow baking dish. Cut larger broccoli spears in half lengthwise and arrange in casserole. Blend together soup, sour cream, savory and onion salt. Pour over broccoli, separating broccoli to allow sauce to run down. Bake uncovered for 40 mins. until tender. Sprinkle onion rings on top the last 3 mins.

Mrs. Lee Kimzey

CABBAGE CASSEROLE
4-6 servings
(2nd Place Bake-Off)

4 cups coarsely-shredded
   cabbage, packed
1 cup celery, sliced
1 cup boiling water
¼ tsp. salt
1 (10¾ oz.) can cream of
   celery soup, undiluted

⅓ cup milk
4 tsp. soy sauce
1 T. onion, minced
dash of Tabasco sauce
½ cup fine cracker crumbs
2 T. butter, melted

Preheat oven to 350F. Grease a 1½ qt. casserole. Cook cabbage and celery in boiling, salted water for 5 mins., covered. Drain. Combine soup, milk, soy sauce, onion and Tabasco; add celery and cabbage, mix well. Turn into casserole. Mix cracker crumbs and butter. Sprinkle over cabbage mixture. Bake uncovered for 35-40 mins.

Mrs. George Vander Wal

RODE KOOL
Red Cabbage

6 servings

2 lbs. red cabbage,
  shredded
5-6 sour apples,
  peeled and sliced
1½ cups water

½ cup light brown
  sugar, packed
½ cup pickled peach juice
¼ cup butter
1½ tsp. salt

Combine cabbage, apples and water in a large saucepan. Cover and cook until just tender, stirring occasionally. Add brown sugar, peach juice, butter and salt. Cook uncovered 5 mins. longer.

Mrs. John Vander Broek

CARROT BAKE

12 servings

3 lbs. tiny whole carrots,
  cooked and drained
1 T. brown sugar
½ lb. bacon, diced

1 medium onion, chopped
1 (10¾ oz.) can tomato soup
1 T. smoked salt

Preheat oven to 350F. Grease a shallow 2 qt. casserole. Arrange carrots in casserole. Sprinkle with brown sugar. Fry bacon and onion until bacon is crisp. Drain all but 2 T. fat and add soup and smoked salt. Pour over carrots. Bake 1 hr.

Mrs. Darold Onstott

GLAZED CARROTS

6 servings

12 small carrots
4 T. butter
2 T. honey
¼ tsp. orange rind, grated

1 T. orange juice
1 T. brown sugar
parsley, chopped

Clean carrots and boil until just tender. Melt butter in fry pan; add honey, orange rind, orange juice and brown sugar, blending well. Add drained carrots and saute slowly over low heat until glazed. Roll in chopped parsley.

Mrs. James Brown

HERBED CARROTS

4 servings

1 lb. new carrots
2 T. butter
2 T. chicken stock
1 clove garlic, finely-chopped
1 medium onion, finely-chopped

1-2 T. parsley, finely chopped
salt and freshly-ground pepper, to taste
½ tsp. rosemary
¼ cup cream

Wash and peel carrots, cut diagonally into thin slices. Melt butter in saucepan, add chicken stock, carrots, garlic, onion and parsley. Season with salt, pepper and rosemary. Cover and cook over low heat 15 mins. or until tender.

Just before serving, stir in cream and season to taste.

Mrs. D. K. Bryant

PENNSYLVANIA DUTCH CARROTS

4 servings

1 lb. carrots
1 tsp. salt
⅛ tsp. pepper

¼ cup sweetened condensed milk
3 T. butter

Peel and cut up carrots. Cook until soft. Drain and mash. Add remaining ingredients. simmer 5 mins. longer. Serve immediately.

If you wish to make this dish ahead, refrigerate. Reheat in a covered 1 qt. greased casserole for 30 mins. at 350F. or reheat on top of stove.

Mrs. Jack DeRoo

BLOEMKOOL
Cauliflower

6 servings

1 medium head cauliflower
1 cup water
¼ cup margarine

¼ cup flour
½ tsp. salt
¼ tsp. nutmeg
2 cups milk

Clean and break cauliflower into flowerets. Boil with water until tender. Drain and place in serving dish. Make white sauce by melting margarine; add flour, salt and nutmeg, stirring until well blended. Add milk slowly, stirring constantly. Cook over low heat until thickened. Pour over cooked cauliflower.

Variation: Add ½-1 cup of grated cheese to white sauce.

Mrs. Ken Kleis

GOLDEN CAULIFLOWER

4-6 servings

1 head cauliflower, separated
    into flowerets
1 (10¾ oz.) can
    cheddar cheese soup,
    undiluted

¼ cup milk
dash nutmeg
2 T. buttered bread crumbs
4 slices bacon,
    cooked, crumbled

Preheat oven to 350F. Use an ungreased 1½ qt. casserole. Cook and drain cauliflower. Place in casserole. Combine soup, milk and nutmeg; pour over cauliflower. Top with crumbs. Bake uncovered 25 mins.; sprinkle with bacon.

Mrs. Del Van Dyke

230

CAULIFLOWER SUPREME
6 servings

1 medium head cauliflower
salt and pepper,
   to taste
1 cup sour cream

1 cup American cheese,
   shredded
1 tsp. sesame seeds, toasted

Preheat oven to 350F. Use an ungreased 1 qt. casserole. Clean cauliflower and break into flowerets. Cook 15 mins. in boiling water. Drain well. Place half of cauliflower in casserole, season with salt and pepper. Spread with ½ cup sour cream, ½ cup cheese and ½ tsp. sesame seeds. Repeat layers. Bake uncovered about 5 mins. until cheese melts and sour cream is heated through.

Mrs. Del Van Tongeren

CHEESY CAULIFLOWER CASSEROLE
6 servings

1 medium head cauliflower,
   separated into flowerets
3 medium tomatoes,
   diced
1 stalk celery, sliced
¼ lb. fresh mushrooms,
   sliced

½ (10 oz.) pkg. frozen
   peas, thawed
1 (10¾ oz.) can cheese
   soup, undiluted
3 T. milk
½ tsp. oregano
⅓ cup Parmesan cheese

Preheat oven to 350F. Grease a 2 qt. rectangular casserole. Cook flowerets to tender-crisp stage; drain. Place all the vegetables in a large bowl. Combine cheese soup, milk and oregano; pour over vegetables and toss gently. Turn into casserole. Sprinkle with cheese. Bake uncovered for 30-40 mins.

Mrs. Beverly Van Genderen

CELERY AND MUSHROOM EXOTICA   *8 servings*

1 lb. mushrooms, sliced
¼ cup margarine
4 cups celery, sliced
     ¾" thick
1 (8 oz.) can water
     chestnuts, sliced
1 (2 oz.) jar pimento, chopped

1 (10¾ oz.) can cream of
     mushroom soup,
     undiluted
¾ cup bread crumbs
¼ cup slivered almonds
2-3 T. butter, melted

Preheat oven to 350F. Use an ungreased 1½ qt. casserole. Saute mushrooms in margarine until tender-crisp. Boil celery in salted water for 6 mins., drain. Combine mushrooms, celery, water chestnuts, pimento and soup. Pour into casserole. Sprinkle with bread crumbs, almonds and melted butter. Bake uncovered for 30 mins. or until bubbly.

Mrs. Johannes Plekker
Mrs. Michael Doyle

CORN-BROCCOLI CASSEROLE   *6 servings*

1 egg, slightly-beaten
1 (10 oz.) pkg. frozen, chopped
     broccoli, partially thawed
1 (8¼ oz.) can cream style corn
1 T. onion, grated

¼ tsp. salt
dash pepper
3 T. butter
1 cup herb seasoned
     stuffing

Preheat oven to 350F. Grease a 1 qt. casserole. Combine egg, broccoli, corn, onion, salt and pepper. Melt butter, stir in stuffing mix. Combine ¾ cup stuffing with vegetable mixture. Pour into casserole. Sprinkle with remaining stuffing. Bake uncovered 30-40 mins.

Mrs. Donald Wassink

CORN PUDDING

6-8 servings

1 (16 oz.) can cream style corn
1 (16 oz.) can whole
kernel corn, drained
1 egg, beaten

⅓ cup dry bread crumbs
½ cup sour cream
½ tsp. salt
⅛ tsp. pepper

Preheat oven to 350F. Grease a 1½ qt. casserole. Mix all ingredients and pour in casserole. Bake 40 mins.

Mrs. William J. Lalley

COUNTRY-STYLE CORN PUDDING

8-10 servings

1 (16 oz.) can whole
kernel corn, drained
1 (16 oz.) can cream style corn
2 eggs, slightly beaten

½ cup margarine, melted
1 cup sour cream
1 (8½ oz.) pkg. corn muffin mix
1 cup cheddar cheese, grated

Preheat oven to 350F. Use an ungreased 9" x 13" pan. Mix together all ingredients except cheese. Pour into pan. Bake 15 mins. Sprinkle top with cheese and bake 20 mins. longer.

Mrs. Jack Dozeman

BAKED CUCUMBERS
10-12 servings

6 cucumbers
4 T. wine vinegar
2½ tsp. salt

¼ tsp. sugar
¼ cup butter, melted
dill

Sauce:
2 T. butter
3 T. flour
1 cup milk

¼ tsp. salt
2 T. Swiss cheese, grated
butter

Peel cucumbers; cut in half lengthwise and scoop out seeds. Mix wine vinegar, salt, sugar. Pour over cucumbers and marinate 30 mins. Drain and pat dry.

Preheat oven to 375F. Grease a 9" x 9" baking dish. Place cucumbers in dish. Baste with melted butter and sprinkle with dill. Bake 1 hr. until crisp.

Melt butter; stir in flour and cook 1 to 2 mins. Remove from heat. Add slowly 1 cup milk and salt, stir until creamy. Add Swiss cheese. Spoon sauce inside cucumbers. Dot with butter and broil 2 to 3 mins. Cut in smaller wedges if desired.

Mrs. Paul Dykema

EGGPLANT PARMESAN
6 servings

1 large eggplant
2 eggs, slightly-beaten
1 T. milk
¾ cup dry bread crumbs

½ cup vegetable oil
2 cups spaghetti sauce
1 (8 oz.) pkg. Mozzarella
 cheese, grated

Preheat oven to 350F. Use a 9" x 13" baking dish. Peel eggplant and cut into ¼" slices. Combine egg and milk. Dip each slice of eggplant in egg mixture and bread crumbs, coating both sides. Brown eggplant in oil. Do not overcook, eggplant should be slightly firm.

Cover bottom of baking dish with a layer of spaghetti sauce, ½ of eggplant, ½ cheese. Repeat layers and end with sauce. Bake 40 mins.

Mrs. Ralph Hensley

STEWED OKRA AND TOMATOES · 4 servings

2 T. bacon drippings or fat
1 small onion, chopped
2 cups okra, sliced

2 cups canned tomatoes
½ tsp. salt
pepper to taste

Melt fat in frying pan. Brown onions and okra in oil, stirring constantly. Add tomatoes and salt. Cook over moderate heat until tender (about 20 mins.) Season with pepper. Stir often to prevent sticking.

Mrs. Don Kuipers

HOLIDAY ONIONS · 6 servings

4 cups onions, sliced
5 T. butter
2 eggs
1 cup light cream

salt and pepper, to taste
²/₃ cup Parmesan cheese,
grated

Preheat oven to 425F. Use an ungreased 1½ qt. casserole. Saute onions in butter until transparent. Put in casserole. Beat eggs until light; add cream, salt and pepper. Pour over onions and sprinkle with cheese. Bake uncovered 15 mins.

Mrs. Robert Sligh

MARINATED ONIONS AND BLUE CHEESE · 6-8 servings

½ cup olive oil
2 T. lemon juice
1 tsp. salt
dash pepper
dash paprika

½ tsp. sugar
¼ cup blue cheese, crumbled
2 cups large red or yellow
onions, thickly-sliced

Mix oil, lemon juice, salt, pepper, paprika and sugar. Stir in cheese. Pour over onions in large bowl. Cover and refrigerate at least 2 days.

Delicious with steak.

Mrs. Ken Lakies

ONION PIE
Excellent With Beef

8 servings

*4 medium onions,
    thinly-sliced*
2 T. flour
1 frozen pie crust
¾ cup light cream

1 cup heavy cream
4 eggs
*salt and pepper to
    taste*

Preheat oven to 400F. Put onions and flour in a paper bag and shake. Place coated onions into frozen pie crust. Mix creams, eggs, salt and pepper and pour over onions. Bake for 10 mins. at 400F. and 30 mins. at 325F. Cool slightly and serve.

Mrs. William G. Beebe

PEAS COINTREAU

4 servings

*1 (10 oz.) pkg. frozen
    green peas, cooked,
    drained*
1 T. butter
1 tsp. salt

½ tsp. pepper
⅛ tsp. nutmeg
1 T. Cointreau
*1-2 T. orange peel,
    grated*

Combine peas, butter, salt, pepper, nutmeg and Cointreau. Heat until butter melts. Place peas in a serving dish and sprinkle with orange peel.

Mrs. Anthony Garofalo

PEAS ORIENTAL

12 servings

1 lb. fresh mushrooms,
  sliced
2 T. butter
2 (16 oz. each) cans
  water chestnuts,
  drained and thinly-sliced
2 (16 oz. each) cans
  bean sprouts, drained

3 (10 oz. each) pkgs.
  frozen peas, cooked,
  drained
2 (10 oz. each) cans
  cream of mushroom soup,
  undiluted
1 (3½ oz.) can French
  fried onion rings

Preheat oven to 350F. Butter a 3 qt. casserole. Saute mushrooms in butter until tender; drain. Combine mushrooms, water chestnuts, bean sprouts and peas with mushroom soup. Place in casserole and bake uncovered ½ hr. Top with onion rings and bake additional 15 mins.

Mrs. Paul Winchester

PEULTJES MET WORTELTJES

4-6 servings

Sugar Peas Mixed With Carrots

4 medium carrots,
  sliced
1 lb. sugar peas

½ tsp. salt
1 T. butter
2 tsp. sugar

Cook carrots in salted water 15 mins. Add sugar peas and cook additional 10 mins. Drain, add salt, butter and sugar.

Mrs. Ken Kleis

GREEN PEAS LORRAINE
5-6 servings

1 (10 oz.) pkg. frozen peas
1/3 cup water
3 T. butter
2 T. onion, chopped
1 T. parsley, chopped
1/2 tsp. salt

1 tsp. sugar
1/8 tsp. pepper
1/4 tsp. nutmeg
4-6 lettuce leaves, finely shredded
1/2 cup light cream

Combine all ingredients, except lettuce and cream in a saucepan. Cover and simmer until peas are almost tender. Stir in lettuce, cook uncovered 5 mins. longer. Blend in cream, heat through. Serve immediately.

Mrs. Jay Freriks

HOPPING JOHN
Truly A Southern Dish
8 servings

1 (10 oz.) pkg. black eyed peas
1 1/2 tsp. salt
8 slices bacon, diced

1 medium onion, chopped
1 cup Minute Rice, uncooked

Cook peas according to pkg. directions along with the salt, bacon and onion. Add rice during the last 10 mins. Cover, cook until rice is tender. Drain.

Mrs. Tom Brown

AARDAPPEL POF
Potato Puff
4-6 servings

2 cups mashed potatoes
3 T. light cream
2 T. butter

2 eggs, separated
1/2 tsp. salt
dash pepper

Preheat oven 375F. Grease a 1 1/2 qt. baking dish. Heat potatoes, cream, butter, beaten egg yolks, salt and pepper in a skillet, stirring until well blended. Beat egg whites until stiff; fold into potato mixture. Put into baking dish and bake uncovered until golden brown.

Mrs. W. C. Vanderberg, Jr.

GERMAN POTATO PANCAKES
14 pancakes

6 medium baking potatoes
2 eggs, beaten
¼ cup onion, finely-grated

⅓ cup oatmeal
1 tsp. salt
vegetable oil

Peel potatoes; drop into cold water to prevent discoloring. In large bowl, combine eggs and onions; gradually beat in oatmeal and salt. Pat potatoes dry; grate coarsely into a sieve. Press out as much moisture as possible. Immediately stir into egg mixture.

Preheat oven to 250F. In a heavy skillet melt ½ cup oil over high heat. Pour in ⅓ cup potato mixture and flatten to make pancake 5" in diameter. Fry over moderate heat 2 mins. on each side. When golden and crisp on edges, transfer to warm oven. Add more oil to pan when necessary. Serve as soon as possible.

Variation: Green pepper, chopped fine may be added to egg mixture.

Delicious served with sauerbraten.

Mrs. Robert Hampson

PARTY POTATOES
8-10 servings

8-10 potatoes, peeled
   and boiled
1 (8 oz.) pkg. cream cheese
1 cup sour cream
milk

salt and garlic salt, to taste
2 T. chives
2 T. butter
⅛ tsp. paprika

Preheat oven 350F. Grease a 2 qt. casserole. In a large bowl beat sour cream and cream cheese until blended. Add hot potatoes, one at a time; beat until light and fluffy. Add milk if potatoes are too stiff. Season with salt and garlic salt; add chives. Spoon into casserole and dot with butter. Sprinkle with paprika. Bake uncovered 30 mins.

Mrs. Terry Nyland

POTATOES BYRON
6-8 servings

6 large baking
  potatoes, baked
½ cup butter, melted
1 tsp. seasoned salt

freshly-ground pepper
½ cup heavy cream
¾ cup Swiss cheese,
  shredded

Preheat oven to 375F. Use a 9" glass pie pan. Cut slice off each potato, scoop out pulp. Break up coarsely. Add butter, salt and pepper. Turn into pie pan, pour cream over and let stand 30 mins. Sprinkle with cheese and bake 20 mins., or until golden.

Mrs. Donald G. Miller

CHEEZY POTATO BAKE
5-6 servings

4 cups potatoes,
  cooked and cubed
1 (10¾ oz.) can cream of
  chicken soup, undiluted
1 cup cheese, shredded
¼ cup onion, minced

2 T. pimento, chopped
salt and pepper
  to taste
½ cup buttered
  bread crumbs
pimento for garnish

Preheat oven to 325F. Grease a 2 qt. casserole. Place layer of potatoes in casserole. Combine soup, cheese, onion, pimento and seasonings. Alternate layers of cheese mixture and potatoes ending with cheese mixture. Edge casserole with buttered crumbs. Garnish with pimento strips. Bake 45 mins. Can be refrigerated until baking time.

Mrs. Doug Neckers

POTATOES FLORENTINE

6-8 servings

6 large potatoes,
  peeled, boiled
¾ cup light cream, heated
1 tsp. sugar
½ cup butter
2 tsp. salt
¼ tsp. pepper
2 T. chives, chopped
1½ tsp. dill seed
1 (10 oz.) pkg. frozen
  chopped spinach, cooked,
  drained well

Preheat oven to 375F. Grease a 2 qt. baking dish. Whip potatoes with cream, sugar, butter, salt and pepper. Add chives, dill seed and spinach. Beat well. Bake for 20 mins.

Mrs. William J. Lalley

TWICE BAKED POTATOES

4 servings

¾ cup evaporated milk
1½ tsp. instant minced onion
4 baking potatoes, baked
2 T. butter
½ tsp. salt
1 T. parsley flakes
1 cup cheddar cheese, grated

Preheat oven to 400F. Combine milk and onions; let stand. Slice top off potatoes and scoop out pulp, saving the shells. Mash potatoes with milk-onion mixture, butter, salt, parsley and cheese. Spoon potato mixture into shells. Bake 10 mins.

Potatoes can be frozen before baking. Thaw and bake 30 mins. at 400F.

Mrs. R.A. Boersma, Jr.

SWEET POTATO CRUNCH   6 servings

3 cups mashed sweet potatoes   ⅓ cup margarine, melted
1 tsp. vanilla

Topping:
1 cup brown sugar   ⅓ cup margarine, melted
1 cup coconut   ⅓ cup flour
1 cup pecans, chopped

Preheat oven 350F. Grease a 1½ qt. shallow casserole. Combine potatoes, vanilla and margarine; place in casserole. Combine topping ingredients; sprinkle over potato mixture. Bake covered 20 mins. and uncovered 15 mins.

Mrs. Robert Hampson

SWEET POTATOES HAWAIIAN   8-10 servings

7-8 sweet potatoes,   ½ cup pineapple juice
  cooked   1½ cups sour cream
flour   1 tsp. salt
butter   light brown sugar
1 (16 oz.) can sliced   butter
  pineapple

Preheat oven to 350F. Grease a 2½ qt. casserole. Cut potatoes into ¾" slices. Flour slices lightly and fry in butter until light brown. Cut pineapple into chunks, reserve several slices for top. Mix pineapple juice with sour cream and salt. Place a layer of potatoes and pineapple chunks in bottom of casserole. Cover with a layer of sour cream mixture and sprinkle with brown sugar. Repeat. Top with a whole slice of pineapple in center. Cut remaining slices in half and tuck around edges of casserole, cut side down. Dot with butter. Cover and bake 30 mins. Uncover and bake a few mins. longer to glaze top. If casserole becomes too dry pour a little pineapple juice around the edge of dish.

This can be prepared the day before and refrigerated.

Mrs. Robert Hall

SWEET POTATOES SUPREME
6 servings

½ cup brown sugar
1 tsp. salt
½ cup crushed
  pineapple

1 (17 oz.) can sweet
  potatoes, sliced
½ cup sherry
¼ cup miniature
  marshmallows

Preheat oven to 375F. Use a 9" x 9" baking dish. Combine brown sugar, salt and pineapple. Arrange potatoes and pineapple mixture in alternate layers in baking dish ending with pineapple mixture. Pour wine over all and bake for 35 mins. Sprinkle marshmallows on top and bake an additional 10 mins. or until brown.

Mrs. Donald Wassink

CARAWAY SAUERKRAUT
4-6 servings

1 (2 lb.) can sauerkraut,
  drained
1 small onion, sliced
2 medium apples,
  peeled and sliced

2 T. brown sugar
1 tsp. caraway
¼ cup margarine,
  melted

Preheat oven to 350F. Use a 1½ qt. casserole. Combine all ingredients in casserole. Bake, covered for 1 hr.

Mrs. Richard Taylor

SAUERKRAUT AND TOMATO CASSEROLE
6 servings

1 (2 lb.) jar sauerkraut,
  rinsed and drained well
⅔ cup sugar
1 (14½ oz.) can stewed tomatoes

6-8 strips bacon, cooked,
  crumbled and undrained

Preheat oven to 350F. Use a 2 qt. casserole. Combine all ingredients in casserole. Bake 1 hr.

Mrs. Gale Schilleman

POPEYE'S SPINACH SPECIAL   *6-8 servings*

1 lb. bacon, diced
1 onion, chopped
½ cup bacon drippings
1 lb. spinach, cooked,
    well drained

1 (8 oz.) pkg. noodles
    cooked, drained
salt and pepper
½ cup buttered bread
    crumbs

Preheat oven to 350F. Grease a 2 qt. casserole. Fry bacon until crisp; drain off all but ½ cup of drippings. Saute onions in ¼ cup of drippings. Combine bacon and onions with the spinach and noodles. Add remaining bacon drippings; season with salt and pepper and toss together. Pour into casserole and top with bread crumbs. Bake 35-45 mins.

Mrs. Paul Van Kolken

SAVORY SPINACH AND
RICE SOUFFLE   *6 servings*

3 eggs, separated
1 (10 oz.) pkg. frozen
    chopped spinach, cooked,
    drained
2 cups cooked rice
¼ cup onion, finely-chopped

1½ cups cheddar cheese,
    grated
¼ cup white wine
2 T. salad oil
½ tsp. seasoned salt
¼ tsp. nutmeg

Preheat oven to 350F. Use a 1 qt. casserole. Beat egg yolks slightly and combine with all ingredients except egg whites. Beat egg whites until stiff; fold into spinach mixture. Turn into casserole and bake 35-40 mins. Serve at once.

Mrs. Herbert Eldean

SPINACH FLORENTINE

6 servings

2 (10 oz. each) pkgs.
  frozen chopped spinach
1 lb. fresh mushrooms
1/3 cup onions, chopped
1/4 cup butter, melted

1/4 tsp. garlic salt
1 tsp. salt
1 cup Old English Sharp
  cheese, grated

Preheat oven to 350F. Use a 1½ qt. casserole. Thaw spinach and press dry. Saute mushrooms and onions in butter; add salt and garlic salt. Place ½ of spinach in casserole; add ½ of mushroom mixture, and ½ of cheese. Repeat. Bake 30 mins., uncovered.

Mrs. Loren Meengs

SCALLOPED SQUASH

4 servings

2 medium summer
  squash, peeled
1 medium onion, chopped
1/4 lb. soda crackers,
  crushed

1 egg
1/4 cup milk
3/8 lb. cheese, grated,
  medium sharp
salt and pepper to taste

Preheat oven to 375F. Grease a 1½ qt. casserole. Slice squash into ¼" slices. Combine squash and onion in a small amount of salted water (approx. 3-4 T.). Cover and simmer until tender, about 15 mins. Cool. Combine soda crackers and squash mixture with juice; pour in casserole. Mix egg and milk together. Pour over squash and cracker mixture, blend; add ½ of the cheese. Season with salt and pepper. Sprinkle remaining cheese on top. Bake uncovered 35-40 mins. until golden.

Mrs. Herbert H. Black

SUMMER SQUASH CASSEROLE

6 servings

*6 cups summer
  squash, sliced
¼ cup onion, chopped
1 (10¾ oz.) can cream
  of chicken soup, undiluted*

*1 cup sour cream
1 cup shredded carrots
1 (8 oz.) pkg. herb
  seasoned stuffing mix
½ cup butter, melted*

Preheat oven to 350F. Use a 12" x 7" x 2" baking dish. Cook squash and onion in a small amount of salted boiling water for 5 mins.; drain. Combine soup and sour cream, stir in carrots, fold in squash and onion. Combine stuffing mix and butter. Spread ½ of stuffing mixture in bottom of pan. Spoon vegetable mixture atop. Sprinkle remaining stuffing over vegetables. Bake uncovered 25-30 mins. or until heated through.

Eet Smakelijk's Best

SURPRIZE SQUASH

4 servings

*½ acorn or butternut squash
5 small potatoes
1 (10 oz.) pkg. frozen peas*

*½ cup chopped walnuts
butter
½-¾ cup beef bouillon*

Preheat oven to 350F. Grease a 1 qt. shallow baking dish.

Peel and remove seeds from squash, cut into ⅛" slices. Peel potatoes and dice fine. Line casserole with squash slices. Spread a layer of potatoes on top leaving a border of squash; layer peas on potatoes. Sprinkle top with walnuts, dot with butter. Pour bouillon over all until it barely reaches top of vegetables. Bake uncovered for 40 to 45 mins. or until vegetables are tender.

Mrs. Robert Hall

ZUCCHINI CASSEROLE

6 servings

3-4 medium zucchini,
sliced ¼" thick
¼ cup margarine
2 onions, thinly-sliced
5-6 fresh tomatoes,
chopped
1 green pepper, thinly-sliced

1 (4 oz.) can button
mushrooms, drained
1 (8 oz.) can tomato
sauce
⅓ tsp. garlic salt
salt and pepper to taste

Preheat oven to 350F. Use a 2 qt. casserole. Saute zucchini in margarine, do not drain. Combine with remaining ingredients. Place in casserole and bake 30 mins. until tender.

Mrs. Norm Lunderberg

ZUCCHINI SOUFFLE

4 servings

6 cups zucchini,
thinly-sliced
½ cup fine dry bread crumbs
4 eggs, separated

¾ cup onions, finely-chopped
3 T. butter
½ tsp. salt
½ cup cheese, shredded

Preheat oven to 350F. Grease a 2 qt. casserole. Boil zucchini in a very small amount of salted water, until tender. Drain and mash. Add bread crumbs and slightly beaten egg yolks. Saute onion in butter until tender. Add to squash mixture; mix in salt. Beat egg whites until stiff, but not dry. Fold into squash mixture. Spoon into casserole; sprinkle cheese over top. Bake uncovered 30 mins.

Mrs. Henry Smith

ZUCCHINI ITALIAN STYLE

6 servings

3 medium zucchini
1 egg, beaten with
 1 T. milk
seasoned dry bread crumbs
olive oil

1 (15½ oz.) jar spaghetti sauce
8 oz. Mozzarella cheese,
 shredded
salt and pepper to taste

Preheat oven to 350F. Use a 1½ qt. baking dish. Slice zucchini lengthwise in ¼" slices. Dip each in egg and coat with bread crumbs. Brush a jelly roll pan generously with olive oil. Arrange zucchini on pan, drizzle lightly with oil. Broil on both sides until brown.

Cover bottom of baking dish with ½ of spaghetti sauce. Add zucchini and cheese, then the remaining sauce. Season with salt and pepper. Bake for 20 mins. until bubbly.

Dolores Haynes

ZUCCHINI AND MUSHROOM CASSEROLE

6 servings

1 lb. zucchini, trimmed
pinch of fresh or dried dill
1 clove garlic
boiling salted water
½ lb. fresh mushrooms, sliced

3 T. butter
2 T. flour
1 cup sour cream
1 (3 oz.) can French
 fried onions

Use a 1½ qt. casserole. Cut the zucchini crosswise into 1" slices; put zucchini, dill and garlic in boiling water to cover. Return to a boil. Reduce heat, cover and simmer until tender; do not overcook. Drain, reserving 2 T. of the liquid. Discard garlic.

Saute mushrooms in butter 5 mins., stirring occasionally. Stir in flour, cook 2 mins. longer. Add sour cream, zucchini, and reserved liquid. Correct seasonings and heat thoroughly but do not boil. Pour into a 1½ qt. casserole, top with French fried onions and quickly brown under broiler.

Mrs. Michael Calahan

CONTINENTAL VEGETABLE CASSEROLE

6 servings

2 T. margarine
1 clove garlic, minced
3 small zucchini, cut
    into ¼" slices
1 small eggplant, cut
    into ¼" slices
2 medium green peppers,
    sliced into rings

2 medium onions,
    thinly-sliced
2 medium tomatoes,
    thinly-sliced
salt and pepper
    to taste
cheese, grated

Preheat oven to 300F. Use an ungreased 2 qt. casserole. Melt margarine, add garlic and cook until brown. Pour into casserole. Layer vegetables in order given. Sprinkle with salt and pepper between layers. Bake, covered 15-20 mins. Uncover, continue baking 15 mins. to reduce sauce. Sprinkle with grated cheese before serving.

Mrs. Norm Lunderberg

FROZEN VEGETABLE CASSEROLE

6-8 servings

1 (10 oz. each) pkg. frozen
    broccoli, Brussels sprouts
    and cauliflower
1 (10¾ oz.) can cream of
    mushroom soup, undiluted

½ cup American
    cheese, grated

Preheat oven to 350F. Use an ungreased 2 qt. casserole. Cook broccoli and Brussels sprouts as directed on pkg.; after 5 mins. add cauliflower, cook until tender. Drain; place in casserole. Cover with soup and sprinkle with cheese. Bake until bubbly.

Mrs. Jay Formsma

CINNAMON APPLES
Good With Pork and Ham

12 servings

1 cup sugar
1½ cups water
1 (2 oz.) bottle cinnamon
  candies

½ tsp. red food coloring
12 Jonathan apples, pared
  and cored

In a large pan combine all ingredients except apples to make a syrup; heat. Add apples one at a time; cook very slowly until tender, about 10 mins. Serve cold with meat.

(Jonathan apples are the only ones that will hold their shape.)

Mrs. John Winter

CONTINENTAL PEACHES

6 servings

1 (1 lb. 13 oz.) can peach
  halves, drained
1 tsp. rum or rum extract

1 cup sour cream
2 T. brown sugar
2 T. slivered almonds

Place peach halves cut side up in a 9" x 9" pan. Sprinkle with rum. Spoon over sour cream, sprinkle with brown sugar and almonds. Broil 4 to 5 inches from heat until sugar caramelizes and almonds are golden.

A good accompaniment with meat, or serve with brunch.

Mrs. R. A. Boersema

CURRIED FRUIT COMPOTE

8 servings

1 (16 oz. each) can of pear
  halves, peach slices, apricot
  halves, pineapple chunks,
  all drained
6 maraschino cherries

1½ T. flour
1½ tsp. curry powder
⅔ cup brown sugar
⅓ cup butter

Preheat oven to 350F. Grease a 2 qt. casserole. Layer fruits in casserole ending with cherries. Mix flour, curry, and brown sugar together and sprinkle over fruit. Dot with butter. Bake uncovered for 45 mins.

Bernadine DeValois

TAGLIATELLE A LA SALVATORE

6-8 servings

½ cup butter
¼ cup olive oil
¾ cup onions, chopped
1 (20 oz.) can tomatoes,
   sieved
1½ tsp. salt
½ tsp. black pepper,
   freshly-ground

1 tsp. oregano
1 (10 oz.) pkg. medium
   noodles, cooked,
   drained
¼ cup Parmesan cheese,
   grated
8 oz. Mozzarella cheese,
   cut in ¼" cubes
½ cup black olives, sliced

Preheat oven to 350F. Use a 2 qt. casserole. Heat ¼ cup butter and oil in a saucepan; saute onions 5 mins. Add the tomatoes, salt and pepper; bring to a boil and cook over high heat 10 mins. Mix in the oregano. Melt remaining butter in casserole. Add the cooked noodles, 2 T. Parmesan cheese and the Mozzarella. Toss well. Pour sauce over the mixture; sprinkle with the remaining Parmesan cheese and arrange the olives on top. Bake uncovered 15 mins. or until Mozzarella cheese melts.

Mrs. Donald G. Miller

CONTINENTAL RICE

4 servings

¼ cup margarine
½ cup raw rice
1 (10¾ oz.) can onion soup,
   diluted with 1 can of water

1 (4 oz.) can mushrooms,
   drained
2 T. parsley flakes

Preheat oven to 325F. Grease a 1½ or 2 qt. casserole. Saute rice in butter for 5 mins. Add soup and water; cook covered for 30 mins. over medium heat. Add mushrooms and parsley and place in casserole. Bake uncovered 10 mins. to fluff rice.

Mrs. Frank Boonstra

NOODLE-SPINACH RING
WITH MUSHROOMS
6-8 servings

1 (8 oz.) pkg. wide noodles
2 (10 oz. each) pkg. frozen,
  chopped spinach, thawed,
  drained
1 onion, chopped
½ cup butter
1 tsp. salt

3 eggs, slightly-beaten
1 cup sour cream
1 lb. fresh mushrooms
¼ cup butter
¼ tsp. salt

Preheat oven to 350F. Grease a 1½ qt. ring mold. Cook noodles until barely tender, drain. Saute onions in butter until golden. Combine noodles, spinach, onions, salt, eggs and sour cream, blending well. Pour into mold. Place mold into pan of hot water in oven. Bake for 45 mins.

Saute mushrooms in butter; add salt. Unmold spinach ring on heated platter and serve with steaming mushrooms in center.

Mrs. John Shepherd

NOODLES ROMANOFF
12 servings

1 (16 oz.) pkg. medium-
  fine noodles, cooked, drained
2 pints sour cream
1 cup small curd
  cottage cheese
2 tsp. garlic powder

2 T. Worcestershire sauce
1 T. parsley, minced
1⅓ T. salt
2 bunches green
  onions, sliced
generous dash Tabasco sauce

Preheat oven to 350F. Grease a 3 qt. casserole. Place noodles in casserole. Combine all other ingredients and toss with noodles. Bake uncovered 30 mins.

Variation: 1 cup grated cheddar cheese can be sprinkled on top before baking.

Mrs. J.C. Petter, Jr.
Mrs. Robert Hampson

PINEAPPLE CASSEROLE
Delicious With Ham

6 servings

1 (20 oz.) can crushed unsweetened pineapple,
  drained
½-¾ cup sugar
3 T. flour

2 eggs, beaten
5 slices dry bread, cubed
½ cup margarine

Preheat oven to 350F. Use an ungreased 1½ qt. casserole. Combine all ingredients except bread and margarine, place in casserole. Brown bread cubes in margarine, place on top of pineapple mixture. Bake 30 mins.

Mrs. James W.F. Brooks

SPICED WINTER FRUIT
Delicious With Roast Chicken

serves 8

1 (16 oz. each) can
  apricot halves, pear
  halves, peach slices,
  pineapple chunks, all
  drained

1 (16 oz.) jar applesauce
¼ cup sherry
⅛ tsp. nutmeg
½ tsp. cinnamon
¼ cup butter

Preheat oven to 300F. Use an ungreased 3 qt. baking dish. Arrange apricots, pears, peaches and pineapple in baking dish in layers, with pineapple on top. In a small saucepan cook applesauce about 5 mins., uncovered to reduce liquid. Cool slightly and add sherry, nutmeg and cinnamon. Pour over fruit, dot with butter. Bake for 4 hrs.

Mrs. William G. Beebe

HONEY RICE
6 servings
Serve With Pork Chops

3 cups cooked rice
½ cup seedless raisins
2½ cups milk
½ cup honey

2 T. butter
1 tsp. lemon peel, grated
1 T. lemon juice

Combine rice, raisins, milk, honey and butter in a saucepan. Bring to boil, reduce heat and simmer 15 mins., stirring occasionally. Stir in lemon peel and juice.

Mrs. Larry Jones

MUSHROOM-WILD RICE CASSEROLE
6 servings

1 (6 oz.) box Uncle Ben's
   wild rice with seasonings
½ green pepper, diced
½ lb. fresh mushrooms,
   sliced
¼ cup margarine, melted

2 T. flour
½ tsp. salt
⅛ tsp. pepper
½ cup chicken bouillon
½ cup dry white wine

Preheat oven to 325F. Grease a 1½ qt. casserole. Prepare rice according to package directions. In skillet, saute green pepper and mushrooms in margarine until mushrooms are lightly browned. Add flour, salt and pepper. Gradually stir in bouillon and wine. Cook over low heat, stirring constantly until slightly thickened. Add cooked rice. Place in casserole and bake uncovered 30 mins.

Mrs. David Vander Leek

ORANGE RICE

3 T. butter
²/₃ cup celery, sliced
2 T. onion, chopped
1½ cups water

2 T. grated orange peel
1 cup orange juice
1½ tsp. salt
1 cup raw rice

Melt butter in a saucepan; add celery and onions and cook until tender and light brown, stirring occasionally. Add water, orange peel, orange juice and salt. Bring to a boil; and rice, cover and steam over low heat for 20-25 mins. or until rice is tender.

Especially good with a breast of chicken main dish.

Mrs. Michael Calahan

OVEN FRIED RICE

¼ cup butter
½ cup onions, minced
1½ cups regular long-grain rice
2 (13¾ oz. each) cans chicken
   broth, heated

¾ tsp. garlic salt
dash pepper
⅓ cup Parmesan
   cheese

Preheat oven to 350F. In a large oven-proof saucepan over medium heat, cook onions in butter, until golden. Add rice stirring until butter is absorbed. Stir in hot chicken broth, salt and pepper and heat, stirring, until broth begins to boil.

Transfer to oven and bake uncovered 30 mins., or until liquid is absorbed and rice is tender (rice will still be moist). Stir in Parmesan cheese. Serve in a heated dish.

Mrs. Lee Kimzey

RICE CASSEROLE
Delicious With Chicken

6-8 servings

1 cup raw rice
1 (10 oz.) can onion soup, undiluted
1 (10 oz.) can chicken broth, undiluted

6 T. margarine
salt and pepper to taste

Preheat oven to 325F. Use a 2 qt. casserole. Combine all ingredients in casserole. Bake 1 hr. Stir once after 30 mins.

Mrs. Robert Bernecker

ROSEMARY RICE

6 servings

1 (10 oz.) pkg. frozen chopped spinach, cooked, drained
2 T. margarine
6 oz. sharp process American cheese, grated
1 cup cooked rice

2 eggs, slightly-beaten
1/3 cup milk
2 T. onion, minced
1/2 tsp. Worcestershire sauce
1 tsp. salt
1/2 tsp. rubbed rosemary

Preheat oven to 350F. Use a 10" x 6" baking dish. Combine butter and cheese with hot spinach. Add remaining ingredients and blend thoroughly. Turn into baking dish and bake uncovered for 20-25 min.

Mrs. Roy J. Kee, Jr.

YORKSHIRE PUDDING

6-8 servings

*roast drippings or butter,
    melted*
2 large eggs or 3 medium

1 cup flour, sifted
1 tsp. salt
1 cup milk

Preheat oven to 400F. Pour enough roast drippings or butter in a 9"
x 9" pan or muffin tins to cover bottom. Place in oven to heat.

Beat eggs 1 min. Combine remaining ingredients and beat 1 min.
longer. Pour batter in hot pan to ¾" high. If muffin tins are used
fill no more than half full. Bake for 20 mins.; reduce heat to 350F.
and bake 10-15 mins. longer. If baked in a flat pan tear the pudding in portions (do not cut). Arrange around roast beef and serve
with gravy.

Mrs. Wesley Small
Mrs. Sherwin Ortman

SAUSAGE STUFFING BALLS

18-20 balls

Good With Pork

*1 (8 oz.) pkg. seasoned
    stuffing mix*
¾ cup hot water
1 lb. fresh pork sausage
½ cup celery, finely-chopped

*½ cup onion, finely-
    chopped*
1 egg, beaten
½ tsp. baking powder

Preheat oven to 325 F. Use a 9" x 13" baking pan. Combine stuffing
mix with hot water. Break sausage into small pieces; add to
stuffing mix. Stir in celery, onion, egg and baking powder. Shape
into balls using ¼ cup mixture for each. Place in baking pan.
Cover with foil securely. Bake for 15 mins. Remove foil; bake at
350F. for 25 mins.

If served with pork, arrange sausage balls around meat on a
platter. Garnish with spiced apples or sauteed peach halves filled
with cranberry sauce.

Mrs. Roger Eldean

257

SCALLOPED OYSTERS
Delicious with Turkey Dinner

4-5 servings

½ cup butter, melted
½ cup stale bread crumbs
1 cup cracker crumbs
1 pt. oysters, drained,
   liquid reserved
salt and pepper to taste

2 T. oyster liquid
2 T. milk or light cream
3 hard boiled eggs,
   finely-chopped
   (optional)

Preheat oven to 375F. Use a buttered 1½ qt. shallow baking dish. Combine butter with bread and cracker crumbs. Spread half of mixture on bottom of baking dish. Cover with half the oysters and sprinkle with salt and pepper. Add half of oyster liquid and cream. Repeat layers saving a small amount of crumbs for the top. Sprinkle chopped eggs over top, and bake 30 mins., uncovered.

Mrs. Robert Bernecker

TOMATO PUDDING
Delicious With Roast Beef

6 servings

2 cups tomato puree
2 cups brown sugar
½ cup water

⅛ tsp. salt
1 cup butter, melted
4 cups dry bread cubes

Preheat oven 375F. Use a 1½ qt. casserole. In a saucepan combine tomato puree, sugar, water and salt; cook together for 5 mins. In baking dish pour melted butter over bread cubes. Pour tomato mixture over top. Set baking dish in a pan of hot water in oven. Bake for 45 to 55 mins.

Mrs. W. A. Butler

Brunch and Lunch

NOTES

SUPERB SWISS CHEESE FONDUE   4-6 servings

½ lb. Gruyere cheese,
  shredded
1 lb. Swiss cheese, shredded
¼ cup flour
1 tsp. nutmeg

1 tsp. black pepper
¼ tsp. garlic powder
2 cups dry white wine
1 loaf French bread,
  torn into bite size pieces

In mixing bowl dredge cheeses with a mixture of flour, nutmeg, pepper, and garlic powder. Pour wine into saucepan; heat over low heat, to the point that air bubbles rise to the surface. Do not cover or boil. Add cheese mixture by handfuls, stir and thoroughly blend after each addition. Stir until smooth, thick, and bubbly. Pour into fondue pot; keep warm over low heat. Dunk bread, with fork, into melted cheese.

Mrs. Jack DeRoo

QUICHE AMERICANA   *8 servings*

10" pastry shell, baked
4 eggs
2 cups milk
½ cup heavy cream
½ tsp. salt
dash pepper

8 oz. Gruyere or Swiss
  cheese, shredded
8 slices bacon, cooked,
  drained and crumbled
½ cup chives, chopped

Preheat oven to 350F. Combine eggs, milk, cream, salt and pepper. Beat until blended. Stir in cheese, bacon, and chives; blend well. Pour into pastry shell. Bake 40 min. or until knife inserted in center comes out clean and top is golden. Let stand 5 min. before cutting. Garnish with cooked bacon slices and parsley, if desired.

Mrs. Delwyn Van Dyke

QUICHE LORRAINE   8-10 servings

9" pastry shell, unbaked
½ lb. bacon, diced
½ green pepper, diced
4 eggs
½ cup half and half
1 T. flour

½ tsp. salt
dash of pepper
⅛ tsp. nutmeg
1 cup Swiss cheese, grated
1 T. butter, melted

Preheat oven to 450F. Bake pie shell for 5 min. Fry bacon until crisp; drain. Spread bacon and green pepper in bottom of shell. Beat eggs and cream together; blend in flour and seasonings. Add cheese. Pour mixture into pie shell. Drizzle butter on top. Bake at 375F. for 35 min. (until filling is firm).

Mrs. John Marquis

SPINACH-CHEESE QUICHE   8 servings

4 frozen patty shells
1 (10 oz.) pkg. frozen
   chopped spinach
6 eggs
1 (3 oz.) pkg. cream cheese,
   softened
¼ cup sharp process
   American cheese, shredded

2 T. green onion,
   sliced
1 T. parsley, snipped
½ tsp. salt
dash pepper
2 T. Parmesan cheese

Thaw patty shells in refrigerator for 2 hrs. Preheat oven to 425F Roll patty shells out on lightly floured surface to fit a 10" pie plate, sealing edges together. Let rest 5 mins. Place in pie plate; flute edges. Cook spinach according to pkg. directions; drain well. Combine eggs, cream cheese and shredded cheese; beat. Stir in spinach, green onion, parsley, salt and pepper. Turn into prepared shell; top with Parmesan. Bake 15 mins. Let stand 10 min. before serving.

Mrs. Jack Dozeman

BRUNCH CHEESE SOUFFLE   12 servings

**8 slices bread, thickly
  buttered and cubed
1 ½ lbs. sharp cheddar cheese,
  sliced
1 T. onion, minced
½ tsp. dry mustard**

**½ tsp. cayenne pepper
1 tsp. brown sugar
½ tsp. salt
¼ tsp. paprika
6 eggs, well beaten
2 ½ cups half and half**

Butter a 2½ qt. souffle dish. Alternate layers of bread and cheese (cheese on top). Add onion and seasonings to eggs; mix in half and half. Blend thoroughly; pour over layers in dish. Cover. Refrigerate overnight.

Preheat oven to 350F. Remove from refrigerator ½ hr. before baking. Place dish in shallow pan of water and bake 20 mins.; reduce heat to 300F. and bake an additional 70 mins.

Mrs. John Hutchinson

EASY CHEESE SOUFFLE   6 servings

**3 eggs
2 cups milk
½ lb. Old English
  sharp cheese, grated**

**8 slices bread, crusts
  trimmed and cubed
½ cup butter, melted**

**Sauce:
1 (10¾ oz.) can mushroom
  soup, undiluted**

**1 (2 oz.) can mushrooms,
  drained
¼ cup milk**

Grease a 1½ qt. baking dish. Beat eggs into milk. Add remaining ingredients. Pour into dish; cover and refrigerate overnight. Preheat oven to 350F. and bake 1 hr.

Combine soup and mushrooms. Add milk; heat. Pour over souffle when ready to serve.

Mrs. Henry Maentz, Jr.

CHEESE SOUFFLE WITH SHERRIED MUSHROOM SAUCE

6 servings

3 T. butter
¼ cup flour
1⅞ cups milk
1 tsp. salt
dash cayenne pepper
1 tsp. dry mustard

2 drops Worcestershire
  sauce
1 cup Old English
  sharp cheese, grated
6 eggs, separated, room
  temperature

Sauce:
1 (10¾ oz.) can mushroom
  soup, undiluted

⅓ cup milk
2 T. dry sherry

Preheat oven to 300F. Butter a 1½ qt. souffle dish. Melt butter in saucepan; blend in flour. Cook until bubbly. Add milk, salt, pepper, mustard, and Worcestershire sauce; bring to boil, stirring constantly. Boil 1 min. Remove from heat; add cheese. Beat egg yolks until thick, slowly add to cheese mixture. Beat egg whites until stiff; fold into cheese mixture carefully. Pour into dish, place in a shallow pan filled with 1" of hot water. Bake 40-50 min., or until browned.

Combine soup, milk, and sherry; heat. Ladle over top of each serving.

Mrs. Lee Kimzey

CHEESE STRATA

12 servings

12 slices white bread
¾ lb. Old English
  cheese, grated
1 (10 oz.) pkg. frozen chopped
  broccoli, cooked and drained
2 cups cooked ham, diced

3½ cups milk
6 eggs
2 T. minced onion
½ tsp. salt
¼ tsp. dry mustard
½ cup cheese, shredded

Arrange 6 slices of bread in bottom of a 9" x 13" baking dish. Place cheese, broccoli and ham in layers and top with remaining bread slices. Combine milk, eggs, onion, salt, and mustard; blend well. Pour over layers. Cover and refrigerate overnight. Allow to return to room temperature before baking. Preheat oven to 325F. Bake 55 min. Sprinkle with cheese and bake 5 min. more. Let stand 10 min. before serving.

Mrs. John Marquis

CHICKEN-AVOCADO SALAD   *6 servings*

1 cup mayonnaise
2 T. fresh lemon juice
1 tsp. salt
¼ tsp. pepper
2 T. blue cheese, crumbled
5 cups cooked chicken, cubed

2 cups celery, chopped
4 bananas, cut into 1"
  pieces
1 avocado, cubed
bibb lettuce

Blend mayonnaise and lemon juice. Add next 3 ingredients, blend well. Add chicken and celery. Mix well and chill. Just before serving add bananas and avocado. Arrange on lettuce leaves.

Mrs. William G. Beebe

CHINESE CHICKEN SALAD   *4 servings*

2 cups cooked chicken, diced
1 cup celery, diced
½ cup slivered almonds,
  toasted
1 (11 oz.) can mandarin
  oranges, drained

½ tsp. salt
¾ cup sour cream
1 (3 oz.) can chow mein
  noodles

Combine chicken, celery, almonds, oranges, and salt. Mix in sour cream. Refrigerate 1-2 hrs. Serve over noodles.

Mrs. Morris Gort

RUSSIAN CHICKEN AND POTATO SALAD

6 servings

1½ lb. whole chicken breasts
1 onion, quartered
2 tsp. salt
½ cup dill pickle, chopped
4 new potatoes, boiled, chopped
3 eggs, hard cooked, chopped
⅛ tsp. white pepper
¾ cup mayonnaise
¾ cup sour cream
lettuce
1 T. dill leaves
6 black olives
1 tomato, sliced

In heavy 2-3 qt. pan combine chicken, onion, and 1 tsp. salt. Cover with 1½ qt. cold water and bring to boil, uncovered, over high heat. Skim off fat. Reduce heat to low and simmer 40 min. or until chicken is tender; cool. Skin and cut meat from bones. Cut into bite size pieces. Combine chicken, pickles, potatoes, eggs, and sprinkle with remaining salt and pepper. Blend mayonnaise and sour cream. Stir half into salad mixture; mix well. Shape salad mixture into pyramid on a lettuce lined platter. Mask with remaining dressing and sprinkle with dill. Garnish with olives and tomato.

Mrs. William Boyer

VIRGINIA CHICKEN APPLE SALAD

6-8 servings

2 cups apples, unpared, cubed
lemon juice
5 cups chicken, cooked and cubed
2 cups celery, sliced
⅔ cup olives, sliced
½ cup slivered almonds
⅓ cup salad dressing
½ cup sour cream
1 T. salt
apple slices

Sprinkle apples with lemon juice. Combine apples, chicken, celery, olives and almonds. Mix together salad dressing, sour cream and salt; add to chicken mixture. Chill. To serve, garnish with apple slices.

Mrs. Jay Freriks

CHICKEN SOUFFLE

8-10 servings

1 (8 oz.) pkg. herb seasoned
  bread stuffing
½ cup margarine, melted
1 cup chicken broth
4 cups chicken, cooked, diced
½ cup onion, chopped
½ cup celery, diced
¼ cup chives or green
  onion tops

½ cup mayonnaise
¾ tsp. salt
2 eggs
1½ cups milk
1 (10¾ oz.) can cream of
  mushroom soup,
  undiluted
1 cup cheddar cheese,
  grated

Grease a 9" x 13" baking dish. Combine bread stuffing, margarine and broth. Spread ½ of mixture in baking dish. Combine chicken, onion, celery, chives, mayonnaise and salt. Spread over stuffing mixture; top with remaining half of stuffing. Beat eggs with milk and pour over mixture in baking dish. Cover and refrigerate overnight. Remove from refrigerator 1 hr. prior to baking. Preheat oven to 325F. Spread soup over top and bake 40 mins. Sprinkle with cheese and bake 10 mins. more.

Mrs. Albert VanLopik

BAKED CHICKEN STRATA

8 servings

6 slices buttered bread,
  crusts removed, cubed
2 cups cooked chicken, diced
⅓ cup celery, chopped
⅓ cup onion, chopped
⅓ cup green pepper, chopped
⅓ cup mayonnaise
salt and pepper to taste

3 eggs
3 cups milk
¼ cup mushrooms
3 T. butter
2 T. flour
¾ cup cheddar
  cheese, grated

continued

Butter a 9" x 9" baking dish. Sprinkle ½ of bread cubes in baking dish. Combine chicken, celery, onion, green pepper and mayonnaise. Add salt and pepper to taste and spread mixture over bread cubes. Sprinkle remaining bread cubes over chicken mixture. Beat eggs and 1½ cups milk; pour over mixture in baking dish. Cover and refrigerate 8 hrs. or overnight.

Let strata come to room temperature. Preheat oven to 350F. Sauté mushrooms in butter for 3 mins. Reduce heat to low, add flour and cook, stirring, for 3 min. Add 1½ cups milk and cook over medium-high heat, stirring constantly until thickened. Pour sauce over chicken mixture and bake 50 mins. Sprinkle cheese on top and bake until melted. Let stand 10 mins. before serving.

Mrs. William Boyer

EGGS AND MUSHROOMS AU GRATIN   *8 servings*

¾ lb. fresh mushrooms, sliced
¼ cup margarine
12 eggs, hard boiled
1 (10 oz.) pkg. frozen peas,
   par cooked, drained
1 (6 oz.) can water chestnuts,
   drained, sliced
1 (10¾ oz.) can cream of
   chicken soup. undiluted

1 cup sour cream
¼ cup milk
1 tsp. instant minced onion
¼ cup sherry
3 T. pimento, chopped
salt and pepper to taste
1 cup soft bread crumbs
3 T. margarine,
   melted

Preheat oven to 375F. Use a 2½ qt. baking dish. Sauté mushrooms until tender in margarine, drain. Cut eggs in fourths lengthwise; arrange eggs, peas, mushrooms, and chestnuts in baking dish. Heat together, but do not boil, soup, sour cream, milk, and onion; remove from heat and add sherry, pimento, salt, and pepper. Pour over ingredients in dish. Mix bread crumbs with margarine; sprinkle over top. Bake 20 mins.

Mrs. Robert Hampson

FLUFFY BLUE CHEESE OMELET WITH BACON AND MUSHROOMS
4 servings

4-5 bacon slices
¼ lb. fresh mushrooms, sliced
1 T. margarine
4 eggs, separated, room
    temperature
½ tsp. salt
¼ tsp. pepper

¼ cup milk
½ cup blue cheese,
    crumbled
2 T. margarine
2 medium size tomatoes,
    thinly sliced
1 T. chives, chopped

Cook bacon until crisp; drain and crumble. Sauté mushrooms in margarine, keep warm. Beat egg whites with ¼ tsp. salt until stiff. Combine yolks, remaining salt, pepper and milk. Stir until well blended; add 1 T. blue cheese. Fold egg yolk mixture into egg whites carefully. Melt margarine in 9" or 10" skillet. Turn egg mixture into skillet and cook slowly over medium-low heat until partially set. Preheat broiler; place omelet 6" from broiler and broil 4 mins. Remove from oven, loosen sides; cut in half, almost all the way through. Quickly spread remaining cheese, bacon, and tomatoes on one half. Lay remaining side on top of filling; tilt pan and let omelet slide onto warm serving platter. Spoon mushrooms around omelet; sprinkle top with chives. Serve immediately.

Mr. Robert Brown

OMELET CHARENTIERE
6 servings

6 bacon slices
½ cup onion, chopped
8 eggs, slightly beaten
1 cup milk
1 T. parsley, chopped
½ tsp. salt

1 cup cheddar cheese,
    shredded
1 cup Swiss cheese,
    shredded
1 T. flour

Preheat oven to 350F. Use a 9" x 9" baking dish. Fry bacon until crisp, remove from skillet and crumble. Drain fat, reserving 1 T. Sauté onion in bacon fat until tender. Combine bacon, onion, eggs, milk, parsley and salt. Toss cheeses in flour; add to egg mixture. Pour into baking dish. Bake 40 min. Serve immediately.

Mrs. Jack Dozeman

TIERED OMELET MORNAY   *8-10 servings*

12 eggs, separated, room temperature	2 T. parsley, minced
1 tsp. salt	¼ cup green onions, chopped
1 tsp. seasoned salt	6 T. flour
freshly ground pepper	4½ T. white wine

Sauce:

6 T. butter	½ cup grated Parmesan cheese
7 T. flour	¼ cup dry sherry
1¾ cups milk	½ tsp. Worcestershire sauce
1 cup chicken bouillon	2 tsp. chives
¾ cup sharp cheddar cheese, diced	salt and pepper to taste

Preheat oven to 350F. Generously grease (1 T. shortening per pan) and line bottoms with wax paper, three 8" cake pans. Beat egg yolks until light. Add salts, pepper, parsley, onions, and flour. Beat until thoroughly blended. Beat egg whites together with wine until stiff but not dry. Carefully fold whites into yolk mixture. Divide egg mixture between cake pans. Bake for 15 mins.

For sauce, melt butter. Stir in flour. Gradually stir in milk and bouillon. Cook over low heat, stirring constantly, until smooth and thickened. Stir in cheese, sherry and remaining seasonings. This sauce may be prepared several hours ahead of time. Reheat prior to serving.

Stack each omelet layer with sauce between; pour sauce over top. Cut in wedges.

Variation: Use sautéed mushrooms between layers.

Mrs. Donald G. Miller

SPANISH EGG AND CHEESE PUFFS · 4 servings

6 eggs
¾ cup flour
1½ tsp. baking powder
½ tsp. salt

½ tsp. onion salt
1½ cups cheddar cheese,
  shredded

Spanish Sauce:
6 T. butter
1 cup green pepper, chopped
1 cup onion, chopped
2 T. flour

2 T. sugar
1 (15 oz.) can tomato sauce
2 (4 oz. each) cans sliced
  mushrooms, drained

Preheat and lightly butter a griddle. Beat eggs until thick (about 10 min.) Sift together flour, baking powder, salt, and onion salt. Blend flour mixture in eggs slowly. Fold in cheese. Drop batter on griddle using ¼ cup for each puff. When puffs are brown turn and finish cooking.

Melt butter; add green pepper and onion; sauté until onion is tender. Blend in flour. Add sugar, tomato sauce and mushrooms. Cook over low heat, stirring constantly, until mixture thickens. Use 3 puffs for each serving; top with ½ cup sauce.

Mrs. Erich Benke

SAVORY EGGS · 6 servings

1 cup cheddar cheese,
  grated
2 T. butter
½ cup cream

¼ tsp. salt
dash of pepper
1 tsp. prepared mustard
6 eggs, slightly beaten

Preheat oven to 325F. Grease an 8" x 8" baking dish. Spread cheese in dish; dot with butter. Combine cream, salt, pepper, and mustard. Pour ½ of mixture over cheese. Pour eggs into baking dish. Add remaining cream mixture. Bake 25 min.

Variation: Add mushrooms, ham, or bacon bits.

Mrs. David VanderWel

BAKED SANDWICHES   8-10 servings

1 lb. cheese, grated
1 lb. ham, ground
1 loaf sandwich bread,
   crusts trimmed

4 eggs
3 cups milk
⅛ tsp. salt

Mushroom Sauce:
⅓ cup onions, sliced
2 T. butter
1 (10¾ oz.) can cream of
   mushroom soup, undiluted

1 cup milk
2 eggs, hard boiled,
   chopped
salt and pepper

Grease a 9" x 13" baking dish. Mix cheese and ham, spread on slices of bread. Make 2 layer sandwiches. Put in baking dish. Beat eggs, milk, and salt together. Pour over sandwiches; cover. Refrigerate overnight. Preheat oven to 300F. Bake uncovered 1 hr.

Sauté onions in butter until tender. Gradually stir in soup and milk. Add eggs, salt and pepper. Serve over sandwiches.

Mrs. Gordon Van Eenenaam

DUTCH LUNCH   6 servings
(2nd Place Bake-Off)

6 Dutch rusks
6 slices balken brij
3 T. margarine
6 eggs, poached
1 (10¾ oz.) can cheddar cheese
   soup, undiluted

3 T. cream
¼ tsp. each, parsley and
   chives or onion
prunes or strawberries

Place rusk on plates. Quick-fry balken brij in margarine and place on top of rusk; then top each slice with an egg. Combine soup, cream and seasonings; cook until heated through. Spoon over eggs. Garnish with a large prune or fresh strawberry.

Mrs. Henry J. Hekman

BALKEN BRIJ

5 lbs. pork liver
5 lbs. fatty pork roast
2 T. salt

1 (1½ oz.) can allspice
1½-2 lbs. buckwheat
flour

Cover meat completely with water. Add salt; cook until tender. Remove meat from broth. Remove bones; chop fine. Return meat to broth; boil. Add allspice; stir in enough flour to make a stiff mixture. Place in 4 loaf pans; cool. Slice and fry on both sides. Serve with maple syrup.

Mrs. Wilbur Prince

PIGS-IN-BLANKET
Easy To Make

4-5 servings

1 lb. pork sausage
2 cups Bisquick mix
¼ cup shortening

½ cup water
1 egg
1 T. cream

Preheat oven to 425F. Make 8-10 sausage rolls, shaped like a hot dog. Mix Bisquick, shortening, and water with fork to soft dough. Spoon dough onto a floured surface, toss lightly and roll to ⅛" thick. Cut squares large enough to roll up sausage rolls. Place on baking sheet. Beat together egg and cream; brush each roll. Bake 30-40 mins.

Mrs. Bill Prince

SCRAPPLE

9 servings

1½ lb. bulk pork
sausage
4 cups cold water
1 tsp. salt

½ tsp. sage
1 cup yellow corn meal
1 cup cold water
fat for frying

In a large saucepan, break sausage into small pieces. Add water, stirring to separate meat. Simmer 20 mins. Drain meat, reserving 3 cups of the stock. Add salt and sage to stock. Refrigerate stock until fat has hardened; remove most of fat. Bring stock to boiling. Combine corn meal and water; gradually add to stock, stirring constantly. Cover; cook over low heat for 10 mins., stirring constantly. Add sausage. Pour mixture into 9½" x 5" x 3" loaf pan. Cover; chill overnight. Slice scrapple ½" thick. Fry slices in a little hot fat until golden brown, turning once. Serve hot with syrup.

Mrs. John Marquis

CRAB-SHRIMP ALMONDINE
6 servings

1 (7½ oz.) can crab meat,
  drained
1 (4½ oz.) can shrimp, drained
¼ cup onion, chopped
1 (6 oz.) can chow mein
  noodles

1 cup celery, diced
1 cup almonds, chopped
1 T. lemon juice
½ cup water
2 (10¾ oz. each) cans
  cream of mushroom soup,
  undiluted

Preheat oven to 375F. Use 1½ qt. baking dish. Combine crab, shrimp, onion, noodles, and celery. Mix in ½ cup almonds and lemon juice. Add water to soup; blend well. Pour soup over crab mixture; toss lightly but thoroughly. Spoon into baking dish. Sprinkle remaining almonds on top. Bake 30 mins.

Mrs. David Linn

PARTY CRAB CASSEROLE
8 servings

1 (7½ oz.) can crab meat,
  flaked
3 eggs, hard boiled, chopped
1 cup cream or evaporated
  milk
1½ cups mayonnaise
1 tsp. onion, grated
½ tsp. salt

⅛ tsp. pepper
dash cayenne pepper
1 (8 oz.) can water
  chestnuts, drained
1½ cups fresh bread
  crumbs
2 T. butter
parsley

Preheat oven to 350F. Use 2 qt. casserole. Combine crab, eggs, and milk. Mix in mayonnaise; add onion, salt, pepper, and cayenne. Slice water chestnuts; add to mixture. Add 1 cup bread crumbs. Turn mixture into casserole. Top with remaining crumbs; dot with butter. Bake 30 mins. Garnish with parsley.

Mrs. Jack Faber

CRAB MEAT QUICHE

6 servings

9" pastry shell, baked
3 eggs, slightly beaten
1 cup sour cream
½ tsp. Worcestershire sauce
¾ tsp. salt

1 cup Swiss cheese, shredded
1 (7½ oz.) can king crab meat,
drained and flaked
1 (3 oz.) can French fried
onion rings

Preheat oven to 300F. Combine eggs, sour cream, Worcestershire sauce, and salt. Stir in cheese, crab meat and onion rings. Pour into pastry shell. Bake 55-60 mins.

Mrs. Leo Jungblut

CRAB MEAT QUICHE SUPREME
(2nd Place Bake-Off)

6 servings

9" deep pastry shell, unbaked
1 cup Swiss cheese, shredded
1 (2 oz.) jar sliced mushrooms,
drained
1 (6 oz.) pkg. frozen crab meat
2 T. chives, chopped
3 eggs, beaten

1 cup light cream
¼ tsp. dry mustard
½ tsp. grated orange peel
½ tsp. salt
pinch of nutmeg
¼ cup almonds, sliced

Preheat oven to 375F. Sprinkle cheese on bottom of pastry shell. Top with mushrooms, then crab meat which has been cut in small pieces. Sprinkle with chives. Combine remaining ingredients except almonds. Pour over crab and cheese. Bake for 45 mins. or until top is golden brown and cracked. Sprinkle on almonds last 15 mins. Let stand 10 mins. before cutting.

Rev. Verne C. Hohl

CRAB WILD RICE SALAD
6 servings

1 (6 oz.) pkg. long grain
  and wild rice mix
1 (7½ oz.) can king crab,
  drained and flaked
1 (4½ oz.) can shrimp,
  drained
1 T. lemon juice

¼ cup green pepper, chopped
¼ cup pimento, chopped
2 T. parsley, snipped
½ cup mayonnaise
2-3 T. Russian
  salad dressing
½ tsp. salt

Cook and cool rice. Combine crab, shrimp and lemon juice. Add rice, green pepper, pimento and parsley. Blend together mayonnaise, Russian dressing, and salt. Add to crab mixture. Toss and chill.

Mrs. Leo Jungblut

HOT CRAB SOUFFLE
10 servings

8-10 slices white bread
2 cups crab, flaked
1 cup mayonnaise
1 small onion, chopped
1 cup celery, chopped
1 green pepper, chopped
1 T. parsley, minced
1 tsp. lemon peel, grated

1 tsp. salt
¼ tsp. pepper
4 eggs
3 cups milk
1 (10¾ oz.) can mushroom
  soup, undiluted
Parmesan cheese, grated
paprika

Butter a 9" x 13" casserole. Dice 4 slices of the bread and place in bottom of casserole. Mix together crab, mayonnaise, onion, celery, green pepper, parsley, lemon peel, salt and pepper. Arrange over bread. Trim crusts from remaining slices of bread and arrange over crab mixture to cover completely. In separate bowl, slightly beat eggs, add milk, and beat until blended; pour over bread. Cover; refrigerate overnight. Preheat oven to 325F. Bake, uncovered 1 hr. 15 mins. Heat soup until just hot; spoon over baked souffle. Sprinkle with cheese; broil for 2 min. Sprinkle with paprika and serve.

Mrs. Jack Dozeman

276

CRAB STROGANOFF

4-6 servings

½ cup onion, chopped
¼ cup butter
½ lb. mushrooms, sliced
1 clove garlic, minced
3 T. flour
1½ cups chicken stock
1 tsp. Worcestershire sauce

¼ tsp. salt
4 drops Tabasco sauce
¼ tsp. dill weed
2 (7½ oz. each) cans crab meat,
   drained
1 cup sour cream
4-6 patty shells

Sauté onions in butter, add mushrooms and garlic; cook until onions are limp. Blend in flour; add chicken stock gradually, stirring until thickened. Add spices and stir to blend. Gently fold in crab meat and heat through. Just before serving, fold in sour cream. Serve over patty shells.

Mrs. John Hutchinson

MOLDED SEAFOOD SALAD

8 servings

1 (4½ oz.) can medium
   shrimp, drained
½ cup water, chilled
6 T. lemon juice
1 envelope unflavored
   gelatin
½ cup cold water
½ tsp. instant minced onion
½ cup chili sauce
few drops of Tabasco

1 cup mayonnaise
1 (7½ oz.) can crab
   meat, drained
1 (6½ oz.) can tuna,
   drained
½ cup celery, chopped
2 T. green pepper, chopped
2 T. pimento-stuffed
   olives, chopped
salad greens

Combine shrimp, chilled water, and 1 T. lemon juice; let stand 30 min. In small saucepan sprinkle gelatin over cold water. Dissolve over low heat, stirring constantly. Stir in onion and remaining lemon juice; set aside to cool. Blend together chili sauce, Tabasco, and mayonnaise. Stir into gelatin mixture; chill to egg white consistency. Combine crab, tuna, drained shrimp, celery, green pepper, and olives; fold into mixture. Pour into 1 qt. mold and chill at least 3 hrs. Serve on salad greens.

Mrs. Kenneth Meunier

QUICK-AS-A-WINK SALMON SOUFFLE   *6 servings*

¼ cup margarine
¼ cup flour
1 cup hot milk
1 T. onion, grated
¼ tsp. salt
⅛ tsp. pepper

1 cup cheddar cheese, grated
3 egg yolks, lightly beaten
12 oz. canned salmon,
    reserve liquid
3 egg whites, room
    temperature

Preheat oven to 400F. Generously butter a 9" pie plate. In saucepan melt margarine. Stir in flour, cook, stirring until mixture is smooth and bubbling. Add milk, stir over medium heat until sauce is smooth and thickened. Stir in onion, salt, pepper, and cheese. Cook, stirring until cheese is melted. Slowly stir in egg yolks and stir over low heat 3 mins. Remove from heat, stir in salmon liquid; cool. Flake and stir in salmon. Place pie plate in oven until butter is sizzling. Beat egg whites and fold into salmon mixture. Pour into hot pie plate. Bake 10-15 mins.

Mrs. Jack DeRoo

SHRIMP SOUFFLE   *6-8 servings*

6 slices of bread
¾ lb. fresh mushrooms,
    sliced
3 T. butter
½ lb. Old English sharp
    cheese, sliced
¾ lb. cooked shrimp

¼ cup butter, melted
3 eggs, beaten
¼ tsp. dry mustard
½ tsp. salt
2 cups milk

Grease a 9" x 13" baking dish. Cube bread; place in dish. Sauté mushrooms in butter until tender; drain. Layer cheese, shrimp, and mushrooms. Pour butter over top. Combine eggs, mustard, salt, and milk. Pour mixture over ingredients in baking dish. Refrigerate, covered, overnight. Remove from refrigerator 1 hr. before baking. Preheat oven to 350F. Bake, covered, 45 mins., uncover and bake 10 mins. longer.

Mrs. Loren Meengs

SHRIMP 'N CRAB BAKE   *8 servings*

1 medium green pepper,
  chopped
1 medium onion, chopped
1 cup celery, chopped
1 (7½ oz.) can crab meat,
  flaked
1 (4½ oz.) can shrimp, drained

½ tsp. salt
⅛ tsp. pepper
1 tsp. Worcestershire
  sauce
1 cup mayonnaise
1 cup crumbs, buttered

Preheat oven to 350F. Combine all ingredients except crumbs. Place in individual sea-shells. Sprinkle with crumbs. Bake 30 mins. (may also be baked in greased 1½ qt. baking dish).

Mrs. G. S. MacKenzie

CREPES WITH PINK SHRIMPS   *8 servings*

3 lbs. shrimp, cooked
½ cup butter
1 large onion, finely-chopped
1 lb. mushrooms, chopped
2 tsp. soy sauce
¼ cup catsup

2 tsp. paprika
2 cups sour cream
¼ cup parsley, chopped
salt and pepper
24-5" crepes

Preheat oven to 375F. Cut shrimp into bite size pieces. Heat butter to bubbling in large skillet, add the onion and sauté until clear. Add mushrooms and sauté 4 mins. Add shrimp and stir to coat with butter and juices. Mix soy sauce, catsup, and paprika with sour cream, combine with the shrimp mixture. Add parsley, salt and pepper. Spread a spoonful or two of shrimp mixture along center of each crepe. Roll and place seam side down in buttered baking dish. Spoon sauce that remains over tops of crepes. Bake uncovered 20 mins.

Mrs. Donald G. Miller

SHRIMP-CRAB DELIGHT
6 servings

¼ cup butter
1 T. minced onion
¼ cup green pepper, chopped
¼ cup celery, chopped
1 (10¾ oz.) can cream of
   mushroom soup, undiluted
¼ cup light cream

8 oz. frozen shrimp, cooked
1 (7½ oz.) can crab
  meat, drained
2 T. parsley, minced
½ tsp. Worcestershire sauce
2-3 T. sherry or white wine
6 patty shells

Melt butter; add onion, green pepper and celery. Sauté until tender. Combine soup and cream and add to first mixture. Add shrimp, crab, parsley, Worcestershire sauce, and sherry. Cook over medium heat until heated, stirring constantly. Serve over patty shells.

Mrs. Gladys Jungling

SHRIMP FLORENTINE
4-6 servings

2 (10 oz. each) pkg. frozen
  spinach, chopped
1½ lbs. jumbo shrimp,
  cooked,
¼ cup margarine
¼ cup flour
½ cup dry white wine

1½ cups milk
¼ cup scallions, chopped
salt and pepper to taste
paprika
1 cup cheddar
  cheese, shredded

Preheat oven to 350F. Use 1½ qt. baking dish. Thaw and drain spinach; spread in baking dish and top with shrimp. In saucepan melt margarine; stir in flour. Gradually add wine, milk, and scallions. Cook, stirring constantly, over low heat until sauce thickens. Add salt, pepper, and enough paprika to make rosy color. Pour sauce over shrimp and sprinkle with cheese. Bake uncovered 35 mins. Can be frozen before baking and baked for 1 hr.

Mrs. Tom Brown

CURRIED SHRIMP SALAD   *4 servings*

⅔ cup mayonnaise
1½ T. catsup
2 T. lemon juice
½ tsp. curry powder
1 (16 oz.) pkg. small frozen
    shrimp, cooked according
    to pkg. directions, well
    drained

½ cup celery, chopped
2 T. onion, finely-chopped
¼ cup chopped almonds
1 T. butter
2 cups head lettuce,
    shredded
1 honeydew melon, cut into
    balls

In a bowl, combine first 4 ingredients. Mix well. Add shrimp, celery and onion. Blend and chill. Sauté almonds in butter until slightly browned. Serve shrimp mixture on a bed of lettuce and melon. Garnish with toasted almonds.

Mrs. William G. Beebe

ORIENTAL SHRIMP SALAD   *4 servings*

1 (16 oz.) can bean sprouts
2 cups cooked tiny shrimp

¼ cup green onions, minced
¼ cup celery, minced

Soy Mayonnaise:
¾ cup mayonnaise
1 T. lemon juice
1 T. soy sauce

⅜ tsp. ground ginger
½ tsp. MSG
1 cup chow mein noodles

Rinse sprouts in cold water. Combine all ingredients.

Mix soy mayonnaise ingredients. Add to shrimp mixture. Add noodles just before serving.

Mrs. John Marquis

TUNA CUPS

12 servings

*12 slices sandwich
   bread, crusts trimmed*
2 T. onion, chopped
½ cup green pepper, chopped
¼ cup margarine
6 T. flour

½ tsp. salt
*1 (10¾ oz.) can chicken
   rice soup, undiluted*
1½ cups milk
1 (7 oz.) can tuna
1 T. lemon juice

Preheat oven to 425F. Grease 12 muffin cups. Place one slice of bread in each cup and bake 10 mins.

Cook onion, green pepper, and margarine together for 5 mins. Blend in flour; gradually add remaining ingredients and cook until thick, stirring constantly. Pour hot mixture into toast shells. Mixture can be made the day before and reheated.

Mrs. Peter Yff

FRENCH APPLE CREPES

8 servings

24   5" or 6" crepes

Apple Filling:
*6 cups Ida Red
   apples, peeled and sliced*
6 T. butter
1¼ cups sugar

½ tsp. cinnamon
¼ tsp. nutmeg
juice of 1 lemon

Honey Glaze:
½ cup butter, melted
¼ tsp. cinnamon

⅛ tsp. nutmeg
½ cup honey

Sour Cream Sauce:
1½ cups sour cream

¼ cup brown sugar

Prepare crepes. Sauté apples in butter for 5 mins. Add remaining ingredients; stir and simmer, covered, 5-7 mins. Drain. Fill crepes with apples; place in baking dish. Crepes can be covered and refrigerated overnight.

continued

Preheat oven to 350F. Bring crepes to room temperature. Combine butter, cinnamon, nutmeg, and honey. Brush glaze generously on crepes. Bake 20 mins.

Combine sour cream and brown sugar and let stand 10 mins. Serve crepes topped with sour cream sauce.

Mrs. Donald G. Miller

ICELAND PONNUKOKUR
Pancakes

8 servings

3 eggs	½ tsp. salt
1 cup milk	½ tsp. vanilla
1 T. sugar	¼ cup butter

Filling:

1½ cups apricot or cherry jam	2 tsp. lemon peel, grated
1 T. brandy	⅓ cup almonds, chopped

Butter and heat a 6-8" fry pan. Combine eggs, milk, and sugar. Add salt, vanilla, and butter; beat well. Pour 2 T. batter into pan. Tilt pan to cover entire bottom. Fry until brown; turn and brown other side. Keep warm in folded towel.

Preheat oven to 250F. Combine filling ingredients. Fold pancakes around divided filling. Heat 10-15 mins.

Variation: Combine cottage cheese and crushed pineapple. Fold pancakes with mixture and top with confectioners' sugar.

Mrs. Mayo Hadden Sr.

ARTICHOKES WITH LAMB STUFFING
4 servings

4 whole fresh artichokes	½ cup fine dry bread crumbs
2 T. white vinegar	¼ cup parsley, snipped
1 lb. lamb, ground	2 eggs, beaten
¾ cup onion, chopped	¼ tsp. cinnamon
2 T. cooking oil	½ tsp. salt

continued

283

Avgolemono Sauce:
2 cups chicken bouillon   *3 T. lemon juice*
3 eggs

Use a 9" x 9" pan. Wash artichokes; cut off stems evenly, close to the base. Cook in boiling salted water, with vinegar, 25-30 mins. or until a leaf can be easily pulled off. Drain upside down. Using kitchen scissors cut off spiny top part of each leaf. Using teaspoon, remove small center leaves and choke.

Preheat oven to 375F. Brown lamb and onion in oil; drain. Add crumbs, parsley, eggs, cinnamon and salt; mix well. Spread artichoke leaves slightly and stuff with lamb mixture. Place in pan; pour in 1" of hot water. Bake 25-30 mins. Can be prepared in advance; extend baking time 10 mins. Serve with sauce.

Heat bouillon in saucepan. In bowl, beat eggs with lemon juice. Add ½ cup bouillon slowly to eggs, beating constantly. Return eggs to remaining bouillon, stirring constantly. Heat, but do not boil. Serve immediately.

Mrs. Stuart Smith

SAVORY ARTICHOKE CASSEROLE   *6-8 servings*

2 (10 oz. each) pkg. frozen   ¼ cup sherry
    artichoke hearts, cooked   1 bay leaf
2 cups cooked ham, diced   ½ tsp. salt
8 eggs, hardboiled, quartered   ¼ tsp. garlic salt
¾ lb. fresh mushrooms, sauteed curry powder to taste
1 (10¾ oz.) can mushroom soup, ¾ cup Swiss cheese, grated
    undiluted   ¼ cup grated Parmesan
1 T. onion, chopped   cheese

Preheat oven to 400F. Use a buttered 9" x 13" baking dish. Arrange artichokes in casserole. Add ham, eggs and mushrooms. Combine soup with onion, wine and seasonings. Pour mixture over ingredients in casserole. Sprinkle cheeses over top. Bake uncovered for 30 mins.

Mrs. Donald Brewer

MUSHROOM TARTS

6 servings

6 tart shells
2 T. shallots
3 T. butter
1 lb. fresh mushrooms,
   quartered
1 tsp. salt
2 T. sherry or Madeira

3 eggs
1½ cups heavy cream
dash nutmeg
⅓ cup Swiss cheese,
   grated
1 T. butter

Preheat oven to 375F. Bake tart shells 5 min. Sauté shallots in butter for 1 min. Add mushrooms, salt, and sherry. Cook 5 min. covered; uncover and cook, stirring until liquid has disappeared. Spoon mixture into tart shells. Beat eggs and cream together, add nutmeg. Pour on top of mushroom mixture. Sprinkle with cheese, dot with butter. Bake 35 mins.

Mrs. Don R. Judd

TACO SALAD
(1st Place Bake-Off)

6 servings

1 lb. ground chuck
1 (1¾ oz.) pkg. Lawry's
   taco seasoning mix
½ large head lettuce, torn
1 avocado or 1 cucumber,
   sliced
½ green pepper, diced
½ large sweet onion, sliced

2 medium tomatoes, diced
½ cup cheddar cheese,
   shredded
¼ cup green or ripe
   olives, sliced
2 cups corn chips
Tabasco sauce

Combine dressing ingredients in blender and set aside.

Prepare meat according to pkg. directions on taco mix and let simmer until ready to serve.

In large bowl, combine lettuce, avocado, pepper, onion, tomatoes, cheese, olives and corn chips. Add meat mixture and toss. Serve with dressing and Tabasco sauce. This is good served with garlic toast.

Dressing:

2½ cups sugar
1 T. salt
1 T. paprika
1 T. celery seed
1 tsp. garlic salt

1 cup vinegar
1 cup catsup
1 cup Mazola oil
1 T. minced onion
½ cup water

Mrs. Alvin DeWeerd

TOMATO SOUFFLE
4 servings

1 (16 oz.) can tomatoes
¼ cup onion, chopped
1 clove garlic, minced
¼ cup parsley, chopped
¼ tsp. sugar
½ tsp. salt

¼ tsp. Tabasco
¼ tsp. dried leaf basil
3 T. margarine
3 T. flour
4 eggs, separated,
    room temperature

Cheese Sauce:
2 T. margarine
2 T. flour
2 cups milk
½ tsp. salt

¼ tsp. Tabasco
1 cup Swiss cheese,
    shredded
1 tsp. lemon juice

Preheat oven to 375F. Grease a 1½ qt. souffle dish. In medium saucepan combine tomatoes, onion, garlic, parsley, sugar, salt, Tabasco and basil. Simmer over medium heat 20-30 mins. or until reduced to 1 cup. Remove from heat. In medium saucepan melt margarine; blend in flour and tomato mixture. Stir constantly until mixture thickens and comes to a boil. Remove from heat; beat in egg yolks one at a time. Beat egg whites until stiff peaks form; fold in. Turn into dish. Bake 20-30 mins.

In medium saucepan melt margarine. Blend in flour; stir in milk. Cook, stirring constantly, until mixture thickens and comes to a boil. Cook 2 mins. Add remaining ingredients. Stir until cheese melts. Serve on top of souffle.

Mrs. Robert Hampson

Outdoor Cookery

NOTES

ARTICHOKE KABOBS

artichoke hearts, canned
Italian dressing
water chestnuts, canned

chicken livers
soy sauce
bacon

Marinate artichoke hearts in Italian dressing for several hrs. Slice water chestnuts in thirds. Cut chicken livers in slices larger than the chestnuts and dip in soy sauce. Sandwich a chestnut between two slices of liver, wrap each in ½ slice bacon and fasten with toothpick. Alternate bacon wrapped chicken livers and artichoke hearts on small skewers. Rotate on hot grill for 8 mins. or until done.

Mrs. Paul Dykema

HILA FRANK NIBBLES

serves 20

1 cup apricot preserves
½ cup seasoned tomato sauce
⅓ cup vinegar
¼ cup sherry
2 T. soy sauce
2 T. honey

1 T. oil
1 tsp. salt
¼ tsp. ground ginger
2 lbs. frankfurters or
  cocktail hot dogs

For sauce, combine all ingredients except frankfurters. Score the frankfurters diagonally and broil slowly over hot coals turning and basting often with the sauce. Broil until hot and glazed. Cut into bite-sized pieces and serve with remaining sauce which has been heated.

This sauce is excellent for glazing roast duck or pork.

Mrs. Darrel Schuurman

MUSHROOM PUFFS   2½ dozen

1 (3 oz.) pkg. cream cheese,
  softened
½ cup mayonnaise
1 T. instant minced
  onion
1 T. tarragon

¼ tsp. Tabasco sauce
1 (3 oz.) pkg. smoked ham,
  shredded
1½ lbs. fresh mushrooms,
  cleaned, stems removed
2 T. butter

Blend cream cheese and mayonnaise. Stir in onion, tarragon, Tabasco, and ham. Mix well and set aside. Sauté mushrooms in butter, fill with cream cheese mixture. Place mushrooms on a large double sheet of foil. Fold foil to seal edges; grill over medium coals 15-20 mins. or until mushrooms are tender.

Mrs. Graham Duryee

BEEF ROLL-UPS   6 servings

6 cube steaks
Kraft red French dressing
¾ cup each onion, green
  pepper, and celery, all
  finely-chopped

1½ cups carrots, shredded
¼ cup water
⅛ tsp. salt
12 strips bacon

Marinate meat for 1 hr. in French Dressing. Simmer vegetables in water and salt for 7-8 mins. Drain steak and vegetables. Cook steaks on one side on hot grill. Remove and put vegetable mixture on cooked side of each steak. Roll up and wrap with bacon. (2 strips on each). Fasten with toothpicks. Grill until done.

Mrs. George Daily

BARBECUED BEEF IN FOIL

serves 4-6

2 lbs. round steak or
   boneless chuck
olive oil
Tomato Barbecue Sauce:
½ small onion, finely
   chopped
1 clove garlic, crushed
1 sprig parsley, chopped

4 medium onions, quartered
4 medium carrots

⅔ cup catsup
2 T. wine vinegar
2 T. olive oil
1 tsp. Worcestershire sauce
freshly ground pepper

Brush round of beef on both sides with oil, and grill until well browned on both sides. Place meat on double sheet of foil large enough to fold over meat; add quartered onions and carrots and coat with sauce. Fold foil over roast and cook on hot grill for 45-60 mins. or until meat is tender.

For sauce, combine all ingredients in screw-top jar. Cover and shake vigorously until all ingredients are well blended. Allow to stand, refrigerated, 24 hrs. before using.

Mrs. Lee Kimzey

BLUE-BURGER SURPRISE

5 large servings

1½ - 2 lbs. ground chuck
1 tsp. seasoned salt
¼ tsp. freshly ground pepper
¼ tsp. dry mustard
5 dashes Worcestershire
   sauce

½ cup blue cheese, crumbled
½ lb. bacon, fried crisp
   and crumbled
1 tsp. garlic salt
2 T. mayonnaise

Combine ground chuck with salt, pepper, mustard, and Worcestershire sauce; form into 10 thin patties. Combine blue cheese, bacon, garlic salt, and mayonnaise. Spoon cheese mixture on 5 patties. Top with remaining patties, pressing meat edges together. Broil burgers on grill 5-10 mins. turning once.

Mrs. Herbert Eldean

HE-MAN BURGERS

4 large servings

1½ - 2 lbs. ground chuck
1 tsp. seasoned salt
freshly ground pepper
20 thin slices of pepperoni

4 slices onion
4 slices Swiss cheese
4 hamburger buns
(optional)

Combine ground chuck with salt and pepper and form into 8 thin patties. Form a small ridge around 4 of the patties; place on each 5 slices of pepperoni and one slice of onion and cheese. Top with remaining patties and seal securely. Cook burgers on grill 5-10 mins. turning once.

Mrs. Herbert Eldean

GIANT STUFFED HAMBURGER

6 servings

2 T. margarine, melted
¾ cup crushed herb-
seasoned stuffing mix
1 egg, beaten
½ lb. mushrooms, sliced,
sautéed, and drained
⅓ cup beef broth

¼ cup onion, chopped
¼ cup toasted almonds,
chopped
¼ cup snipped parsley
1 tsp. lemon juice
2 lbs. ground chuck
1 tsp. salt

Combine all ingredients except ground chuck and salt. Mix well and set aside. Combine ground chuck and salt; divide meat in half. On sheets of waxed paper, pat each half to an 8" circle. Spoon stuffing over one circle of meat to within 1" of edge. Top with second circle of meat; peel off top sheet of paper and seal edges. Invert meat patty into well-greased grill basket; peel off remaining paper. Grill over medium coals 10-12 mins. on each side. Cut into wedges.

Mrs. James W. F. Brooks

CHARCOALED CHUCK ROAST

6-8 servings

2½ - 3½ lbs. chuck roast,
2½ - 3" thick
salt and pepper
garlic salt
1 (5 oz.) bottle soy sauce
¼ cup brown sugar
¼ cup bourbon, wine or
whiskey
1 T. lemon juice
1 tsp. salt
1 T. Worcestershire sauce
1½ cups water

Season meat with salt, pepper, and garlic salt. Combine remaining ingredients and pour over roast. Refrigerate 6 hrs. or overnight. Broil meat on hot grill 45-60 mins. per pound. Baste frequently with marinade.

Mrs. Ronald L. Doolittle

CHUCK WAGON PEPPER STEAK

6-8 servings

3 lbs. round steak,
cut 2" thick
2 tsp. unseasoned meat
tenderizer
2 T. instant minced onion
2 tsp. thyme
1 tsp. marjoram
1 bay leaf, crushed
1 cup wine vinegar or
red Burgundy wine
½ cup oil
1 T. lemon juice
1-2 T. peppercorns,
crushed

Sprinkle both sides of meat with tenderizer (use no salt); pierce meat with fork and place in shallow pan. Combine remaining ingredients, except peppercorns, and pour over meat. Let stand at room temperature 2-3 hrs. turning meat occasionally. Pound the peppercorns into meat and grill for 15 mins. per side at 6" from coals. Carve meat diagonally into ½" slices.

Mrs. William Boyer

FLANK STEAK TOURNEDOS
4 servings

1 - 1½ lbs. beef flank
  steak
1 (⅞ oz.) pkg, meat marinade
  red wine
½ lb. bacon

1 tsp. garlic salt
½ tsp. freshly ground
  pepper
2 T. parsley, chopped
2 T. onion, chopped

Pound flank steak to even thickness, about ½". Use meat marinade according to package directions using red wine for the liquid. Meanwhile, cook bacon till almost done, but not crisp. Sprinkle flank steak with salt and pepper. Score steak diagonally on both sides making diamond-shaped cuts. Place bacon strips lengthwise on flank steak. Sprinkle with parsley and onion. Roll up jelly roll fashion, starting at narrow end. Skewer with wooden picks at 1" intervals, cut in 1" slices (about 8 pinwheel steaks). Grill over medium coals 15 mins., turning once, for rare.

Mrs. Herbert Eldean

GRILLED STUFFED FLANK STEAK
6 servings

2 lbs. flank steak
⅓ cup A. 1. sauce
1 cup red wine
1 medium onion, chopped

¼ cup oil
½ tsp. salt
¼ tsp. pepper

Stuffing:
3 T. butter
¼ lb. fresh mushrooms,
  chopped
½ cup onion, minced

1½ cups seasoned stuffing
  crumbs
salt and pepper to taste

Cut pocket in steak and score surfaces. Combine A.1. sauce, wine, onion, oil, salt and pepper and pour over meat. Refrigerate overnight.

For stuffing, sauté mushrooms and onion in butter. Add stuffing crumbs, salt, and pepper. Place stuffing in pocket and skewer. Broil 8-10 mins. per side. Carve meat diagonally in ½" slices.

Mrs. John Hutchinson

294

LONDON BROIL
6-8 servings

2 flank steaks

1½ tsp. meat tenderizer

Marinade:

⅔ cup olive oil

⅓ cup salad oil

¼ cup dry white
   wine or wine vinegar

¼ cup lemon juice

½ tsp. salt

¼ tsp. pepper

1 tsp. sugar

½ tsp. thyme

Arrange steaks in shallow dish. Use tenderizer, following directions on package. Combine all ingredients for marinade in jar and shake well. Pour over steak and let stand 1 hr. or more.

Adjust grill to 4". Grill 10 mins. on one side, basting frequently; 5 mins. on other side. Serve medium rare and slice very thinly on an angle. Marinade can be kept in refrigerator and used for basting other meats or chicken.

Mrs. William J. Lalley

PEPPERY BEEF SHISH KABOBS
8-10 servings

1¼ cups oil

¾ cup soy sauce

¼ cup Worcestershire sauce

2¼ tsp. salt

2 T. dry mustard

½ cup wine vinegar

2 T. black pepper

⅓ cup fresh lemon juice

2 garlic cloves, crushed

3-4 lbs. beef sirloin
   tip, cubed

¼ lb. large mushroom

2 green peppers, cut
   in 2" pieces

2 onions, cut in chunks

Combine all ingredients except meat and vegetables. Marinate meat in mixture for several hours or overnight. On skewers, alternate meat with vegetables. Broil over hot coals turning frequently 10-20 mins. depending on desired degree of doneness.

Mrs. Herbert Eldean

STEAK AND MUSHROOMS ON SKEWERS 4 servings

½ cup Burgundy *wine*	1 tsp. sugar
1 tsp. Worcestershire sauce	½ tsp. each: salt, MSG,
1 clove garlic, minced	rosemary, & marjoram
½ cup oil	12 large mushrooms
2 T. catsup	2 lbs. sirloin steak,
1 T. vinegar	cut in 1" cubes

Combine all ingredients except mushrooms and steak. Pour over steak and mushrooms and marinate for 2 hrs. at room temperature. Alternate mushrooms and steak on skewers. Grill over hot coals.

Mrs. William Boyer

SUKIYAKI SKEWERS   2 servings

⅓ cup soy sauce	½ lb. fresh *whole*
¼ cup honey	green beans
¼ tsp. ground ginger	4-5 large carrots,
1 clove garlic, minced	cut into 3" sticks
1 lb. sirloin tip, cut	melted butter
in thin strips	

For marinade combine soy sauce, honey, ginger and garlic. Add meat and refrigerate 3-4 hrs. Cook vegetables until just tender. Wrap half of meat strips around bundles of 3-4 beans; repeat with remaining meat and bundles of 3 or 4 carrot sticks. Thread kabobs on 2 parallel skewers, ladder-fashion. Brush with melted butter. Broil over hot coals about 10-12 mins., turning once. Serve with rice.

Mrs. Michael Calahan

TERIYAKI
serves 8-10

2 tsp. M.S.G.
6 T. sugar
1 cup soy sauce
1 T. fresh lemon juice
2 jiggers bourbon

3 cloves garlic, crushed
1 tsp. ginger
4-5 lbs. top round
   of sirloin, 1¾" thick
sautéed mushrooms (optional)

Combine all ingredients except meat and mushrooms. Pour over meat and marinate 24 hrs. in refrigerator. Drain marinade. Grill 16 mins. on one side; turn, grill 14 mins. more for medium rare. Slice diagonally and serve with sautéed mushrooms.

Mrs. Robert Hall
Mrs. Paul Dykema

GREEK LAMB SHISH KABOBS
6 servings

3 T. oil
3 T. vinegar
3 dashes Worcestershire
   sauce
¼ tsp. oregano
⅛ tsp. pepper
1 clove garlic, crushed
2 lbs. lamb, cut in 1" cubes

whole mushrooms
lemon slices
bay leaves
cherry tomatoes
potato slices
green pepper slices
small onions, skinned

Combine oil, vinegar, Worcestershire sauce, oregano, pepper and garlic. Pour over lamb and marinate in refrigerator overnight. Drain meat and reserve marinade. Alternate lamb on lightly greased skewers with remaining ingredients. Broil over hot coals 15-20 mins. basting with sauce. Turn skewers frequently. Serve with rice and Greek salad.

Mrs. William Baum

MARINATED LAMB CHOPS
4 servings

4 lamb chops,
  cut 1" thick
¼ cup peanut or
  vegetable oil
salt and pepper
Butter Sauce:
  ¼ cup butter
  2 T. shallots, chopped

1 tsp. rosemary
1 tsp. oregano
fresh lemon juice (optional)
chopped fresh parsley
  (optional)

1 small clove garlic,
  minced

Place lamb chops in plastic bag. Combine remaining ingredients, pour over chops, and marinate at least 1 hr. Turn occasionally to blend flavors. Drain chops and broil 8-10 mins. or till done. Remove chops to serving plate. Spoon butter sauce on top and sprinkle with lemon juice and chopped parsley.

For butter sauce, combine ingredients and cook until it begins to brown.

Mrs. William Baum

HAWAIIAN HAM STEAK
8 servings

½ cup oil
1 cup honey
½ cup cider vinegar
1 tsp. ground ginger
½ tsp. pepper
1 tsp. dry mustard

pinch ground cloves
3 lbs. ham steak, cut
  1½" thick
8 canned pineapple slices
2 T. pecans, chopped

Combine oil, honey, vinegar, ginger, pepper, mustard and cloves in a small saucepan; heat to boiling stage. Grill ham over hot coals 10 mins. Brush with glaze; turn. Grill ham 10-15 mins. more brushing with sauce. Grill pineapple slices alongside ham, brushing with sauce. Place pineapple atop ham during last 5 mins. of grilling. When nicely glazed and hot, sprinkle with nuts.

Mrs. Jack Dozeman

HOT HAM AND CHEESE SANDWICHES

12 sandwiches

½ lb. ham, cubed
½ lb. sharp cheese, cubed
⅓ cup green onion, sliced
2 hard-boiled eggs, sliced
½ cup stuffed olives, sliced

3 - 4 T. mayonnaise
½ cup chili sauce
12 hamburger or hot dog
buns split

Combine all ingredients except buns. Fill each bun with mixture and wrap in aluminum foil. Place on grill 10 mins. or in 400F. oven for 15 mins.

Mrs. Douglas Neckers

BARBECUED PORK CHOPS

4 servings

4 thick center-cut loin
pork chops, 1½ lbs.
1 tsp. dry mustard
1 tsp. ginger
¼ cup soy sauce

¼ cup oil
¼ cup steak sauce
3 garlic cloves, minced
1 T. brown sugar

Place chops in a glass casserole. Mix remaining ingredients and pour over chops. Cover and refrigerate. Marinate overnight, turning several times. Grill over medium coals and baste occasionally with the marinade.

Mrs. Thomas Buis

PORK STACK-UPS

8 servings

3 lbs. boned pork loin
roast, tied in 8 places
16 strips of bacon
8 slices onion, ½" thick

8 tomato slices, ½" thick
1 (10 oz.) pkg. Cracker
Barrel Cheddar Cheese,
cut into 8 pieces

Slice pork roast into 8 pieces, each slice tied by a string. Take 2 pieces of bacon and crisscross them. On top of bacon, center a slice of pork, onion, tomato, and top with cheese. Bring ends of bacon up and over stack and toothpick in place. Repeat for remainder of ingredients. Adjust grill several inches from fire. Bake over low heat in a covered grill for 50 to 60 mins.

Mrs. Herbert Eldean

299

PLUM-SAUCED SPARERIBS
10 servings

10 lbs. spareribs
1 T. salt
2 T. butter
1 onion, chopped
1 (17 oz.) can purple plums
⅓ cup chili sauce
⅓ cup soy sauce

1 (6 oz.) can lemonade
   concentrate, thawed
   and undiluted
1½ tsp. ginger
2 tsp. mustard
1 tsp. Worcestershire sauce
3 drops hot sauce

Several hrs. before serving, cut up ribs into 3 rib portions; put in large pan with water and salt. Simmer, covered, 1½ hrs. Drain. Meanwhile sauté onion in butter until tender. Remove pits from plums and puree plums with syrup in blender. Add plums and remaining ingredients to onions and simmer 15 mins. Place ribs on grill over medium heat and cook 30-45 mins. or until fork tender. Baste with sauce often and turn occasionally.

Mrs. James Nelson

HONEY GLAZED CHICKEN
6-8 servings

1 (8 oz.) can tomato sauce
½ cup olive oil
½ cup orange juice
¼ cup vinegar
1½ tsp. oregano, crushed

1 tsp. salt
6 peppercorns
1 clove garlic, minced
2 whole chicken breasts, split
4 chicken legs & thighs

Honey-Mustard Glaze:
¼ cup honey

½ tsp. dry mustard

Combine all ingredients, except chicken, in screw top jar. Pour mixture over chicken and marinate 2 hrs. at room temperature or overnight in refrigerator. Drain and reserve marinade. Grill chicken 45-50 mins. over medium coals brushing frequently with marinade. Just before serving brush chicken with honey and mustard mixture.

Mrs. William Mendenhall

LEMON GRILLED CHICKEN

6 servings

2 young frying chickens,
  quartered

salt and freshly ground
  pepper

Lemon Barbecue Sauce:
⅔ cup olive oil
½ cup fresh lemon juice
¾ cup white wine
3 T. onion, finely-chopped
1-3 tsp. dried tarragon

1-3 tsp. parsley, finely
  chopped
salt and pepper
dash Tabasco

Sprinkle chicken with salt and pepper. Combine all ingredients for lemon barbecue sauce and pour over chicken. Marinate for at least 4 hrs. When ready to grill, drain chicken pieces, reserving juices. Grill 6" from coals over low heat until tender about 45-60 mins. Turn chicken pieces from time to time and baste with marinade.

Mrs. L. C. Miller

PATIO CHICKEN

serves 4

3 cups cooked rice
1(1¼) pkg. dried onion
  soup mix

1 broiler-fryer chicken,
  cut up about 2½-3 lbs.
½ cup evaporated milk
4 tsp. butter

Cut 4 pieces of heavy duty foil each 8" x 12". Put ¼ rice on each piece of foil. Sprinkle 1 T. onion soup mix over each. Put chicken pieces on rice. On each pour 2 T. evaporated milk, 1 T. onion soup mix, and 1 T. butter. Fold foil securely. Place on grill over medium heat. Cook on covered grill about 1 hr. 15 min.

Mrs. Gerald Boeve

BARBECUED TURKEY

10-14 servings

10-15 lb. turkey
½ cup butter, melted
½ cup oil
2 cups cider vinegar
1 cup catsup
⅓ cup fresh lemon juice
¼ cup Worcestershire sauce

½ cup sugar
2 medium onions, grated
2 T. dry mustard
2-3 T. chili powder
2 tsp. pepper
2 tsp. salt
2 garlic cloves, crushed

Wash turkey, pat dry. Insert spit rod in turkey, running it through tail and diagonally through breastbone. Fasten turkey with spit forks. Wings and legs should be tied closely to body. Be sure turkey is properly balanced. Insert meat thermometer. Make a drip pan of foil to catch drippings and place under turkey. Combine remaining ingredients. Cook turkey over medium heat basting with sauce every 15-20 mins. while it rotates. Cook about 20 mins. per pound or until meat thermometer registers 185F. Serve with remaining barbecue sauce.

Mrs. Robert Bauspies

BARBECUED FISH

4-6 servings

3 lbs. fresh fish fillets
  (halibut, flounder, salmon)
⅔ cup olive oil
¼ cup wine vinegar
¼ cup dry sherry
2 T. soy sauce

1-2 garlic cloves,
  finely minced
1 bay leaf, finely crushed
½ tsp. ground ginger
1 T. sugar

Arrange fish fillets in shallow dish. Combine remaining ingredients and pour over fish. Marinate for at least 2 hrs. To cook, place drained fish on a well-oiled grill over glowing charcoal. Cook for 10-15 mins., brushing from time to time with marinade. Cook until fish is tender. Remove carefully to heated serving dish. Brush with remaining marinade and serve immediately.

Mrs. Donald G. Miller

FISH IN CORN HUSKS

small whole fish, cleaned
(perch, bluegills etc.)
butter
lemon juice

salt and pepper
bacon strips (optional)
de-silked corn husks

In the cavity of each fish, place a lump of butter, a generous squirt of lemon juice, salt and pepper. Place a strip of bacon down each side of fish. Wrap each fish in a whole de-silked corn husk; (if husks are dry soak in water 5 mins.) tie with string on silk end. Place on bed of hot coals; top with more hot coals. Cook about 15 mins. or until fish flakes when tested with fork.

Mrs. Darrel Schuurman

FOIL-BAKED FISH   4 servings

3 lbs. fresh or frozen halibut
steak, 1-1½" thick or any
comparable white, firm
fleshed fish or fillets
1 tsp. salt
¼ tsp. pepper
¼ tsp. paprika

¼ cup margarine, melted
5 slices bacon, minced
1 large green pepper, minced
1 large red pepper, minced
1 large onion, minced
1 cup sour cream

Cut fish in 4 serving-size portions. Sprinkle with salt, pepper, and paprika. Use 4 pieces of heavy duty foil each about 18" x 24". Fold in half crosswise. Brush one side with butter. Place portion of fish on buttered side of each foil. Fry bacon until almost crisp. Add peppers and onion and cook until tender not brown. Stir in sour cream. Spoon ¼ of sour cream mixture on top of each fish portion. Seal foil and grill close to hot coals 20-25 mins. Open one packet to see if fish flakes when tested with a fork. Fillets will take less time than fish steaks.

Mrs. Wm. Beebe

GRILLED COHO SALMON   *10 servings*

10-12 lbs. coho salmon   **1 tsp. lemon juice**
⅓ cup brown sugar   **salt and pepper**
⅔ cup butter

Clean and fillet fish leaving skin intact if possible. Combine remaining ingredients. Over a hot bed of coals, put a layer of aluminum foil on grill. Poke holes in foil so fat will drain through. (If skinned fish are used, no holes need to be made in foil.) Lay fish fillet on foil, skin side down. Spread with brown sugar mixture. Grill 10-15 mins. in covered grill. Then lift up fish (the skin will remain on the foil) turn over replacing fish on skin and repeat basting with sauce and seasonings. Let grill 10-15 mins. longer or until fish flakes. Serve hot or cold. Very rich and very good.

Mrs. Earl Welling

TROUT GRILL AU VIN   *4 servings*

4 fresh or frozen trout   **¼ cup dry white wine**
4 slices bacon   **2 T. almonds, chopped**
salt and pepper   **¼ cup grated Parmesan**
¼ cup butter, melted   **cheese**

Season trout with salt and pepper. Wrap a bacon slice around each trout. Place on grill over hot coals. Brush with mixture of butter and wine. Broil, basting frequently. Turn and continue basting. Just before trout is done, sprinkle with almonds and cheese. Leave on grill until cheese melts.

Mrs. Donald G. Miller

BARBECUED CORN   *12 servings*

12 ears corn, husked   **½ cup barbecue sauce**
and silked   **½ tsp. salt**
1 cup margarine, melted   **¼ tsp. pepper**

Place each ear on a thick sheet of foil. Combine margarine, barbecue sauce, salt and pepper; brush over corn. Wrap foil around corn; twist ends. Place ears on grill over hot coals. Turn often, 15-25 mins., depending on temperature of coals.

Mrs. Jack Dozeman

ROASTED CORN

corn on the cob with husks   **butter**

Clean corn by throwing away outer husks and stripping inner husks to the end of cob (but do not tear off). Clean off silk. Soak corn with husks pulled back in ice water for 20-25 mins. (lay cubes right on top of ears). Spread corn with plenty of butter; do not salt until after it is cooked. Pull husks up around the buttered corn, making certain all kernels are covered with husks. Then wrap ears in double thickness of aluminum foil. Cook on hot grill 8-10 mins. on each side.

Mrs. Thomas DePree

GRILLED ONIONS

large sweet onions   *freshly ground pepper*
butter   *bacon*
salt

Pare large sweet onions and remove a thin slice from top and bottom of each. Make 4 cuts ¾ of the way through onion from top to bottom, forming 8 uniform pie-shape wedges. Carefully cut out centers of onions to a depth of 1". Place 1 T. butter in hollow and sprinkle generously with salt and freshly ground pepper. Crisscross 2 half strips of bacon over each onion. Wrap each in foil and bake 1 hr. or until tender.

Mrs. Robert De Bruyn

ONION AND POTATOES IN FOIL   *4 servings*

4 medium baking potatoes   *½ cup soft butter*
4 medium onions, thinly   *2 tsp. seasoned salt*
  sliced   *paprika*

Cut 4 rectangles of heavy duty foil, each 12" x 18". Slice a potato crosswise into ¼" thick slices. Place a potato in center of a foil rectangle, keeping original shape of potato. Insert an onion slice between each 2 potato slices. Spread each top with 2 T. butter; sprinkle with ½ tsp. salt and a dash paprika. Seal packages by folding sides and ends twice. Place packages directly on hot coals. Roast 40 mins., turning occasionally.

Mrs. James Nelson

FOILED PARMESAN POTATOES   *4 servings*

3 large new baking potatoes   ⅓ cup grated Parmesan
onion salt   cheese
celery salt   ⅓ cup butter
salt and pepper

Scrub potatoes (do not pare). Cut each potato into ¼" lengthwise slices. Spread out on a heavy duty foil 18" x 20". Sprinkle generously with salts, pepper, and cheese. Overlap potato slices and dot with butter. Bring edges of foil together, leaving room for expansion of steam. Seal with a double fold. Place packet on grill and cook 30-45 mins. or till done. Turn frequently.

Mrs. Darrell Schuurman

CRUNCHY-TOPPED TOMATOES   *6 servings*

6 large ripe tomatoes   ⅓ cup sharp process
salt and pepper   American cheese, shredded
⅓ cup crushed seasoned   1½ T. margarine, melted
   croutons   snipped parsley

Slice tops off of tomatoes. Cut zigzag edges; season with salt and pepper. Combine crouton crumbs, cheese and margarine; sprinkle over tomatoes. Heat tomatoes on foil over coals till warm through. Garnish with snipped parsley. Serve immediately.

Mrs. Herbert Eldean

SKEWERED VEGETABLES

6 servings

3 medium zucchini,
    cut in 2" chunks
12 small red onions,
    peeled
12 jumbo pitted black
    olives

3 T. oil
3 T. vinegar
1 tsp. garlic salt
1 T. oregano
2 T. red pepper flakes

Place vegetables in shallow dish. Combine remaining ingredients and pour over vegetables. Marinate about 1 hr. Reserving marinade, alternate vegetables on lightly greased skewers and wrap in foil. Place on grill 6" from heat; cook 8-10 mins., turning frequently. Open foil and brush with marinade. Cook until zucchini is tender.

Mrs. James Nelson

ZUCCHINI CREOLE

8-10 servings

8 medium zucchini,
    cut into ½" pieces
1 large onion, sliced
1 large green pepper, sliced
½ lb. fresh mushrooms, sliced
1 clove garlic, crushed
4 tsp. butter
½ tsp. Worcestershire sauce

1 (1 lb.) can tomatoes,
    drained
½ tsp. sugar
1 tsp. salt
¼ tsp. pepper
½ tsp. oregano
pinch sweet basil

Combine all ingredients and place on a large rectangle of heavy duty foil. Seal foil with a double fold and place on grill over medium heat. Cook 45-60 mins. or till vegetables are tender. Turn occasionally.

Mrs. Herbert Eldean

PINEAPPLE ON A SPIT
6-8 servings

1 medium pineapple   **½ cup maple syrup**
whole cloves   **½ tsp. cinnamon**

Pare pineapple leaving leafy crown intact. Remove eyes and stud with cloves. Center pineapple on spit and secure tightly. Wrap leafy end in foil. Let rotate over hot coals 45 mins. to 1 hr. basting frequently with sauce made by combining syrup and cinnamon.

Mrs. Paul Dykema

HERBED BREAD
8 servings

½ cup butter   **¼ tsp. tarragon**
¼ tsp. basil   **¼ tsp. parsley**
¼ tsp. marjoram   **loaf of French bread**

Cut bread into 1" slices, cutting to but not quite through bottom crust. Melt butter; add herbs. Brush herb mixture on slices and across top. Wrap in double thickness of foil; seal with double fold on top and ends. Heat in covered grill 15-20 mins. For a crisp crust loosen foil on top and ends 5 mins. before end of heating time.

Parmesan Herb Bread Variation: Omit the herbs above and use ¼ cup Parmesan cheese, 4 tsp. chopped parsley, 1 tsp. oregano, and ¼ tsp. garlic salt.

Mrs. Wm. Lalley
Mrs. George Daily

ALL-PURPOSE BARBECUE SAUCE — 3 cups

2 cups oil
½ cup soy sauce
½ cup Worcestershire sauce
2 cloves garlic, crushed
8-10 drops liquid smoke
1 tsp. paprika
1 T. oregano, crumbled
salt and pepper to taste

Combine all ingredients in large jar; refrigerate for several hrs. to blend flavors. This sauce can be brushed on any meat but is especially good for chicken. For a distinct flavor, marinate meat in sauce overnight before grilling. Sauce may be stored in refrigerator.

Mrs. William Boyer

FAST AND EASY BARBECUE SAUCE — 1½ cups

1 T. margarine
¼ cup onion, chopped
⅛ tsp. pepper
4 tsp. sugar
1 tsp. mustard
4 tsp. Worcestershire sauce
½ cup catsup
½ cup water
¼ cup vinegar

Sauté onion in butter until clear. Add remaining ingredients and simmer uncovered for about 10 mins.

Mrs. Randall Vande Water

SOUTHERN BARBECUE SAUCE

3 T. prepared mustard
2 T. Worcestershire sauce
2 T. barbecue sauce
½ tsp. Tabasco sauce
¼ tsp. cayenne pepper
1 tsp. garlic salt or
   small clove garlic, crushed
½ tsp. allspice
2 T. onion juice
   (or chopped onion)
1 tsp. parsley (optional)
1 (14 oz.) bottle catsup
½ cup vinegar
1¾ cups sugar

Mix all ingredients together and chill overnight.

Mrs. Charles Knowles

FRESH TOMATO BARBECUE SAUCE   *1 qt.*

4 lbs. fresh tomatoes, peeled   *1 cup chili sauce*
* and chopped*   *¼ cup Worcestershire sauce*
1 cup onions, chopped   *¼ cup fresh lemon juice*
2 cloves garlic, minced   *2 tsp. salt*
1 cup brown sugar, packed   *1 tsp. dry mustard*
¼ cup butter

Combine all ingredients in large saucepan. Bring to a boil. Reduce heat and simmer uncovered, 1½ hrs., or until thickened.

Mrs. John Hutchinson

SWEET-SOUR STEAK SAUCE

1 (14 oz.) bottle catsup   *½ cup water*
¼ cup bottled steak sauce   *¼ cup pineapple juice*
⅔ cup brown sugar   *1 tsp. horseradish*
¼ cup cider vinegar   * (optional)*

Combine all ingredients and simmer 5-10 mins.

Mrs. Paul Dykema

WINE BASTING SAUCE AND MARINADE $3\frac{1}{2}$ cups

1 ½ cups peanut or
   salad oil
1 cup dry red wine
¾ cup soy sauce
⅓ cup lemon juice
2 T. Worcestershire sauce

2 T. salt
1 T. freshly ground pepper
2 tsp. dried parsley
   flakes
2 T. dry mustard

Combine all ingredients in quart jar. Shake vigorously. Marinade can be drained from meat and reused. It can be frozen for future use. Wonderful flavor for sirloin steaks and will help tenderize economical cuts of meat.

Mrs. Robert King

VERMOUTH BASTING SAUCE 1 cup

½ cup olive or salad oil
½ cup dry Vermouth

2 tsp. salt
dash of pepper

Combine all ingredients. Excellent for basting almost anything, but especially good on grilled pork chops or fish that may be dry.

Mrs. William Lalley

NOTES

Our Best Breads

NOTES

ALMOND BREAD

2 loaves

1 cup Grape Nuts cereal
3 cups milk
1 cup almond paste, cut into
small pieces
1 tsp. butter
2 eggs, beaten

1½ cups sugar
3 cups flour
2 tsp. baking powder
1 tsp. baking soda
1 tsp. salt

Combine cereal and milk; soak for 1 hr. Preheat oven to 350F. Grease 2 8x4x2" loaf pans. Cream almond paste, butter, eggs and sugar. Add milk mixture; sift together flour, baking powder, soda and salt. Add to creamed mixture. Pour into loaf pans. Bake 1 hr. Cool 10 min.; remove from pan.

Mrs. Robert Van Wieren

APPLE BREAD

1 loaf

1 cup sugar
⅓ cup shortening
1 egg, beaten
1 cup apple, finely chopped
¾ cup small raisins
¼ cup nuts, chopped

⅓ cup orange juice
1 tsp. orange peel, grated
2 cups flour
1 tsp. baking powder
½ tsp. salt
1 tsp. baking soda

Preheat oven to 350F. Grease a 9x5x3" loaf pan or 3 (1 lb. each) food cans. Cream sugar and shortening. Add beaten egg. Add fruit, nuts, juice and peel. Sift together flour, baking powder, salt and soda. Add sifted ingredients and mix well. Pour into loaf pan; bake 1 hr. Cool 10 min.; remove from pan. Fill cans ¾ full; bake 35-40 min. Leave in cans until cold.

Mrs. Russell Klaasen

DUTCH APPLE BREAD   *1 loaf*

1 cup sugar	1 tsp. baking soda
½ cup margarine	1 tsp. salt
2 eggs, unbeaten	1 tsp. vanilla
2 T. sour milk	2 cups apples,
2 cups flour	finely chopped

Topping:
2 T. sugar	1 tsp. cinnamon
2 T. flour	chopped nuts, optional
2 T. butter	

Preheat oven to 350F. Grease a 9x5x3'' loaf pan. Cream sugar and margarine. Blend in eggs and sour milk. Sift together flour, soda and salt; add to creamed mixture. Mix in vanilla and apples. Pour into pan. Combine topping ingredients; cut through until crumbly. Sprinkle over batter in pan. Bake 1 hr. Cool 10 min.; remove from pan.

"Eet Smakelijk's Best"

SPICED APPLESAUCE BREAD   *1 loaf*

1½ cups applesauce	½ tsp. baking powder
1 cup sugar	¼ tsp. salt
½ cup oil	¼ tsp. allspice
2 eggs	½ tsp. cinnamon
3 T. milk	¼ tsp. nutmeg
2 cups flour	½ cup pecans, chopped
1 tsp. baking soda	

Topping:
¼ cup pecans, chopped	½ tsp. cinnamon
¼ cup brown sugar	

Preheat oven to 350F. Grease a 9x5x3'' loaf pan. Combine applesauce, sugar, oil, eggs and milk. Sift together flour, soda, baking powder, salt and spices. Add to first mixture; beat well. Fold in nuts. Pour into pan. Combine topping ingredients; sprinkle on top. Bake 50-60 min. Cool 10 min. Remove from pan.

Mrs. Gary Jalving

BLUEBERRY ORANGE BREAD   *2 loaves*

2 T. margarine	*1 cup sugar*
¼ cup boiling water	*2 cups flour*
½ cup orange juice (remove	*1 tsp. baking soda*
1 T. for glaze)	*1 tsp. salt*
3 T. orange rind, grated	*1 cup blueberries*
1 egg	

Glaze:
½ cup confectioners' sugar	*1 T. hot water*
1 T. orange juice	

Preheat oven to 350F. Grease 2 7⅜ x 3⅝" loaf pans. Melt margarine in water. Add juice and rind. Beat in egg and sugar. Sift together flour, soda and salt; add to mixture. Fold in blueberries. Pour into pan. Bake 50-60 min.

Combine ingredients for glaze. Drizzle over bread while hot. Cool 10 min.; remove from pans.

Barb Zoet
Mrs. Henry Bouwman

BOSTON BROWN BREAD   *6 small loaves*

1½ cups raisins	*2 T. molasses*
1½ cups water	*2¾ cups flour*
2 T. shortening	*2 tsp. baking soda*
1 cup sugar	*1 tsp. salt*
1 egg	

Preheat oven to 325F. Grease and flour 6 (1 lb. each) food cans. Cook raisins in water for 7 min. over medium heat in covered pan; set aside. Cream shortening and sugar. Add egg and molasses; mix thoroughly. Sift together flour, soda and salt. Add to creamed mixture alternately with raisins and water. Fill cans ½ full. Cover tightly with foil. Bake 1 hr. Cool 10 min.; remove from cans. Wrap and store overnight.

Mrs. Clyde Line

RAISIN BROWN BREAD
6 small loaves

2 lb. dark raisins
1 cup yellow raisins
4 tsp. baking soda
2 heaping T. shortening
3 cups boiling water
1½ cups sugar

1 tsp. salt
2 T. molasses
2 eggs, beaten
3 cups flour
1½ cups All-Bran

Preheat oven to 350F. Use 6 (1 lb. each) ungreased food cans. Combine raisins, soda, shortening and water; set aside to cool. Combine remaining ingredients; add to cooled raisin mixture. Mix well. Fill cans ¾ full. Bake 1 hr. Remove from cans when cooled. This freezes well. After freezing, wrap in foil and heat to serve warm.

Mrs. Jack DeRoo

CARROT BREAD
1 loaf

1 cup sugar
½ cup oil
2 eggs
1½ cups flour
1 tsp. baking soda

½ tsp. salt
1 tsp. vanilla
1 cup carrots, grated
½ cup nuts, chopped
¾ tsp. cinnamon (optional)

Preheat oven to 350F. Grease an 8x4x2" loaf pan or 3 (1 lb. each) food cans. Mix sugar, oil and eggs together. Sift together flour, soda and salt; add to mixture. Add vanilla, carrots, nuts and cinnamon. Mix well. Pour into pan; bake 1 hr. Fill cans ⅔ full; bake 45 min. Cool 10 min.; remove from pan.

Mrs. Norman Japinga
Mrs. Charles Vander Meulen

CINNAMON BREAD
1 loaf

1 egg
1 cup sugar
¼ cup Wesson Oil
2 cups flour
½ tsp. salt

1 tsp. baking soda
1 cup buttermilk or
  sour milk
½ cup sugar
1 T. cinnamon

Preheat oven to 350F. Grease a 9x5x3" loaf pan. Beat egg, sugar and oil. Sift together flour, salt and soda; add to mixture alternately with buttermilk. Place ½ batter in pan; sprinkle with half the sugar-cinnamon mixture. Repeat; swirl with knife. Bake 1 hr. Cool 10 min.; remove from pan.

Mrs. Ken Michmerhuizen

CREAMY DOUBLE CORN BREAD
8 servings

3 eggs
1 cup sour cream
⅓ cup oil
1 (8¾ oz.) can cream
  style corn

½ tsp. salt
1 T. baking powder
1 cup yellow corn meal

Preheat oven to 375F. Grease a 9x9" baking pan. Combine eggs, sour cream, oil and corn; mix well. Add salt, baking powder and corn meal, mixing well. Turn into pan. Bake 30-35 min. Cut in serving pieces and serve at once.

Mrs. Charles Kramer

YULETIDE CRANBERRY LOAF
1 loaf

2 cups flour
½ tsp. salt
1½ tsp. baking powder
½ tsp. baking soda
1 cup sugar
¼ cup margarine, melted

½ cup orange juice
1 egg, well beaten
1 T. grated orange rind
1½ cups fresh cranberries, halved
¾ cup nuts, chopped

Preheat oven to 350F. Grease well an 8 x 4 x 2" loaf pan. Sift together flour, salt, baking powder, baking soda and sugar. Combine margarine with orange juice and egg. Add to dry ingredients, stir just to moisten. Stir in cranberries and nuts. Bake 1 hr.

Mrs. Morris Rogers

DATE WALNUT LOAF BREAD
1 loaf

1 (8 oz.) pkg. pitted dates, cut in small pieces
1¼ cups boiling water
1½ cups brown sugar, firmly packed
6 T. margarine

1 egg, beaten
¾ cup walnuts, chopped
2¼ cups flour
1½ tsp. baking soda
1½ tsp. salt

Preheat oven to 350F. Grease a 9x5x3" loaf pan. Pour boiling water over dates. Stir in sugar and margarine; cool to room temperature. Stir in egg and walnuts. Sift together flour, soda and salt; stir quickly into date mixture until just blended. Pour into pan. Bake 1 hr. or until center is firm. Cool 10 min.; remove from pan. Serve with Orange Butter.

Mrs. James Crozier

ORANGE BUTTER
1 pound
Delicious with quick breads

4 oranges
1½ cups confectioners' sugar

2 cups butter

Grate rind from 2 oranges. Extract juice from all 4 oranges; strain. Add rind and sugar to juice, dissolving sugar as much as possible. Add to butter with electric beater. Mix until well blended. Either remold or place in a jelly jar. Chill before serving.

Mrs. J.K. Brown

FRUIT NUT BREAD
1 loaf

Freezes beautifully

3 cups walnuts, whole
1 lb. dates, halved
1 (8 oz.) jar maraschino
  cherries, drained and halved
¾ cup flour
¾ cup sugar
½ tsp. baking powder
½ tsp. salt
3 eggs
1 tsp. vanilla

Preheat oven to 300F. Grease a 9x5x3" loaf pan or 3 (1 lb. each) food cans. Combine walnuts and fruits. Sift together flour, sugar, baking powder and salt; add to fruit mixture. Mix in eggs and vanilla. Mixture will be very lumpy and not too moist. Spoon into pan; bake 1 hr. or until done. Fill cans ¾ full; bake 45 min. or until done. Cool 10 min.; remove from pan or cans.

Mrs. Robert Hulst

HOLIDAY FRUIT BREAD
9 small loaves

1 lb. raisins
2¼ cups water
1 lb. pitted dates, cut up
1 cup flour
¼ cup shortening
2 cups sugar
2 eggs
1 tsp. vanilla
1 (20 oz.) can crushed
  pineapple, drained
  (save juice)
32 maraschino cherries,
  halved
1 cup nuts, chopped
4½ cups flour
4 tsp. baking soda
1 tsp. salt

Preheat oven to 375F. Grease 9 (1 lb. each) food cans. Simmer raisins with water for 15 min. Drain, saving juice. Mix dates with warm raisins. When cool, shake flour through mixture. Cream shortening, sugar, eggs and vanilla. Add pineapple, cherries and nuts. Sift together flour, soda and salt. Combine raisin juice with enough pineapple juice to make 2 cups. Add alternately with sifted ingredients to creamed mixture. Add raisins and dates. Fill cans ⅔ full; bake 40-45 min. or until done. Cool 10 min.; remove from cans.

Mrs. Rufus Van Omen

VRUCHTENBROOD
Dutch Harvest Bread

1 loaf

2 cups flour
4 tsp. baking powder
¼ tsp. salt
¾ cup sugar
¼ cup each, citron
   and currants
2 T. candied cherries, chopped

2 T. candied
   lemon peel, chopped
½ cup nuts, chopped
2 eggs, beaten
1 cup milk
3 T. shortening, melted

Preheat oven to 375 F. Grease a 9x5x3" loaf pan. Sift together flour, baking powder, salt and sugar. Add fruits and nuts. Combine eggs, milk and shortening; add to flour mixture stirring just enough to moisten flour. Turn into pan. Bake 1 hr. Cool 10 min.; remove from pan.

Miss Alice V. Althuis

LEMON BREAD

1 loaf

1 cup margarine
1 cup sugar
2 eggs
1½ cups flour

1 tsp. baking powder
½ tsp. salt
½ cup milk
rind of 1 lemon, grated

Glaze:
juice of 1 lemon

½ cup sugar

Preheat oven to 350F. Grease an 8x4x2" loaf pan. Cream margarine, sugar and eggs. Sift together flour, baking powder and salt; add to creamed mixture alternately with milk. Stir in lemon rind. Pour into pan. Bake 45-50 min.

Combine ingredients for glaze. Pour over bread while hot. Cool 10 min.; remove from pan.

Mrs. Michael Calahan

324

ORANGE NUT BREAD

1 loaf

¾ cup sugar
3 T. margarine, softened
2 eggs
1 cup orange rind,
    finely chopped (2 oranges)

½ cup walnuts, chopped
2¼ cups flour
1 T. baking powder
1 tsp. salt
1 cup milk

Preheat oven to 350F. Grease a 9x5x3" loaf pan. Cream sugar and margarine until fluffy. Beat in eggs, one at a time. Mix in orange rind and nuts. Sift together flour, baking powder and salt. Add small amounts to first mixture alternately with milk, until blended. Pour into pan. Bake 55-60 min. Cool 10 min; remove from pan.

If kept in freezer, slice while frozen. To "waffle" it, toast unbuttered half-inch slices in hot waffle baker until just nicely browned.

Mrs. Carl Harrington

PINEAPPLE NUT BREAD

1 loaf

2 cups flour
½ cup sugar
1 tsp. baking powder
1 tsp. baking soda
½ tsp. salt
1 cup raisins

½ cup walnuts, chopped
1 egg, beaten
1 tsp. vanilla
2 T. shortening, melted
1 cup crushed pineapple,
    slightly drained

Preheat oven to 350F. Grease a 9x5x3" loaf pan. Sift together flour, sugar, baking powder, soda and salt into mixing bowl; add raisins and nuts. Combine egg, vanilla and shortening; add to above mixture. Stir in pineapple. Pour into pan. Bake 1 hr. Cool 10 min.; remove from pan.

Mrs. Paul Hooker

PRUNE BREAD
2 loaves

2 cups cooked prunes, cut up
  or combination of dates
  and raisins
1 ¾ cups hot juice or water
1 cup sugar
2 T. shortening

1 egg
1 tsp. vanilla
3 cups flour
1 tsp. salt
2 tsp. baking soda
dash cinnamon

Preheat oven to 350F. Grease 2 7⅜ x 3⅝" loaf pans. Combine prunes and juice; set aside. Cream sugar and shortening; add egg and vanilla. Sift together flour, salt, soda and cinnamon; add to mixture. Stir in prunes and juice. Pour into pans. Bake 1 hr. Cool 10 min.; remove from pans.

Mrs. Robert Slocum

PRUNE NUT BREAD
1 loaf

2 T. shortening
1 cup sugar
1 egg, beaten
1 (7 oz.) jar baby food prunes
½ cup milk

1½ cups flour
1 tsp. baking soda
1 tsp. salt
½ cup nuts, chopped,
  or raisins

Preheat oven to 375F. Grease a 9x5x3" loaf pan. Cream shortening, sugar and egg. Mix in prunes and milk. Sift together flour, soda and salt; add to mixture. Stir in nuts. Pour into pan. Bake 1 hr. Cool 10 min.; remove from pan.

Mrs. Robert Dykstra
Mrs. Terry Hofmeyer

GLAZED PUMPKIN BREAD   1 loaf

2 cups biscuit mix
½ cup sugar
½ tsp. cinnamon
½ tsp. allspice
¼ tsp. ground cloves

½ cup canned pumpkin
½ cup golden raisins
1 egg, slightly beaten
¾ cup milk
2 T. oil

Glaze:
1 cup confectioners' sugar
1 T. cream

few drops yellow food color

Preheat oven to 350F. Grease a 9x5x3" loaf pan. Blend biscuit mix with sugar and spices. Combine pumpkin and raisins with egg, milk and oil. Add to dry ingredients, stirring just until blended. Pour into pan. Bake 45-50 min. Cool 10 min., remove from pan. Combine ingredients for glaze. Spread over cooled bread.

Mrs. Brian Ward

PUMPKIN BREAD   2 large loaves

3 cups sugar
1 cup vegetable oil
4 eggs, beaten
2 cups pumpkin
3 cups flour
2 tsp. baking soda
1½ tsp. salt
1 tsp. cinnamon

1 tsp. nutmeg
1 tsp. ground cloves
½ tsp. baking powder
⅔ cup water
¾ cups raisins
1 cup walnuts, chopped
rind of 1 lemon, grated

Preheat oven to 350F. Grease 2 9x5x3" loaf pans. In a large bowl mix sugar, oil, eggs, and pumpkin. Beat well. Sift together flour, baking soda, salt, cinnamon, nutmeg, cloves and baking powder. Add dry ingredients alternately with water to pumpkin mixture. Fold in raisins, nuts and lemon rind. Pour into pans. Bake 1 hr., 20 mins., or until done.

Mrs. James Hobler
Mrs. Willis Streur

327

RAISIN ORANGE BREAD   *1 loaf*

1 medium orange
boiling water
1 cup raisins
2 T. margarine, melted
1 tsp. vanilla
1 egg, well beaten
2 cups flour

¼ tsp. baking powder
½ tsp. baking soda
1 cup sugar
½ tsp. salt
½ cup nuts,
   chopped (optional)

Preheat oven to 350F. Grease a 9x5x3" loaf pan. Squeeze juice from orange; save peel. Add boiling water to juice to make 1 cup. Remove most of white membrane from orange peel. Put peel and raisins through food chopper, using coarse blade. Add diluted orange juice. Stir in margarine, vanilla and egg. Sift together flour, baking powder, soda, sugar and salt; add to mixture, mixing well. Stir in nuts. Pour into pan. Bake 1 hr. Cool 10 min.; remove from pan.

Mrs. J.J. Brower

RHUBARB BREAD

1½ cups brown sugar
⅔ cup oil
1 egg
1 cup buttermilk or sour milk
1 tsp. baking soda
2½ cups flour

1 tsp. salt
1½ cups raw rhubarb, cut
   in pieces
1 tsp. lemon extract
1 tsp. lemon rind, grated
½ cup nuts, chopped

Topping:
½ cup sugar
¼ cup nuts, chopped

1 T. margarine
dash of cinnamon

Preheat oven to 350F. Grease 2 7⅜ x 3⅝" loaf pans or a 10" tube pan. Mix sugar, oil, egg, milk and soda. Sift together flour and salt; add to mixture. Fold in rhubarb, lemon extract, rind and nuts. Pour into pans. Combine topping ingredients; sprinkle over batter. Bake 50-60 min. Cool 10 min.; remove from pans.

Mrs. Gary Jalving

SOUTHERN SPOON BREAD
Famous from Boone Tavern Hotel

1 loaf

1¼ cups white corn meal
3 cups boiling milk
3 eggs, well beaten

1 tsp. salt
1¾ tsp. baking powder
2 T. butter, melted

Grease well a 2-qt. casserole. Stir corn meal into rapidly boiling milk. Cook until very thick, stirring constantly to prevent scorching. Remove from heat to cool. Mixture should be cold and very stiff.

Preheat oven to 375F. Add eggs, salt, baking powder and butter. Beat with electric beater for 15 min. Pour into casserole. Bake 30 min. Serve from casserole by spoonfuls.

Mrs. L. W. Lamb, Jr.

FRESH STRAWBERRY BREAD

1 loaf

1 pt. fresh strawberries,
  washed and hulled
1¾ cups flour
1 tsp. baking soda
¾ tsp. salt
½ tsp. cinnamon
¼ tsp. baking powder

1 cup sugar
⅓ cup shortening
2 eggs
⅓ cup water
½ cup walnuts, chopped
cream cheese,
  softened (optional)

Preheat oven to 350F. Grease a 9x5x3" loaf pan. Crush enough berries to make 1 cup crushed. Pour into small saucepan. Heat to boiling over medium heat. Cook one minute, stirring constantly. Cool. Slice remaining strawberries; chill.

In medium bowl combine flour, soda, salt, cinnamon and baking powder. In large mixing bowl cream sugar, shortening and eggs with electric mixer until light and fluffy. Add flour mixture alternately with water to creamed mixture, mixing well after each addition. Stir in crushed strawberries. Fold in walnuts. Spread batter in pan. Bake 50-60 min. or until pick inserted in center comes out clean. Cool in pan 10 min.; remove and cool completely on wire rack.

To serve, cut in thin slices, spread with cream cheese and top with reserved sliced strawberries.

Mrs. Wm. G. Beebe

APPLE PAN WALNUT
12-16 servings

1 (20 oz.) can apple pie filling
2 cups flour
1 cup sugar
1 ½ tsp. baking soda
1 tsp. salt

2 eggs, beaten
1 tsp. vanilla
⅔ cup safflower oil
½ cup walnuts or
   pecans, broken

Topping:
1 cup sugar
½ cup sour cream

½ tsp. baking soda

Preheat oven to 350F. Use an ungreased 9x13" pan. Mix together pie filling, flour, sugar, soda and salt. Add eggs, vanilla, oil and nuts, mixing till blended. Spread in pan. Bake approximately 30 min. Watch carefully as it burns easily. When there are about 10 min. baking time left, prepare topping.

Combine sugar, sour cream and soda in saucepan. Cook, stirring constantly, until it boils. Texture may be funny and brown flecks may appear. When cake is done, prick with fork, pour topping over and sprinkle with nuts. Serve warm or reheat.

Mrs. Anthony Garofalo

BLUEBERRY COFFEE CAKE
12-16 servings

¾ cup sugar
¼ cup butter
1 egg
½ cup milk or ½ cup sour
   cream

2 cups flour
2 tsp. baking powder
¼ tsp. salt
2 cups blueberries

Topping:
½ cup sugar
⅓ cup flour

½ tsp. cinnamon
¼ cup butter
confectioners' sugar glaze

Preheat oven to 375F. Grease a 9x13" pan or 2 8" round pans. Mix the sugar, butter, egg and milk. Sift together flour, baking powder and salt; stir well into mixture. Fold in blueberries. Spread in pan. Combine ingredients for topping. Sprinkle over batter. Bake 50 min. Drizzle with confectioners' sugar glaze, if desired.

Mrs Kenneth Etterbeek
Mrs. Tom Carey

SPICED BUTTERMILK COFFEE CAKE   *12-16 servings*

3 cups sifted flour
2 cups sugar
¾ cup margarine
1 tsp. cloves
½ tsp. cinnamon

½ tsp. nutmeg
2 tsp. baking soda
2 cups buttermilk
¾ cup raisins

Preheat oven to 350F. Grease 2 9" square pans or a 9x13" pan. Cut flour, sugar and margarine with pastry blender until crumbly. Take out ½ cup. To remainder add spices and soda; mix well. Add buttermilk, then raisins. Pour into pan. Sprinkle ½ cup crumbs on top. Bake 45 min.

Mrs. Robert Bernecker

CINNAMON COFFEE CAKE   *8 servings*

1 cup sifted flour
2 tsp. baking powder
1 egg
2 T. oil

1 tsp. vanilla
½ cup sugar
pinch of salt
⅔ cup milk

Topping:
⅓ cup brown sugar
1 tsp. cinnamon

½ cup pecans, chopped
½ cup butter, melted

Preheat oven to 375F. Grease and flour an 8x8" baking pan. Combine all ingredients; beat until smooth. Pour into pan. Combine brown sugar, cinnamon and pecans. Sprinkle over batter. Bake 20-25 min. Pour melted butter on top; return to oven for 5 min.

Mrs. Frank Boonstra

DUTCH COFFEE CAKE   *8 servings*

1½ cups sifted flour
2 tsp. baking powder
¾ tsp. salt
¼ cup sugar
⅓ cup shortening

1 egg, well beaten
⅓ cup milk
3 firm bananas, cut
  diagonally into ¼-½" slices

continued

Streusel Topping:

3 T. butter

⅓ cup sugar

⅓ cup flour

1 tsp. cinnamon

½ cup nuts, chopped

Preheat oven to 375F. Grease well an 8x8x2" cake pan. Sift together flour, baking powder, salt and sugar into mixing bowl. Cut in shortening. Combine egg and milk; add to flour mixture stirring until blended. Turn the stiff dough into pan, spreading evenly over bottom of pan. Cover surface of dough with bananas, overlapping slices.

Cream butter, gradually add sugar and beat well. Blend in flour, cinnamon and nuts. Sprinkle topping over cake. Bake 30 min. This cannot be tested for doneness by the conventional methods. Serve warm.

Mrs. Geroge VanderWal

GERMAN COFFEE CAKE

12-16 servings

½ cup butter

½ cup margarine

1¼ cups sugar

2 eggs, well beaten

1 cup sour cream

2 tsp. vanilla

2¼ cups flour

1 tsp. baking powder

½ tsp. baking soda

Topping:

1 cup nuts, chopped

⅓ cup brown sugar

¼ cup sugar

1 tsp. cinnamon

Preheat oven to 325 F. Grease a 13x9" pan. Cream the butter, margarine and sugar. Beat until fluffy. Mix in eggs, sour cream and vanilla. Sift together flour, baking powder and soda; add to mixture, beating well. Mix together topping ingredients. Put ½ batter in pan. Sprinkle with ½ topping. Repeat with remaining batter and topping. Bake 40 min.

Mrs. Marie Saunders

332

RASPBERRY CREAM
CHEESE COFFEE CAKE
8 servings

1 (3 oz.) pkg. cream cheese
¼ cup margarine
2 cups biscuit mix

⅓ cup milk
½ cup raspberry preserves
confectioners' sugar glaze

Preheat oven to 425F. Grease a baking sheet. Cut cream cheese and margarine into biscuit mix until crumbly. Blend in milk. Turn onto floured surface; knead 8-10 strokes. On waxed paper, roll dough to 12x8" rectangle. Turn onto baking sheet; remove paper. Spread preserves down center of dough. Make 2½" cuts at 1" intervals on long sides. Fold strips over filling. Bake 12-15 min. Drizzle with glaze while warm.

Mrs. James Nelson

RHUBARB COFFEE CAKE
12-16 servings

½ cup margarine
1¼ cups sugar
1 egg
2 cups flour
1 tsp. baking soda

½ tsp. salt
1 cup buttermilk
1 tsp. vanilla
2 cups rhubarb, chopped
  (fresh or frozen)

Topping:
1 tsp. cinnamon
½ cup sugar

2 T. margarine
½ cup nuts, chopped

Preheat oven to 350F. Grease a 9x13" pan or 2 round 9" cake pans. Cream margarine and sugar until light; beat in egg. Sift dry ingredients together and add to creamed mixture alternately with buttermilk. Fold in vanilla and rhubarb. Pour into pan. Combine topping ingredients and sprinkle over batter. Bake 40 min.

Mrs. Richard Taylor

STREUSEL COFFEE CAKE
12-16 servings

Delicious warm or cool

2 eggs, beaten
1 cup sugar
1 cup milk
¼ cup shortening, melted

2 cups flour
1 tsp. salt
1 T. baking powder

Topping:
2 T. butter, melted
⅔ cup brown sugar
2 tsp. cinnamon

2 T. flour
confectioners' sugar glaze

Preheat oven to 375F. Grease a 9x13" pan. Mix eggs, sugar, milk and shortening. Sift together flour, salt and baking powder; add to mixture. Pour into pan. Combine butter, brown sugar, cinnamon and flour. Sprinkle atop batter. Bake 30 min. Glaze while warm.

Mrs. Conrad Eckstrom

SURPRISE COFFEE CAKE
12-16 servings

2 eggs
1½ cups sugar
¼ cup margarine, melted
1 (16 oz.) can fruit cocktail,
  undrained
2¼ cups flour

1½ tsp. baking soda
1 tsp. salt
1 tsp. vanilla
1½ cups coconut
½ cup nuts, chopped

Glaze:
¾ cup sugar
½ cup margarine, melted

¼ cup evaporated milk
½ tsp. vanilla

Preheat oven to 350F. Grease and flour a 13x9" or 15½x10½" pan. Beat eggs and sugar together until light; add margarine. Mix in fruit cocktail. Sift together flour, soda and salt; add, mixing thoroughly. Add vanilla. Turn into pan. Top with coconut and nuts. Bake 30-35 min. for 13x9" pan or 20-25 min. for 15½x10½" pan. Do not overbake. About 5 min. before end of baking time prepare glaze.

Mix ingredients for glaze in saucepan; boil 2 min. Drizzle over coffee cake after removing from oven.

Mrs. Walter Kimberley

DUTCH APPLE FLAPPEN
A traditional holiday specialty

12-18 flappen

6 large cooking apples
1 cup flour, sifted
2 tsp. baking powder
¼ tsp. salt
1 T. sugar

1 egg, beaten
½ cup milk
shortening
confectioners' sugar

Peel and core apples. Slice the apples in ⅓" thick round slices. Combine dry ingredients; add egg to milk and gradually add to dry ingredients. Mix well for 2-3 min. Dip apple slices in batter and deep fry in hot shortening for 1-2 min. or until golden. Sprinkle with confectioners' sugar. Serve warm or cold.

Gladie VerBeek

CORN FRITTERS
Delicious with syrup or fried chicken

8 fritters

1 cup corn, drained
2 eggs, beaten
½ cup flour

½ tsp. baking powder
¼ tsp. salt
pepper

Preheat shortening in skillet to 375F. Combine corn and eggs. Sift together flour, baking powder, salt and pepper; add to mixture, beating until smooth. Drop by tablespoon into fat; fry until brown. This is also good served with bacon.

Mrs. F. K. Macdonald

FAT BALLEN

1 cup sugar
1 T. shortening
2 eggs
2 cups milk
4 cups flour

4 tsp. baking powder
1 tsp. salt
1 cup raisins
1 lg. apple, sliced thin
¼ tsp. nutmeg

Preheat shortening in skillet to 375F. Mix ingredients in order given. Drop by tablespoons into hot fat and deep fry.

Mrs. Fred DeWilde

OLIE BOLLEN
Dutch Fritters

1 pkg. active dry yeast
1 tsp. sugar
¾ cup warm water
3 eggs, beaten
2 cups warm milk

3 T. light corn syrup
1 (1 lb.) pkg. raisins
4 cups flour
1 T. salt

Dissolve yeast and sugar in water; let stand in warm place for 30 min. Combine eggs, milk, syrup, raisins and yeast mixture in large kettle. Sift flour and salt into mixture and mix well for 2 to 3 min. Test a spoonful of dough to see if it will fall in lump form from the spoon. If not, add a little more water or milk. Let rise in warm place for 2 hours. Drop by tablespoon into deep, hot fat; fry until brown.

SUE'S BAKED APPLE MUFFINS   *12 muffins*

1½ cups flour
1¾ tsp. baking powder
½ tsp. salt
¼ tsp. nutmeg
½ cup sugar
1 egg, beaten
⅓ cup oil

¼ cup milk
½ cup apple, grated, or
   ¾ cup applesauce
¼ cup margarine, melted
⅔ cup sugar
2 tsp. cinnamon

Preheat oven to 350F. Grease a 12-cup muffin pan. Sift together flour, baking powder, salt, nutmeg and sugar. Add egg, oil and milk; blend well. Add apple. Fill muffin cups ⅔ full. Bake 20-25 min. Remove from pan while still warm. Brush with margarine and roll in sugar-cinnamon mixture.

Mrs. Ron Boeve

BLUEBERRY MUFFINS

12 muffins

½ cup shortening
½ cup sugar
½ cup milk
1 egg
1½ cups flour

1½ tsp. baking powder
pinch of salt
¾ cup fresh blueberries
or frozen, thawed and
drained

Preheat oven to 375F. Grease a 12-cup muffin pan. Cream shortening and sugar. Beat milk and egg together; add to creamed ingredients. Sift flour, baking powder and salt into creamed mixture. Fold in berries. Fill muffin cups ⅔ full. Bake 20-25 min.

Mrs. Tracy Stockman
Mrs. Jack Lamb

BRAN MUFFINS

about 5 dozen muffins

A large recipe

2 cups boiling water
2 cups All Bran
4 cups Bran Buds
5 tsp. baking soda
1 qt. buttermilk
3 cups sugar

1 cup shortening
5 cups flour
3 tsp. salt
4 eggs, slightly beaten
dates or nuts, optional

Preheat oven to 375F. Grease muffin pan. Pour boiling water over All Bran and Bran Buds; cool. Dissolve soda in buttermilk; stir and set aside. Cream sugar and shortening. Add flour, salt, eggs and buttermilk mixture. Add bran mixture. Fold in dates or nuts. Fill muffin cups ⅔ full. Bake 20 min. Batter may be refrigerated 6-8 weeks.

Mrs. Robert VanWieren
Barb Zoet

OATMEAL MUFFINS

12 muffins

1 cup flour
½ tsp. salt
2 tsp. baking powder
½ tsp. baking soda
1 cup sour milk

1 cup rolled oats, quick cooking
½ cup brown sugar
1 egg, beaten
½ cup vegetable oil or
  melted shortening

Preheat oven to 375F. Grease a 12-cup muffin pan. Sift together flour, salt, baking powder and soda; set aside. Pour sour milk over oats. Add brown sugar, egg and oil; mix well. Stir in sifted ingredients. Fill muffin cups ⅔ full. Bake 25-30 min.

Mrs. W.A. Butler

PINEAPPLE MUFFINS

12 muffins

1 (9 oz.) can crushed
  pineapple, undrained
1 cup rolled oats,
  quick cooking
½ cup sour cream
⅓ cup shortening
⅓ cup brown sugar,
  firmly packed

1 tsp. orange rind, grated
1 egg, beaten
1¼ cups flour
1 tsp. baking powder
½ tsp. baking soda
1 tsp. salt

Preheat oven to 400F. Grease a 12-cup muffin pan. Combine pineapple, oats and sour cream; let stand at least 15 min. Cream shortening, brown sugar and orange rind. Add egg. Sift together flour, baking powder, soda and salt. Add sifted ingredients alternately with pineapple mixture to creamed mixture. Fill muffin cups ⅔ full. Bake 25 min.

Mrs. David Kempker

PINEAPPLE POPPINS

16 muffins

1 T. baking powder
½ tsp. salt
½ cup sugar
2 cups flour
1 cup crushed pineapple,
   drained

¼ cup margarine
¾ cup milk
1 egg, beaten
¼ cup pineapple juice

Topping:
½ cup flour
¼ tsp. cinnamon
⅓ cup brown sugar,
   firmly packed

¼ cup margarine, melted
maraschino cherries, optional
chopped nuts, optional

Preheat oven to 375F. Grease muffin pans. Sift together baking powder, salt, sugar and flour; set aside. Combine pineapple, margarine, milk, egg and pineapple juice. Stir in sifted ingredients. Fill muffin cups ¾ full. Combine flour, cinnamon, brown sugar and margarine. Sprinkle over unbaked poppins. Garnish with cherries and nuts. Bake 30 min.

Mrs. Jay Formsma

BLUEBERRY PANCAKES

½ cup flour
½ cup whole wheat flour
2 tsp. baking powder
¾ tsp. salt
¼ cup dark brown sugar
4 egg yolks

1 cup sour cream
about ½ cup buttermilk
4 egg whites, room
   temperature
1 cup blueberries, washed
butter

Serving Suggestion:
blueberries
sour cream

Sift together the flours, baking powder and salt into a bowl; stir in sugar and make a well in the center. Add egg yolks, sour cream, and a little buttermilk, beat until mixture is smooth. Beat 2 min.; then stir in enough buttermilk to make a batter that pours easily. Beat egg whites to a stiff peak; fold into batter with blueberries.

Fry pancakes over medium heat on buttered griddle or skillet, turning them when bubbles rise to the surface. Serve at once with additional berries and sour cream.

Mrs. Mike Myers

CORN PANCAKES

1 (16 oz.) can creamed corn   2 T. butter, melted
1 egg, slightly beaten   1 cup pancake mix
2 T. milk   dash salt and pepper

Mix together all ingredients. Bake on hot griddle. Can be served with either bacon or pork sausage for a quick, satisfying luncheon.

Mrs. John J. VandeWege

COTTAGE CHEESE PANCAKES

4 eggs   1 cup cottage cheese
1 cup flour   ½ tsp. salt
1 cup sour cream   1 tsp. sugar

Combine all ingredients. Fry until light brown; turn and brown other side. Serve with butter and syrup.

Mrs. Willis Diekema

DANISH PANCAKES   16 pancakes

4 egg yolks, well beaten   1 T. butter, melted
1 T. sugar   1 ¼ cups flour
½ tsp. salt   4 egg whites, room
2 cups coffee cream   temperature, stiffly beaten

Beat together egg yolks, sugar, salt, ½ cup cream and butter. Add flour; mix until smooth. Add remaining cream and fold in egg whites. Fry on hot griddle, turning when bubbles rise to the surface.

Mrs. Ralph Miller

ENGLISH PANCAKES
12 pancakes

1 cup flour
½ tsp. salt
1 tsp. baking powder
2 eggs, beaten
1 cup milk

1 T. margarine, melted
1 tsp. margarine
about 3 T. sugar
fresh lemon juice

Sift together flour, salt and baking powder. Combine eggs with milk and add gradually to dry ingredients, beating until smooth. Stir in melted margarine. Melt 1 tsp. margarine in small frying pan. When hot, pour in batter, paper thin. Turn when light brown. Sprinkle each with ½ tsp. sugar and a little lemon juice. Roll into a long strip.

Mrs. Sherwin Ortman

BAKED GERMAN PANCAKES
2 servings

¼ cup margarine
3 eggs
½ cup flour

½ cup milk
½ tsp. salt

Preheat oven to 400F. Melt margarine in 9x9'' pan; this can be done in oven while preheating. Mix eggs, flour, milk and salt well. Pour into pan. Bake 20 min.; don't peek before 12 min. Serve with syrup.

Mrs. John Madison

GERMAN APPLE PANCAKES
12 pancakes

2 cups pancake mix	1 egg, beaten
¼ cup light brown sugar	2 cups apples, pared and
½ tsp. cinnamon	sliced very thin
¼ tsp. nutmeg	½ cup sugar
1½ cups milk	2 tsp. cinnamon
2 T. margarine, melted	

Combine pancake mix, brown sugar, cinnamon and nutmeg. Add milk, margarine and egg; beat until blended. Fold in apple slices. Bake on hot, lightly greased griddle.

Combine sugar and cinnamon. When pancakes have baked on one side, turn and sprinkle with sugar mixture. Do not stack. Serve warm with warm applesauce, honey or syrup. Link sausages, sausage patties or Canadian bacon are perfect accompaniments.

Mrs. Delwyn VanDyke

OATMEAL PANCAKES
12 pancakes

1½ cups rolled oats,	1 tsp. sugar
quick cooking	1 tsp. baking soda
2 cups buttermilk	1 tsp. salt
½ cup flour	2 eggs, separated

Mix together rolled oats and buttermilk. Beat in flour, sugar, soda, salt and egg yolks. Fold in stiffly beaten egg whites. Bake on hot griddle until light brown; turn.

Mrs. L.M. McCarthy

PANNEKOEKEN
Pancakes

12 eggs	1 tsp. salt
1 qt. milk	1 cup flour

Beat eggs to a froth; add milk and salt. Slowly stir in flour. Cook very thin layers on buttered griddle; turn. Roll up with butter and brown sugar or serve with maple syrup.

Pancakes are almost always used for dessert in the Netherlands.

Miss Alice V. Althuis

SEVEN-UP PANCAKES

1 egg	*2 cups pancake mix*
2 T. oil	*1½ - 2 cups Seven-Up*

Beat egg and shortening. Add pancake mix. Add 1 cup Seven-Up. Stir until most lumps have disappeared. Gently stir in additional Seven-Up until batter is consistency of medium heavy cream. Bake on medium heat griddle. Turn once when edges start to dry. Serve with butter, syrup and bacon or sausage.

Mrs. Tom Carey

GARLIC-CHEESE BREAD
8 servings

¾ cup Romano cheese, grated	*butter*
6 T. mayonnaise	*1 loaf French bread, sliced*
2 cloves garlic, crushed	*in ½" slices*
1½ T. parsley, chopped	

Preheat oven to broiling. Use a broiler pan. Mix cheese, mayonnaise, garlic and parsley. Refrigerate, covered, for 10-15 min.

Spread both sides of each slice of bread with butter; spread a thin amount of cheese mixture on each side. Arrange on broiler pan and broil until lightly browned; turn and broil other side.

Note: This may be prepared up to 4 hr. prior to serving. Refrigerate, loosely covered, until time to broil.

Mrs. Donald G. Miller

SAVORY CHEESE BREAD
8 servings
Delicious for a Buffet

1 loaf sandwich bread,	*2 T. onion, grated*
unsliced, all but bottom	*2 T. prepared mustard*
crust trimmed	*1 T. sesame seed*
½ cup butter, softened	*¼ - ½ lb. Swiss cheese,*
	sliced

Preheat oven to 400F. Make diagonal cuts 1¼ inches apart almost through loaf. Blend butter, onion, mustard and seed. Spread on slices, saving some for outside. Fill with cheese slices. Press loaf together. Spread outside with remaining butter mixture. Bake uncovered 15 to 20 min.

Mrs. Jay Formsma
Mrs. David Paulson

HERB SEASONED CROUTONS   *13 cups*

30 slices firm textured bread
½ cup cooking oil
3 T. dried minced onion
3 T. dried parsley flakes
2 tsp. garlic salt

¾ tsp. ground sage
½ tsp. seasoned pepper
⅓ cup Parmesan
  cheese, optional

Preheat oven to 300F. Use a large roasting pan. Trim crusts and cut bread into ½ inch cubes. Toast in oven 45 min. Remove; cool slightly. Stir in oil. Add remaining ingredients, tossing lightly to coat bread cubes. Store in covered container. These freeze well.

Mrs. Hal Thornhill

ANSONIA (LARD) BREAD   *4 round 6-8" loaves*
Delicious served with an Italian dinner.

1 crusty white bread recipe
1 lb. unpurified lard (can be
  obtained at butcher shop)
½ cup Romano or
Parmesan cheese

1 tsp pepper
1 (8 oz.) pkg. Italian salami
  or pepperoni, cut into bits

Heat lard to liquid form; drain off liquid leaving hard solid pieces. Prepare any crusty white bread recipe; during first kneading add solid pieces of lard and remaining ingredients. Proceed with bread recipe.

Mrs. Ralph Hensley

BOUNTIFUL WHITE BREAD   *3 loaves*

1 cup milk, scalded
6 T. margarine
⅓ cup sugar
4 tsp. salt

2 pkg. active dry yeast
3 cups warm water
12 cups flour (approximately)
melted margarine

continued

Add margarine, sugar and salt to scalded milk. Let cool to lukewarm. In large mixing bowl, dissolve yeast in warm water 5 min. Add milk mixture and 6 cups flour; beat with electric mixer at high speed for 3 min. By hand, stir in enough of remaining flour to make a stiff dough. Turn on lightly floured surface; knead 8 min. Place in greased bowl, turning once. Cover; let rise in warm place till double, about 1¼ hrs. Punch down; let rest 10 min. Divide dough into 3 parts; shape each part into a loaf. Place in 3 greased 9"x5"x3" loaf pans. Cover; let rise until double, about 45 to 60 min. Bake at 350F. for 1 hr. or till done. Remove from pans to rack; brush with melted margarine. Cover with towel until cool.

Mrs. Rol Bartels

CHEESE-ONION-BACON BREAD   2 loaves

5½ - 6½ cups flour
2 pkg. active dry yeast
½ cup warm water (105-115F)
1¾ cups warm milk
2 T. sugar
1 T. salt

3 T. margarine
¾ cup sharp cheddar
* cheese, grated*
⅓ cup (6 slices) bacon, fried
* crisp and crumbled*
¼ cup onion, minced

Grease 2 9x5x3" loaf pans. Measure flour and set aside. In large warm bowl, dissolve yeast in water. Add milk, sugar, salt and margarine. Stir in 2 cups flour. Beat mixture with rotary beater until smooth (about 1 min.). Add 1 cup more flour. Beat vigorously with wooden spoon until smooth (150 strokes), scraping sides of bowl occasionally. Stir in cheese, bacon and onion. Gradually stir in 2½ to 3 cups of remaining flour. Use enough flour to make a soft dough which leaves sides of bowl, adding more if necessary. Turn out onto floured board. Cover, let rest 10 to 15 min. Knead 10 min., until smooth and blistered. Cover, set in warm place until double, about 1 to 2 hr. Punch down, cover and let rise again until almost double, about 45 min. Divide into 2 parts; round up each and place in pans. Cover; let rise in warm place until dough reaches top of pan and corners are filled, about 1 to 1½ hr. Preheat oven to 400F. Bake 30 to 40 min. or until done. Remove from pans immediately. Brush top crust with margarine, if desired. Cool on racks. This is delicious served warm with the Sharp Cheese Spread.

Mrs. David Credo

SHARP CHEESE SPREAD
1½ cups

2 jars Old English cheese
dash of salt
½ cup butter

1 loaf unsliced bread,
crusts trimmed

Preheat oven to 350F. Mix cheese, salt and butter. Place loaf on baking sheet; spread top and sides with cheese mixture. Bake 10-12 min. or until cheese turns a little brown. Cut loaf into quarters the long way, then cut each quarter into 6 slices the short way.

Mrs. Andrew Dalman

DILL-ONION BREAD
3 loaves

¼ cup honey
3½ tsp. salt
¼ cup oil
1 cup milk, scalded
2 pkg. active dry yeast
1 cup warm water (105-115F.)
1 cup creamed cottage
  cheese, blenderized smooth

1 cup onion, finely chopped
1 T. dried dillweed
2 cups rye flour
5-5½ cups unbleached flour
corn meal
light cream
coarse salt (optional)

Stir honey, salt and oil into milk; cool to lukewarm. Dissolve yeast in warm water, stir into milk mixture. Stir cottage cheese, onion, dillweed and rye flour into milk mixture; beat 2 min. Mix in enough unbleached flour to make dough easy to handle.

Knead dough on board lightly floured with rye flour for 5 min. Place dough in greased bowl; turn. Cover; let rise in warm place until double, about 1½ hr. Punch dough down; fold in edges. Cover; let rise until double, about 1 hr. Grease 2 large baking sheets. Punch dough down and divide into 3 portions. Roll each portion into 13" x 8" rectangle. Roll up from long side; press ends to seal and fold ends under loaves. Sprinkle bottoms of loaves with corn meal. Place on baking sheets. Cover; let rise until double, about 1 hr. Preheat oven to 350F. Brush loaves with cream and sprinkle lightly with salt. Bake until loaves sound hollow when tapped, about 50 min. Cool on wire rack.

Mrs. Herbert Eldean

DILLY CASSEROLE BREAD   1 loaf

1 pkg. active dry yeast	1 tsp. salt
¼ cup warm water	¼ tsp. baking soda
1 cup creamed cottage cheese	1 egg, well beaten
¼ cup shortening	2¼-2½ cups flour
2 T. sugar	margarine, melted
1 T. instant minced onion	dill seed or salt
2 tsp. dill seed, more if desired	

Grease an 8" round (1½ or 2 qt.) casserole. Soften yeast in water. In saucepan, heat cottage cheese to lukewarm. Stir in shortening, sugar, onion, dill seed, salt, soda and the softened yeast. Beat in egg. Add flour, a little at a time, stirring to make a soft dough. Knead on lightly floured surface till smooth and elastic, about 5 min. Place in greased bowl, turning once to grease surface. Cover; let rise in warm place until doubled in size, about 1 hr. Punch down; cover. Let rest 10 min. Turn into casserole. Cover; let rise again till almost double, 30 to 45 min. Preheat oven to 350F. Bake 40-50 min., until brown. Remove from pan; brush with melted margarine. Sprinkle with additional dill seed or salt.

Mrs. David Windemuller
Mrs. Dale Anthonsen

HOBO BREAD   2 loaves

1 pkg. active dry yeast	1 (13 oz.) can evaporated milk
⅛ tsp. ginger	1 T. salt
1 T. sugar	2 T. oil
½ cup warm water	4 cups flour
2 T. sugar	butter

Grease well 2 (1 lb. each) coffee cans and their plastic lids. Dissolve yeast, ginger and sugar in warm water. Let stand in warm place until bubbly (about 15 min.) Stir in 2 T. sugar, milk, salt, oil and flour. Dough should be heavy and too sticky to knead. Place dough in cans; cover with lids. Let stand in warm place until dough rises and lids pop off (1½-2 hr.) Preheat oven to 350F. Bake, without lids, for 45 min. Crust will be very brown when done. Brush top well with butter immediately. Let cool about 10 min. before removing from cans; cool on rack.

Mrs. Don Judd

MAPLE OATMEAL BREAD   *2 loaves*

1½ cups quick oatmeal
1 cup warm water
1½ cups milk, scalded
2 pkg. active dry yeast
3 T. margarine

2 tsp. salt
⅓ cup maple syrup
2 T. sugar
3 cups flour, approximately

Soak oatmeal in water for 5 min. Add milk; cool to lukewarm. Add yeast. Mix in margarine, salt, syrup and sugar. Add enough flour so that when stirred with wooden spoon it comes loose from edge of bowl. Put on floured board; knead for 5 min. or until no longer sticky. Put in greased bowl; turn. Cover; let rise in warm place until double in bulk, about 1½ hr. Turn over; let rise again, about 45 min. Grease 2 9x5x3" loaf pans. Put dough on floured board; shape into 2 loaves. Put in pans. Let rise another 45 min. Preheat oven to 350F. Bake 30-35 min. Remove from pans. Cool on wire rack.

Mrs. Herbert J. Thomas, III

POP UP BREAD   *2 loaves*

3 to 3¼ cups flour
1 pkg. active dry yeast
½ cup milk
½ cup water

½ cup oil
¼ cup sugar
1 tsp. salt
2 eggs

Grease well 2 (1 lb. each) coffee cans. Stir together 1½ cups flour and yeast. Heat milk, water, oil, sugar and salt over low heat only until warm, stirring to blend; add to flour-yeast mixture and beat until smooth (about 2 min. on medium speed). Blend in eggs. Stir in the remaining flour to make a stiff batter. Beat until batter is smooth and elastic (about 1 min. on medium speed). Divide dough into 2 cans; cover with plastic lids. Let rise in warm place (80-85 degrees) until batter reaches ¼ to ½" below lids. Preheat oven to 375F. Remove lids. Bake 30-35 min. or until brown and done. Cool in cans 15 min. before removing.

Mrs. John Van Dyke, Jr.

SWEDISH RYE BREAD   *2 loaves*

2 T. lard
1 cup brown sugar
2 T. molasses
2 cups warm water
1 pkg. active dry yeast

1 tsp. orange rind, grated
2 tsp. salt
¾ cup rye flour
3 cups white flour

Grease a large baking sheet. Put lard, sugar and molasses in warm water; add yeast. Add rind and salt. Mix in flour. Knead on well floured surface till smooth, about 10 min. Place in greased bowl, turning once to grease surface. Cover; let rise in warm place till double, 1½ to 2 hrs. Punch down. Turn out onto lightly floured surface. Shape into 2 loaves. Place on baking sheet. Cover; let rise again till double, about 1 hr. Preheat oven to 350F. Bake 1 hr. or until brown.

Mrs. C.R. Laitsch

ANISE SWEET BREAD   *7 or 8 loaves*

3 pkg. active dry yeast
3½ cups milk, scalded
    and cooled
5 lb. flour
2 cups sugar
2 tsp. salt

¼ tsp. cinnamon
pinch of baking soda
1 cup margarine, melted
1 cup oil
⅓ cup anise seed
2 eggs, beaten

Dissolve yeast in 1½ cups of the milk. Sift together flour, sugar, salt, cinnamon and soda. Make a well in the dry ingredients; add yeast mixture, remaining 2 cups milk, margarine, oil, and anise seed. Mix well. Knead slightly; let rest 5-10 min. Knead well. Cover; let rise until double.

Preheat oven to 350F. Form dough into 7 or 8 loaves on greased baking sheets. Brush tops with beaten eggs. Bake 35-40 min. This is also delicious when toasted.

Mrs. Dale Anthonsen

CINNAMON COFFEE CAKE

3 - 9" cakes

2 pkg. active dry yeast
¼ cup lukewarm water
1 cup boiling water
¾ cup shortening
1 cup cold water

2 eggs, well beaten
½ cup sugar
1 tsp. salt
7 cups flour

Filling and Frosting:
butter
brown sugar
cinnamon

nuts, chopped
raisins
confectioners' sugar frosting

Dissolve yeast in lukewarm water; set aside. Pour boiling water over shortening, stir until dissolved. Add cold water, eggs, sugar, yeast, salt and flour. Mix well and knead. Let rise in warm place until doubled in size. Grease 3 9" pie pans. Knead; roll out on floured surface to a rectangle about 1" thick. Spread with butter; sprinkle with brown sugar, cinnamon, nuts and raisins. Roll up and twist into a ring. Place in pan. Let rise again until doubled in size. Preheat oven to 375F. Bake 20 min. Turn onto board; spread top with butter. When partially cool, spread lightly with frosting.

Mrs. Larry Den Uyl

DATE PASTRY CRESCENT

3 crescents

1 pkg. active dry yeast
¼ cup warm water
4 cups flour
½ cup sugar
½ tsp. salt

1 cup margarine
3 eggs, beaten
½ cup cold water
½ cup hot milk

Filling and Glaze:
1 lb. dates, pitted
   and chopped
½ cup sugar

1 cup water
¼ cup margarine
confectioners' sugar glaze

continued

350

Soften yeast in warm water. Blend flour, sugar, salt and margarine like pie crust. Add eggs, cold water, milk and yeast mixture. Cover with wet cloth; place in refrigerator overnight.

Combine dates, sugar and water; boil until thick. Divide dough into 3 portions; roll each into rectangle ½" thick. Spread with margarine and filling. Roll lengthwise as for a jelly roll, shape into crescent and seal edges. Place on 2 greased baking sheets. Cut through ring almost to center at 1½" intervals. Let rise for 1 hr. Preheat oven to 350F. Bake 30-35 min. Drizzle with glaze while warm.

Mrs. Henry J. Derksen

ENGLISH TEA RING   *2 rings*

1 pkg. active dry yeast
¼ cup warm water
½ cup milk, scalded
3 T. shortening
3 T. sugar

½ tsp. salt
1 egg, beaten
½ tsp. vanilla
3 cups flour

Filling:
melted butter
¼ cup sugar
2 tsp. cinnamon

¾ cup walnuts, broken
¾ cup candied fruit peel

Soften yeast in water; set aside. Combine milk, shortening, sugar and salt. Cool to lukewarm; add yeast mixture. Add egg, reserving 2 tsp. Add vanilla and enough flour to make a soft dough. Knead lightly and place in greased bowl, turning once to grease top. Cover, let rise until double.

Divide dough into 2 portions; roll to oblong shape ½ inch thick, Brush with melted butter. Combine filling ingredients; spread evenly on dough. Roll lengthwise as for a jelly roll. Seal edge. Shape each roll in a circle on a greased baking sheet. Snip almost to center at 2" intervals with scissors. Pull sections apart and twist slightly. Brush with egg which has been set aside; let rise until double. Preheat oven to 375F. Bake 25 min.

Mrs. John H. Jones

FRUITED SWEET BREAD
1 loaf

2 pkg. active dry yeast	*4 cups flour*
½ cup lukewarm water	*1 tsp. cinnamon*
1 cup lukewarm milk	*1 tsp. nutmeg*
½ cup sugar	*1 cup figs, finely chopped*
1½ tsp. salt	*½ cup candied orange*
½ cup soft margarine	* peel, chopped*
2 eggs	*½ cup white raisins*
	1 cup nuts, finely chopped

Frosting:
1 cup confectioners' sugar   *orange peel, finely slivered*
orange juice

Grease and flour a 2½ qt. mold or Bundt pan. Dissolve yeast in water. Stir in milk, sugar, salt and margarine. Beat in eggs. Add flour, cinnamon and nutmeg; beat until flour is just mixed into dough. Add fruits and nuts; beat until smooth and well mixed. Spoon batter into pan. Let rise, covered in warm place, until double in bulk. Preheat oven to 375F. Bake 35 to 40 min. or until richly browned. Unmold and cool.

For frosting, mix sugar with enough juice to the consistency of heavy cream. Spoon over top of cooled loaf, letting it drizzle down sides. Sprinkle with orange peel.

This can be wrapped after cooling (do not frost) and frozen until needed. When ready to serve, unwrap and thaw at room temperature for 2 hrs. Frost as directed.

Mrs. Jack DeRoo

GERMAN STOLLEN (CHRISTMAS BREAD)   *2 braids*

The shape of the German Stollen is supposed to represent the Christ child. The folds of dough on the top of the loaf should remind you of swaddling clothes. When you bake your stollen, give it plenty of room on the baking sheet so the shape will be sure.

1 cake compressed yeast	*2 eggs*
1 tsp. sugar	*2 cups scalded milk,*
¼ cup lukewarm water	*cooled to lukewarm*
1 cup shortening	*1 cup raisins*
1¼ cups sugar	*1 cup currants*
6 cups flour	*½ cup citron, chopped*
1 tsp. salt	*½ cup blanched almonds*
½ tsp. nutmeg	*1½ tsp. lemon extract*

Dissolve yeast and tsp. of sugar in lukewarm water; cover and allow to rise. Cream shortening and sugar. Sift together flour, salt and nutmeg. Add to creamed mixture alternately with eggs and milk. Add yeast mixture; knead until smooth. Add fruits, nuts and extract. Cover; let dough rise to double its bulk. Knead dough again. Shape into ropes about 1½" in diameter. Preheat oven to 400F. Grease 2 large baking sheets. For each large stollen make 1 rope 3 ft. long and 2 that are 2½ ft. long. Braid the dough. Bring the braid to a point at either end. Place braid on baking sheet. Cover; let rise again about 1 hr. Bake 25 min. or until brown.

Mrs. Peter Heydens

EGG BAGELS

32 bagels

2 pkg. active dry yeast
2 cups warm potato water
4 eggs, beaten
1 T. salt
1 T. sugar
¼ cup oil

8 cups flour, approximately
2 T. sugar
2 qt. boiling water
2 egg yolks beaten with
2 T. water

Soften yeast in ½ cup of the potato water (water in which peeled potatoes have been cooked). In large bowl blend together eggs, softened yeast, remaining potato water, salt, sugar, oil and 2 cups of the flour. Stir in remaining flour. Turn out on a lightly floured board and knead for about 10 min., adding more flour as needed to make a firm dough. Place dough in a greased bowl, cover lightly, and let rise in a warm place until doubled in bulk (or place covered dough in refrigerator where it will rise slowly overnight — in about 10 to 12 hr.) Punch the dough down; knead for a few min. on a lightly floured board until it is smooth. Roll the dough out to a rectangle and divide into 32 pieces of equal size. Roll each piece between the palms to form a strand about 6 inches long and ¾ inch in diameter. Moisten ends and seal together firmly to make doughnut-shaped rolls of uniform thickness. Let them rise on board for about 15 min.

Preheat oven to 425F. Grease a large baking sheet. Dissolve sugar in boiling water in a deep pot. Drop bagels in, one at a time. Do not crowd. As bagels rise to the surface, turn them over. Boil for 3 min. on the second side. Remove with slotted spoon and place on baking sheet; brush with egg yolk glaze. Bake 20 to 25 min., or until golden.

For a breakfast variation, add cinnamon, nutmeg and raisins as desired to the given recipe.

Mr. Bob Brown

CINNAMON ROLLS

48 rolls

2 pkg. active dry yeast	2 tsp. salt
1 T. sugar	4½ cups flour
⅓ cup warm water	margarine, melted
½ cup margarine	brown sugar
1 cup scalded milk	pecans, broken
½ cup cold water	margarine, melted
2 eggs or 4 egg yolks	cinnamon-sugar mixture
½ cup sugar	raisins, optional

Soften yeast and sugar in warm water. Melt margarine in scalded milk; add cold water. Beat eggs and sugar until thick. Add dissolved yeast and warm milk. Add salt and 2½ cups of the flour, then add remaining flour and mix well. Place bowl in warm water; let dough rise until double in bulk. Punch down and stiffen with a little flour until it loses its stickiness. Let rise again.

Prepare each muffin tin with 1 tsp. melted margarine, 1 tsp. brown sugar and pecans. Roll dough into rectangle ½" thick. Brush with melted margarine, sprinkle with cinnamon-sugar mixture and raisins. Roll up lengthwise as for a cake roll. Slice in ½" slices; place sliced side down in muffin tins. Brush each slice with melted margarine and cinnamon-sugar mixture. Let rise until light, 30-40 min. Preheat oven to 375F. Bake 10-12 min.

Mrs. W.C. Kools

OLD ENGLISH HOT CROSS BUNS

2½ dozen

1 cup sugar	7½ cups flour
½ cup butter, melted	1½ tsp. salt
3 egg yolks, beaten	1 tsp. nutmeg
2¼ cups milk, scalded, cooled to lukewarm	3 egg whites, room temperature, well beaten
1 pkg. active dry yeast	butter, melted
¼ cup lukewarm water	confectioners' sugar glaze

continued

Grease a large bowl. At 9 p.m. mix sugar, butter, yolks and milk. Soften yeast in water; add to mixture. Sift together flour, salt and nutmeg; add half to first mixture and beat well. Stir in remaining flour and egg whites until blended. Place in bowl; oil top of dough. Cover with cloth; let stand overnight in warm place.

Grease 2 large baking sheets. At 6 a.m. knead dough on lightly floured surface using not more than ½ cup additional flour. Roll dough out ½" thick; cut in rounds with 3" floured cookie cutter. Place on baking sheets. Brush with melted butter, cover with clean towel and let rise 1½ hr. more or until doubled in size. Preheat oven to 375F. With a knife or scissors, cut a deep cross on each bun. Bake 20-25 min. Brush with glaze while warm.

Mrs. Ernest Penna

LUNCH ROLLS

40 rolls

2 pkg. active dry yeast	1 egg
½ cup warm water	1 T. salt
½ cup lard	½ cup sugar
1 cup boiling water	7 cups flour
1 cup cold water	butter, melted

Dissolve yeast in warm water, set aside. Melt lard in boiling water; add cold water. Beat together egg, salt and sugar; add to lard mixture. When lukewarm, add yeast; stir in flour. Cover; let rise 1 hr.

Grease a large baking sheet. Knead dough. Shape into 40 balls (walnut size) and roll in flour; dough will be stiff. Place on baking sheet and flatten slightly. Cover; let rise in warm place until double in bulk, about 1 hr. Preheat oven to 400F. Bake 12-15 min. Brush with butter.

Mrs. Thomas Buis

HUNGARIAN POPPY SEED ROLLS

24 rolls

2 pkg. active dry yeast *1 tsp. salt*
2 T. sugar *1 cup margarine*
1 scant cup lukewarm water *2 eggs, separated*
4 cups flour

Filling:
1 cup milk *1 tsp. vanilla*
½ lb. ground poppy seed *confectioners' sugar*
½ cup sugar

Grease a large baking sheet. Dissolve yeast and sugar in water. Mix flour, salt and margarine with pastry blender until coarse. Make a well in the center; drop in egg yolks and add yeast mixture. Mix dough until it leaves side of bowl.

Heat milk until just warm; add poppy seed. Just let poppy seed absorb the milk. Remove from heat. Add sugar and vanilla.

Preheat oven to 425F. Divide dough into 4 portions; roll out each into a 15x6" rectangle. Spread on poppy seed filling. Roll up like jelly roll, put on baking sheet and brush with slightly beaten egg whites. Let stand 20 min. Bake 15 to 18 min. or until brown. Slice rolls; sprinkle with confectioners' sugar.

Mrs. William DeVries
Mrs. David Credo

NOTES

Windmill

DeZwaan
and the
Windmill Section

For two hundred years in the verdant lowlands of the Zaan district of the Netherlands a giant windmill has toiled her days grinding grain into flour to be used by the Dutch "haus fraus".

Two centuries later a dream was realized as that windmill, "De Zwaan", complete with World War II bullet scars in her wings, was dismantled in her homeland for shipment and restoration in a new Dutch land. Today she stands proudly towering twelve stories high on an island among the spongy lowlands of the Black River bottoms.

With flags of the United States and the Netherlands flying from her halyards, she is an impressive sight as she heads into the wind and rotates her eighty foot beams as if flexing her muscles while the five foot grindstones spin out streams of grahom flour.

De Zwaan is the last windmill that can leave the homeland. Once the Netherlands had thousands upon thousands: now their numbers have so dwindled that all Dutch mills are preserved as national monuments. It was only through perseverance and belief in a dream that Holland now has the only authentic operating Dutch windmill in the United States.

Visitors to the windmill receive "visas" which are stamped with the official seal of the "De Zwaan" miller, who is always in attendance. Bags of graham flour ground by the windmill can be purchased.

Today, with the help of De Zwaan to grind the flour and the authentic Dutch recipes in our Windmill section, modern day "haus fraus" can again bake the breads, waffles, cookies and muffins that our Dutch ancestors baked generations ago. "Eet Smakelijk" indeed means "Eat well and with taste!"

Mrs. Randall Baar

NUBBY PEANUT LOAF   *1 loaf*

1 pkg. active dry yeast
¼ cup warm water (110F)
¾ cup milk, scalded
2 T. sugar
¾ tsp. salt
2 T. shortening

1 egg, slightly-beaten
1½ cups whole wheat
*   flour (graham)*
½ cup salted peanuts,
*   chopped*
1½ to 2 cups white flour

Soften yeast in water in a small bowl. Combine milk with sugar, salt and shortening in a large bowl; cool to lukewarm. Stir in yeast mixture and egg, mixing well. Add wheat flour, peanuts and half of the white flour; beat until smooth, about 100 strokes. Add enough of the white flour to make a moderately stiff dough. Turn onto a lightly floured surface; knead until smooth and satiny (8-10 mins.). Shape dough into a ball; place in a lightly greased bowl, turning once to grease surface. Cover; let rise in a warm place until doubled (about 1 hr.) Punch down bread. Shape into a loaf and place in a greased 8½" x 4½" x 2½" loaf pan. Cover and let rise about 45 mins. or until center of dough rounds slightly over top of pan. Preheat oven to 400F. Bake bread 30-40 mins. Cover with brown paper if necessary the last 20 mins. of baking to prevent crust from burning.

Spread with peanut butter for a double peanut treat.

Mrs. William Gargano

WHOLE WHEAT BATTER BREAD   *1 loaf*

1 pkg. active dry yeast	*2 tsp. salt*
1¼ cups warm water	*2 T. soft shortening*
2 T. honey or brown sugar	*1 cup whole wheat*
2 cups flour	*flour (graham)*

In a large bowl dissolve yeast in water. Add the honey, half of the flour, salt and shortening. Beat with mixer for 2 mins. at medium speed. Blend in remaining flours with spoon. Cover and let rise in a warm place until doubled in size, about 30 mins. Stir batter down and spread evenly in a greased 9" x 5" x 3" loaf pan. Let rise in a warm place until batter reaches ½" from the top of the pan, about 40 mins. Bake at 375F. for 40-50 mins. Brush top of loaf with butter and cool on rack before cutting.

Mrs. Henry J. Hekman

APRICOT BREAD   *1 loaf*

¾ cup boiling water	*½ tsp. almond extract*
¾ cup dried apricots, ground	*½ cup whole wheat flour*
1 T. margarine	*(graham)*
½ cup sugar	*¾ cup white flour*
¼ tsp. salt	*½ tsp. baking soda*
1 egg, beaten	*½ tsp. baking powder*
½ tsp. orange extract	*½ cup slivered almonds*

Preheat oven to 350F. Grease a 8" x 4" x 2" loaf pan. Add boiling water to apricots. Add margarine, sugar and salt. Cool. Mix in egg and extracts. Sift together flours, baking soda and baking powder. Add to apricot mixture along with the almonds. Mix ingredients with a few quick strokes. Pour into pan and bake 40 mins. Cool 10 mins. and remove from pan.

Serve with honey-butter or softened cream cheese.

Mrs. William Gargano

BOSTON BROWN BREAD

2 loaves

1 cup rye flour
1 cup whole wheat flour
 (graham)
1 cup corn meal
2¼ tsp. baking soda

1 tsp. salt
½ cup raisins
¾ cup light molasses
2 cups buttermilk

Grease 2 (1 lb. each) food cans. Sift dry ingredients together; add raisins and mix. Combine molasses with buttermilk; add to dry ingredients and beat until batter is smooth. Fill the cans ⅔ full. Fill a large kettle ½ full of water, cover cans of bread dough with aluminum foil and place in kettle. Cover kettle and steam bread for 2-2½ hours.

Mrs. William Gargano

BROWN BREAD

3 loaves

1 cup seedless raisins
1 cup water
¾ cup sugar
1 egg, beaten
1 cup sour milk or
 buttermilk

1 cup All Bran or Bran Buds
1 cup oatmeal
1 cup whole wheat flour
 (graham)
1 tsp. baking soda
1 tsp. salt

Preheat oven to 350F. Grease and flour 3 (1 lb. each) food cans. Combine raisins and water in a saucepan and boil for 5 mins. In a large bowl combine sugar, egg, buttermilk, bran and oatmeal. Sift together flour, baking soda and salt, add to mixture. Add raisins and water mixing well. Pour into cans. Bake 1 hr. Cool 10 mins; cut around bread in cans and remove.

Mrs. William Gargano

CRACKED WHEAT BREAD
2 loaves

½ cup cracked wheat
2½ cups buttermilk or
  sour milk
½ cup light molasses
½ cup rye flour

3 cups whole wheat flour
  (graham)
1 tsp. salt
2 tsp. soda

Combine the cracked wheat and buttermilk; refrigerate overnight.

The next day preheat oven to 300F. Grease 2 9" x 5" x 3" loaf pans. Add the molasses to the cracked wheat mixture. Sift together the rye flour, whole wheat flour, salt and soda. Add sifted ingredients; mix until batter is evenly moistened. Pour into loaf pans. Bake for 1½ hrs. Cool about 1 hr. before slicing.

Delicious served with honey or cheese.

GRAHAM BREAD
1 loaf

2 T. sugar
2 T. margarine
½ cup light molasses
1 cup buttermilk
1 tsp. baking soda

1 tsp baking powder
½ tsp. salt
⅔ cup flour
1 cup whole wheat flour
  (graham)

Preheat oven to 350F. Grease a 8" x 4" x 2½" loaf. Cream sugar and shortening. Combine molasses and buttermilk; add to the creamed mixture. Sift together baking soda, baking powder, salt and flour. Add to creamed mixture. Add whole wheat flour and mix well. Pour into loaf pans, bake 45 mins. Cool 10 mins. and remove from pans.

Mrs. Robert Cooper

HONEY BROWN NUT BREAD
2 loaves

1 cup honey	1 tsp. salt
1 T. margarine	1 tsp. baking soda
1 egg, beaten	1 cup buttermilk
1½ cups flour	1 cup dates, chopped
1½ cups whole wheat flour (graham)	1 cup walnuts, chopped

Preheat oven to 300F. Grease and flour 2 8" x 4" x 2" loaf pans. Heat honey to lukewarm, add margarine. Stir in egg. Sift flours, salt and soda. Add dry ingredients alternately with buttermilk to honey mixture. Add dates and walnuts, mix well. Pour into loaf pans. Bake 1 hr. Cool 10 mins; remove from pan.

Mrs. William Gargano

MAPLE DATE NUT BREAD
1 loaf

1 cup dates, chopped	1 tsp. baking powder
¼ tsp. baking soda	1 cup flour
1 T. shortening	1 cup whole wheat flour (graham)
1 cup boiling water	¾ cup pecans, chopped
1 egg, beaten	maple syrup
½ tsp. salt	
½ cup maple syrup	

Preheat oven to 350F. Grease a 9" x 5" x 3" loaf pan. Combine dates, soda and shortening with boiling water; set aside. In a large bowl beat together egg, salt and syrup. Add date mixture, blending thoroughly. Sift together baking powder and flours. Add dry ingredients. Fold in pecans. Pour into loaf pans. Bake 1 hr. Let cool 10 mins. Remove from pans and brush with maple syrup.

Delicious for party sandwiches.

ORANGE-NUT BREAD   *1 loaf*

2 cups flour
2 cups whole wheat flour
  (graham)
4 tsp. baking powder
2 tsp. salt
½ cup sugar

½ cup candied orange peel or
  orange gum drops, chopped
½ cup nuts, chopped
1 egg, beaten
2 cups milk

Preheat oven to 350F. Grease a 9" x 5" x 3" loaf pan. Sift together dry ingredients. Add fruit and nuts. Add egg and blend in milk. Beat well. Pour into pan. Bake 1 hr. Cool 10 mins. Remove from pan.

Mrs. William Gargano

WINDMILL BROWN BREAD   *9 loaves*

1 lb. raisins
3 cups water
2 cups sugar
½ cup lard
3 eggs
1 tsp. salt
4 cups flour

2 cups whole wheat flour
  (graham)
4 tsp. soda
½ cup nuts, chopped
2 cups canned fruit, drained,
  chopped
citron, chopped, to taste

Preheat oven to 350F. Grease and flour 9 (16 oz. each) food cans. Combine raisins and water, bring to a boil and cool. Combine sugar, lard, eggs and salt. Add liquid from the raisins. Sift together the flours and soda. Add to sugar mixture. Add raisins, nuts, fruit and citron mixing well. Pour into cans and fill to a little over ½ full. Bake 1 hr. Cool 10 mins., remove from cans. Wrap in foil leaving the top of foil open until cool.

Mrs. Raymond Warden

DE ZWAAN KOEKJES
Cookies

3½ doz.

Filling:

1 cup dates, chopped
½ cup sugar
½ cup water

2 T. lemon juice
½ tsp. salt

2 cups brown sugar,
  firmly packed
1 cup shortening, melted
2 eggs, beaten
1 cup sour milk

2 cups whole wheat flour
  (graham)
2½ cups flour
½ tsp. baking soda
1 tsp. cinnamon

Simmer dates, sugar and water for 5 mins. or until thick. Stir in lemon juice and salt. Set aside.

Preheat oven to 375F. Grease a cookie sheet. Mix sugar and shortening. Blend in eggs and milk. Sift together flours, baking soda and cinnamon. Add to sugar mixture, mixing well. If necessary add more flour to make dough stiff enough to roll out. Roll dough ⅛'' thick on a floured surface and cut out cookies with a round cookie cutter. Place ½ of the cookie rounds on the cookie sheet and top each with a spoonful of filling. Add the top cookie round which has been decorated by four small knife slits at right angles to resemble windmill sails. Bake for 10 mins.

Mrs. Gerritt Vanderwood

BRAN MUFFINS

2 doz. muffins

2 cups brown sugar,
  firmly packed
1 cup flour
1 cup whole wheat flour
  (graham)
1 cup quick oatmeal

1 cup Bran Buds
1 tsp. salt
2 eggs, slightly-beaten
3 T. oil
2 cups buttermilk
2 tsp. soda

Preheat oven to 375F. Grease muffin tins. Combine dry ingredients. Add eggs. Mix together oil, buttermilk and soda until it foams; add to dry ingredients. Mix but don't beat. Bake 15 mins. Batter will keep in refrigerator.

Mrs. Richard Oudersluys

WHOLE WHEAT MUFFINS
1 doz. muffins

1 egg
½ cup brown sugar,
  firmly packed
2 T. molasses
2 cups whole wheat flour
  (graham)

½ tsp. salt
1 tsp. baking soda
1 cup sour milk or
  buttermilk
2 T. shortening, melted
½ cup raisins

Preheat oven to 400F. Grease a muffin tin. Blend together egg, brown sugar and molasses. Sift together flour, salt, and baking soda; add to sugar mixture. Mix in sour milk and shortening. Add raisins, blending evenly. Fill muffin cups ½ full. Bake for 20 mins.

Mrs. Willis M. Oosterhof

WHOLE WHEAT WAFFLES
4 waffles

2 eggs, separated
1 cup milk
1 T. brown sugar,
  firmly packed
1 T. oil

1 cup whole wheat flour
  (graham)
1 tsp. baking powder
½ tsp. salt

Beat egg whites until stiff, set aside. Beat egg yolks until fluffy. Add milk and mix well. Add sugar, oil, flour, baking powder and salt; blend well. Fold in egg whites. Bake in waffle griddle.

Mrs. Willis M. Oosterhof

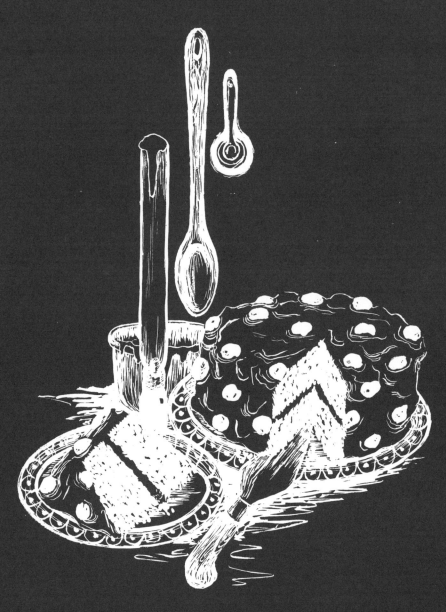

Cakes and their Toppings

NOTES

APPLE DAPPLE CAKE

12-15 servings

1¾ cups sugar
1½ cups oil
3 eggs
3 cups flour, sifted
1 tsp. salt

1 tsp. baking soda
3 cups apples, chopped
1 tsp. vanilla
1 cup nuts, chopped

Glaze:
1 cup brown sugar
½ cup margarine
¼ cup milk

1 tsp. vanilla
walnut halves

Preheat oven to 350F. Grease and flour a 10" tube pan. Mix together sugar, oil and eggs. Sift together dry ingredients and add to creamed mixture. Add apples, vanilla, and nuts. Pour into pan and bake 1 hr. 15 min. Cool 15 min. and remove from pan. Poke holes with toothpick in top of cake.

Boil together brown sugar, margarine, and milk for 2½ min., stirring constantly. Add vanilla. Cool 15-20 min. or until thickened. Carefully spoon over top of cake, allowing glaze to drizzle over sides. Garnish with walnut halves.

Variation: After removing cake from oven cool 15 min. in pan. Pour hot glaze over cake. Cool several hours in pan.

Mrs. C. Lynn Vincent

APPLE DATE CAKE   *9 servings*

1 cup hot water
1 cup dates, chopped
1 cup apples, chopped
1 tsp. baking soda
½ cup shortening
1 cup sugar

1 egg, beaten
1 tsp. salt
1 tsp. vanilla
1½ cups flour
1 cup nuts, chopped

Topping:
2 T. butter
1 cup flaked coconut

1 cup brown sugar
4 T. hot milk

Preheat oven to 350F. Grease a 9" x 9" pan. Pour water over dates, apples, baking soda, and shortening. Cool. Add remaining ingredients to date mixture. Pour into pan and bake 40 min.

Mix together topping ingredients and spread on hot cake. Broil until lightly browned.

Mrs. Roger Macleod

APPLE PUDDING CAKE   *16 servings*

2 cups sugar
½ cup oil
1 (20 oz.) can
   apple pie slices
2 eggs
½ cup nuts, chopped

½ cup raisins
1 tsp. vanilla
2 cups flour
2 tsp. baking soda
2 tsp. salt
2 tsp. cinnamon

Frosting:
1 (3¾ oz.) pkg.
   vanilla instant
   pudding mix

1 envelope dessert
   topping mix
1½ cups milk

Preheat oven to 325F. Grease a 9" x 13" pan. Mix together sugar, oil, apples, eggs, nuts, raisins and vanilla. Add flour, baking soda, salt, and cinnamon; blend well. Spread in pan and bake 35 min.

Beat together pudding mix, topping mix, and milk for 5 min. Frost cooled cake and refrigerate for several hours.

Mrs. Jay Freriks

APPLE RAISIN LOAF

12-15 servings

½ cup butter
1 cup sugar
2 cups flour
2 cups apples, diced
2 eggs, beaten
½ tsp. salt

½ cup nuts, chopped
1 tsp. baking soda
2 T. sour cream
½ tsp. lemon extract
½ cup raisins
½ cup citron

Topping:
2 T. butter
2 T. sugar

2 T. flour

Preheat oven to 350F. Line a 1½ qt. loaf pan with wax paper. Cream together butter and sugar. Add remaining ingredients and mix well. Pour into pan. Combine topping ingredients and sprinkle on batter. Bake 1 hr.

Mrs. Leo Jungblut

APPLESAUCE CAKE

16 servings

½ cup shortening
1 cup sugar
1 egg
1½ cups applesauce
1 tsp. vanilla
½ tsp. nutmeg

1 tsp. cinnamon
½ tsp. cloves
2 cups flour
1 tsp. baking soda
½ cup nuts, chopped
½ cup raisins or dates

Frosting:
¾ cup butter
¾ cup sugar

¾ cup evaporated milk
½ tsp. vanilla

Preheat oven to 350F. Grease a 9" x 13" pan. Cream shortening and sugar. Mix in egg, applesauce, and vanilla. Sift together nutmeg, cinnamon, cloves, flour, and baking soda; add to first mixture. Blend in nuts and raisins. Spread in pan and bake 30 min. Cool.

Cream butter and sugar. Gradually add milk and beat. Add vanilla. Spread on cooled cake.

Mrs. Hollis Clark, Jr.
Mrs. Barb Lamb

TROPICAL BANANA CAKE   *12-15 servings*

½ cup butter	½ cup buttermilk
1½ cups sugar	2 cups flour
2 eggs, beaten	1 tsp. baking soda
1 cup mashed bananas	½ tsp. salt
1 tsp. vanilla	½ cup pecans, chopped

Frosting:

1 (3 oz.) pkg. cream cheese	⅛ tsp. salt
¼ cup warm milk	1 tsp. vanilla
3 cups confectioners' sugar	

Preheat oven to 350F. Grease a 9" x 13" pan. Cream butter and sugar until light and fluffy. Mix in eggs, bananas and vanilla. Sift dry ingredients together and add alternately with buttermilk. Fold in nuts. Pour batter into pan and bake for 30-35 min.

Beat cream cheese and milk. Add remaining ingredients and beat until smooth. Frost cooled cake.

Mrs. Morris Peterson

BUTTERSCOTCH SPICE CAKE   *12-15 servings*

2 cups water	2 tsp. ground cloves
2 cups sugar	½ tsp. salt
1 egg, beaten	1 cup white raisins
1 cup butter, melted	2 cups cake flour, sifted
2 tsp. cinnamon	2 tsp. baking soda, sifted

Frosting:

¼ cup butter	2 cups confectioners' sugar
1 cup brown sugar	½ tsp. vanilla
⅛ tsp. salt	¼ cup nuts, chopped
4-5 T. evaporated milk	

Preheat oven to 350F. Grease a 9" x 13" pan. Simmer the first eight ingredients together for 5 min. Cool to lukewarm. Add flour and soda; mix well. Pour into pan and bake 30 min.

Boil butter, brown sugar, salt, and evaporated milk for 1 min. Cool slightly; beat with sugar and vanilla until consistency to spread. Add nuts and spread on cooled cake.

Mrs. John Marquis

CARROT CAKE 12-15 servings

2 cups flour
2 tsp. baking powder
2 tsp. baking soda
2 tsp. cinnamon
1 tsp. salt

2 cups sugar
1½ cups cooking oil
2 cups carrots, grated
4 eggs
½ cup walnuts, chopped

Frosting:
1 (3 oz.) pkg. cream cheese
¼ cup warm milk
3 cups confectioners' sugar

⅛ tsp. salt
1 tsp. vanilla

Preheat oven to 350F. Grease and flour a 10" tube pan. Sift together first 5 ingredients. Mix remaining ingredients and combine the two mixtures. Mix well. Pour into pan and bake 1 hr.

Beat cream cheese and milk. Add remaining ingredients and beat until smooth. Spread on cooled cake.

Miss Karen Kaiser

BLACK FOREST CHERRY TORTE 12-15 servings

1½ cups heavy cream
3 eggs
1½ tsp. vanilla
2 cups flour

1½ cups sugar
2 tsp. baking powder
½ tsp. salt

Filling:
2 T. cornstarch
2 T. sugar

1 (1 lb.) can pitted dark red
    cherries, drained,
    reserving juice
1 T. brandy

Topping:
1½ cups heavy cream
¼ cup confectioners' sugar

2 oz. sweet cooking
    chocolate, grated

Preheat oven to 350F. Grease and flour two 8" or 9" layer pans. In chilled bowl, beat cream until stiff. Beat eggs until thick and lemon colored. Fold eggs and vanilla into whipped cream. Stir together remaining ingredients and fold gently into creamed mixture; blend. Pour into pans and bake 30-35 min. Cool.

continued

Stir together cornstarch and sugar in pan. Add enough water to cherry juice to measure 1 cup; stir into sugar mixture. Cook, stirring constantly, until it bubbles. Boil and stir 1 min. Cool to lukewarm; add brandy. Dip 36 cherries into syrup; set aside. Cut remaining cherries in ¼ and stir into syrup. Chill.

Beat cream and confectioners' sugar until very stiff. To assemble cake place one layer upside down on serving plate. With decorator's tube or spoon, form thin rim of whipped cream around outer edge of layer. Fill center with cherry filling. Place other layer top side up on filling. Gently spread whipped cream on sides and top of cake. Garnish side of cake with chocolate. If desired, place whipped cream in decorator's tube with star tip. Place border of cream around edge of cake. Beginning from center of cake, outline individual portions in a spoke-fashion design. Place desired number of reserved dipped cherries in outline portion. Keep refrigerated.

Mrs. Leo Jungblut

CHERRY CAKE WITH ALMOND SAUCE   9 servings

1 ½ cups sugar
1 ½ cups flour
1 tsp. baking soda
1 tsp. cinnamon
½ tsp. salt

1 egg
3 T. butter, melted
2 cups sour cherries,
    drained, reserving juice

Sauce:
1 cup cherry juice
1 T. butter
½ cup sugar
¼ tsp. salt

¼ cup toasted slivered
    almonds
2-3 drops almond extract
1 T. cornstarch

Preheat oven to 350F. Grease an 8" x 8" pan. Mix first six ingredients; add butter and cherries. Pour into pan and bake 45 min.

Combine sauce ingredients and cook until thickened. Serve over cake.

Mrs. Joel VerPlank

SCOTTISH CHERRY CAKE

1 cup butter, softened
1 cup sugar
4 eggs
2½ cups flour
½ tsp. baking powder

½ tsp. salt
½ tsp. vanilla
½ lb. candied maraschino
    cherries, halved and floured

Preheat oven to 350F. Grease and flour a 9" x 5" loaf pan. Cream together butter and sugar. Add eggs one at a time. Sift together flour, baking powder, and salt; gradually add to creamed mixture. Blend 3 min., scraping bowl constantly. Add vanilla and cherries. Pour into pan and bake 1¼-1½ hrs.

Mrs. Staff Keegin
Mrs. Anthony Garofalo

CHOCOLATE SPICE CAKE   *12-15 servings*

2 (1 oz. each) squares
    unsweetened chocolate
¼ cup water
2 cups cake flour, sifted
½ tsp. salt
¾ tsp. baking soda
1 tsp. baking powder

2 tsp. cinnamon
½ tsp. cloves
½ cup butter
1½ cups sugar
2 eggs, beaten
1 cup buttermilk

Frosting:
¼ cup butter
1 tsp. strong coffee
1½ cups confectioners' sugar

⅓ cup Droste's cocoa
1 egg white, room
    temperature

Preheat oven to 325F. Grease an 8" x 12" pan. Cook chocolate and water over low heat until chocolate is melted, stirring constantly. Cool. Sift together flour, salt, baking soda, baking powder and spices. Cream butter; gradually add sugar. Add chocolate mixture; mix well. Add eggs. Add dry ingredients alternately with buttermilk. Mix until smooth. Pour into pan and bake 55 min. Cool.

Cream butter. Add coffee, 1 cup sugar and cocoa; mix well. Beat egg white until stiff; gradually beat in remaining sugar. Fold into butter mixture. Spread on cooled cake.

Mrs. William Lang

377

FUDGE CAKE

12-15 servings

4 (1 oz. each) squares
  unsweetened chocolate
½ cup butter
2 cups sugar
1 cup water
2 eggs, beaten
2 cups flour

1 tsp. baking powder
½ tsp. salt
1 tsp. baking soda
½ cup sour cream
  or buttermilk
1 tsp. vanilla

Frosting:
¼ cup butter
1 tsp. vanilla
2 (1 oz. each) squares
  unsweetened chocolate,
  melted

1 (1 lb.) box confectioners'
  sugar
light cream

Preheat oven to 375F. Grease two 9" round cake pans. Melt together chocolate and butter; add sugar and water. Cool; add eggs. Sift together flour, baking powder, and salt. Add to first mixture; beat. Dissolve baking soda in sour cream. Add to mixture with vanilla. Pour in pans and bake 25-30 min. Cool.

Cream butter, vanilla, and chocolate. Add sugar and enough cream to reach desired spreading consistency. Fill and frost cooled cake.

Mrs. Pat Mass

MIAMI BEACH BIRTHDAY CAKE

12-15 servings

½ cup butter
1½ cups sugar
2 eggs
⅓ cup semi-sweet
  chocolate chips, melted

2 cups flour, sifted
1 tsp. baking soda
1 tsp. salt
1¼ cups buttermilk
1 tsp. vanilla

Topping:
½ cup graham cracker
  crumbs
⅓ cup butter, melted

½ cup walnuts, chopped
⅔ cup semi-sweet
  chocolate chips

continued

Frosting:

1 cup milk

3 T. flour

1 cup sugar

½ cup butter

½ cup margarine

1 tsp. vanilla

Preheat oven to 375F. Grease and flour two 9'' round cake pans. Cream butter, gradually adding sugar. Add eggs one at a time, beating well after each. Blend in chocolate chips. Combine dry ingredients; add at low speed alternately with the buttermilk, beginning and ending with dry ingredients. Add vanilla. Pour into pans.

Combine topping ingredients and sprinkle on top of cake batter in pans. Bake 30-35 min.

Combine milk and flour; cook until thick, stirring constantly. Cool. Mix together sugar, butter, margarine, and vanilla; beat until fluffy. Beat in milk mixture. Frost cooled cake.

Mrs. David Vanderwel

NO FROST CUP CAKES

20 servings

1 (8 oz.) pkg. cream cheese

1 egg

⅓ cup sugar

⅛ tsp. salt

1 (6 oz.) pkg. semi-sweet
chocolate chips

½ tsp. salt

¼ cup cocoa .

1½ cups flour

⅓ cup cooking oil

1 tsp. baking soda

1 cup sugar

1 cup water

1 T. vinegar

1 tsp. vanilla

Preheat oven to 350F. Grease 20 cupcake cups. Mix cream cheese, egg, sugar, and salt; beat well and set aside. Mix remaining ingredients together. Fill muffin tins ⅓ full. Spoon 1 heaping tablespoon of cheese mixture in middle of batter. Bake 25 min.

Mrs. Ron Bergman

RED CAKE
12-15 servings

3 tsp. cocoa	1 tsp. vanilla
1 (½ oz.) bottle	2 cups flour
red food coloring	½ tsp. salt
½ cup shortening	1 cup buttermilk
1½ cups sugar	1 T. vinegar
2 eggs	1 tsp. baking soda

Frosting:

5 T. flour	1 cup sugar
1 cup milk	½ tsp. salt
½ cup margarine	1 tsp. vanilla
½ cup shortening	confectioners' sugar to taste

Preheat oven to 325F. Grease and flour two 8" or 9" round cake pans. Mix cocoa and food coloring into paste. Cream shortening, sugar, eggs, and vanilla. Mix in paste. Mix together flour and salt; add to mixture alternately with buttermilk. Blend thoroughly. Add vinegar and soda. Pour into pans and bake 45 min.

Combine flour and milk; cook, stirring constantly, until a thick paste is formed; cool. Cream margarine, shortening, sugar, salt, and vanilla. Add paste and beat until creamy. Spread part of this mixture between cake layers. Beat confectioners' sugar in remaining frosting for top and sides of cake.

Mrs. James Brooks

SAUERKRAUT CHOCOLATE CAKE
12-15 servings

⅔ cup margarine	1 tsp. baking soda
1½ cups sugar	¼ tsp. salt
3 eggs	1 cup water
1 tsp. vanilla	⅔ cup sauerkraut,
½ cup cocoa	rinsed, drained and
2¼ cups flour	chopped
1 tsp. baking powder	

continued

380

Frosting:
1 cup milk
¼ cup flour
½ cup shortening
½ cup margarine

1 cup sugar
½ cup confectioners' sugar
⅛ tsp. salt
1 tsp. vanilla

Preheat oven to 350F. Grease and flour two 8'' round pans. Cream margarine and sugar; beat in eggs and vanilla. Sift dry ingredients together; add alternately with water to first mixture. Stir in sauerkraut. Pour into pans and bake 30 min. Cool.

Cook milk and flour until thick, stirring constantly. Cool. Cream shortening, margarine, sugar and confectioners' sugar; add cooked mixture, salt, and vanilla. Beat until fluffy. Spread on cooled cake.

Mrs. Lynn Hoepfinger

TEXAS SHEET CAKE
24 servings

1 cup water
1 cup margarine
¼ cup cocoa
2 cups flour, sifted
2 cups sugar

1 tsp. baking soda
½ tsp. salt
2 eggs
½ cup sour cream

Frosting:
½ cup margarine
¼ cup cocoa
6 T. milk

1 (1 lb.) box confectioners'
*   sugar*
1 cup nuts, chopped
1 tsp. vanilla

Preheat oven to 400F. Grease and flour a 10½'' x 15½'' jelly roll pan. Bring water, margarine, and cocoa to a boil; cool. Combine flour, sugar, soda and salt; add to cocoa mixture. Add eggs and sour cream. Pour into pan and bake 20 min. Frost while warm.

Bring margarine, cocoa and milk to a boil; cool. Beat in sugar until smooth. Add nuts and vanilla. Spread on warm cake.

Mrs. Clyde Line

WACKY CAKE
9 servings

1½ cups flour
1 cup sugar
3 T. cocoa
½ tsp. salt
1 tsp. baking soda

1 T. vinegar
6 T. margarine, melted
1 tsp. vanilla
1 cup cold water

Preheat oven to 350F. Use an ungreased 9" x 9" x 2" pan. Sift dry ingredients into pan. Level off and punch 3 holes into mixture with back of spoon. Into one hole pour vinegar, into the next pour margarine, and into the last hole the vanilla. Pour water over all and stir thoroughly with a fork. Bake 25 min. This is a fine moist devil's food cake that will keep 4 or 5 days and is a man's favorite.

Mrs. Richard Johnson
Mrs. Alvin Vander Kolk

CRANBERRY CAKE
16 servings

3 T. butter
1 cup sugar
½ cup water
1 cup sweetened
condensed milk

2 cups flour
1 tsp. salt
2 tsp. baking soda
2 cups raw cranberries,
sliced

Sauce:
¼ cup butter
1 cup sugar

½ cup sweetened
condensed milk
1 tsp. vanilla

Preheat oven to 350F. Grease a 9" x 13" pan. Cream together butter and sugar. Combine water and milk and add to creamed mixture alternately with dry ingredients. Add cranberries. Pour into pan and bake 30-35 min.

Combine sauce ingredients and cook over medium-low heat. Serve hot over cake squares.

Mrs. John Suby

KRUIMEL KOEK
Dutch Crumb Cake

9 servings

2½ cups flour
½ tsp. salt
½ tsp. baking soda
½ cup shortening
¾ cup brown sugar,
    firmly packed

1 cup raisins, ground
1 egg, beaten
¾ cup thick sour milk
2 T. sugar
⅛ tsp. cinnamon

Preheat oven to 350F. Grease an 8" x 8" pan. Sift together flour, salt, and soda. Cream shortening, gradually add brown sugar; mix until light and fluffy. Blend in dry ingredients. Reserve ¾ cup mixture. Combine raisins, egg, and milk; add to remaining mixture. Beat well. Pour into pan. Sprinkle reserved mixture over batter. Sprinkle sugar and cinnamon on top. Bake 25 min.

ITALIAN CREAM CAKE
So Good and Moist

16 servings

2 cups sugar
½ cup shortening
½ cup margarine
5 eggs, separated,
    room temperature
1 T. vanilla

2 cups cake flour, sifted
1 tsp. baking soda
½ tsp. salt
1 cup buttermilk
2 cups flaked coconut
1 cup pecans, chopped

Frosting:
1 (8 oz.) pkg. cream
    cheese
½ cup margarine

1 (1 lb.) box
    confectioners' sugar
1 tsp. vanilla

Preheat oven to 350F. Generously grease and flour 3 9" layer cake pans. Cream sugar, shortening and margarine until light and fluffy. Add egg yolks, one at a time, beating well after each addition; add vanilla. Sift together flour, soda and salt and add to creamed mixture alternately with buttermilk. Fold in coconut and pecans. Beat egg whites until stiff; gently fold into cake batter. Pour into pans and bake for 30-35 min.

continued

Prepare frosting by creaming cream cheese and margarine until well blended. Slowly beat in confectioners' sugar; add vanilla. Fill and frost top and sides of cake.

Idea! Use 4 8" cake pans and freeze 2 layers.

Mrs. Uel Kimzey

GEVULDE KOEK
Filled Cake

12 servings

¹/₃ cup butter
¹/₈ tsp. salt
¹/₂ cup sugar
4 egg yolks, beaten

1 tsp. baking powder
1 cup flour, sifted
¹/₄ cup milk

Meringue:
4 egg whites, room
   temperature
1 cup confectioners' sugar

¾ cup almonds,
   chopped

Custard:
1 cup milk
2 T. sugar
1 T. cornstarch
¹/₈ tsp. salt

1 egg, slightly beaten
1 tsp. vanilla
1 cup heavy cream,
   whipped

Preheat oven to 325F. Line two 9" layer cake pans with wax paper. Cream butter, salt, and sugar; add egg yolks and blend well. Sift baking powder with flour and add alternately with milk. Beat well. Spread in pans. Beat egg whites, add sugar gradually. Spread over batter; sprinkle with almonds. Bake 25 min. Increase heat to 350F. and bake 30 min. longer. Cool in pans.

Heat milk in double boiler. Mix sugar, cornstarch and salt; blend with a little of the milk. Return to double boiler and cook 10 min., stirring as needed. Pour a little hot mixture into egg, return to double boiler and cook 2 min., stirring constantly. Add vanilla. Cool. Place 1 layer, meringue side down, on serving plate, cover with custard and place second layer on top, merinque side up. Garnish with whipped cream.

FRUIT CAKE
18 servings

1 cup shortening
½ cup sugar
½ cup honey
5 eggs, beaten
1½ cups flour, sifted
1 tsp. salt
1 tsp. baking powder
1 tsp. allspice
½ tsp. nutmeg
½ tsp. ground cloves
¼ cup rum (brandy
   or orange juice)

1 (8 oz.) jar candied
   fruit, chopped
½ lb. candied cherries
½ lb. walnuts, chopped
½ lb. pecans, chopped
½ lb. dates, chopped
½ lb. candied
   pineapple
½ lb. seeded raisins
¼ cup flour
brandy

Preheat oven to 250F. Line a 10" tube pan with aluminum foil. Cream shortening and sugar; add honey and eggs. Sift together flour, salt, baking powder, allspice, nutmeg, cloves, and add alternately with rum; beat. Combine fruits and dredge with flour. Fold batter into fruits and mix well. Pour into pan. Do not flatten batter. Place pan in 1" of water and bake 3 hrs. Cool. Brush with brandy and wrap tightly in foil. Make 3 to 6 weeks prior to serving and moisten with brandy 3 times.

Mrs. William Mendenhall

TULBAND
18 servings

Light Fruit Cake

1 cup sugar
½ cup shortening
2 eggs, beaten
1 cup milk
2 tsp. baking powder
2 cups flour, sifted
1 cup raisins

¼ lb. citron
juice and grated rind
   of 1 orange
2 oz. walnuts, chopped
1 tsp. vanilla or
   almond flavoring
confectioners' sugar

Preheat oven to 350F. Grease and flour 10" tube pan. Cream sugar and shortening, add eggs. Gradually add milk, baking powder, and flour. Mix in fruit, nuts, and flavoring. Pour in pan and bake 1 hr. Cool. Dust with confectioners' sugar or serve plain.

SOUTHERN SPICY GINGERBREAD   *12-15 servings*

¾ cup shortening,
  melted
¾ cup brown sugar
¾ cup molasses
2 eggs, beaten
2½ cups flour
2 tsp. baking soda
2 tsp. ginger

1½ tsp. cinnamon
½ tsp. cloves
½ tsp. nutmeg
½ tsp. baking powder
1 cup boiling water
2 cups heavy cream,
  whipped

Preheat oven to 350F. Grease a 9" x 13" pan. Combine shortening, sugar, and molasses; add eggs. Sift together dry ingredients and add to first mixture. Add water. Pour into pan and bake 30-40 min. Serve warm with whipped cream.

Mrs. Lyle Sanders

TROPISCHE GEMBERKOEK   *12-15 servings*
Tropical Gingerbread

½ cup butter
½ cup sugar
2 eggs, beaten
1 tsp. baking soda
½ cup molasses
1 tsp. ginger

1 tsp. cinnamon
¼ tsp. salt
1½ cups flour
½ cup cold water
1 cup coconut

Frosting:
1 cup sugar
1 cup water
2 egg whites, room
  temperature

1 tsp. orange or
  lemon extract
1 cup coconut

Preheat oven to 350F. Grease a 9" x 13" pan. Cream butter and sugar; add eggs. Dissolve soda in molasses and add to first mixture. Sift dry ingredients and add alternately with water. Add coconut. Pour into pan and bake 30-35 min.

Boil sugar and water without stirring, until syrup forms a long thread. Beat egg whites; slowly add boiling syrup. Add extract. Mix in ½ cup coconut. Frost cooled cake; sprinkle remaining coconut on top.

MOCHA TORTE CAKE

12-15 servings

3 egg yolks
1 cup sugar
⅔ cup milk
1 cup flour, sifted

1 tsp. baking powder
⅛ tsp. salt
3 egg whites, room
  temperature

Frosting:
1 cup prepared
  vanilla pudding
½ cup butter,
  softened

½ cup sugar
1 tsp. instant coffee
1 T. water, room
  temperature

Preheat oven to 375F. Grease a 9" x 13" pan. Beat egg yolks until light and fluffy. Gradually add sugar and milk. Sift together dry ingredients and add to mixture. Fold in stiffly beaten egg whites. Pour into pan and bake 30-35 min. Cool and slice cake crosswise into 2 layers.

Spread pudding between cake layers. Cream butter and sugar. Dissolve coffee in water and add to creamed mixture. Spread on cake top and sides.

Mrs. Arndt Garretson

OATMEAL CAKE

12-15 servings

1 cup quick oats
1¼ cups water, boiled
½ cup shortening
1 cup brown sugar
1 cup white sugar
2 eggs

1½ cups flour, sifted
1 tsp. salt
1 tsp. baking soda
1 tsp. cinnamon
1 tsp. vanilla

Topping:
6 T. butter
1 cup brown sugar
1 cup flaked coconut

5 T. cream
1 cup pecans, chopped

continued

Preheat oven to 350F. Grease a 13" x 9" pan. Mix oats and boiling water; cool. Cream shortening and sugars; add eggs. Sift together dry ingredients; add alternately with oatmeal to creamed mixture. Add vanilla. Pour into pan and bake 45 min.

Mix ingredients for topping. Put on warm cake, set under broiler until it bubbles.

Mrs. Don Hillebrands
Mrs. Frank Conley

ORANGE COCONUT CAKE   12-15 servings

½ cup shortening
1 cup sugar
2 eggs, beaten
2 cups cake flour,
  sifted

3½ tsp. baking powder
½ tsp. salt
1¼ cups milk
1 tsp. vanilla

Frosting:
2 egg whites
1½ cups sugar
¼ tsp. salt
3 T. orange juice

2 T. water
1 T. orange rind,
  grated
1 cup coconut, grated

Preheat oven to 375F. Grease two 8" layer cake pans. Cream shortening, gradually adding sugar. Add eggs. Sift together flour, baking powder, and salt; add alternately with milk, mixing well after each addition. Add vanilla. Pour into pans and bake 30 min.

Mix unbeaten egg whites, sugar, salt, orange juice and water in top of double boiler. Place over rapidly boiling water and beat with a rotary beater 7 min. or until frosting holds in peaks. Remove from boiling water; add orange rind and mix well. Beat with spatula until frosting is thick and creamy. Spread between layers and on top and sides of cooled cake; sprinkle with coconut.

Mrs. Michael Calahan

PECAN CAKE WITH RUM SAUCE   *10-12 servings*

3 cups flour
1½ cups sugar
4½ tsp. baking powder
1½ tsp. salt
1⅓ cups milk

⅓ cup butter
⅓ cup shortening
3 eggs
2 tsp. vanilla
½ cup pecans, ground

Sauce:
1½ cups apricot
   nectar
1 cup sugar
2-3 T. cornstarch
2 T. cold water

½ cup light or
   dark rum
1 (1 lb.) can mandarin
   oranges, drained

Preheat oven to 350F. Grease and flour a 12 cup bundt or 10" tube pan. Combine all ingredients in large mixing bowl. Blend ½ min. on low speed, scraping bowl constantly. Beat 3 min. on high speed, scraping bowl often. Pour into pan and bake 55-60 min. Cool.

Bring to boil apricot nectar and sugar, stirring often. Simmer 8 min. Blend cornstarch and water; stir into sauce. Cook, stirring constantly, until sauce thickens and clears. Cool. Add rum and oranges. Drizzle cooled cake with a little sauce. Serve slices topped with remaining sauce.

Mrs. Michael Calahan

TOASTED BUTTER PECAN CAKE   *12-15 servings*

2 cups pecans,
   chopped
1¼ cups butter
2 cups sugar
4 eggs

3 cups flour
2 tsp. baking powder
½ tsp. salt
1 cup milk
2 tsp. vanilla

Frosting:
¼ cup butter
1 lb. confectioners'
   sugar

4-6 T. evaporated milk
   or cream
1 tsp. vanilla

continued

Preheat oven to 350F. Grease and flour three 8" or 9" round pans. Toast pecans in ¼ cup butter in oven 20 min.; stir frequently. Cream remaining butter, gradually adding sugar; beat well. Blend in eggs, one at a time, beating well after each. Sift together flour, baking powder, and salt. Add alternately with milk, beginning and ending with dry ingredients. Stir in vanilla and 1⅓ cups pecans. Pour into pans and bake 25-30 min.

Cream butter and sugar. Gradually add milk until desired spreading consistency is reached. Add vanilla and remaining pecans. Frost cooled cake between layers and on top.

Mrs. Howard Perry

PINEAPPLE FEATHER CAKE   *10-12 servings*

**6 eggs, separated,
  room temperature**
¾ cup sugar
½ cup pineapple juice
1 T. lemon juice

¼ tsp. salt
¾ cup sugar
1½ cups flour
1 tsp. baking powder

Topping:
1½ cups light cream
1 egg yolk, beaten
¾ cup sugar
**1 T. unflavored
  gelatin**

2 T. cold water
**2 cups heavy cream,
  whipped**
1 tsp. vanilla

Preheat oven to 325F. Grease and flour a 10" tube pan. Beat egg yolks until lemon colored; gradually add sugar. Add pineapple and lemon juice. Beat egg whites until stiff; gradually add salt and sugar. Combine yolk mixture with whites; fold in flour and baking powder. Pour in pan and bake 1 hr. Cool.

Warm cream in top of double boiler; blend in yolk and sugar. Dissolve gelatin in water; add to hot custard. Beat until cooled. Add whipped cream and vanilla. Spread on cooled cake.

Mrs. Harold Vander Bie

390

PINEAPPLE UPSIDE DOWN CAKE   9 servings

2 T. margarine
½ cup brown sugar
4 pineapple slices,
   halved
4 maraschino
   cherries, halved
⅓ cup shortening
1¼ cups flour, sifted

½ cup sugar
2 tsp. baking powder
½ tsp. salt
½ cup pineapple syrup
½ tsp. lemon peel,
   grated
1 egg
1 cup heavy cream, whipped

Preheat oven to 350F. Melt margarine in an 8" x 8" pan. Stir in brown sugar. Arrange pineapple in mixture, placing a cherry half in each hollow. Combine shortening and dry ingredients. Add syrup, lemon peel, and egg; mix well. Beat 2 min. Pour batter over pineapple and bake 30-35 min. Let stand 10 min., invert on plate. Serve warm with whipped cream.

Mrs. George Lievense

POPPY SEED CAKE   12-15 servings

¾ cup poppy seeds
¾ cup milk
¾ cup margarine
1½ cups sugar
1 tsp. vanilla

Filling:
½ cup sugar
1 T. cornstarch
1 cup milk, scalded
4 egg yolks

Frosting:
2 (1 oz. each) squares
   unsweetened chocolate
1 egg

2 cups cake flour, sifted
2 tsp. baking powder
½ tsp. salt
4 egg whites, room
   temperature

¼ tsp. salt
1 tsp. vanilla
¾ cup nuts, chopped

1 cup sugar
5 T. cream

continued

Preheat oven to 350F. Grease two 9" layer cake pans. Blend poppy seeds and milk; allow to stand 2 hrs. Cream margarine, sugar and vanilla until light and fluffy. Sift together dry ingredients and add alternately with poppy seed mixture. Fold in stiffly beaten egg whites. Spread in pans and bake 25-35 min. Cool.

Combine sugar and cornstarch. Blend in scalded milk and cook, stirring constantly, until slightly thickened. Beat egg yolks; add a small amount of hot mixture to yolks, then stir into remaining custard. Cook and stir until thickened. Stir in salt, vanilla, and nuts. Cool. Spread filling between layers.

Mix frosting ingredients in saucepan. Cook, stirring constantly, to a boil; then boil 2 min. Cool slightly and spread on sides and top of cake.

Mrs. Jack Dozeman

POUND CAKE
10 servings

2¼ cups cake flour,
  sifted
1 cup sugar
2 tsp. baking powder
1 tsp. salt
¼ cup margarine

¼ cup shortening
1 tsp. vanilla
1 lemon rind, grated
5 egg yolks
¾ cup milk

Preheat oven to 350F. Line a 9" x 5" loaf pan with wax paper. Sift flour, sugar, baking powder, and salt. Add margarine, shortening, vanilla, lemon rind, yolks and ½ cup milk. Beat 2 min. at medium speed. Add remaining milk; beat 2 more min. Pour into pan and bake 60 min.

Mrs. Dale Anthonsen

EENVOUDIGE KOEK
Sour Cream Pound Cake

12 servings

1 cup butter,
 softened
2⅔ cup sugar
6 eggs
3 cups flour, sifted
½ tsp. salt

¼ tsp. baking soda
1 cup sour cream
1 tsp. vanilla
confectioners' sugar glaze
red and green
 maraschino cherries

Preheat oven to 350F. Line bottom of 9'' tube pan with paper. Cream butter and sugar until light. Add eggs, one at a time, beating thoroughly after each. Sift dry ingredients together and add alternately with sour cream to first mixture; beat until smooth. Add vanilla. Pour into pan and bake 1 hr. 20 min. Let stand in pan for 5 min., turn out and cool. Cover cake with frosting, allowing it to run down sides. Decorate with whole red cherries and quartered green (leaves) cherries.

Mrs. Miriam VanEyl

RICH 'N MOIST PRUNE CAKE
(2nd Place Bake-Off)

12-15 servings

3 eggs
1½ cups sugar
1 cup oil
½ tsp. salt
1 tsp. cinnamon
1 tsp. nutmeg
1 tsp. ground cloves

1 cup prunes, cooked,
 drained and chopped
2 cups flour
1 tsp. baking soda
1 cup buttermilk
1 cup nuts, chopped

Sauce:
1 cup sugar
½ cup buttermilk
½ tsp. baking soda

3 T. butter
2 tsp. vanilla
1 T. light corn syrup

continued

Preheat oven to 350F. Grease a 9" x 13" pan. Cream eggs and sugar. Blend in oil and next 4 seasonings; add prunes. Combine flour and soda and add to cream mixture alternately with buttermilk; blend well. Fold in nuts. Pour into pan and bake for 40-50 min.

Combine sauce ingredients and boil for 3 min. Prick cake and pour sauce over, letting sauce soak through.

Mrs. Terri Granskog

PEPER KOEK
Dutch Spice Cake

12 servings

1 cup brown sugar	½ cup cold water
½ cup shortening	2 cups flour
2 eggs, beaten	1 tsp. ginger
1 tsp. baking soda	1 tsp. cinnamon
½ cup molasses	⅛ tsp. salt

Sauce:

2 cups brown sugar	2 T. butter
2 T. flour	2 tsp. vanilla
2 cups hot water	

Preheat oven to 300F. Grease a 7½" x 11¼" pan. Cream sugar and shortening; add eggs. Stir soda into molasses; add to mixture. Blend in water. Sift together flour and spices; add to mixture. Pour into pan and bake 40 min.

Mix brown sugar and flour; add water. Cook over medium heat until mixture thickens. Remove from heat; add butter and vanilla. Serve hot over cake.

RAISIN CAKE
12-15 servings

1 cup raisins
3 cups water
1 cup sugar
½ cup shortening
2 eggs
½ tsp. cinnamon

½ tsp. nutmeg
½ tsp. cloves
½ tsp. salt
1 tsp. baking soda
2 cups flour
1 tsp. vanilla
1 cup nuts, chopped

Preheat oven to 350F. Grease a 13" x 9" pan. Boil raisins in water until 1 cup water remains; cool. Cream sugar and shortening; add eggs. Sift dry ingredients into mixture. Add raisin mixture, vanilla and nuts. Pour into pan and bake 30 min.

Mrs. Billy J. Boes

SOUR CREAM CAKE
12 servings

1 cup butter
3 cups sugar
6 egg yolks
3 cups flour, sifted
¼ tsp. baking soda

1 cup sour cream
6 egg whites, room
   temperature
fresh fruit

Preheat oven to 300F. Grease and flour a 10" tube pan. Cream butter and sugar. Add yolks, one at a time, beating after each addition. Add flour and baking soda alternately with sour cream. Beat egg whites until stiff; fold into mixture. Pour into pan and bake 1½ hrs. Turn out immediately and serve with fresh fruit spooned over cake slices.

Mrs. Ginny Pollock

SUNSHINE CAKE

12-15 servings

10 egg whites, room
   temperature
1 ½ cups sugar
7 egg yolks

1 cup flour, sifted
½ tsp. cream of tartar
1 tsp. vanilla

Frosting:
3 egg yolks,
   slightly beaten
1 cup milk
½ cup sugar

1 envelope unflavored
   gelatin
¼ cup cold water
2 cups heavy cream, whipped

Preheat oven to 350F. Grease and flour a 10'' tube pan. Beat egg whites until frothy; add ¾ cup sugar and beat until peaks form. Beat egg yolks, gradually adding ¾ cup sugar until lemon colored. Fold yolk mixture into whites. Sift together flour and cream of tartar; fold into mixture. Add vanilla. Pour into pan and bake 45 min. Invert to cool. Slice cooled cake crosswise into 3 layers.

Cook yolks, milk and sugar in double boiler until thick. Remove from heat. Dissolve gelatin in cold water and add to yolk mixture. Cool to room temperature; add whipped cream. Spread frosting between layers and on top and sides. Cool and store in refrigerator.

Mrs. Morris Peterson

The Candy and Cookie Jar

NOTES

BUTTER CREAM CHOCOLATE BARS 3-4 doz.

½ cup margarine
1 (4 oz.) pkg German sweet
  chocolate
1 egg, beaten
1 tsp. vanilla
2 cups graham cracker crumbs
1 cup coconut

½ cup nuts, chopped
2 cups confectioners' sugar
¼ cup margarine
2 T. instant vanilla pudding
milk

Melt margarine and ½ bar of chocolate; add egg and vanilla. Let stand till thick; add cracker crumbs, coconut and nuts. Press in an ungreased 8'' x 8'' pan and refrigerate. For the second layer, mix sugar, margarine, pudding and enough milk to make stiff. Spread over first layer. Melt the remaining ½ bar of chocolate and pour over top. These bars must be kept in refrigerator.

Mrs. Justin Brower

CARAMEL CORN 8 quarts

2 cups brown sugar
1 cup butter
½ cup light corn syrup
1 tsp. salt

1 tsp. vanilla
½ tsp. baking soda
8 qts. popped corn
(approximately 2 cups raw)

In a 2-qt. saucepan, combine sugar, butter, corn syrup and salt. Over low heat, bring to a boil and cook 5 mins. Remove from heat; add vanilla and baking soda. Pour syrup over corn; mix well. Bake in large roaster pan at 250F. for 1 hr. stirring every 15 mins. Spread on waxed paper to cool. Caramel corn can be kept for weeks, if stored in an air-tight container.

Mrs. Jay Freriks

CHOCOLATE CLUSTER
about 30 pieces

2 cups sugar
½ cup milk
¼ cup margarine
1 tsp. vanilla
5 T. cocoa or 2 (1 oz. each)
   squares unsweetened
   chocolate or 1 (6 oz.) pkg. semi-
   sweet chocolate chips

3 cups quick cooking
   rolled oats
1 cup coconut or nuts,
   optional

In a 2-qt. saucepan, combine sugar, milk and margarine; boil 1 min. Add vanilla and cocoa. Combine oatmeal and coconut; add chocolate mixture and mix well. Drop by teaspoonful on waxed paper.

Variation: substitute 1 (6 oz.) pkg. butterscotch chips for the cocoa and 3 cups chow mein noodles for the oatmeal.

Mrs. Ward Perry

CHOCOLATE COVERED CREAMS
150 pieces

½ cup margarine
2 (1 lb. each) boxes
   confectioners' sugar
1 (14 oz.) can sweetened
   condensed milk
1 T. vanilla or other flavoring

1 cup pecans or walnuts,
   chopped
2 cups large flaked coconut
2 (12 oz. each) pkg. semi-
   sweet chocolate chips
¾ bar paraffin

Cream together margarine, confectioners' sugar, condensed milk and vanilla. Mix in nuts and coconut. Shape into small balls; place on wax paper and chill.

In a double boiler, melt chocolate and paraffin. Using a toothpick or fork, dip each piece of candy into chocolate and set on wax paper. Store in cool place.

Mrs. Clyde Line

CHOCOLATE PEANUT BUTTER BALLS   70 to 80 balls

2 cups creamy peanut butter
½ cup margarine, melted
1 (1 lb.) box confectioners'
   sugar
3 cups Rice Krispies

1 (6 oz.) pkg. semi-sweet
   chocolate chips
1 (7 or 8 oz.) plain
   Hershey bar
½ cake paraffin wax

Mix together peanut butter, margarine, sugar and Rice Krispies and form into balls. In a double boiler, melt chocolate chips, chocolate bar and the paraffin wax. Dip balls into chocolate mixture, using 2 forks and put on waxed paper.

Mrs. Robert Hulst

DATE NUT CANDY   about 1½ lbs.

2 cups sugar
1 (5½ oz.) can evaporated milk
¼ tsp. cream of tartar

¾ lb. dates, chopped
1 cup nuts, chopped

In a saucepan, combine sugar, evaporated milk and cream of tartar. Cook until mixture reaches soft ball stage. Add dates and nuts; stir until stiff and creamy. Drop by teaspoonfuls on waxed paper. Sometimes this will be chewy but creams after setting.

Mrs. W. A. Hower

DIVINITY   30 pieces

2 cups sugar
½ cup light corn syrup
½ cup water

2 egg whites, room
   temperature
1 tsp. vanilla
1 cup walnuts, chopped

In a 2-qt. saucepan, combine sugar, corn syrup and water. Cook until mixture reaches hard ball stage. Beat egg whites to stiff peaks. Slowly pour hot syrup into egg whites, beating constantly at high speed on electric mixer. When mixture begins to stiffen, add vanilla. Stir in nuts. Drop by teaspoonfuls onto waxed paper.

Mrs. W. A. Hower

BROWN SUGAR FUDGE

about 1 ¼ lbs.

1 cup brown sugar
1 cup sugar
1 scant cup milk
½ tsp. baking soda

1 T. butter
1 tsp. vanilla
½ cup nuts

Butter sides of heavy 2-qt. pan. In it, combine sugars and milk. Bring to a boil and simmer at low temperature until mixture reaches soft ball stage. Remove from heat, add baking soda, butter, vanilla and nuts. Cool to lukewarm. Beat until thick and pour into buttered 9" x 5" x 3" pan.

Mrs. L. M. McCarthy

DOUBLE DELIGHT FUDGE

2 ¾ lbs.

2 ½ cups sugar
1 cup evaporated milk
¼ cup margarine
¼ tsp. salt
1 ½ cups miniature
marshmallows

1 cup nuts, chopped
1 tsp. vanilla
1 cup milk chocolate chips
1 cup semi-sweet chocolate
chips

In a 3-qt. saucepan, combine sugar, evaporated milk, margarine and salt. Bring to a full rolling boil over moderate heat; boil for 6 mins. Remove from heat and stir in marshmallows, nuts and vanilla until well blended. Divide in half; add milk chocolate chips to one half and pour it in buttered 8" x 8" pan. Add semi-sweet chips to the other half and pour on top of other mixture. Chill until firm, about 4 hrs.

Mrs. James W. F. Brooks

402

DUTCH FUDGE
about 1 ¼ lbs.

2 cups sugar
2-3 T. Droste's cocoa
2 T. margarine
1 cup milk
1 tsp. vanilla

pinch of salt
1 heaping T. marshmallow
   cream
½ cup nuts, chopped
(optional)

Butter sides of heavy 2-qt. pan. In it, combine sugar, cocoa, margarine and milk. Bring to a boil and cook slowly to the soft ball stage. Remove from heat, add vanilla, salt and marshmallow cream. Cool until lukewarm. Beat until candy starts to thicken and loses gloss. (If using nuts, add after beating candy just a little.) Turn out onto buttered platter.

Mrs. Phillip Enstam

VANILLA PUDDING FUDGE
1 ½ lbs.

1 pkg. regular vanilla
   pudding
2 T. butter

½ cup sweetened condensed
   milk
1 cup sugar
1 cup salted peanuts

Combine pudding, butter, milk and sugar. Cook 7 mins. Place peanuts in a 8" x 8" greased pan. Pour pudding mixture on top of peanuts. For variety, other flavored puddings and nuts may be used.

Mrs. Edward Damson

VELVET FUDGE
1¾ lbs.

3 cups sugar
¼ cup cocoa
pinch salt
⅞ cup milk
2 T. butter

½ tsp. cream of tartar
⅓ cup peanut butter and/or
½ cup nuts, chopped
1 tsp. vanilla

Butter sides of heavy 3-qt.pan. In it, combine sugar, cocoa and salt. Add milk and mix thoroughly. Heat to boiling without stirring; simmer at low temperature until mixture reaches soft ball stage. Remove from heat; add butter, cream of tartar, peanut butter and nuts without stirring. Cool by placing pan of fudge in pan of cold water. When fudge is lukewarm, add vanilla and beat vigorously; pour into buttered 8" x 8" tin before it becomes too stiff to pour.

Mrs. Bill Prince

GRANDMA'S FAVORITE HARD CANDY
3 lbs.

3¾ cups sugar
1¼ cup light corn syrup
1 cup water

1 tsp. flavoring oil (available
from pharmacist)
food coloring
confectioner's sugar

In 3-qt. saucepan, combine sugar, corn syrup and water; stirring, cook rapidly until syrup reaches 300F. Remove from heat and add flavoring oil, stirring quickly. Pour onto confectioners' sugar-covered flat surface (formica counter or marble slab). When mixture begins to harden, cut into pieces with kitchen shears.

Mrs. Clyde Line

MARSEPEIN ALMOND CANDY
about 1 lb.

1 egg white
1 cup almond paste

2 cups confectioners' sugar
1 tsp. salt

continued

Beat egg white until fluffy and combine with almond paste, confectioners' sugar and salt. Let stand 30 mins. to soften the paste. Mix 5 to 10 mins. until well blended. Place in covered earthen jar for 24 hrs. Using food colorings, make any shape of candy you prefer, ie. bananas, carrots and sausages. For small potatoes, shape into half-inch balls and roll into mixture of 1 T. cocoa and 3 T. sugar.

Mrs. Ken Kleis

OLD FASHIONED BUTTER CRUNCH

about 5 doz. pieces

2 cups almonds,
  finely chopped
1 cup margarine
1¼ cups sugar

2 T. light corn syrup
2 T. water
1 cup semi-sweet chocolate
  chips, melted

Spread almonds in shallow pan; toast in 350F. oven until golden. Melt margarine in large, heavy saucepan; add sugar, corn syrup and water. Cook, stirring often, to hard-crack stage. Remove from heat; stir in 1 cup toasted almonds. Pour quickly into 13" x 9" pan. Cool completely. When set, turn out on piece of waxed paper. Spread ½ of melted chocolate over top. Sprinkle with ½ cup almonds; let set. Turn over and repeat above. Let stand until chocolate sets. Break into pieces.

Mrs. Landis Zylman

PEANUT BRITTLE

2 lbs.

2 cups sugar
1 cup light corn syrup
½ cup water
2 cups raw peanuts

1 heaping tsp. butter
1 tsp. vanilla
1 tsp. baking soda

In saucepan, combine sugar, syrup and water and cook to hard ball stage. Add peanuts and butter; continue cooking until it browns. Remove from heat, add vanilla and baking soda, mixing well. Spread thinly on two (10" x 15") buttered cookie sheets. When cool, break into serving pieces.

Mrs. Harvey Kronemeyer
Mrs. Landis Zylman

PRALINES
20 pieces

1 cup buttermilk
2 cups sugar
1 tsp. baking soda

2 T. butter
1 tsp. vanilla
1 cup pecans chopped

In a 2-qt. saucepan, combine buttermilk, sugar and baking soda. Bring to a boil and simmer until mixture reaches soft ball stage. Add butter and vanilla; beat and add pecans. Drop by teaspoonfulls on waxed paper.

Mrs. Howard Poll

PEPERMUNTKUSSENTJES
about ½ lb.
After-dinner mints

½ egg white, room
temperature

1 or 2 drops peppermint oil
1 cup confectioners' sugar,
sifted

Beat egg white until fluffy. Constantly stirring, add egg white and oil to the sugar until a stiff, smooth paste forms. Roll the paste out into long rolls like a pencil on a board sprinkled with confectioners' sugar. Cut these long strips with a scissors into small square pieces. Let stiffen in cool place.

Mrs. Ken Kleis

TOFFEE CANDY
about 1 lb.

1 cup pecans
¾ cup brown sugar
½ cup butter

½ cup semi-sweet
chocolate chips

Sprinkle pecans in a buttered 9" x 9" pan. In a saucepan, combine sugar and butter. Stirring constantly, boil for 7 mins. Spread mixture over nuts. Sprinkle the chocolate chips over hot mixture; cover pan to keep warm. After chips are melted, spread with a knife. Cut while warm. Refrigerate to set.

Mrs. Fred Leaske

ENGLISH TOFFEE
about 3 lbs.

2 cups butter
2 cups sugar

6 (1.2 oz. each) milk chocolate
Hershey bars, melted
1 cup walnuts, chopped

In saucepan, combine butter and sugar; boil until mixture reaches hard crack stage. Pour on greased cookie sheet; cool. Spread with melted milk chocolate and sprinkle with nuts. When hard, break into pieces.

Mr. Jay W. Formsma

SALT WATER TAFFY
1¼ lbs.

2 cups sugar
1 T. cornstarch
¾ tsp. salt
½ T. butter

1 cup light corn syrup
¾ cup water
1 tsp. vanilla

In 2-qt. saucepan, melt together sugar, cornstarch, salt and butter. Add corn syrup and water; stir only until mixture boils rapidly. Continue boiling until mixture reaches hard ball stage. Add vanilla; pour onto a large, buttered platter. When cool enough to handle, butter hands and pull taffy until light in color and hard to pull. Pull into a rope and cut in inch lengths. Wrap in waxed paper.

Mrs. Harold Buter

SUGAR-COATED WALNUTS
2 lbs.

1 cup sugar
5 T. water
1 tsp. cinnamon
1 tsp. salt

1 tsp. vanilla
2 (1 lb. each) bags shelled
walnut halves

In saucepan, combine sugar, water, cinnamon and salt; boil until mixture reaches soft ball stage. Stir in vanilla and walnuts. Pour mixture onto waxed paper to dry. When cool, separate. Especially nice for the holidays.

Mrs. David Paulson

VERSNAPERING
Puffed Cereal Snacks

1 qt.

½ cup sugar
1 T. butter

4 cups Puffed barley, Kix,
Krispies or any
puffed cereal

In heavy skillet, brown sugar and butter until light brown. Remove from burner and quickly add cereal. Spread on buttered cookie sheet. If mixture sticks to spoon when spreading, dip spoon into cold water frequently. Cut or break into bite-sized pieces when cold.

ZEEUWSE BABBELAARS
Hard Candy

1 lb.

1 cup brown sugar
1 cup sugar
2 T. butter

⅓ cup vinegar
⅓ cup water

In a saucepan, combine sugars, butter, vinegar and water. Boil without stirring, until mixture reaches hard crack stage. Pour onto large, buttered pan. When cool enough to handle, butter hands and pull candy into long strips. Cut at once into small square pieces. Wrap in waxed paper.

Mrs. Chris Sas

ALMOND BARK SWEETIES

4 doz.

2 lbs. almond bark candy or
white chocolate stars candy
2 cups chunky peanut butter
2 cups miniature marshmallows

2 cups Rice Krispies
2 cups roasted peanuts,
chopped

Melt candy in double boiler, stirring until melted. Remove from heat and add peanut butter. Cool 5 mins.; add marshmallows, Rice Krispies and peanuts. Drop by teaspoonfuls on waxed paper. Dry. These cookies freeze well.

Mrs. Joseph Gartner

APRICOT BALLS   *about 6 doz.*

1½ cups dried apricots, ground   ⅔ cup sweetened condensed
2 cups coconut, ground   milk
¼ cup sugar   sugar for coating balls

Mix together apricots, coconut, sugar and milk. Form into balls and roll in granulated sugar.

Mrs. J. E. Campbell

CHOCOLATE NUGGETS   *4 doz.*

½ cup margarine   2 cups quick-cooking rolled
2 cups sugar   oats
½ cup Dutch cocoa   2 cups flaked coconut
½ cup milk   1 T. dark rum (optional)
⅓ tsp. salt

Bring to a rolling boil margarine, sugar, cocoa and milk. Remove from heat; stir in salt, rolled oats, coconut and rum. Drop by rounded teaspoonfuls onto waxed paper. Cool.

Mrs. Leo Jungblut

COCONUT CUTIES   *3-4 doz.*

2½ cups graham cracker   ½ cup nuts, chopped
  crumbs   3 cups miniature
1 (10 oz.) jar maraschino   marshmallows
  cherries, drained and halved   1 (13 oz.) can evaporated milk
1 cup dates, chopped   flaked coconut

Mix crumbs, cherries, dates, nuts, marshmallows and milk; form into balls. Roll in flaked coconut. Set on waxed paper.

Mrs. Richard Flaherty

DATE COOKIES

3-4 doz.

½ cup sugar
1 egg
½ cup margarine, melted
½ lb. dates, chopped
1 tsp. vanilla

2½ cups Rice Krispies
½ cup nuts, chopped
confectioners' sugar
   for coating

In saucepan, combine sugar and egg; beat in margarine. Add dates. Cook mixture until it turns brown, stirring constantly. Cool. Add vanilla, Rice Krispies and nuts. Roll in small balls and then in confectioners' sugar.

Mrs. Norman Kalkman

GRAHAM CRACKER NIBBLERS

60 squares

14-16 graham crackers
1 cup margarine
1 cup milk
1 cup sugar

1 egg, slightly beaten
1 cup shredded coconut
1 cup pecans, chopped
1 cup graham cracker crumbs

Frosting:
1 cup confectioners' sugar
½ cup margarine

lemon juice

With half of graham crackers, cover bottom of 9" x 13" pan. In saucepan, combine margarine, milk, sugar and egg; bring to a boil. Add coconut, pecans, and crumbs. Cool. Pour mixture over crackers in pan. Use remainder of graham crackers to form top layer.

Frosting: Combine confectioners' sugar and margarine with enough lemon juice for spreading consistency. Frost. Chill overnight and cut into 1" squares.

Mrs. Charles Knowles

NONAIMO BARS   24 bars

½ cup butter
½ cup sugar
3 T. cocoa
1 egg, beaten
1 tsp. vanilla

2 cups crushed graham
crackers
1 cup coconut
½ cup walnuts, chopped

Topping:
¼ cup butter, softened
2 cups confectioners' sugar

1 tsp. vanilla
2 - 3 T. hot water

Glaze:
1 (1 oz.) square
unsweetened chocolate

1 T. butter

Heat butter, sugar, cocoa in double boiler. Stir till smooth; add egg and vanilla. Remove from heat. Add graham crackers, coconut and nuts. Spread in buttered 8" x 12" or 10" round pan and refrigerate.

Mix together topping and spread over first layer.

For glaze, melt together chocolate and butter. Drizzle on top. Cut into bars when firm. Refrigerate.

Mrs. Michael Doyle

ORANGE COOKIES   about 4 doz.

3 cups vanilla wafer crumbs
(about 66)
¾ cup shredded coconut
¾ cup confectioners' sugar

3 oz. frozen orange juice,
thawed and undiluted
confectioners' sugar for
coating

Combine wafer crumbs, coconut, confectioners' sugar; add orange juice. Form into small balls and roll in additional confectioners' sugar. Let stand a few days to mellow.

Mrs. Martin Japinga

RUM BALLS   5 - 6 doz.

2 cups vanilla wafer crumbs   ¼ tsp. salt
2 cups confectioners' sugar   ½ cup light rum
2 cups pecans, chopped   1 tsp. vanilla
¼ cup cocoa   confectioners' sugar for
¼ cup light corn syrup   coating

Combine crumbs, sugar, pecans, cocoa, corn syrup, salt, rum and vanilla. Shape into balls and roll in confectioners' sugar. Store in tightly-covered container. Especially nice for the holidays.

Mrs. J. E. Campbell

SPECIAL K SQUARES   25 squares

½ cup light corn syrup   1 (6 oz.) pkg. semi-sweet
½ cup sugar   chocolate chips
¾ cup crunchy peanut butter   1 (6 oz.) pkg. butterscotch
3½ cups Special K   chips
1 tsp. vanilla

In a large saucepan, bring syrup and sugar to a boil. Quickly add peanut butter. Then stir in Special K and vanilla. Spread in a greased 8" x 8" pan; cool. In a double boiler, melt chocolate and butterscotch chips, spread on top of cookie mixture. When cool, cut into squares. Store in refrigerator.

Mrs. Wm. Buis, Jr.
Mrs. George Worden

STRAWBERRY COOKIES
Very decorative

4 - 5 doz.

6 cups grated coconut
1 (14 oz.) can sweetened
    condensed milk
2 (3 oz. each) pkg. strawberry
    gelatin

¼ tsp. vanilla
1 T. sugar
20-25 drops red food coloring
green toothpicks

Frosting:
1 T. butter
½ cup confectioners' sugar,
    sifted

1 tsp. milk
green food coloring, few drops

Mix coconut, milk, all but 2 T. of gelatin, vanilla, sugar and food coloring. Shape mixture in the shape of strawberries and roll in the 2 T. of gelatin. Trim the strawberries with leaves using green decorative frosting.

Combine all ingredients for frosting. Beat. Place a little ball on top of the strawberry cookie and work down to make the leaves. Insert green toothpicks as stems. If green toothpicks are not available, place white ones in a bowl with green food coloring and add a little water.

Mrs. Joan Brieve

ALMOND BARS

32 bars

1 cup margarine
½ lb. almond paste
    (about 1 cup)
2 cups sugar

2 eggs
½ tsp. salt
2 cups flour
½ cup nuts, chopped

Preheat oven to 300F. Grease a 9" x 13" pan. Cream together margarine and almond paste; beat in sugar and eggs. Add flour and salt. Pour in pan; sprinkle with nuts. Bake for 40 mins.

Mrs. Audrey Penna

COCONUT-ALMOND BARS   24 squares

1½ cups flour   pinch of salt
3 T. sugar   ¾ cup margarine, melted

Filling:
6 eggs, beaten   1 (12 oz.) can almond cake and
2 cups sugar   pastry filling
2 cups coconut

Preheat oven to 350F. Grease a 9" x 13" pan. Combine flour, sugar, salt and margarine; press lightly in pan. Bake for 25 mins.

While crust is baking, combine eggs, sugar, coconut and almond filling. Pour over hot crust. Bake at 325F for 40 mins. more. While hot, cut into squares.

Mrs. Ray Backus

EASY ALMOND BARS   32 pieces

2 cups flour   2 tsp. almond extract
2 cups sugar   pinch of salt
1 cup margarine, melted   1 T. sugar
4 eggs   ½ cup sliced almonds
                                     (approximately)

Preheat oven to 350F. Grease a 9" x 13" pan. Combine flour, sugar, margarine, eggs, almond extract and salt. Pour into pan. Sprinkle with sugar and almonds. Bake for 30 mins.

Mrs. John Schmidt

APRICOT BARS
2½ doz. bars

1½ cups flour, sifted
1 tsp. baking powder
¼ tsp. salt
1½ cups quick-cooking rolled
   oats

1 cup brown sugar
1 cup margarine
¾ cup apricot preserves
   or jam

Preheat oven to 375F. Use an 9" x 9" pan. Sift together flour, baking powder and salt; stir in rolled oats and sugar. Cut in margarine until crumbly. Pat ⅔ of crumb mixture into pan. Spread with preserves. Cover with remaining crumb mixture. Bake for 35 mins. or until browned. Cool. Cut in bars or squares.

Mrs. Jack Miller

CREAM CHEESE BROWNIES
24 bars

1 (3 oz.) pkg. cream cheese
2 T. butter
¼ cup sugar

1 egg, slightly beaten
1 T. flour
1 tsp. vanilla

Chocolate Layers:
1 (4 oz.) pkg. German
   sweet chocolate
3 T. butter
2 eggs, well beaten
¾ cup sugar
½ tsp. baking powder

¼ tsp salt
½ cup flour
1 tsp. vanilla
1 tsp. almond extract
½ cup nuts, chopped
confectioners' sugar (optional)

Preheat oven to 350F. Grease a 9" x 9" pan. Combine cream cheese, butter, sugar, egg, flour and vanilla; set aside. Melt chocolate and butter together; cool. Combine and mix remainder of ingredients. Beat in chocolate mixture. Pour half of mixture in pan. Cover with cream cheese mixture, top with chocolate mixture. Zig-zag with knife to marbleize. Bake 35-40 mins. When cool, sprinkle with confectioners' sugar.

Mrs. Jay Freriks

CROWD PLEASER BROWNIES   35 squares

4 eggs, beaten
2 cups sugar
¼ cup cocoa
2 tsp. vanilla

1 cup margarine, melted
1½ cups flour
1 tsp. baking powder
1 cup nuts, chopped (optional)

Frosting:
2 T. margarine
1 tsp. vanilla
2 T. cocoa

8 oz. confectioners' sugar
(about 2¼ cup)
milk

Preheat oven to 350F. Grease a 10½" x 15½" pan. Combine eggs and sugar; mix well. Add cocoa, vanilla and margarine. Sift flour and baking powder together; add to chocolate mixture. Stir in nuts. Pour into pan and bake 22 mins. Frost immediately after removing from oven. Cut when cool.

For frosting, combine margarine, vanilla, cocoa and confectioners' sugar and enough milk to get a spreading consistency.

Mrs. Ray Backus

ONE POT BROWNIES   24 bars

4 (1 oz. each) squares
    unsweetened chocolate
1 cup margarine
2 cups sugar
4 eggs

1½ cups flour
2 tsp. vanilla
1 cup nuts, chopped and/or
1 cup raisins (optional)

Preheat oven to 375F. Grease a 9" x 13" pan. In a heavy pot, melt chocolate and margarine. Cool slightly. Add sugar and eggs, mixing well. Beat in flour and vanilla. Stir in nuts and raisins. Pour in baking pan. Bake for 20-25 mins. Do not overbake. Cut while warm (not hot.)

Mrs. Stuart Padnos

416

BUTTERSCOTCH BARS *40 bars*

½ cup margarine
2 cups brown sugar
2 eggs
1 tsp. vanilla
2 cups flour, sifted

2 tsp. baking powder
¼ tsp. salt
1 cup coconut
1 cup nuts, chopped (optional)

Preheat oven to 350F. Grease a 10½" x 15½" pan. Combine margarine and brown sugar; cook over low heat till bubbly. Add eggs, one at a time, beating well after each addition. Add vanilla. Sift together flour, baking powder and salt and add to first mixture. Stir in coconut and nuts. Pour into pan. Bake for 20 mins.

Mrs. John Suby

CELESTIAL SQUARES *16 squares*

½ cup margarine
2 cups brown sugar
1 tsp. vanilla
½ tsp. almond extract
3 eggs

2 cups flour
½ tsp. salt
1½ cups walnuts, chopped
2 (1 oz. each) squares
    unsweetened chocolate,
    melted

Frosting:
1 (6 oz.) pkg. semi-sweet
    chocolate chips
½ cup margarine

⅓ cup evaporated milk
5 cups confectioners' sugar
1 tsp. vanilla extract

Preheat oven to 350F. Grease a 9" x 13" pan. Cream together margarine, brown sugar, vanilla, and almond extract. Add eggs, one at a time, beating after each egg. Blend in flour and salt, stir in walnuts. Divide batter in half. Add chocolate to half of batter and pour this mixture into pan. Spread remaining batter over top and marbleize with a knife. Bake for 15-18 mins. Cool. Top with frosting.

For frosting, melt chips; add remaining ingredients and beat until smooth. Drizzle over cake.

Mrs. Lee Beyer

417

CHEESECAKE SQUARES   16 squares

⅓ cup margarine	1 (8 oz.) pkg. cream cheese,
⅓ cup brown sugar	softened
1 cup flour	1 egg
½ cup nuts, chopped	2 T. milk
¼ cup sugar	1 T. lemon juice
	½ tsp. vanilla

Preheat oven to 350F. Use an 8" x 8" pan. Cream together margarine and brown sugar; add flour and nuts. Mix to make a crumb mixture. Reserving 1 cup of mixture for topping, press remainder into bottom of pan. Bake for 12-15 mins. or until lightly browned. Blend sugar with cream cheese until smooth. Add egg, milk, lemon juice and vanilla; beat well. Spread over baked layer and sprinkle with reserved crumb mixture. Bake for 20-25 mins. Cool, cut into 2" squares.

Mrs. Delwyn Van Dyke

CHERRY COCONUT BARS   20 bars

1 cup flour	3 T. confectioners' sugar
½ cup butter	

Filling:

2 eggs, slightly beaten	1 tsp. vanilla
1 cup sugar	¾ cup nuts, chopped
¼ cup flour	½ cup coconut
½ tsp. baking powder	½ cup maraschino cherries,
¼ tsp. salt	quartered

Preheat oven to 350F. Use a 10" x 6" pan. With hands, combine flour, butter and confectioners' sugar until smooth. Spread thinly with fingers in pan. Bake 25 mins.

For the filling, combine all ingredients well. Spread over top of pastry and bake 25 mins.

Mrs. Tom DeVries

CHOCOLATE MINT STICKS
40 sticks

½ cup margarine
1 cup sugar
2 eggs
1 tsp. vanilla

2 (1 oz. each) squares unsweetened chocolate, melted
½ cup flour, sifted
½ cup walnuts, finely chopped

Mint frosting:
1 cup confectioners' sugar,
sifted
2 T. margarine, softened
1 T. light cream

¼ - ½ tsp. peppermint
extract
green food coloring (optional)

Chocolate Glaze:
1 (1 oz.) square unsweetened
chocolate

1 T. butter

Preheat oven to 350F. Grease an 8'' x 8'' pan. Cream together margarine and sugar until light and fluffy; beat in eggs and vanilla. Blend in chocolate; stir in flour, then nuts. Pour into pan and bake for about 25 mins. Cool, then spread with frosting, then glaze.

For frosting, combine all ingredients; beat well. Spread over cooled brownie layer, let stand till set.

For glaze, melt the 1 square chocolate with 1 T. margarine and spread over frosting. Chill until firm. Cut into 2'' x ¾'' bars.

Mrs. Jack Miller

CHOCOLATE OATMEAL SQUARES
32 bars

1 cup brown sugar
1 egg
½ cup margarine
½ tsp. salt

½ tsp. vanilla
1½ cups flour
1½ cups oatmeal

Filling:

1 (6 oz.) pkg. semi-sweet
   chocolate chips
1 (14 oz.) can sweetened
   condensed milk

1 T. butter
¼ tsp. salt
¼ tsp. vanilla

Preheat oven to 350F. Use an ungreased 9" x 13" pan. Combine brown sugar, egg, margarine, salt, vanilla, flour and oatmeal. Reserving ¼ of mixture for topping, pat remainder into pan. Combine chocolate chips, milk, butter, salt and vanilla and cook over low heat until chocolate is melted. Pour chocolate mixture over crust. Top with remaining crumb mixture. Bake for 25 mins.

Mrs. Don Tietsma

DATE BARS
30 bars

1 cup sugar
1 T. butter
3 eggs, beaten
1 cup flour
1 tsp. baking powder

½ tsp. salt
1 tsp. vanilla
1 cup nuts, chopped
1 cup dates, chopped
confectioners' sugar

Preheat oven to 350F. Grease a 9" x 13" pan. Cream together sugar, butter and eggs. Sift together flour, baking powder and salt; add to creamy mixture. Stir in nuts and dates; pour into pan. Bake 20 mins. Cool slightly and cut into bars. Cool completely before sprinkling with confectioners' sugar and removing from pan.

Mrs. William G. Winter

FRENCH PASTRY
24 bars

1 cup flour
1/3 cup margarine

1/4 cup brown sugar

Topping:
2 eggs, well beaten
2 T. flour
1 tsp. baking powder

1 1/2 cups brown sugar
1/2 cup shredded coconut
1 tsp. vanilla

Preheat oven to 350F. Use a 9" x 13" pan. Combine flour, margarine and brown sugar. Pat in bottom of pan. Bake for 10 mins.

Mix eggs, flour, baking powder, brown sugar, coconut and vanilla. Spread over baked layer. Continue baking 20-25 mins. Will keep well in refrigerator for weeks.

Mrs. Henry Maentz, Jr.
Mrs. Norman Kalkman

JAN HAGEL
about 6 doz. bars

Sugar cookies - very delicate!

1/2 cup butter
1/2 cup margarine
3/4 cup sugar
1 egg, separated

2 cups flour
1 tsp. cinnamon
1/4 tsp. baking soda
1 cup almonds, sliced

Preheat oven to 325F. Grease two (14" x 16") cookie sheets. Cream together butter, margarine and sugar; beat in egg yolk. Sift together flour, cinnamon and baking soda; add to first mixture. If dough is too thick, add a few drops water. Place half the dough in middle of cookie sheet, flatten. Place a sheet of waxed paper over the dough and roll very thin. Remove the paper, brush dough with slightly-beaten egg white; sprinkle with almonds. Press almonds into dough. Repeat with other half of dough. Bake for 25 mins. Cut immediately into bars and remove from cookie sheet.

Mrs. Cornelius Vander Kuy, Sr.
Mrs. Terry Hofmeyer

421

LEMON BARS
24 squares

2 cups flour
1 cup margarine
½ cup confectioners' sugar

Filling:
4 eggs, beaten
¼ cup flour
2 cups sugar
1 tsp. baking powder
dash salt
confectioners' sugar
6 T. lemon juice

Preheat oven to 350F. Grease a 9" x 13" pan. Combine flour and confectioners' sugar, cut in margarine. Pat into pan. Bake 20 mins. For filling, combine eggs, sugar, salt, lemon juice, flour and baking powder. Pour over hot crust. Bake 25 mins. Cool; sprinkle with confectioners' sugar. Cut into squares.

Variation: Confectioners' sugar can be omitted and a confectioners' sugar frosting with lemon juice can be substituted.

Mrs. Ray Backus

MARBLE SQUARES
24 squares

½ cup butter, softened
1 cup plus 2 T. sifted flour
6 T. sugar
½ tsp. baking soda
6 T. brown sugar
½ tsp. salt
½ tsp. vanilla
½ cup walnuts, chopped
¼ tsp. water
1 (6 oz.) pkg. semi-sweet
1 egg
chocolate chips

Preheat oven to 375F. Grease a 9" x 13" pan. Beat butter, sugars, vanilla and water until creamy. Mix in egg. Sift together flour, baking soda and salt; add to creamy mixture. Stir in walnuts. Spread in pan and sprinkle with chips. Bake 1 min. Run knife through dough to marbleize. Bake 12-14 mins. more.

Mrs. Carl S. Cook
Mrs. Bruce Van Dyke

PINEAPPLE BARS

35 bars

1 cup margarine	2½ cups flour
½ cup sugar	

Filling:

2 (1 lb. each) cans crushed pineapple, drained	1 cup sugar
	2 T. butter, melted
2 eggs, beaten	3 cups coconut

Preheat oven to 350F. Use an ungreased 10" x 15" pan. Combine margarine, sugar and flour as for pie crust. Press into pan and prick with fork. Bake 15 mins. Cool.

Spread pineapple on cooled crust. Combine eggs, sugar, butter and coconut and place on top of pineapple. Bake 20 mins. or till coconut is brown.

Mrs. David Kempker

AMANDEL KOEKJES

3 doz.

Almond Paste Cookies

½ cup butter	1½ cups flour
½ cup margarine	½ tsp. baking soda
¾ cup sugar	1 cup almond or kernel paste
2 eggs	½ cup nuts, chopped

Preheat oven to 325F. Cream butter, margarine, and sugar together; beat in eggs. Add flour and baking soda and then paste. If dough gets too stiff, add a few drops of water. Mix in nuts. Drop by teaspoonfuls on greased cookie sheet. Bake for 15 mins.

Mrs. Cornelius Vander Kuy, Sr.

AMERICAN CRISPS   7 doz.

1 cup sugar	3½ cup flour
1 cup brown sugar	1 tsp. baking soda
1 cup oil	1 tsp. salt
1 cup shortening, softened	1 cup corn flakes
1 egg, beaten	1 cup oatmeal
1 T. sour cream	½ cup coconut
or buttermilk	½ - 1 cup nuts, chopped
2 tsp. vanilla	

Preheat oven to 350F. Cream together sugars, oil, and shortening; add egg, sour cream, and vanilla. Sift together flour, baking soda and salt. Add to creamed mixture. Stir in corn flakes, oatmeal, coconut, and nuts. Drop by teaspoonfuls on greased cookie sheet; flatten with fork. Bake 10-12 mins.

Mrs. Marie Saunders
Mrs. Wm. Buis, Jr.

BITTER KOEKJES   3 doz.
Almond Cookies

1 heaping cup almond paste	3 egg whites, room
¾ cup sugar	temperature and beaten stiff

Preheat oven to 350F. Mix together paste and sugar and add egg whites. Drop by teaspoonfuls onto waxed paper lined cookie sheet; bake 30 mins. or until brown. Remove from waxed paper when taken from oven.

DAINTY DATE-NUT COOKIES   2 doz.

1 cup dates, chopped	1 cup confectioners' sugar
1 cup pecans, chopped	1 egg white, unbeaten

Preheat oven to 350F. Combine all ingredients and mix well. Drop by teaspoonfuls on greased cookie sheet. Bake 8-10 mins. Do not overbake. Cookies will be soft when removed from oven but will become firmer when cool. Do not try to remove until completely cool. Then remove gently.

Mrs. Tom Vander Kuy

DUIMPJES

4 doz.

Cookies

½ cup butter
¾ cup sugar
2½ cups flour, sifted
¼ tsp. salt

2 tsp. baking powder
1 cup milk
½ cup almonds, chopped
1 tsp. anise seed, crushed

Preheat oven to 400F. Cream butter and sugar together until light and fluffy. Sift flour, salt, and baking powder together and add alternately with the milk to creamed mixture. Add almonds and anise seed. Drop from tip of a teaspoon onto cookie sheet. Bake 12 mins.

GLAZED FRESH APPLE COOKIES

4 doz.

½ cup butter
1⅓ cups brown sugar
1 egg
2 cups flour
½ tsp. baking soda
1 tsp. baking powder
½ tsp. salt

1 tsp. cinnamon
½ tsp. nutmeg
¼ cup apple juice or milk
1 cup nuts, chopped
1 cup raisins
1 cup unpeeled apple,
  finely chopped

Glaze:
1 T. butter
1½ cups confectioners' sugar
⅛ tsp. salt

2½ T. apple juice or milk
¼ tsp. vanilla

Preheat oven to 400F. Thoroughly cream butter and sugar. Add egg and beat well. Sift together flour, baking soda, baking powder, salt, cinnamon and nutmeg; add to creamed mixture alternately with apple juice. Stir in nuts, raisins, and apples. Drop by tablespoonfuls on greased cookie sheets. Bake 10-12 mins. Remove cookies from pan at once and glaze while cookies are hot.

For glaze, cream butter, sugar, and salt. Stir in apple juice and vanilla.

Mrs. Hollis Clark

HEATH ENGLISH TOFFEE COOKIES

3 doz.

½ cup margarine
½ cup sugar
¼ cup brown sugar
1 egg
1 tsp. vanilla

1⅛ cups flour, sifted
½ tsp. salt
¼ tsp. baking soda
5 Heath Toffee Bars,
    finely broken

Preheat oven to 375F. Mix together margarine, sugars, egg and vanilla. Sift flour, salt, and baking soda together; stir into creamed mixture. Stir in Heath Bars. Drop by teaspoonful 2" apart on greased baking sheet. Bake 8-10 mins. Cool slightly before removing from sheet.

Mrs. Lee Beyer

M & M NIBBLERS

2 doz.

Kids love 'em

1 cup confectioners' sugar
¾ cup dates, chopped
½ cup crunchy peanut butter
½ cup semi-sweet chocolate
    chips

1 cup plain M & M candies
2 egg whites, unbeaten
plain M & M candies

Preheat oven to 350F. Mix together sugar, dates, peanut butter, chips, 1 cup M & M's, and egg whites. Drop by teaspoonfuls onto greased cookie sheet. Decorate with more M & M's. Bake 15 mins.

Mrs. Edyn Evans

MACAROONIES
3 doz.

2 eggs
1/8 tsp. salt
3/4 cup sugar
1/2 cup flour
1 T. butter, melted
2 cups flaked coconut

1 (6 oz.) pkg. semi-sweet
   chocolate chips
1 tsp. grated lemon or
   orange rind
1 tsp. vanilla

Preheat oven to 325F. Beat eggs and salt until foamy. Gradually add sugar and continue beating until thick and ivory colored, 5-7 mins. Fold in flour and butter. Stir in coconut, chocolate chips, lemon rind and vanilla. Drop dough by teaspoonfuls onto greased cookie sheet. Bake 12-15 mins. or until lightly browned. Cool 1 min. and remove from pan.

Mrs. Leo Jungblut

MERINGUE COOKIES
2 doz.

2 egg whites,
   room temperature
1/8 tsp. salt
1/8 tsp. cream of tartar
1 tsp. vanilla

3/4 cup sugar
1 (6 oz.) pkg. semi-sweet
   chocolate chips
1/4 cup nuts, chopped

Preheat oven to 300F. Beat egg whites, salt, cream of tartar and vanilla until soft peaks appear. Add sugar gradually until soft peaks appear. Stir in chocolate chips and nuts. Drop by teaspoonfuls onto brown paper-covered cookie sheet. Bake 25 mins.

Mrs. Chandler Oakes

PEANUT-CEREAL COOKIES   6 doz.

1 cup shortening	1 tsp. cream of tartar
1 cup sugar	1 cup corn flakes or any
1 cup brown sugar	other cereal
3 eggs	1 cup oatmeal
1 tsp. vanilla	1 cup salted peanuts
2 cups flour	1 cup semi-sweet chocolate
1 tsp. baking soda	chips (optional)

Preheat oven to 350F. Cream together shortening and sugars; add eggs and vanilla. Sift together flour, baking soda, and cream of tartar and add to creamy mixture. Stir in cereals, peanuts, and chips. Drop by teaspoonfuls on greased cookie sheet. Bake 12-14 mins.

Mrs. Russell Klaasen
Mrs. John Percival

PUMPKIN SPICE COOKIES   5 doz.

½ cup shortening	1 tsp. salt
1 cup sugar	1 tsp. baking powder
2 eggs	1 tsp. baking soda
1 cup pumpkin	1 tsp. cinnamon
1 tsp. vanilla	1 cup raisins
2 cups flour	½ cup nuts, chopped

Frosting:

1 cup confectioners' sugar	1 tsp. maple flavoring
1 T. butter	coffee

Preheat oven to 350F. Cream shortening, sugar, and eggs. Add pumpkin and vanilla. Sift together flour, salt, baking powder, baking soda, and cinnamon; add to creamy mixture. Stir in raisins and nuts. Drop by teaspoonfuls, onto greased cookie sheet. Bake 10-12 mins. When cool, frost.

Frosting: Mix sugar, butter, and flavoring. Add enough coffee to make a nice spreading consistency.

Mrs. Dale Shearer

RICE KRISPIE COOKIES   5 doz.

1 cup shortening	½ tsp. baking powder
1 cup sugar	1 tsp. baking soda
1 cup brown sugar	½ tsp. salt
2 eggs	1½ cups rolled oats
1 tsp. vanilla	2 cups Rice Krispies
2 cups flour	1 cup coconut

Preheat oven to 350F. Cream together shortening and sugars. Beat in eggs and vanilla. Sift together flour, baking powder, baking soda, and salt; add to creamed mixture. Stir in oats, Rice Krispies and coconut. Drop from teaspoon onto greased cookie sheet. Bake 10-12 mins.

Mrs. George Becker

SCHUIMPJES   2 doz.
Foam Cookies

3 egg whites, room temperature	½ tsp. vanilla or other flavoring
1 cup sugar	

Preheat oven to 225F. Beat egg whites until foamy; gradually add sugar until stiff peaks form. Add flavoring. Drop by teaspoonfuls on greased cookie sheet. Place on low rack in oven and bake 75 mins. Turn oven off and leave in oven until cool.

Mrs. Ken Kleis

SOUR CREAM COOKIES   4 doz.

1 cup margarine   1 tsp. baking soda
2 cups brown sugar   4 tsp. baking powder
2 eggs   1 cup sour cream
4½ cups flour   1 cup raisins
½ tsp. salt   1 cup nuts, chopped
½ tsp. nutmeg

Preheat oven to 400F. Cream together margarine and sugar. Add eggs. Sift together flour, salt, nutmeg, baking soda, baking powder; add alternately with the sour cream to the creamed mixture. Stir in raisins and nuts. Drop by teaspoonfuls onto greased cookie sheet. Bake 15 mins.

Mrs. J. K. Brown

SWEDISH OATMEAL WAFERS   3 doz.

½ cup butter   1 cup rolled oats
¾ cup sugar   1 T. flour
1 egg, beaten   1 tsp. baking powder

Preheat oven to 375F. Cream together butter and sugar. Add egg and oatmeal. Mix together flour and baking powder and add to creamed mixture. Drop by teaspoonfuls onto greased cookie sheet. Bake 8-10 mins.

Mary Lubbers

VANILLA COOKIES   2-3 doz.

½ cup margarine   ½ tsp. baking soda
1½ cups brown sugar   1 tsp. salt
2 eggs   1 cup sour cream or
1 tsp. vanilla   evaporated milk
2¾ cups flour   ⅔ cup nuts, chopped, or
                                  coconut

continued

430

Glaze:
¾ cup confectioners' sugar   ½ cup margarine, melted
½ tsp. vanilla   1-2 tsp. hot water

Preheat oven to 375F. Cream together margarine and sugar; add eggs and vanilla. Sift together flour, baking soda, and salt; add alternately with sour cream to creamed mixture. Stir in nuts. Drop by teaspoonfuls onto lightly greased cookie sheet. Bake 10 mins.

For glaze, blend sugar and vanilla with margarine. Stir in hot water. Spread over cooled cookies.

Mrs. Ken Michmerhuizen

BANKET   *4 - 13" sticks*
Almond roll

1 cup almond or macaroon   ¼ cup cornstarch
   paste   2 cups flour
1 cup sugar   1 cup butter
1 egg   ¼ cup water
1 egg, separated

Let paste, sugar, egg, egg yolk and cornstarch stand in bowl for 30 mins. Preheat oven to 400F. Blend flour, butter and water in bowl like pie crust. Dough may be refrigerated overnight if desired. When ready to prepare, divide dough into 2 equal parts. Roll each part on floured board to 8" x 13" rectangle. Cut lengthwise into 2 equal strips (4 strips, each 4" x 13", in all.)

Prepare the filling by mixing the almond paste, sugar, eggs and cornstarch. Form into 4 cylinders, each 12" long and the diameter of a dime. Place filling rolls on length of dough. Fold over the ends and then the long sides, moistening one side to seal before pressing.

Place with the seam side down on cookie sheet. Prick holes on top for air. Beat egg white and brush the top of the rolls. Bake for 14 mins. and then at 325F. for 20 mins. or until light brown.

Mrs. Howard VandeVusse

CANDY CANE COOKIES
4 doz.

½ cup butter, softened
½ cup shortening
1 cup confectioners' sugar, sifted
1 egg
1½ tsp. almond extract

1 tsp. vanilla
2½ cups flour, sifted
1 tsp. salt
½ tsp. red food coloring
½ cup sugar

Preheat oven to 375F. Mix shortenings, sugar, egg, and flavorings well. Combine flour and salt and add to creamed mixture. Divide dough in half. Blend coloring into one half. On a floured board, roll 1 tsp. of each color dough into a 4" long strip. Place strips side by side; press lightly together at one end and twist like a rope. Put on an ungreased baking sheet. Curve top so that each cookie looks like a candy cane. Continue making candy canes with remainder of dough. Bake 9 mins. While cookies are warm, sprinkle with sugar.

Variation: Color ¼ of dough with ½ tsp. red food coloring and ¼ of dough with ½ tsp. green food coloring and leave ½ of the dough plain. Shape some cookies like candy canes and some like wreaths. Add a small red bow, if you like.

Mrs. John Marquis

CHRISTMAS COOKIES
3 doz.

1 cup sugar
½ cup margarine
1 egg
1 tsp. grated lemon rind

⅓ cup sour cream
⅓ tsp. baking soda
¼ tsp. salt
2 cups flour, sifted

Cream together sugar and margarine. Add egg, lemon rind and beat well. Combine sour cream, baking soda, and salt; stir in flour and add to creamed mixture gradually and beat until smooth. Divide dough into 3 parts, wrap in waxed paper, and refrigerate 24 hrs.

Preheat oven to 375F. Flour pastry sheet well and roll dough ⅛" thick. Cut with cookie cutters. Bake on greased cookie sheet 8-10 mins. Cool. Decorate with colored frostings.

Mrs. Ray Backus

DATE FILLED COOKIES
6 doz.

1 cup shortening
1 cup sugar
1 cup brown sugar
3 eggs
2 tsp. vanilla
1 T. sour milk

5 cups flour, sifted
1 tsp. baking powder
1 tsp. salt
1 tsp. baking soda
¼ tsp. nutmeg

Filling:
½ cup sugar
3 T. flour
1½ cup dates, chopped

1½ cups cold water
2 tsp. lemon juice

Preheat oven to 375F. Cream shortening and sugars together; add eggs, vanilla, and sour milk. Sift together flour, baking powder, salt, baking soda, and nutmeg; add to creamed mixture. Roll on a floured surface to about 1/16" thickness and cut out in 2½" circle. Place 1 tsp. filling on one cookie, cover with another cookie and press edges together. Bake 12-15 mins.

For filling, mix sugar and flour together. Add dates and water. Bring to a boil and simmer uncovered 5 mins. Add lemon juice.

Mrs. James W. F. Brooks

JACKIE'S OLD FASHIONED SUGAR COOKIES

1 cup confectioners' sugar
1 cup sugar
1 cup margarine
1 scant cup oil
2 eggs, beaten

2 tsp. vanilla
4½ cups flour
1 tsp. baking soda
1 tsp. cream of tartar
¼ tsp. salt

Preheat oven to 350F. Cream together confectioners' sugar, sugar and margarine. Blend in remaining ingredients well. Place by rounded teaspoonfuls on greased cookie sheets. Press each cookie down with a decorative design bottom glass that is dipped in sugar. Repeat with each cookie. If using cut glass, lightly brush with oil before dipping in sugar. Bake 10-12 mins.

Mrs. Richard Streur

FRY-PAN COOKIES   3 doz.

1½ cups dates, chopped   2 cups Rice Krispies
1 cup sugar   1 cup coconut
2 eggs   1 T. sugar
1 tsp. vanilla

Over medium-low heat, fry dates, sugar, and eggs stirring constantly. Cool 1 min. Add vanilla and Rice Krispies. On a sheet of waxed paper spread the coconut and sugar. Shape date mixture into balls and roll in coconut and sugar.   Mrs. Norm Japinga

GERMAN FROZEN BRAZIL COOKIES   about 3 doz.

¾ cup sugar   2 scant cups flour
¾ cup brown sugar   1 tsp. baking soda
¾ cup shortening (½ cup   1 cup finely shredded coconut
   if butter)   1 cup Brazil nuts, chopped
1 egg   ½ cup candied cherries,
1 tsp. vanilla   chopped

Cream together sugars and shortenings. Beat in egg and vanilla. Sift together flour and baking soda; add to creamed mixture. Stir in coconut, nuts and cherries. Form into 2 or 3 rolls and freeze. Preheat oven to 375F. Slice rolls and bake for 8-10 mins. or until light brown.

Mrs. Arnold Dood

434

HOLIDAY ALMOND SURPRISES

about 4 doz.

¾ cup margarine
¼ cup confectioners' sugar
2 cups flour, sifted
1 cup ground almonds
¼ tsp. salt
1 tsp. vanilla
48 whole candied cherries
confectioners' sugar

Preheat oven to 325F. Cream margarine until light and fluffy. Blend in confectioners' sugar. Add flour, almonds, salt, and vanilla and blend thoroughly. Use teaspoon of dough to roll around each whole cherry to form a ball. Place on ungreased cookie sheet and bake 20 mins. When slightly cool, roll in confectioners' sugar.

Mrs. Gerald Boeve

ICE BOX COOKIES

4 doz.

1 cup sugar
1 cup light brown sugar
½ cup butter
1 cup shortening
2 eggs
2 T. hot water
4 cups flour
1 tsp. salt
1 tsp. baking soda
1 cup walnuts, chopped

Cream together sugars and shortenings. Add eggs and water. Sift together flour, salt and baking soda; add to creamy mixture. Shape into 2 rolls; wrap in waxed paper. Refrigerate overnight. Preheat oven to 350F. Thinly slice rolls and place on baking sheet. Bake about 5 mins. or until brown.

Mrs. Michael Calahan

CHOCOLATE CRINKLES   4 doz.

½ cup shortening
1 ⅔ cups sugar
2 tsp. vanilla
2 eggs
2 (1 oz. each) squares
   unsweetened chocolate,
   melted

2 cups flour, sifted
2 tsp. baking powder
½ tsp. salt
⅓ cup milk
½ cup walnuts, chopped
confectioners' sugar,
   sifted

Preheat oven to 350F. Cream shortening, sugar, and vanilla thoroughly. Beat in eggs, then chocolate. Sift together flour, baking powder and salt; add to creamed mixture alternately with milk. Stir in nuts. Chill 2-3 hrs. Form into 1" balls and roll in confectioners' sugar. Place on greased cookie sheet 2" to 3" apart. Bake 15 mins. Cool slightly before removing from pan.

Mrs. Dale Grissen

DANISH PUFF COOKIES   4 doz.

1 cup flour
½ cup margarine

2 T. water

Top Layer:
1 cup water
½ cup margarine
1 tsp. almond extract

1 cup flour
3 eggs

Frosting:
1 cup confectioners' sugar
2 T. margarine
pinch of salt

1 tsp. vanilla
2 T. brown sugar
hot coffee

Preheat oven to 350F. Mix flour, margarine, and water; divide into 2 parts. Place half of dough on a greased cookie sheet and flatten. Repeat with other half.

continued

For top layer, boil water and margarine. Remove from heat, add extract and flour. Add eggs, 1 at a time, beating well after each addition. Beat until smooth; spread on crusts. Bake for 1 hr.

For frosting, mix sugar, margarine, salt, vanilla, and brown sugar. Add hot coffee by teaspoonfuls until frosting is right consistency. Spread on cooled cookies.

Mrs. Kenneth Etterbeek

DOUBLE CRUNCHER COOKIES 3½ doz.

½ cup shortening
½ cup sugar
½ cup brown sugar, packed
1 egg
½ tsp. vanilla
1 cup sifted flour

½ tsp. baking soda
¼ tsp. salt
1 cup corn flakes, crushed
1 cup quick-cooking
  rolled oats
½ cup coconut

Filling:
1 (6 oz.) pkg. semi-sweet
  chocolate chips
½ cup confectioners' sugar

1 T. water
1 (3 oz.) pkg. cream cheese

Preheat oven to 350F. Combine shortening and sugars until light and creamy. Blend in egg and vanilla. Sift together flour, baking soda, and salt; add to creamed mixture. Add corn flakes, oats, and coconut. Remove ⅓ of dough and set aside. Shape remaining ⅔ of dough into balls using level teaspoonfuls; place on greased cookie sheet. Flatten with bottom of a glass dipped in flour. Bake 8-10 mins. Shape remaining ⅓ of dough into balls using half teaspoonfuls. Bake on greased cookie sheet 8-10 mins. Cool.

For filling, melt chips, sugar, and water in double boiler. Blend in cream cheese; beat until smooth. Cool. Spread filling over larger cookies and top with small ones.

Mrs. John Van Dyke, Jr.

KANEEL KOEKJES
Cinnamon Snaps

6 doz.

1 cup sugar
1 cup shortening
1 cup molasses
2 tsp. baking soda, dissolved
   in 2 T. warm water

6 cups cake flour
1 T. cinnamon
1 T. ginger
½ tsp. salt

Preheat oven to 350F. Cream sugar with shortening, add molasses, then baking soda dissolved in water. Sift together flour, cinnamon, ginger and salt, and add to creamed mixture. These cookies can either be rolled out very thin or can be used in a cookie press. Place cookies on greased cookie sheets and bake 8 to 10 mins.

Mrs. W. Tappan

NUTJAMMER COOKIES

3 doz.

1 cup butter
1 (8 oz.) pkg. cream cheese
2 cups flour

½ tsp. baking powder

Filling:
1 (12 oz.) jar apricot or
   peach jam
2 tsp. sugar

2 cups walnuts,
   finely chopped
confectioners' sugar

Cream together butter and cream cheese. Sift together flour and baking powder and add to creamed mixture. Chill dough 3 hrs. Preheat oven to 375F. Divide dough into 4 parts (work with ¼ at a time, chilling rest.) Roll very thin (1/16") on a lightly floured board. Cut into 2" squares. Place on greased baking sheet. Place 1 tsp. nut filling in center of square and top with another square of dough. Press together with floured tines of a fork. Brush edges with milk to seal. Bake 15 to 20 mins. or till lightly brown. When cooled, sprinkle with confectioners' sugar.

For filling, combine all ingredients.

Mrs. George Daily

SOUR CREAM TWISTS
4 doz.

3½ cups flour
1 tsp. salt
1 cup shortening, part butter
1 pkg. active dry yeast
¼ cup warm water
¾ cup sour cream

1 egg, beaten
2 egg yolks, beaten
1 tsp. vanilla
1 cup sugar
cinnamon to taste (optional)

Sift flour and salt in bowl. Cut in shortening. Dissolve yeast in water and stir into flour mixture. Add sour cream, eggs and vanilla. Mix thoroughly and form a ball. Cover bowl with cloth; refrigerate until dough is cold and firm.

Preheat oven to 350F. Divide dough in half and roll half into 8" x 12" rectangle; sprinkle with sugar and cinnamon, fold sides in, roll again into rectangle, repeat 2 more times. Cut rectangle in half lengthwise. Cut into 1" strips, twist ends and place on ungreased cookie sheet. Repeat with remaining dough. Bake for 10 mins. or until slightly browned.

Mrs. Roxy Wieland
Mrs. Ronald Appledorn

STROOP KOEKJES
8 doz.
Syrup Cookies

1 cup margarine
1 cup brown sugar
2 cups molasses
4 to 5 cups flour

1 tsp. ginger
1 tsp. baking soda
1 tsp. salt

Preheat oven to 375F. Cream margarine and sugar until light and fluffy. Add molasses. Sift 2 cups of flour with ginger, baking soda and salt 3 times. Add to creamed mixture. Add enough of remaining flour to allow handling. Roll out on a floured board and cut with floured cookie cutter. Place on ungreased cookie sheet and bake 10-12 mins.

KLETS KOEKJES
Caramel Cookies

2 doz.

½ cup butter
1½ cups brown sugar
1 cup sifted flour

⅛ tsp. salt
½ cup almonds, chopped

Preheat oven to 400F. Cream butter and sugar together. Sift together flour and salt; add to creamed mixture. Stir in almonds. Form into balls the size of marbles. Place on greased cookie sheet 1½" apart. Bake for 15 mins.

KRAKELINGEN
Butter cookies in shape of 8

6 doz.

2 cups butter
4 cups flour

½ cup water
sugar

Cut butter into flour. Gradually stir in water forming a dough similar to pastry. Cover and refrigerate overnight. Preheat oven to 375F. Roll small amount of dough into a pencil shape, bring ends together and twist like figure 8. Dip both sides in sugar; place on ungreased cookie sheet. Bake until brown on bottom.

Mrs. G. J. Van Zoeren

LEMON BUTTER TARTS   4 doz.

1 cup butter
2 (3 oz. each) pkg. cream cheese

2 cups flour
½ tsp. salt

Filling:
½ cup butter
1 cup sugar
juice of 3 lemons

grated rind of ½ lemon
3 eggs, beaten

Preheat oven to 350F. Cream together butter and cream cheese. Add flour and salt and form a large ball. Pinch off small pieces of dough and press on bottom and sides of mini-muffin tins. Bake 15-20 mins.

For filling, melt butter and sugar in a double boiler. Add lemon juice, lemon rind, and eggs. Cook until thick. Fill pastry shells. Refrigerate. This lemon filling can be refrigerated separately for 6 weeks.

Mrs. Donald G. Miller

MOLASSES COOKIES   5 doz.

1½ cups sugar
1 cup shortening
6 T. molasses
3 eggs yolks
3 cups flour
1 T. baking soda

1½ tsp. cinnamon
1½ tsp. ginger
¾ tsp. ground cloves
1½ tsp. salt
sugar

Preheat oven to 375F. Cream together sugar, shortening, and molasses. Beat in egg yolks. Sift together flour, baking soda, cinnamon, ginger, cloves, and salt; add to creamed mixture. Form 1" balls, roll in sugar, and place 2" apart on greased cookie sheet. Bake 8 mins. or until large cracks appear.

Mrs. Eugene Worrell

OATMEAL ICE BOX COOKIES   *6-7 doz.*

1 cup sugar	1 tsp. baking soda
1 cup brown sugar	1 tsp. salt
1 cup margarine	3 cups quick cooking
2 eggs	rolled oats
1 tsp. vanilla	½ cup walnuts, chopped
1½ cups flour	

Cream together sugars and margarine; add eggs and vanilla. Sift together flour, baking soda, and salt; add to creamed mixture. Stir in oats and nuts. Shape into 3 long rolls and refrigerate 4 or more hrs. Preheat oven to 350F. Cut roll into thin slices and bake on greased sheet 10-12 mins.

Mrs. Robert Fitzsimmons
Barb Zoet

PEANUT BUTTER COOKIES   *3-4 doz.*

½ cup shortening	1 egg, beaten
½ cup crunchy peanut butter	1¼ cup flour, sifted
½ cup sugar	¾ tsp. baking soda
½ cup brown sugar,	¼ tsp. salt
firmly packed	½ tsp. baking powder

Cream shortening, add peanut butter and cream thoroughly. Add sugars gradually and beat until light and fluffy. Add egg. Sift flour, baking soda, salt and baking powder together and add to creamed mixture. Chill dough thoroughly in refrigerator.

Preheat oven to 375F. Shape dough into balls the size of walnuts. Place on slightly greased baking sheet and flatten into round cookies with a fork dipped in flour, making a criss cross pattern. Bake for 8-10 mins.

Mrs. Russell Klaasen

ROYAL SCOTCH SHORTBREAD   4 doz.

1 ½ cups flour, sifted   1 cup margarine
1 ½ cups confectioners'   silver candies
   sugar, sifted

Preheat oven to 300F. Sift flour and sugar together into bowl; cut in margarine with pastry blender. Work dough into a ball with hands and knead about 10 mins. Pat dough into ¼" thick rectangle 14" x 12" on large ungreased cookie sheet; cut into 2" diamonds or squares with sharp knife. Decorate points of each piece with silver candies. Bake for 45 mins. or until firm. Recut cookies at marks and separate very carefully. Remove from sheet and cool on rack. These are delicate. Store with waxed paper between layers in air tight container. The flavor becomes better with storing.

Mrs. Arnold Dood

SPECULAASJES KOEKJES   5 doz.
Santa Claus Cookies

2 cups butter   ½ tsp. ground cloves
2 cups sugar   ½ tsp. baking soda
4 cups flour, sifted   ¼ tsp. salt
4 tsp. cinnamon   ½ cup sour cream
½ tsp. nutmeg   ½ cup almonds, chopped

Cream butter with sugar. Sift flour with cinnamon, nutmeg, cloves, baking soda, and salt; add alternately with sour cream to creamed mixture. Stir in nuts and knead well. Shape into a loaf, wrap in waxed paper and refrigerate overnight. Preheat oven to 400F. Slice loaf and bake on greased cookie sheet until browned.

SWEDISH HEIRLOOM COOKIES 4½ doz.

1 cup butter
1 cup sugar
1 tsp. vanilla

1¼ cup ground almonds
2 cups flour, sifted
½ tsp. salt

Preheat oven to 325F. Cream butter and sugar; add vanilla and almonds. Sift together flour and salt and add to creamed mixture. Shape dough into balls or crescents using a rounded teaspoon and place on ungreased baking sheet. Decorate if desired. Bake 15-18 mins.

Mrs. Ralph Stolp

SWEDISH SNICKERDOODLES 4 doz.

1 cup shortening, softened
1½ cups sugar
2 eggs
2¾ cups flour, sifted
2 tsp. cream of tartar

1 tsp. baking soda
½ tsp. salt
2 T. sugar
2 tsp. cinnamon

Cream shortening and sugar together; add eggs and beat until light. Sift together flour, cream of tartar, baking soda, and salt; add to creamed mixture. Chill. Preheat oven to 400F. Form into walnut size balls, roll in mixture of sugar and cinnamon. Place on ungreased cookie sheet, 2'' apart. Bake 8-10 mins.

Mrs. C. R. Laitsch

THIMBLE COOKIES   *3 doz.*
A rich cookie treat for any special occasion.

½ cup brown sugar
1 cup margarine
2 eggs, separated
2 tsp. vanilla
2 cups flour

¼ tsp. salt
finely chopped nuts
jelly
confectioners' sugar frosting

Preheat oven to 350F. Combine sugar and margarine; beat in egg yolks and vanilla. Sift together flour and salt; add to creamed mixture. Roll in balls the size of walnuts; dip in unbeaten egg whites, then in finely chopped nuts. Make a depression in the center with a thimble. Bake on ungreased cookie sheet for 10-15 mins. Fill holes with jelly and frost with confectioners' sugar frosting.

Miss Esther Kooyers

NOTES

Delectable Desserts

NOTES

ALMOND PASTRY SQUARES 12-16 servings

2 cups flour
¼ tsp. baking powder

1 cup margarine
6 T. ice water

Filling:
2 cups sugar
½ cup flour
½ cup milk
2 T. almond extract

3 egg yolks, slightly beaten
cream
sugar

Preheat oven to 350F. Use an ungreased 9" x 13" baking dish. Combine flour and baking powder; cut margarine into mixture. Add water; mix well. Divide into 2 parts; roll out. Put ½ in bottom of pan and partly up sides. Roll out remaining crust for top.

Mix together filling ingredients; pour into crust. Put second crust over top and seal edges. Brush with cream and sprinkle with sugar. Bake 1 hr.

Mrs. Lee Beyer

BUCHE DE NOEL 10 servings

Christmas Log
5 eggs, separated, room
   temperature

1 cup confectioners' sugar
3 T. cocoa

Frosting and Filling:
½ cup butter
½ cup sugar
2 tsp. strong coffee
1 T. dark cocoa

2 cups heavy cream
½ cup sugar
Pistachio nuts, chopped

Preheat oven to 375F. Butter and flour a 15½" x 10½" jelly roll pan. Sprinkle a damp towel with sugar. Beat egg yolks until thick and pale. Add sugar and cocoa; beat well. Beat egg whites until stiff; fold into mixture. Spread batter evenly in pan. Bake 12-15 mins., until toothpick inserted in center comes out clean. Quickly turn cake out on towel. Trim edges, roll cake in towel and cool. Cream butter with sugar; add coffee and cocoa. Whip heavy cream with sugar until stiff. Unroll cake; spread lightly with 3 T. frosting and thickly with all the whipping cream. Roll again. Spread frosting over the roll using a spatula to make a rough surface in imitation of bark. Decorate with swirls of frosting forced through pastry tube. Sprinkle ends of log with nuts.

Mrs. Ed Nyland

CHOCOLATE CHIP DATE SQUARES   *12-16 servings*

1 (6½ oz.) pkg. dates,	
* chopped*	*2 eggs*
1 cup boiling water	*1¾ cups flour*
1 tsp. baking soda	*⅛ tsp. salt*
½ cup shortening	*½ (6 oz.) pkg. semi-sweet*
1 cup sugar	* chocolate chips*
1 T. cocoa	*½ cup nuts, chopped*

Preheat oven to 350F. Grease a 13" x 9" baking pan. Mix dates, water and soda; set aside. Cream shortening and sugar; add cocoa. Beat in eggs, one at a time. Sift together flour and salt; add to creamed mixture. Stir in date mixture. Put in pan; top with chocolate chips and nuts. Bake 35 mins.

Mrs. Norman Japinga

DREAMY CREAM PUFFS   *24 puffs*

½ cup butter	*1 cup flour*
1 tsp. salt	*5 eggs*
1 cup boiling water	

Filling and Topping:

2 (3 oz. each) pkg. cream	*1 cup heavy cream, whipped*
* cheese, softened*	*1 tsp. vanilla*
½ cup confectioners' sugar	*confectioners' sugar,*
	* sifted, or fudge sauce*

Preheat oven to 450F. Grease 2 large baking sheets. Add butter and salt to boiling water. When butter melts, add flour all at once until paste leaves sides of pan and forms a ball. Remove from heat; cool slightly. Beat in eggs, one at a time, beating briskly after each. Drop paste by rounded tablespoon on baking sheet. Bake 15 mins.; reduce heat to 325F. and bake 25 mins. longer. Cool; cut out soft insides carefully.

Combine ingredients for filling; beat till well blended. Spoon into puffs. Dust with confectioners' sugar or top with fudge sauce.

Mrs. Keith Lankheet

HOT OR COLD FUDGE SAUCE
2½ cups

6 T. margarine
1 cup sugar
5 T. cocoa

1 (13 oz.) can evaporated
milk
1 tsp. vanilla

Mix together butter, sugar and cocoa in saucepan; cook over low heat until butter is completely melted. Slowly add milk; let boil for 1 min., stirring constantly. Remove from heat; add vanilla.

Mrs. Joseph Borgman, Jr.

CRUMB DELIGHT
9 servings

Serve with slices of butter pecan ice cream.

4 egg whites, room
  temperature
¼ tsp. salt
1 tsp. vanilla
1 cup sugar

1 cup graham cracker
  crumbs
½ cup coconut
½ cup walnuts, chopped
1 tsp. baking powder

Preheat oven to 350F. Grease and flour a 9" x 9" pan. Beat egg whites until stiff, slowly adding salt, vanilla and sugar. Mix remaining ingredients together; fold into egg whites. Spread in pan. Bake 30 mins.

Mrs. William Venhuizen

GRAND SLAM
12 servings

½ cup butter
1 cup confectioners' sugar
4 eggs, separated, room
   temperature
1 cup flour, sifted

1 tsp. baking powder
3 T. milk
1 tsp. vanilla
¾ cup sugar
1 cup walnuts, chopped

Filling:
2 T. sugar
1 T. cornstarch
1 cup sour cream

1 egg yolk, beaten
1 T. butter
1 tsp. vanilla

Preheat oven to 350F. Grease and flour two 8'' round pans. Cream butter and sugar; stir in egg yolks. Sift flour with baking powder and add alternately with milk and vanilla. Place in pans. Beat egg whites until stiff, gradually add sugar and continue beating. Spread meringue over batter; sprinkle with nuts. Bake 35 mins. Cool.

Combine sugar, cornstarch and sour cream in top of double boiler; add egg yolk. Cook until mixture coats spoon. Add butter and vanilla. Cool. Place this filling between layers of cake. This needs no frosting. Should be served the same day as prepared.

Mrs. Robert King

NECTARINE RUM RING
8 servings

1 (9 oz.) or ½ (18.5 oz.) pkg.
   yellow cake mix
¼ cup orange or pineapple juice

¼ cup light rum or 2 tsp. rum
   extract + 3 T. water

Filling and Glaze:
1½ cups (3 to 5) fresh
   nectarines, finely chopped
½ cup roasted almonds, diced

1 (10 oz.) jar apricot preserves
sliced nectarines for garnish

Preheat oven to 350F. Grease and flour a 5-cup ring mold. Prepare cake mix as package directs. Pour into mold. Bake 30 mins. or until cake tests done. Cool 10 mins.; remove from pan onto platter. When cake is lukewarm, split it into 2 layers, placing each layer, cut side up, on separate plates. Combine fruit juice and rum; drizzle over both layers. Refrigerate cake layers until serving time.

continued

Combine nectarines, almonds and half of preserves; set aside. Just before serving heat remaining preserves in saucepan. Spread half of filling on bottom cake layer; top with remaining layer. Spoon warm preserves over top and sides of cake to glaze. Spoon remaining filling over top of cake. Arrange sliced nectarines around cake for garnish.

Mrs. Sherwin Ortman

GOLDEN PECAN TASSIES
24 Tassies

½ cup margarine, softened   1 cup flour, sifted
1 (3 oz.) pkg. cream cheese

Filling:
1 egg, slightly beaten   ⅛ tsp. salt
¾ cup brown sugar   1 tsp. vanilla
1 T. butter, melted   ⅔ cup pecans, chopped

Use ungreased 1¾" muffin pans. Blend margarine and cream cheese. Add flour; work with fingers into smooth, blended dough. Chill about 1 hr. Shape into 2 dozen 1" balls; press dough into bottoms and sides of cups.

Preheat oven to 350F. Beat together egg, sugar, butter, salt and vanilla till smooth. Divide half the pecans among pastry-lined pans. Add filling and top with remaining pecans. Bake 15-17 mins., reduce heat to 250F. and bake 10 mins. longer. Cool; remove from pan to rack.

Mrs. Ted Boeve

PUMPKIN DESSERT SQUARES
12-16 servings

1 (18.5 oz.) pkg. yellow
  cake mix

½ cup margarine, melted
1 egg

Filling:
3 cups (1 lb. 14 oz. can)
  pumpkin pie mix*

2 eggs
⅔ cup milk

Topping:
1 cup cake mix (from
  pkg. above)
¼ cup sugar

1 tsp. cinnamon
¼ cup margarine
1 cup heavy cream, whipped

Preheat oven to 350F. Grease a 9" x 13" baking pan. Reserve 1 cup cake mix for topping. Combine cake mix, margarine and egg; press in pan. Beat together pumpkin pie mix, eggs and milk; pour over crust.

Mix together cake mix, sugar and cinnamon; cut in margarine with fork to make crumbs. Sprinkle over filling. Bake 45 to 50 mins. Serve with whipping cream.

*For use with 1 lb. can solid pack pumpkin, add 2½ tsp. pumpkin pie spice and ½ cup brown sugar.

Mrs. Jay Freriks

RUMMIE PUDDING
9 servings

For pecan pie lovers

1 cup sugar
½ cup butter
2 eggs
¾ cup milk
1 T. flour

½ tsp. baking powder
1 cup dates, finely chopped
½ cup pecans, broken
whipping cream or ice cream

Preheat oven to 350F. Grease an 8" x 8" baking pan. Cream sugar and butter; beat in eggs and milk. Sift together flour and baking powder; add to mixture. Fold in dates and pecans. Bake 45 mins. Serve warm with whipping cream or ice cream.

Mrs. Ginny Pollock

ANGEL CHEESECAKE PIE

8 servings

1¼ cups flour
½ cup nuts, chopped
   or coconut

½ cup brown sugar, firmly
   packed
½ cup butter

Cheese Filling:
⅓ cup sugar
1 envelope unflavored
   gelatin
½ tsp. salt
1 egg, separated,
   room temperature
½ cup milk

12 oz. cream cheese or 12 oz.
   small curd cottage
   cheese, sieved
1 T. lemon juice
1 tsp. vanilla
2 T. sugar
1 cup heavy cream, whipped

Preheat oven to 450F. Use an ungreased 9" pie pan. Combine flour, nuts and brown sugar. Cut in butter to make a crumb mixture. Place in pie pan. Bake 10-12 mins., stirring occasionally, until golden brown. Cool. Remove ¼ cup. Press remainder into pan.

Combine sugar, gelatin and salt in saucepan. Blend in egg yolk and milk. Cook over low heat until it comes to a boil and gelatin is dissolved. Remove from heat. Blend in cheese, lemon juice and vanilla; beat until creamy. Chill until mixture is very thick but not set. Beat egg white until soft peaks form; gradually add 2 T. sugar and beat until stiff peaks form. Fold into cheese mixture. Fold in whipped cream. Spoon into shell; sprinkle with reserved crumbs. Chill 4 to 6 hrs.

Mrs. Millicent Benke

BLENDER CHEESECAKE

crumb crust
2 eggs
½ cup sugar
2 tsp. vanilla
1½ cups sour cream

2 (8 oz. each) pkgs. cream
   cheese, softened and cut
   into pieces
2 T. butter, melted

Preheat oven to 325F. Line a 9" cake pan with crumb crust. Put eggs, sugar, vanilla and sour cream into blender; blend 15 seconds. Gradually add cheese, then butter. Pour into cake pan. Bake 35 mins. or until set in center. Filling will be soft but will firm up as the cake cools. Chill thoroughly before serving.

Mrs. William Boyer

CHEESECAKE

10 servings

*10 graham crackers, finely
crushed*

¼ cup butter, melted
¼ cup sugar

Filling:
*2 (8 oz. each) pkgs. cream
cheese, softened*

3 eggs
½ cup sugar

Topping:
2 cups sour cream
¼ cup sugar

½ tsp. vanilla

Preneat oven to 350F. Use an ungreased 10'' pie pan. Combine crackers, butter and sugar. Press over bottom and sides of pan. Combine cream cheese, eggs and sugar; beat until smooth. Pour over crust. Bake 30 mins. or until knife inserted in center comes out clean. Cool 15 mins.

Increase oven temperature to 475F. Mix together sour cream, sugar and vanilla carefully by hand; spread on top. Bake 5 mins. Cool and refrigerate overnight.

Mrs. Robert Bernecker

CHEESECAKE TARTS

6 servings

Rich and Fussy

Pastry Rounds:
1½ cups flour
¾ tsp. salt

½ cup shortening
3 T. water

Lemon Filling:
*2 (3 oz. each) pkgs. cream
cheese, softened*
1 T. lemon juice

1 T. lemon rind (optional)
2-3 T. sugar
slivered almonds

Sauce:
*1 (10 oz.) pkg. frozen sliced
strawberries*

1 T. lemon juice
½ tsp. almond extract

continued

Preheat oven to 400F. Use a large ungreased baking sheet. Sift together flour and salt; cut in shortening until crumbly. Gradually add water and mix. Roll pastry into ball; divide in half. On lightly floured, cloth covered board, roll each half ⅛" thick. Cut 9 (4") rounds from each half. Place on baking sheet; prick with fork. Bake 7 to 8 mins. or until lightly browned.

Combine cream cheese, lemon juice, rind and sugar; beat until fluffy. Place 3 rounds together with 1 T. filling between each layer. Spread small dab of filling on top. Sprinkle with almonds. Bake 10 mins.

Combine strawberries, lemon juice and almond extract. Serve sauce over hot tarts.

Mrs. George Steininger

CHOCOLATE CHEESECAKE   *8 servings*

1½ cups graham cracker crumbs   **½ cup butter, melted**

Filling:

1 cup semi-sweet chocolate chips   **¼ tsp. salt**

2 (3 oz. each) pkgs. cream cheese   **2 egg yolks**

½ cup sugar   **1 cup heavy cream, whipped**

1 tsp. vanilla   **2 egg whites, room temperature**

                                           ¼ cup sugar

Use a 9" springform or pie pan. Mix together crumbs and butter; press firmly onto sides and bottom of pan. Melt chips over hot water; stir in cream cheese, sugar, vanilla and salt. Beat in egg yolks, one at a time, mixing well after each; beat until smooth. Add whipped cream. Beat egg whites until soft peaks form; gradually add sugar until stiff peaks form. Fold into mixture. Place in shell and freeze. Remove 15 mins. before serving. Serve with a dollop of whipped cream, if desired.

Mrs. Gregory Burhans

GELATIN CHEESECAKE

12-16 servings

2 cups graham cracker
   crumbs

¼ cup margarine, melted
6 T. sugar

Filling:
1 (3 oz.) pkg. lemon gelatin
1 cup boiling water
1 (8 oz.) pkg. cream cheese,
   softened
1 cup sugar

1 tsp. vanilla
1 (13 oz.) can evaporated
   milk, whipped
¼ cup graham cracker crumbs

Lightly grease two 9" pie pans or a 13" x 9" baking pan. Mix together crumbs, margarine and sugar. Press into pan.

Dissolve gelatin in boiling water; cool. Cream cheese with sugar and vanilla; add gelatin mixture. Fold whipped milk into gelatin. Pour into crust. Sprinkle with crumbs. Chill overnight. For a special treat top with a can of fruit pie filling.

Eet Smakelijk's Best

JEWISH CHEESECAKE

8 servings

Graham cracker crust
   using 1 cup crumbs
5 medium eggs, separated,
   room temperature
1 cup sugar
2 T. cornstarch

3 (8 oz. each) pkgs. cream
   cheese, softened
1 cup sour cream
1 cup milk
1 tsp. cream of tartar
1 tsp. vanilla

Preheat oven to 350F. Butter a 9 or 10" springform pan. Prepare crust; line pan. Beat egg yolks; add sugar and cornstarch, then cream cheese, sour cream and milk. Beat this mixture at least 10 mins. Beat egg whites until stiff. Add cream of tartar and vanilla to yolk mixture; fold in whites. Pour into pan. Bake 60-70 mins. Cake will be very high. Turn off oven and leave cake in at least 2 hrs. or overnight. The cake will not be as high as it was when baking.

Mrs. Fred Leaske

PINEAPPLE CHEESECAKE

12-16 servings

1½ cups graham cracker
crumbs

¼ cup sugar
6 T. margarine, melted

Filling:
1 envelope unflavored gelatin
3 egg yolks, beaten
1 (13¼ oz.) can crushed
pineapple, drained,
reserving ½ cup syrup
1½ cups creamed cottage
cheese

1 (8 oz.) pkg. cream cheese,
softened
2 T. lemon juice
3 egg whites, room temperature
3 T. sugar
½ cup heavy cream, whipped

Preheat oven to 375F. Use a 9" x 13" pan. Combine cracker crumbs, sugar and margarine. Reserve ¼ cup mixture. Press remainder in pan. Bake 8 mins. Chill.

Combine gelatin, egg yolks and ½ cup syrup in a saucepan. Cook and stir till slightly thickened. Chill till partially set. Combine cottage cheese, cream cheese, lemon juice and pineapple. Beat until all ingredients are blended. Gradually add gelatin mixture to the cheese mixture. Beat egg whites to soft peaks. Gradually add sugar, beating to stiff peaks. Fold into cheese and gelatin mixture. Fold in whipped cream. Turn into prepared crust. Sprinkle with reserved crumb mixture. Chill.

Mrs. David Windemuller

BAKED ALASKA DELIGHT

15 servings

⅓ cup butter
½ cup nuts, finely
  chopped

1½ cups vanilla wafers,
  crushed
¼ cup sugar

Filling:
½ gal. chocolate ice cream
½ gal. strawberry ice cream

Meringue:
8 egg whites, room
  temperature
½ tsp. cream of tartar

1 cup sugar
1 tsp. vanilla

Hot Fudge Sauce:
3 T. butter, melted
3 T. cocoa

1 cup sugar
1 (13 oz.) can evaporated milk

Use an ungreased 9" x 13" pan. Melt butter; add nuts, wafers and sugar. Press into pan.

Slice chocolate ice cream over crust. Place in freezer until firm. Slice strawberry ice cream over chocolate ice cream. Place in freezer until firm.

Preheat oven to 475F. Beat egg whites with cream of tartar until frothy. Gradually beat in sugar until stiff and glossy. Beat in vanilla. Place meringue on strawberry ice cream being careful to seal edge. Bake 2 or 3 mins. till lightly browned. Cover lightly with foil; freeze.

Melt butter over low heat; stir in cocoa. Add sugar slowly. Gradually add milk, stirring constantly. Bring to a boil; cook until thick. Serve hot over individual squares of Baked Alaska.

Mrs. Morris Gort

FLAMING STRAWBERRY BAKED ALASKA

8 servings

1 qt. strawberry ripple ice
  cream, softened
2 cups biscuit mix
3 T. sugar
½ cup milk
1 egg
3 T. butter, melted

4 egg whites, room temperature
½ tsp. cream of tartar
½ tsp. vanilla
½ cup sugar
1 pt. fresh strawberries, sliced
sugar cubes presoaked in
  rum extract

Preheat oven to 425F. Line an 8" round pan with foil. Spoon in ice cream. Freeze hard.

Grease a 9" round pan. Combine biscuit mix, sugar, milk, egg and butter. Blend until smooth. Pour into pan. Bake 15 mins. Cool; remove from pan and place on cake plate.

Preheat oven to 500F. Beat egg whites, cream of tartar and vanilla to soft peaks; by tablespoon add ½ cup sugar, beating to very stiff peaks. Place hardened ice cream on cake. Spoon on sliced strawberries and top with meringue, being sure to cover sides of cake completely. Place in oven 3-5 mins. to brown lightly. Place sugar cubes in meringue and ignite. Serve immediately.

Mrs. Keith Lankheet

ALMENDRADO

9 servings

A light, colorful Mexican dessert.

1 envelope unflavored gelatin
¼ cup cold water
¼ cup boiling water
6 egg whites, room
  temperature
1 cup sugar

1 tsp. vanilla
red and green food coloring
¼ cup almonds, chopped
1 cup semi-sweet chocolate
  chips

Custard Sauce:
6 egg yolks, beaten
2 cups milk
½ cup sugar

1 tsp. salt
1 tsp. almond extract
1 tsp. vanilla

continued

Use an ungreased 9" x 9" baking pan. Soak gelatin in cold water. Then dissolve in boiling water; cool. Beat egg whites until soft peaks form; gradually add sugar and vanilla; beat until stiff. Slowly beat in gelatin. Divide egg whites into 3 bowls; color one part red and one part green. Add almonds and chocolate chips to the white part. Spread into pan with red on bottom, white in middle and green on top. Refrigerate.

Combine egg yolks, milk, sugar, salt and almond extract in top of double boiler. Cook, stirring constantly, until mixture thickens and coats spoon; do not boil. Cool; add vanilla. Strain and chill. Serve over dessert squares.

Mrs. Lyle Sprik

BANANA SPLIT DESSERT
8 servings

2 cups vanilla wafer or
   graham cracker crumbs

⅓ cup butter, melted

Filling:
½ cup butter
1½ cups confectioners' sugar

2 eggs

Topping:
¼ cup sugar
2 T. cocoa
1 cup heavy cream, whipped
½ cup nuts, chopped

2 ripe bananas, sliced
   or mashed
½ cup maraschino cherries,
   halved

Use an ungreased 8" or 9" square pan. Mix crumbs and butter; reserve 2 T. and pat rest into pan. Cream butter and sugar; add eggs, one at a time, beating well. Spread over crumbs. Mix sugar and cocoa; add to whipped cream. Stir in nuts, bananas and cherries. Spread over creamed mixture. Top with reserved crumbs. Chill 24 hrs.

Mrs. Jacob Van Hoff, Jr.

BROKEN GLASS TORTE
12 servings

1 (3 oz.) pkg. lemon or orange gelatin
1 (3 oz.) pkg. lime gelatin
1 (3 oz.) pkg. cherry, raspberry or strawberry gelatin
1½ cups hot water for each pkg. of gelatin

1 pkg. lady fingers, split
1 envelope unflavored gelatin
¼ cup cold water
1 cup hot pineapple juice
2 cups heavy cream
½ cup sugar
1 tsp. vanilla

Dissolve each pkg. of gelatin in hot water and chill in separate cake pans until firm. Cut into ½" cubes. Line an angel food cake pan with ladyfingers. Soften unflavored gelatin in cold water; add pineapple juice. Whip cream with sugar and vanilla; fold in unflavored gelatin mixture. Carefully blend in colored cubes; turn into lined pan. Chill about 12 hours. Slice to serve. The cut slices give the broken glass effect.

Mrs. T. Vande Water

BUTTER PECAN SUMMER COOLER
10-12 servings

1½ cups graham cracker crumbs
½ cup margarine
1 qt. butter pecan ice cream, softened
2 (3¾ oz. each) pkg. instant vanilla pudding

2 cups milk
2 envelopes dessert topping mix
6 Heath bars, broken

Combine crumbs and margarine; spread in 8" x 12" pan. Whip together ice cream, pudding and milk; pour over crust. Chill. Prepare topping mix according to package directions; fold in Heath bars. Spread over filling. Chill until firm.

Mrs. Robert Bauspies
Mrs. Jerome Essink

CHERRIES IN THE SNOW   10 servings

1 cup flour	¼ cup brown sugar
½ cup margarine	½ cup nuts, chopped

Filling and Topping:

1 (8 oz.) pkg. cream cheese, softened	2 tsp. vanilla
	1 cup heavy cream, whipped
2 cups confectioners' sugar	1 (32 oz.) can cherry pie filling

Preheat oven to 375F. Use an ungreased 9" x 12" pan or 10" pie pan. Combine flour, margarine, brown sugar and nuts. Place in pan. Bake 15 mins. Crumble and pat down into pan; cool.

Cream the cheese, sugar and vanilla; fold in whipped cream. Spoon over crust. Spoon pie filling over cheese mixture; chill several hrs.

Mrs. Fred Leaske

CHOCOLATE CHIFFON TOPPED CAKE DESSERT   10 servings

1 envelope unflavored gelatin	1 tsp. vanilla
¼ cup cold water	⅓ cup sugar
⅓ cup sugar	1 baked 8" cake layer (see
¼ tsp. salt	Velvet Cocoa cake below)
1¾ cups milk	1 cup heavy cream, whipped
1 (4 oz.) pkg. German Sweet Chocolate	and sweetened or 1 envelope dessert topping mix
3 eggs, separated, room temperature	

continued

464

Soften gelatin in cold water. Combine ⅓ cup sugar with salt and milk in medium saucepan. Add ⅔ of the chocolate; cook over medium heat, stirring constantly until chocolate is melted. Blend mixture well with egg beater. Beat egg yolks slightly; add small amount of hot mixture, stirring vigorously. Gradually add remaining hot mixture, stirring constantly. Return to saucepan; cook over low heat until mixture is slightly thickened, about 5 min. Remove from heat; add softened gelatin and stir until dissolved. Pour into large bowl; chill until partially thickened. Stir in vanilla.

Beat egg whites until foamy; add ⅓ cup sugar, 2 T. at a time, and continue beating until stiff peaks form. Fold into chilled chocolate mixture. Spoon into greased 1½ qt. mixing bowl and chill until firm, about 2½ hrs. Loosen mold at top edge with sharp knife. Place in warm water a few seconds, shaking bowl gently. Unmold on cake layer. Trim any overlapping edges with sharp knife. Frost with whipping cream. Garnish with chocolate curls made by using a carrot scraper and the remaining ⅓ of the chocolate.

Mrs. Tom Vander Kuy

VELVET COCOA CAKE   9 servings

⅓ cup margarine
1 cup brown sugar,
  firmly packed
1 egg
1 tsp. vanilla
1½ cups flour

1 tsp. baking soda
½ tsp. baking powder
¼ tsp. salt
¼ cup cocoa
1 cup hot water

Preheat oven to 350F. Grease and flour a 9" x 9" baking pan. Cream margarine and sugar until light and fluffy. Add egg and vanilla; beat thoroughly. Sift together flour, soda, baking powder, salt and cocoa; add to creamed mixture alternately with water in thirds, blending smooth after each addition. Pour into pan; bake 25 min.

Mrs. Tom Vander Kuy

ENGLISH TOFFEE
8 servings

1 ½ cups vanilla wafers,
  crushed

Filling:
½ cup margarine
1 cup confectioners' sugar
3 egg yolks, beaten
1 ½ (1 oz. each) squares
  unsweetened chocolate,
  melted and cooled

¼ cup butter, melted
1 cup walnuts, chopped

1 tsp. vanilla
3 egg whites, room
  temperature, beaten stiff

Use an ungreased 8" x 8" pan. Mix together the wafers, butter and walnuts; press into pan, reserving ¼ cup.

Cream margarine and sugar; add egg yolks. Add chocolate and vanilla. Fold in egg whites. Spread over crust. Sprinkle with reserved crumbs. Refrigerate overnight.

Mrs. David Linn

FRENCH MINT TORTES
24 servings
Rich and attractive dessert, wonderful for a ladies' tea.

3 egg whites, room
  temperature
1 cup sugar
1 tsp. vanilla

15 single saltines, finely
  crushed
1 cup nuts, finely chopped

Filling:
1 cup butter, softened
2 cups confectioners' sugar
4 (1 oz. each) squares
  unsweetened chocolate,
  melted and cooled

4 eggs
1 tsp. peppermint extract
2 tsp. vanilla

Garnish: whipped cream and chocolate curls

Preheat oven to 350F. Insert cupcake papers into two 12-cup muffin tins. Beat egg whites until stiff; gradually add sugar and vanilla while continuing to beat. Fold in crackers and nuts. Put 1 T. of mixture into each paper. Bake 20 mins.; do not overbake or they will be too hard.

continued

Blend butter and sugar; beat 5 mins. Add chocolate; beat 5 mins. more. Add eggs, one at a time, beating 5 mins. after each egg. Add extracts; beat 5 mins. Do not underbeat, or the tortes will stick to the papers when they are unmolded. Spoon mixture on top of baked layer and freeze. Thaw 5 mins. before serving. Garnish with whipped cream and chocolate curls.

Mrs. John Marquis

GRASSHOPPERS IN THE STRAWBERRY PATCH

6-8 servings

1 envelope unflavored gelatin
¼ cup cold water
½ cup lime juice, heated
¼ cup white Creme de Cacao

¼ cup green Creme de Menthe
¼ cup sugar
2 egg whites, room temperature
 cup heavy cream, whipped

Meringue:
½ cup (3-4) egg whites, room
   temperature
1 cup fine granulated sugar

½ tsp. vanilla
⅛ tsp. salt

Filling and Garnish:
1 qt. strawberries, crushed
   and sweetened

whole strawberries

Soften gelatin in cold water; let stand 5 min. Add lime juice; stir. Add Creme de Cacao and Creme de Menthe with sugar, blending until sugar dissolves. Chill. When slightly thickened, beat with rotary beater. Beat egg whites till stiff peaks form. Fold egg whites and cream into chilled mixture. Pour into 6-8 individual molds. Chill.

Preheat oven to 250F. Grease a large baking sheet. Beat egg whites with salt and vanilla until stiff, adding sugar gradually. Spoon onto baking sheet and spread into 3½" rounds; depress in center. Bake 1 hr. Cool.

To serve, place meringues on plates. Fill with crushed strawberries. Unmold grasshoppers in center. Garnish with a whole strawberry.

Mrs. Delwyn Van Dyke

467

LEMON FLUFF   12-16 servings

8 oz. vanilla wafers, crushed   ½ cup hot water
4 egg yolks, well beaten   4 egg whites, room
1 ½ lemons, juiced   temperature
½ cup sugar   ½ cup sugar
3 T. lemon gelatin   1 cup heavy cream, whipped

Line a 9" x 13" cake pan with crumbs, reserving ½ cup. Combine the egg yolks and juice in top of double boiler; beat well. Add sugar; cook until thick. Dissolve gelatin in hot water; add to egg mixture while hot. Let cool. Beat egg whites until stiff peaks form, gradually adding sugar; fold into lemon mixture. Fold in whipped cream. Pour into crust and top with remaining crumbs. Chill 24 hrs.

Mrs. Lyle Sanders

FOUR GENERATION LEMON TORTONI   8 servings

2 doz. ladyfingers, separated   3 egg whites, room
½ cup sugar   temperature
3 egg yolks, beaten   ½ cup sugar
juice of 1 lemon   whipped cream topping
juice and rind, grated,
   of 1 orange

Separate and stand ladyfingers on long edge in 9" x 9" pan. Mix sugar and egg yolks. Add juices and rind. Beat egg whites until stiff, gradually adding remaining ½ cup sugar. Fold into egg yolk mixture. Pour over ladyfingers. Refrigerate overnight or 24 hrs. Serve with whipped cream.

Mrs. A. Leenhouts
Mrs. Mayo Hadden
Mrs. William Hakken
Mrs. Michael Zeedyk

PEPPERMINT BAVARIAN
8 servings

1 cup flaked coconut
¼ cup margarine, melted
1 cup milk
1 cup peppermint candy, crushed

⅛ tsp. salt
1 envelope unflavored gelatin
¼ cup cold water
1 cup heavy cream, whipped

Preheat oven to 350F. Combine coconut and margarine; pat into bottom of a 9" x 9" baking pan. Bake 10 mins. or till golden; cool. Combine milk, ¾ cup candy and salt. Cook over low heat, stirring frequently, till candy dissolves; remove from heat. Soften gelatin in cold water; dissolve in the hot mixture. Chill till partially set. Fold in whipped cream. Pour over crust. Chill 4 to 5 hrs. or till firm. Cut in squares; top with remaining candy.

Mrs. Jack De Roo

LIKO-LIKO DESSERT
12 servings

This king of the island dessert is light and rich.

32 marshmallows or
  4 cups miniature
½ cup milk
¼ lb. pecans, broken
½ cup chunk pineapple, drained

½ cup maraschino cherries, drained
2 tsp. lemon juice
2 cups heavy cream, whipped
frozen raspberries

Melt marshmallows in milk; cool. Add pecans, pineapple, cherries and lemon juice. Fold in whipped cream; freeze. Serve in sherbet glasses topped with frozen raspberries. Will keep in freezer 2 or 3 weeks. Serve with cookies.

Mrs. Charles Vander Meulen

PINEAPPLE MERINGUE DESSERT   12-16 servings

1½ cups graham cracker   ½ cup butter, melted
    crumbs

Meringue:
4 egg whites, room   ½ tsp. cream of tartar
    temperature   1 cup sugar
¼ tsp. salt

Filling:
1 (20 oz.) can crushed   1 cup flaked coconut
    pineapple, well drained   1 cup heavy cream, whipped

Preheat oven to 325F. Combine crumbs and butter; line a 9" x 13" pan. Beat egg whites, salt and cream of tartar until foamy; gradually add sugar, beating until stiff peaks form. Spread meringue on crust. Bake 30 mins. Cool. Combine pineapple, coconut and whipped cream; spread on top of meringue. Chill overnight.

Mrs. Norman Wangen

RASPBERRY DANISH DESSERT   8 servings

1 cup flour   3 T. sugar
½ cup margarine

Cream Layer:
1 (3 oz.) pkg. cream cheese   1 tsp. vanilla
6 T. sugar   1 cup heavy cream, whipped

Fruit Layer:
1 (16 oz.) pkg. frozen   water
    raspberries, thawed,   1 (4¾ oz.) pkg. Raspberry
    reserving juice   Danish Junket Dessert

continued

Preheat oven to 350F. Combine flour, margarine and sugar; pat into an ungreased 9" x 9" baking pan. Bake until light brown, 12-15 mins. Cool.

Cream together cream cheese, sugar and vanilla; blend in whipped cream. Spread on crust.

Add enough water to raspberry juice to make 1¾ cups; add Junket and cook until thick. Let partially cool, then fold in berries. Spread on top of cream layer. Refrigerate.

Mrs. Don Teitsma
Mrs. Jerry DeVries

STRAWBERRY BAVARIAN CROWN — *12 servings*

1 (3 oz.) pkg. strawberry gelatin
1 cup hot water
½ cup ice water

2 (10 oz. each) pkg. frozen or 2½ cups sliced, sweetened fresh strawberries
2 cups heavy cream, whipped
1 10" angel food cake

Glaze:
1 T. cornstarch
1 cup reserved strawberry juice

2 or 3 drops red food coloring
1 tsp. butter, softened

Use an ungreased 10" tube pan. Dissolve gelatin in hot water; add ice water and chill until slightly congealed. Beat until light and fluffy. Drain berries, reserving juice for glaze. Fold in berries and whipped cream. With fork, tear cake into pieces, cutting off browned edge, if desired. Alternate cake pieces and gelatin mixture in cake pan. Chill until firm.

Blend cornstarch with a little juice. Gradually add to remaining juice in saucepan. Cook until clear, 3-5 mins. Remove from heat; add food coloring and butter. Cool. Unmold bavarian mold; drizzle with glaze. Chill.

Mrs. Vern Schipper

STRAWBERRY CROWN

½ cup butter
¼ cup brown sugar, packed

1 cup flour
½ cup pecans or walnuts
   chopped

Berry Mixture:
1 envelope unflavored gelatin
½ cup cold water
1 qt. strawberries, halved
1 tsp. lemon juice

¾ cup sugar
few drops red food coloring
1 cup heavy cream, whipped

Preheat oven to 400F. Mix together butter, sugar, flour and nuts. Spread in an ungreased 9" x 9" pan. Bake 15 min. Stir with spoon; cool.

Soften gelatin in cold water. Mash 1 cup of the berries in saucepan. Add lemon juice and sugar. Bring to a boil, stirring occasionally. Remove from heat; stir in gelatin until dissolved. Add red food coloring. Put a thin layer of this mixture on bottom of 1½ qt. mold; let set. Chill rest of mixture until partially set. Fold in remaining berries, reserving a few for garnish, and whipped cream. Fill mold in layers by alternating the berry and nut mixtures, starting with berry and ending with nuts. Chill. Unmold by dipping quickly in hot water. Garnish with remaining strawberries. May be made a day ahead.

Mrs. Vern Schipper

STRAWBERRY SWIRL

8 servings

1 cup graham cracker
   crumbs (6 double crackers)

1 T. sugar
¼ cup butter

Filling:
2 T. sugar
2 cups fresh strawberries,
   sliced or 1 (10 oz.) pkg.
   frozen strawberries, thawed
1 (3 oz.) pkg. strawberry gelatin

1 cup boiling water
½ lb. marshmallows
½ cup milk
1 cup heavy cream, whipped

continued

Combine crumbs, sugar and butter; press in a 9" x 9" pan. Chill.

Sprinkle sugar over fresh berries; let stand 30 min. Dissolve gelatin in boiling water. Drain berries, reserving juice. Add water to juice to make 1 cup; add to gelatin. Chill until partially set. Heat marshmallows and milk, stirring until marshmallows melt. Cool thoroughly, fold in whipped cream. Add berries to gelatin, then swirl in marshmallow mixture. Pour into crust. Chill until set.

Mrs. Norman Japinga

CRANBERRY ICE
8-10 servings

1 cup sugar
2½ cups boiling water
1 pkg. unflavored gelatin
3 T. cold water
2 T. orange rind, grated

⅔ cup orange juice
⅔ cup cranberry juice
or puree
3 T. lemon juice

Dissolve sugar in boiling water, heat to boiling point and cook 10 mins. Soften gelatin in cold water for 5 mins. Add cooked syrup. Cool 30 mins. Combine gelatin mixture with orange rind and juices. Pour into 2 shallow refrigerator trays; place in freezing compartment. When mixture is consistency of mush, remove from refrigerator and beat well with fork. Return to freezer and complete freezing, about 3 hrs.

Mrs. Ralph Stolp

CALIFORNIA ORANGE ICE
4-6 servings

A simple dessert with old fashioned orange ice flavor

1¼ cups water
1 cup sugar
juice of 2 lemons

1½ cups orange juice
(3-4 oranges)

Boil water and sugar for 5 mins.; cool. Stir in citrus juices and place in freezer tray. Stir about every hour until all is evenly frozen.

Mrs. Ronald Dalman

PINEAPPLE COCONUT ICE CREAM 1¾ qt.

¾ cup sugar
2 T. flour
¼ tsp. salt
2 cups milk
2 eggs, beaten

3 cups crushed pineapple,
    drained
½ cup sugar
2 cups heavy cream
½ cup coconut
1½ tsp. vanilla

In saucepan combine sugar, flour and salt; stir in milk. Cook until mixture thickens and bubbles. Stir small amount into eggs and return all to saucepan. Cook one min. more. Chill.

Combine pineapple and remaining sugar. Stir cream, coconut, vanilla and pineapple mixture into chilled mixture. Freeze in ice cream freezer. Can be served with blueberry sauce.

Mrs. Betty Sprick

BLUEBERRY SAUCE 2 cups

½ cup sugar
2 tsp. cornstarch
⅛ tsp. salt
½ cup water

1 pt. blueberries
1 T. lemon juice
1 tsp. lemon rind, grated

Combine sugar, cornstarch and salt in saucepan. Stir in water and blueberries. Bring to boil; simmer until clear and thickened, about 4 mins. Remove from heat; add lemon juice and rind. Chill.

Serve cold or warm over ice cream, pudding, custard, waffles, and cake.

Mrs. Michael Calahan

HOMEMADE STRAWBERRY ICE CREAM   2 qts.

2 (3¾ oz. each) pkgs. instant
vanilla pudding mix
4 eggs
½ cup sugar
2 cups heavy cream

4 (10 oz. each) pkgs. frozen
strawberries, thawed
1 tsp. vanilla
½ tsp. red food coloring

Prepare pudding mix according to package directions; chill till set. Beat eggs till light and fluffy. Beat in sugar, cream and pudding. Stir in strawberries, vanilla and food coloring. Freeze in ice cream freezer according to manufacturer's directions.

Mrs. William Buis

HOMEMADE VANILLA ICE CREAM

1 qt. half and half
2 cups sugar
3 T. vanilla

few drops of lemon juice
⅛ tsp. salt
7 eggs

Combine ingredients and mix well. Fill a 1 gallon freezer to 4" from top, adding whole milk, if necessary, to make desired height. Follow freezer instructions.

Mrs. Fred Leaske

EASY BUTTERSCOTCH SAUCE   1 cup

¾ cup brown sugar
⅓ cup corn syrup
2 tsp. butter

⅓ cup heavy cream
or evaporated milk

Combine sugar, syrup and butter in saucepan; boil 1 min. Remove from heat; stir in cream.

Mrs. Paul Dykema

CHRYSANTHEMUM SUNDAES
2 cups

1 cup sugar
2 T. cornstarch
⅛ tsp. salt
⅓ cup orange juice
1 T. butter

1 (11 oz.) can mandarin
  oranges, drained
¼ cup pomegranate seeds
  (optional)
½ cup walnuts, chopped
vanilla ice cream

Combine sugar, cornstarch and salt in heavy saucepan. Add orange juice, cook until clear and smooth, stirring constantly. When mixture foams up, add butter. Cool. If mixture seems to sugar when cool, heat slightly before serving.

Just before serving, add oranges, pomegranate seeds and walnuts. Spoon over vanilla ice cream.

Mrs. Jack H. Miller

HOT FUDGE SAUCE
2½ cups
Pudding Consistency

2 cups sugar
3 T. cocoa
3 T. cornstarch
½ tsp. salt

2 cups milk
1 tsp. vanilla
2 T. butter

Combine sugar, cocoa, cornstarch, salt and milk in saucepan or top of double boiler; cook over low heat until thick or in double boiler 45 min. Remove from heat; add vanilla and butter.

Mrs. Donald Broene

HOT FUDGE SAUCE   4 cups
Smooth and Creamy

½ cup margarine
4 (1 oz. each) squares
   unsweetened chocolate
3 cups sugar

½ tsp. salt
1 (13 oz.) can evaporated
   milk
2 tsp. vanilla

Melt margarine and chocolate in double boiler; slowly stir in sugar and salt. Mixture will be thick. Add milk gradually and cook over boiling water 6-10 mins., stirring frequently. Remove from heat; add vanilla and cool. Store in refrigerator.

Mrs. John Van Zoeren
Mrs. William Mendenhall

HOT FUDGE SAUCE   about 1¼ cups
Thick and Rich

2 (1 oz. each) squares
   unsweetened chocolate
2 T. butter
1 cup sugar

1 T. light corn syrup
1 (5¼ oz.) can evaporated milk
1 tsp. vanilla

Melt chocolate and butter in double boiler; slowly stir in sugar. Add corn syrup and milk gradually. Stir over boiling water until it thickens. Add vanilla. This can be stored in a jar in the refrigerator for several months.

Mrs. Don Judd

ICE CREAM FUDGE SAUCE
2-2½ cups
Thick and Fudgy

2 (1 oz. each) squares
  unsweetened chocolate
1 (15 oz.) can sweetened
  condensed milk
⅛ tsp. salt

½-1 cup hot water
1 cup walnuts, finely
  chopped (optional)
2-3 drops peppermint
  extract (optional)

Melt chocolate in top of double boiler. Add milk; stir over boiling water 5 mins. until mixture thickens. Add salt and hot water depending on consistency desired. If desired, add walnuts or peppermint.

Mrs. Lyle Sanders

PEANUT BUTTER SUNDAE SAUCE
about 3½ cups

1¼ cups brown sugar
¾ cup light corn syrup
1¼ cups peanut butter

¼ cup margarine
1½ cups light cream,
  approximately

Combine brown sugar and syrup in saucepan; boil until sugar is thoroughly dissolved. Add peanut butter and margarine; combine thoroughly. Cool; add cream using enough to make the sauce a proper consistency. Good when served slightly warm.

Mrs. Kenneth Elhart

RUM SAUCE
about 1½ cups

½ cup sugar
1 T. cornstarch
⅛ tsp. salt
⅛ tsp. nutmeg

1 cup boiling water
2 T. butter
1½ T. rum extract

Blend together sugar, cornstarch, salt and nutmeg in a saucepan. Add water and butter. Cook 5 mins., stirring constantly. Remove from heat; stir in extract.

Mrs. Paul Klomparens

OLD FASHIONED APPLE CRISP
6 servings

5½ cups cooking apples,
   peeled and sliced
¼ cup water
½ cup sugar
½ cup light brown sugar,
   firmly packed
½ tsp. nutmeg

½ tsp. cinnamon
¼ tsp. salt
¾ cup flour
½ cup butter
⅓ cup pecans, chopped
   (optional)

Preheat oven to 350F. Use an 8" x 10" casserole. Put apples in casserole; add water. Combine sugars, nutmeg, cinnamon, salt and flour. Cut in butter with pastry blender. Stir in nuts. Spoon evenly over apples. Cover; bake 30 mins. Uncover; bake 30 mins. longer. Serve warm with vanilla ice cream or hard sauce.

Mrs. Donald G. Miller

APPLE DUMPLINGS
8 servings

pie crust dough for 1
   2-crust pie
8 medium Spy apples,
   peeled and cored

½ cup sugar
1½ tsp. cinnamon
4 tsp. butter

Sauce:
1 cup sugar
2 cups water

3 T. butter
1½ tsp. cinnamon

Preheat oven to 425F. Use a 9" x 13" baking pan. Roll out pie dough in 2 sections, each 12" x 12". Cut each into 4 equal parts, each 6" x 6". Place 1 apple on each of the 8 squares of dough. Combine sugar and cinnamon; divide mixture into center of each apple. Top each with ½ tsp. butter. Wrap pastry square around the apple, pressing closed at the top. Place in baking pan.

Combine sauce ingredients in saucepan; heat. Pour into baking pan around apples. Bake 40-45 mins., basting occasionally with the sauce. Serve hot.

Mrs. Ken Kleis

APPLE HARVEST
8 servings

4 cups apples, peeled
    and diced
1 cup sugar
½ cup flour, sifted
1 egg, beaten
2 tsp. baking powder

1 T. margarine, melted
1 tsp. vanilla
½ cup nuts, chopped
½ cup dates, chopped
whipping cream or ice cream

Preheat oven to 400F. Grease a 9" x 9" baking pan. Combine all ingredients; stir until mixed. Bake 35-40 mins. Serve warm with whipping cream or ice cream.

Mrs. Bill Penna
Mrs. Bruce Van Dyke

GLAZED APPLE SQUARES
15 servings

3 cups flour, sifted
1 cup lard
½ cup water

1 egg
1 T. vinegar

Filling:
15 medium size cooking
    apples
2 cups sugar
6 T. flour

2 tsp. cinnamon
¼ tsp. salt
½ cup pecans, chopped
¼ cup butter

Glaze:
2 T. butter, melted
1 cup confectioners' sugar

½ tsp. vanilla
milk as needed for
    thin glaze

Cut flour into lard until size of a pea. Combine water, egg and vinegar; blend into flour mixture. Divide dough in half.

Preheat oven to 375F. Use an ungreased jelly roll pan. Roll half of dough out; place on pan. Slice peeled apples and place on crust. Combine sugar, flour, cinnamon, salt and nuts; sprinkle over apples, dot with butter. Roll out remaining dough; place over top of apples and seal crust. Make several slits on top. Bake for 1 hr.

Combine topping ingredients and drizzle over warm apple squares.

Mrs. Roger Smith

480

BLUEBERRY CRUMBLE
8 servings

6 cups fresh blueberries, washed

⅔ cup sugar
juice of 1 lemon

Topping:
½ cup butter
⅔ cup sugar

1 ⅓ cups flour
vanilla ice cream

Preheat oven to 375F. Place blueberries in 9" x 9" baking dish. Sprinkle with sugar and lemon juice.

Blend butter, sugar and flour. Sprinkle over berries. Bake 40-60 min. until brown and bubbly. Serve warm with ice cream.

Mrs. Adrian Trimpe

CHERRY CINNAMON COBBLER
8 servings

½ cup sugar
2 T. cornstarch
2-4 T. red cinnamon candy

1 (16 oz.) can sour cherries
¼ cup water

Topping:
1 ½ cups flour
½ tsp. salt
2 tsp. baking powder
6 T. brown sugar
¼ cup shortening

1 egg, slightly beaten
2 T. milk
1 T. butter, melted
¼ tsp. cinnamon
⅓ cup pecans, chopped

Lemon Glaze:
½ cup confectioners' sugar, sifted

1 T. lemon juice

Preheat oven to 400F. Grease an 8" x 8" baking dish. Combine sugar, cornstarch, candy, cherries and water in a saucepan; cook until thickened. Pour into baking dish. Sift the flour, salt and baking powder into a mixing bowl. Add 3 T. brown sugar. Cut in shortening until particles are fine. Combine egg and milk; add to flour mixture and stir until moistened. Add a few more drops of milk, if necessary. Roll out to a 12" x 14" rectangle on floured surface. Brush with butter. Combine the remaining brown sugar, cinnamon and nuts; sprinkle over the dough. Roll up from the 12" side. Cut into ¾" slices; put on cherry filling. Bake 25 mins. Combine sugar and lemon juice. Glaze while warm.

Mrs. Erich Benke

CHERRY CRUNCH
8 servings

1 egg, slightly beaten
1¼ cups sugar
1 T. shortening, melted
1¼ cups flour
1 tsp. baking soda

1 tsp. cinnamon
¼ tsp. salt
1 (16 oz.) can pitted sour
   cherries, drained, reserving
   juice
½ cup nuts, chopped

Cherry Sauce:
1 cup cherry juice (add
   water to make 1 cup)
½ cup sugar

1 heaping T. flour
1 T. butter
vanilla ice cream

Preheat oven to 350F. Grease an 8" x 8" pan. Cream the egg, sugar and shortening. Sift together the flour, soda, cinnamon and salt; add to creamed mixture. Stir in cherries and nuts. Bake 45 mins.

Combine ingredients for cherry sauce in saucepan; cook until thickened. Serve the crunch with a dip of ice cream and sauce on top.

Mrs. Richard Forwood

CHERRY DUMPLINGS
8 servings

2 (16 oz. each) cans pitted sour
   cherries, undrained

1 heaping T. cornstarch
1 cup sugar

Dumplings:
2 cups flour
1 tsp. salt
4 tsp. baking powder

1 egg, beaten
milk

Combine cherries, cornstarch and sugar in saucepan; bring to boil.

Sift together flour, salt and baking powder. Add egg and enough milk to make batter moist. Drop by spoonfuls onto cherry mixture. Cook gently uncovered about 10 min. Cover and cook 10 min. more or until dumplings look dry on top and test done with a toothpick.

Mrs. James Chamness

HEAVENLY HASH

8 servings

2 eggs, slightly beaten
1 cup sugar
2 heaping T. flour

Fruit Filling:
1½ pt. strawberries
3 bananas

Topping:
1 cup heavy cream, whipped
sugar

½ tsp. baking powder
1 tsp. vanilla
½ cup pecans, chopped

or any other combination as blueberries and pineapple or raspberries and bananas

whole pecans

Preheat oven to 325F. Use a 9" x 9" baking pan. Combine eggs, sugar, flour, baking powder, vanilla and nuts; put in pan. Bake 30 mins. Let cool; break into chunks on a plate with an edge, such as a pie plate.

Combine fruits; spread atop base. Sweeten whipping cream to taste or use commercial whipped topping. Top fruit mixture with whipping cream and whole pecans. The base freezes well.

Mrs. William Vander Bilt

CALIFORNIA PEACH COBBLER

8 servings

1 cup flour, sifted
1 tsp. baking powder
½ tsp. salt
2 eggs
1½ cups sugar
2 T. margarine

2 T. milk
½ cup sherry
3 cups fresh peaches, sliced
whipped cream or
ice cream

Preheat oven to 375F. Grease a 9" x 9" baking pan. Sift together flour, baking powder and salt; set aside. Beat together eggs and 1 cup sugar. Add margarine and milk. Add flour mixture; mix well. Pour into pan.

Simmer together sherry and remaining ½ cup sugar for 3 to 4 min.; add peaches. Pour hot peach mixture over batter in pan. Bake 30 min. Serve warm with dollop of whipped cream or vanilla ice cream.

Mrs. David Vander Leek

FRESH PEACH COBBLER

6-8 servings

4½ cups fresh peaches,
    sliced
1 cup sugar
1 T. cornstarch

¼ tsp. almond extract
1 T. lemon juice
2 tsp. lemon rind, grated

Shortcake:
1 cup flour
½ cup sugar
1 tsp. baking powder
¼ tsp. salt

1 egg, beaten
¾ cup sour cream
2 T. butter, melted
cream or ice cream

Preheat oven to 375F. Grease a 9" x 9" baking dish. Arrange peaches in dish. Combine sugar, cornstarch, extract, juice and rind; sprinkle on peaches. Heat in oven while preparing short-cake.

Sift together flour, sugar, baking powder and salt; set aside. Combine egg, sour cream and butter; blend well into flour mixture. Drop by spoonfuls onto fruit. Bake 30-40 mins. If desired, serve with cream or ice cream.

Mrs. Donald G. Miller

FRESH PEACH CRUMBLE

6-8 servings

3 eggs
1½ cups soda cracker
    crumbs or rusk crumbs
1½ tsp. baking powder
1½ cups brown sugar

1½ tsp. vanilla
½ cup nuts, chopped
4 cups fresh peaches, sliced
    and sweetened

Preheat oven to 375F. Use an ungreased 9" x 9" baking dish. Combine all ingredients except peaches; place in dish. Bake 15 mins. Cool. Cut into squares and top each square with sliced peaches and a dollop of whipped cream, if desired. This may be baked in a 12-cup muffin tin.

Eet Smakelijk's Best

PEACH KUCHEN
Peach Cake

6 servings

2 cups flour
¼ tsp. baking powder
½ tsp. salt
1 cup sugar
½ cup butter

12 peach halves, fresh or
    frozen
1 tsp. cinnamon
2 egg yolks, slightly beaten
1 cup cream or half and half

Preheat oven to 400F. Grease an 8" x 8" baking dish. Sift together flour, baking powder, salt and 2 T. sugar. Work in butter until mix is like cornmeal. Pat evenly over bottom and halfway up sides of baking dish. Place peaches over pastry. Mix remaining sugar and cinnamon; sprinkle over peaches. Bake 15 mins. Mix egg yolks and cream; pour over peaches and bake 30 mins. longer. Serve warm.

Mrs. Kenneth Louis

WALNUT PEACH MERINGUE

1 cup soft shortening
2 cups sifted flour

1 tsp. salt
1 egg

Filling:
3 egg yolks
1¼ cups sugar
2 tsp. lemon juice

4 cups fresh peaches, sliced
3 T. quick cooking tapioca

Meringue:
3 egg whites
¼ tsp. cream of tartar
¾ cup sugar

1 cup walnuts, coarsely
    chopped
12 walnut halves

Preheat oven to 425F. Use an ungreased 2 qt. oblong dish. Blend shortening, flour and salt; add egg. Stir to combine. Pat into dish. Bake 15 min.

In saucepan combine egg yolks, sugar, lemon juice, 3 cups peaches and tapioca. Cook over medium heat until it comes to a full rolling boil; cook 1 min. longer. Cool slightly and add remaining peaches. Pour over baked crust.

Reduce oven heat to 350F. Beat egg whites with cream of tartar until frothy. Slowly add sugar, beating until stiff. Fold in nuts. Cover fruit mixture with meringue; arrange walnut halves on top. Bake 15-20 mins. or until lightly browned.

RASPBERRY DESSERT SQUARES 12 servings

1 cup flour	½ cup butter, softened
⅓ cup sugar	

Filling:

1 (8 oz.) pkg. frozen raspberries, drained, reserve juice	1 cup sugar
	½ tsp. salt
	½ tsp. baking powder
¾ cup nuts, chopped	¼ cup flour
2 eggs	1 tsp. vanilla

Sauce:

reserved raspberry juice	2 T. cornstarch
½ cup water	1 T. lemon juice
½ cup sugar	vanilla ice cream

Preheat oven to 350F. Use an ungreased 9" x 13" pan. Blend flour, sugar and butter; press in bottom of pan. Sprinkle raspberries and nuts over top. Beat eggs and sugar until fluffy. Add salt, baking powder, flour and vanilla; mix well. Spread over raspberries. Bake 30 min. Combine juice, water, sugar and cornstarch in saucepan; cook until thickened, stirring constantly. Remove from heat; add lemon juice. Cool.

Place a square of dessert on plate. Top with a scoop of ice cream and sauce.

Mrs. Thomas Buis

486

RHUBARB-MANDARIN CRISP   *8 servings*

**6 cups rhubarb, cut in
    1" pieces
1½ cups sugar
5 T. tapioca
1 (11 oz.) can mandarin
    oranges, drained**

**½ cup butter
1 cup brown sugar
½ cup flour
1 cup quick oatmeal**

In a 9" x 12", lightly buttered baking dish, place rhubarb and cover with sugar and tapioca. Cover and refrigerate 3 hrs. or overnight. Preheat oven to 350F. Sprinkle mandarin oranges over rhubarb mixture. Combine butter, brown sugar, flour and oatmeal; put crumb mixture on top and bake uncovered for 40 min. Extra good served warm with ice cream.

Mrs. Linda Anderson

STRAWBERRY TURNOVERS

**¼ cup sugar
1½ T. cornstarch**

**2 cups fresh strawberries,
    sliced**

**Dough:
1¼ cups flour, sifted
¼ cup corn meal
¾ tsp. salt**

**½ cup + 2 T. shortening
3 T. water**

**Glaze:
½ cup confectioners' sugar,
    sifted**

1 T. water

Mix sugar and cornstarch; add strawberries. Cook over medium heat, stirring until thick. Cool.

Preheat oven to 425F. Use an ungreased baking sheet. Mix together flour, corn meal and salt; cut in shortening. Sprinkle water on dough; mix until moist. Press into ball. On floured board roll to 4" circle. Place dough on 16" x 8" piece of foil. Roll out to larger circle; transfer on foil to baking sheet. Place filling on ½ of circle, 1½" from edge. Bring dough over, seal edges and slash top of pastry. Turn up edges of foil. Bake 35 min.

Combine sugar and water; drizzle atop turnover. To serve, cut in triangle shapes.

Mrs. Richard Oudersluys, Jr.

SUMMER DESSERT
6 servings

¾ cup sour cream
½ cup brown sugar

3 cups (1½ lbs.) white
   seedless grapes
sour cream

Mix sour cream and brown sugar. Then mix gently with grapes. Spread in a shallow pan and refrigerate at least 4 hrs. Top each serving with a dab of sour cream. Other fruits may be substituted for the grapes.

Mrs. John Marquis

CHOCOLATE RUM MOUSSE
8 servings

¼ cup cold milk
1 envelope unflavored gelatin
¾ cup milk, scalded
6 T. dark rum
1 egg
¼ cup sugar

⅛ tsp. salt
1 (6 oz.) pkg. semi-sweet
   chocolate chips
1 cup heavy cream
2 ice cubes
1 tsp. vanilla

Place cold milk and gelatin in blender; cover and blend low to soften gelatin. Add milk, rum, egg, sugar, salt and chocolate chips. Cover; turn to high and blend until smooth. Add cream, ice cubes and vanilla; continue blending until ice is liquified. Pour into parfait or sherbet glasses. Chill.

Mrs. John Tysse

COFFEE MOUSSE
8 servings

2 envelopes unflavored
   gelatin
6 T. cold water
2 cups strong hot coffee
¾ cup sugar

pinch of salt
1 cup heavy cream
1 tsp. vanilla
whipped cream topping,
   optional

continued

488

Soften gelatin in cold water. Add coffee; stir until gelatin is dissolved. Add sugar and salt. Cool. When gelatin mixture is firm, whip cream to moderately stiff; add vanilla. Whip gelatin mixture until soft; beat in whipped cream and blend well. Turn into serving dishes or large mold. Chill. Unmold. Top with whipped cream, if desired.

Mrs. Robert King

BUTTERSCOTCH BREAD PUDDING   *6 servings*

3 cups soft bread crumbs
2 cups milk, scalded
¼ cup butter, melted
½ cup brown sugar

2 eggs, slightly beaten
¼ tsp. salt
1 tsp. cinnamon
½ cup raisins

Preheat oven to 350F. Place bread crumbs in 1½ qt. baking dish. Blend in the milk and butter. Add brown sugar, eggs, salt, cinnamon and raisins; mix well. Place dish in a pan of hot water 1" deep. Bake until knife inserted 1" from edge comes out clean, 40-45 mins. Serve warm, with or without hard sauce.

Mrs. Don Hillebrands

HARD SAUCE

½ cup butter
1 cup confectioners'
*   sugar*

1 egg white, unbeaten
½ tsp. vanilla
nutmeg

Cream butter until soft. Blend in sugar. Beat in egg white. Stir in vanilla. Put in serving dish and sprinkle with nutmeg. Chill in refrigerator for 1 hr.

Mrs. Don Hillebrands

CHOCOLATE BLENDER PUDDING 6 servings

1 cup semi-sweet
    chocolate chips
2 egg yolks

1¼ cups evaporated
    milk, scalded
3 T. creme de cacao

Put all ingredients into blender and process at high speed until smooth. Pour into 6 small sherbets, filling ⅔ full. Cover and chill at least 3 hrs.

Mrs. Frank Boonstra

CRANBERRY PUDDING 8-10 servings

2 tsp. baking soda
½ cup molasses
½ cup boiling water

1⅓ cups flour
1 tsp. baking powder
1 cup cranberries

Sauce:
1 cup sugar
½ cup butter

½ cup heavy cream
1 tsp. vanilla

Grease and flour a 1 qt. metal can or heat-proof jello mold. Add soda to molasses; stir in boiling water. Sift flour with baking powder; combine all but ⅓ cup with molasses mixture. Toss cranberries in remaining flour and add to mixture. Pour into can; cover tightly with aluminum foil. Place on rack in pan of water. Steam 2 hrs., keeping at 2" water level.

About ½ hour before serving, place foil covered pudding in warm oven. Combine sugar, butter and cream in top of double boiler. Cook over simmering water 15-20 mins. Remove from heat; add vanilla. Serve over cranberry pudding.

The pudding may be prepared ahead of time, wrapped in aluminum foil and placed in refrigerator or freezer.

Janet Heydens

DUTCH TEA RUSK PUDDING
4 servings

4 rusks

1 cup canned strawberry
juice, heated

Pudding:
1 T. cornstarch
2 T. water
1 cup milk

¼ cup sugar
½ tsp. butter
¼ tsp. vanilla
12 fresh strawberries

Dip both sides of each rusk in juice and place on serving dishes. Pour on remaining juice, reserving ¼ cup for topping, if desired.

Moisten cornstarch in water. Heat milk in saucepan; add sugar and cornstarch. Bring to boil, stirring constantly. Remove from heat; add butter and vanilla. Pour over rusk, dribbling over the edges. Cool. Before serving, garnish each with 3 berries and 1 T. juice, if desired.

Mrs. Louis Garvelink

JAN IN DE ZAK
Dutch Pudding

1 cake compressed yeast
1 cup lukewarm milk
1 egg, beaten
3 cups flour

1 cup raisins
½ tsp. salt
1 T. candied lemon peel

Dissolve yeast in milk. Add egg, flour, raisins, salt and peel; mix well. Let stand 1-1½ hrs. in warm place.

Sprinkle flour on a piece of cheesecloth large enough to hold dough. Pour in batter and tie, leaving a little room to allow for swelling. Put in large kettle of hot water; boil for 2-2½ hrs. Untie, remove from bag and slice pudding with a thread. Serve with butter and sugar.

Mrs. Matthew Rozema

VICTORIAN PLUM PUDDING   12 servings

4 slices bread, torn in pieces
1 cup prepared mincemeat
½ cup milk
2 eggs, slightly beaten
1 cup light brown sugar,
   firmly packed
¼ cup brandy
4 oz. (about 1 cup) suet,
   finely chopped
1 tsp. vanilla
1 cup flour

1 tsp. baking soda
½ tsp. salt
2 tsp. cinnamon
1 tsp. ground cloves
1 tsp. ground mace
1½ cups (8 oz.) mixed candied
   fruits and peels, chopped
1 cup raisins
½ cup slivered almonds
1 recipe Brandy Hard Sauce

Garnish:
green grapes and holly

Grease well a 2 qt. mold. Combine bread, mincemeat and milk; beat. Stir in eggs, brown sugar, brandy, suet and vanilla. Sift together flour, soda, salt, cinnamon, cloves and mace into a bowl; add candied fruits and peels, raisins and almonds. Stir in bread mixture. Pour into mold. Cover. Place on rack in deep kettle; add boiling water to kettle 1" deep. Cover; steam 3½ hrs., adding more boiling water, if needed, to maintain 1" level. Cool 10 mins.; unmold. Serve with Brandy Hard Sauce. Garnish with green grapes and holly, if desired.

Mrs. Robert Hampson

BRANDY HARD SAUCE   1¾ cups

½ cup margarine
2 cups confectioners'
   sugar
1 egg yolk, beaten

2 T. brandy
1 tsp. vanilla
1 egg white, stiffly beaten

Garnish:
orange peel twist

Thoroughly cream margarine and sugar. Beat in egg yolk, brandy and vanilla. Fold in egg white. Chill. Garnish with an orange peel twist, if desired. Serve with Victorian Plum Pudding.

Mrs. Robert Hampson

CARLOTA DE CAFE
12-16 servings

A rich and attractive dessert cake.

3 dozen ladyfingers, split
2 cups butter
2 (14 oz. each) cans sweetened
  condensed milk
2 T. strong coffee

1 T. cognac
½ lb. blanched almonds,
  pulverized in blender
1 tsp. almond extract
1 (16 oz.) can cherry pie filling

Line bottom and sides of a 9" springform pan with ladyfingers; set aside. Beat butter until soft. Add milk, coffee and cognac. Fold in almonds and almond extract. Pour ½ of mixture into pan. Top with a layer of ladyfingers. Repeat with remaining mixture and ladyfingers. Top with pie filling. Chill overnight unmold onto a serving plate.

Mrs. John Marquis

CHOCOLATE CHARLOTTE RUSSE CAKE 12 servings

4 (1 oz. each) squares
  unsweetened chocolate
¾ cup sugar
⅓ cup milk
6 eggs, separated, room
  temperature

1½ cups unsalted butter
1½ cups confectioners' sugar
⅛ tsp. salt
1½ tsp. vanilla
3 doz. ladyfingers, split

Garnish:
1 cup heavy cream, whipped

unsweetened chocolate,
  shaved

Use an ungreased deep 9" flat springform or loose bottomed pan. Melt chocolate over hot water in top of double boiler. Mix sugar, milk and egg yolks. Add to chocolate; cook until smooth and thickened, stirring constantly. Cool. Cream butter well; add ¾ cup confectioners' sugar and cream thoroughly. Add chocolate mixture and beat well. Beat egg whites with salt until stiff; gradually beat in remaining confectioners' sugar. Fold into chocolate mixture. Add vanilla. Line sides and bottom of pan with split ladyfingers. Put in alternate layers ⅓ of the mixture and remaining ladyfingers. Chill overnight. Remove to cake plate. Garnish with whipped cream and shaved chocolate. This freezes well.

Mrs. Robert Weber

493

LEMON LUSCIOUS SUPREME

12 servings

3 dozen ladyfingers, split
1 envelope unflavored gelatin
1/2 cup fresh lemon juice
4 eggs separated, room
   temperature
1 cup sugar
1 1/2 tsp. lemon peel, grated

1/8 tsp. salt
3 T. butter
1 cup heavy cream, whipped
1 cup heavy cream, whipped
   and sweetened to taste
whole strawberries (optional)

Line sides and bottom of 9" springform pan with ladyfingers. Soften gelatin in lemon juice. Beat egg yolks; slowly add 1/2 cup sugar, beating until light and thick. Combine egg mixture with gelatin mixture, lemon peel, salt and butter in top of double boiler; cook, stirring constantly until thickened and smooth. Cool. Beat egg whites until foamy; gradually add 1/2 cup sugar, beating until stiff peaks form. Gently fold in yolk mixture, then fold in 1 cup whipped cream. Pour 1/2 of custard into pan. Layer broken ladyfingers over custard; add remaining custard. Chill 24 hrs. Before serving top with sweetened whipped cream and garnish with whole strawberries.

Mrs. Leo Jungblut

MAI TAI MOUSSE

12-16 servings

18 ladyfingers, split
2 envelopes unflavored
   gelatin
1/2 cup pineapple juice
   (reserved from pineapple)
5 egg yolks
3/4 cup sugar
1/4 tsp. salt
1 cup milk, scalded
1/3 cup lime juice
1/3 cup light rum

1 (20 oz.) can crushed pineapple, well drained,
   reserving juice
5 egg whites, room
   temperature
1/2 cup sugar
1 cup heavy cream, whipped
1 cup heavy cream, whipped,
   to garnish
1/4 cup macadamia nuts,
   walnuts or toasted almonds,
   chopped

continued

Line sides and bottom of a 9" springform pan with ladyfingers. Soften gelatin in pineapple juice. Beat egg yolks in top of double boiler; stir in sugar and salt. Blend in milk and cook over boiling water, stirring constantly, until thickened, about 5 min. Blend in lime juice, rum, pineapple and gelatin mixture. Chill till thickened but not set.

Beat egg whites until stiff peaks form, adding sugar gradually. Fold in pineapple custard and whipped cream. Pour into lined pan. Chill several hours or overnight. Before serving, remove from pan; garnish with whipped cream and nuts.

Mrs. Landis Zylman

PEANUT BRITTLE REFRIGERATOR CAKE

12-15 servings

2 envelopes unflavored gelatin
½ cup cold water
2 cups milk, scalded
¾ tsp. salt
2 dozen ladyfingers, split or 1 angel food cake, crusts trimmed, cut into strips 1" x ½"
½ lb. marshmallows, diced

1 lb. peanut brittle, crushed
2 cups heavy cream, whipped
2 T. lemon juice
1 tsp. vanilla
additional peanut brittle, crushed
walnut halves, pineapple chunks and galax leaves (optional)

Soften gelatin in cold water. Dissolve in hot milk and add salt. Chill until partially set.

Line bottom and sides of greased angel food cake pan with ladyfingers. Fold marshmallows and peanut brittle into whipped cream. Beat gelatin until light and fluffy; fold in whipped cream mixture and add lemon juice and vanilla. Pour into pan; chill until set. Unmold and garnish top with peanut brittle. Garnish plate with walnuts, pineapple and leaves.

Note: This dessert may also be made by breaking the ladyfingers into tiny pieces, folding them into the gelatin and then placing into a mold or 9" x 13" pan.

Mrs. Robert Hall

STRAWBERRY-RHUBARB RUSSE

10-12 servings

*6 cups rhubarb, cut in
½" pieces*
½ cup sugar
1 cup water
*2 (3 oz. each) pkg. strawberry
gelatin*

*2 cups heavy cream,
whipped*
1 tsp. vanilla
3 dozen ladyfingers, split

Rhubarb Glaze:
1 cup reserved rhubarb syrup
¼ cup sugar
1½ T. cornstarch
1½ T. cold water

*few drops red food coloring,
if desired*
whole fresh strawberries
fresh mint sprigs

Combine rhubarb, sugar and water in saucepan. Bring to boil and simmer 6-8 mins., or until rhubarb is very soft. Drain off 1 cup syrup, reserving for glaze. Blenderize rhubarb and remaining syrup or force through food mill to make pulp (about 3½ cups); bring to boil, pour over gelatin and stir until gelatin is dissolved and well blended. Chill until slightly thickened, but not firm. Fold in whipped cream until well blended; add vanilla.

Line bottom and sides of a 9" springform pan with ladyfingers. Alternate layers of rhubarb mixture and ladyfingers, ending with rhubarb mixture. Chill overnight or until firm.

In saucepan combine reserved syrup and sugar; bring to boil. Blend cornstarch with water; stir into syrup. Bring to boil and cook, stirring constantly, until thickened and clear. Add food coloring. Cool.

Before serving, spread glaze over cake. Split whole strawberries from tip almost to stem end in 4 to 6 places and open out to resemble flower petals. Arrange on glaze. Garnish with mint sprigs.

Mrs. Roger Scholten

WHISKEY CAKE   *10-12 servings*
An elegant dessert for a special occasion.

2 envelopes unflavored gelatin
1 cup cold water
6 eggs, separated, room
   temperature
½ cup Scotch

1 cup sugar
1 T. lemon juice
2 cups heavy cream, whipped
3 pkg. ladyfingers, split

Soak gelatin in cold water; heat over hot water to dissolve. Beat egg yolks; add whiskey slowly, beating well. Beat in sugar. Add lemon juice. Blend in gelatin. Chill briefly, until slightly congealed. Fold in whipped cream and stiffly beaten egg whites.

Line sides and bottom of a 9" springform pan with ladyfingers. Add half of the mixture. Top with layer of ladyfingers. Add remaining mixture and top with more ladyfingers. Chill overnight.

Mrs. Hal Thornhill

BAVARIAN BANANA TORTE   *12 servings*

4 eggs, separated, room
   temperature
1 cup sugar
1 cup graham cracker crumbs

½ tsp. baking powder
½ cup pecans, chopped
½ cup flaked coconut
1 tsp. vanilla

Filling and Topping:
1 (18 oz.) can ready to serve
   vanilla pudding
2 bananas

lemon juice
½ cup heavy cream or
   topping, whipped

Preheat oven to 350F. Grease 2 round 8" cake pans. Beat egg yolks with sugar until thick. Add crumbs, baking powder, pecans, coconut and vanilla. In another bowl beat egg whites until stiff; fold into crumb mixture. Pour into cake pans. Bake 20-25 mins. Cool.

Spread half the pudding on one layer. Slice one banana, brush with lemon juice and arrange on pudding. Put on top cake layer. Spread remaining pudding on top; refrigerate. Just before serving garnish top with whipped cream around edge and second banana sliced, in center.

Mrs. Sherwin Ortman

CHOCOLATE CHANTILLY TORTE   16-18 servings

1 (18½ oz.) pkg. Lemon Chiffon cake mix	6 T. water
1 T. lemon peel, finely-grated	4 eggs, separated, room temperature
4 (4 oz. each) pkg. sweet cooking chocolate	¼ cup confectioners' sugar
	3 T. sugar
	3½ cups heavy cream

Prepare cake mix according to package directions, adding lemon peel to cake batter. Place sweet cooking chocolate and water in saucepan over low heat; stir until chocolate is melted and mixture is smooth. Remove from heat, cooling slightly. Add egg yolks, beating vigorously until smooth. Add, and mix well, confectioners' sugar. Fold in stiffly beaten egg whites; set mixture aside to finish cooling. Combine sugar and heavy cream and whip until stiff.

Split chiffon cake into seven layers. Put layers together spreading each with part of whipped cream first and following with part of chocolate mixture. On top layer spread chocolate mixture to edge of cake so it runs down sides in several places. Chill in refrigerator 4 to 5 hrs. or overnight. Can be frozen.

Mrs. C. Vandekerck

CHOCOLATE COFFEE TORTE   12 servings

6 eggs, separated, room temperature	1 cup cake flour
	1 tsp. baking powder
1 cup sugar	1 T. instant coffee
1 tsp. vanilla	

Filling and Topping:

2 cups heavy cream	2 T. instant coffee
5 T. sugar	

Glaze:

⅓ cup semi-sweet chocolate chips	2 T. margarine
	2 T. cream or milk

continued

498

Preheat oven to 325F. Grease 3 round 8" cake pans. Beat egg whites until soft peaks form; gradually add sugar, beating until stiff peaks form. Beat egg yolks and vanilla; fold into egg whites. Sift together flour and baking powder into bowl. Fold in coffee and egg mixture. Bake 15 mins.

Beat heavy cream with sugar and coffee until stiff. Spread between cookie layers and over top and sides.

Melt together chocolate chips, margarine and cream. When cool, pour over top and drizzle down sides. Chill.

Mrs. Richard Taylor

CHOCOLATE PASTRY TORTE   *12 servings*

*2 (4 oz. each) pkg. German
  sweet chocolate*
½ cup sugar
½ cup water
1½ tsp. instant coffee

2 tsp. vanilla
*1 (9 or 10 oz.) pkg. pie
  crust mix (2 sticks)*
2 cups heavy cream
stick candy

In saucepan, combine chocolate, sugar, water and coffee. Cook over low heat, stirring constantly until smooth. Add vanilla; cool to room temperature.

Preheat oven to 425F. Use ungreased 8" round cake pans. Mix ¾ cup chocolate sauce into pie crust mix; blend well. Divide pastry into 6 equal parts; press each part over bottom of an inverted cake pan to within ½" of edge. (Do in relays according to the number of pans you have). Bake 4-5 mins. or until done. If necessary, trim layers to even the edges. Cool; then run tip of knife under edges of layers to loosen and lift off carefully.

Whip cream until it just begins to form soft peaks; fold in remaining chocolate sauce. Stack baked pastry, spreading chocolate cream between layers and over top. Chill at least 8 hrs. or overnight. Trim with stick candy. Serve with Rum Mocha Sauce, if desired.

Mrs. Arnold Dood

RUM MOCHA SAUCE

2 cups

¼ cup butter
1 cup sugar
⅛ tsp. salt
1 tsp. instant coffee
3 T. light rum

⅓ cup Dutch cocoa
1 cup heavy cream or
  evaporated milk
2 tsp. vanilla

Melt butter in saucepan; blend in sugar, salt, coffee, rum and cocoa. Add cream; bring to a boil. Lower heat and simmer 5 min. Add vanilla.

Mrs. Donald G. Miller

HAZELNUT TORTE

10-12 servings

6 eggs, separated,
  room temperature
1 cup sugar
2 tsp. lemon peel, grated

2½ cups hazelnuts,
  ground
2 T. dry bread crumbs
1 tsp. baking powder

Filling:
2 cups heavy cream, whipped
½ cup sugar

½ cup hazelnuts, ground

Frosting:
2 egg yolks
2 T. sugar
¼ cup margarine, softened

2 sq. (1 oz. each) semi-sweet
  chocolate, melted
1 T. hazelnuts, finely chopped

Preheat oven to 350F. Line two 8" round pans with waxed paper. Beat egg whites until soft peaks form. Gradually beat in ½ cup sugar, beating until stiff. Beat yolks until thick and light; gradually add remaining ½ cup sugar. Stir lemon peel, hazelnuts, bread crumbs, and baking powder into egg yolks; mix well. At low speed, beat yolk mixture into whites, just until combined. Pour into pans; bake 30 min. Cool. Split each layer in half crosswise.

continued

Combine filling ingredients. Put layers together using ⅔ of the filling.

In small bowl beat yolks and sugar until thick and light. Add margarine and chocolate; beat until smooth. Cover top of cake with frosting and cover sides with remaining filling. Sprinkle top with hazelnuts. Refrigerate 1 hr.

Mrs. Michael Calahan

RUSSIAN TEA LOAF   *12 servings*

9 egg whites, room
    temperature
⅛ tsp. salt
1 tsp. cream of tartar

5 egg yolks
1½ cups sugar, sifted 5 times
1 cup cake flour, sifted 5
    times

Custard Filling and Topping:
5 egg yolks
¾ cup sugar
1½ cups light cream
1 envelope unflavored gelatin

¼ cup cold water
2 cups heavy cream, whipped
1 tsp. vanilla

Preheat oven to 200F. Use an ungreased 10" tube pan. Beat egg whites with salt until stiff; add cream of tartar and finish beating. Beat yolks until light and lemon colored; beat in sugar. Fold in half the whites; fold in flour and remaining whites. Turn into pan. Bake 1 hr., increasing heat 25 degrees every 15 mins.; leave at 300F. for another 15 mins. Invert and cool.

Beat egg yolks until light; add sugar. Heat cream in double boiler. Add egg yolk mixture and cook until thick. Dissolve gelatin in cold water; add to hot custard. Cool; fold in whipped cream and vanilla.

Cut cake in 3 layers; put custard between layers and over entire cake. Chill.

Mrs. William G. Winter

SWEET MOUTHFUL
8-10 servings

As delicious as it is beautiful.

5 egg whites, room
   temperature
½ tsp. cream of tartar

¼ tsp. salt
1¼ cups superfine
   sugar

Filling:
1 (6 oz.) pkg. semi-sweet
   chocolate chips
3 T. water
3 cups heavy cream

2 tsp. vanilla
⅓ cup sugar
1-2 pints fresh strawberries,
   sliced

Beat egg whites with cream of tartar and salt until soft peaks form. Gradually add sugar, a small amount at a time, beating until very stiff peaks form and sugar is dissolved.

Preheat oven to 275F. Cover 2 cookie sheets with brown (grocery bag type), ungreased paper. Using an 8" round cake pan as a guide, draw 3 circles on the paper (2 circles on one sheet and 1 circle on the other.). Divide the meringue into thirds and spread evenly over the circles. Bake 1 hr. Turn off heat and let dry in oven (door closed) at least 2 hrs. or overnight.

Melt chocolate chips with water; cool to room temperature. Whip cream stiff with vanilla and sugar. To assemble torte, place 1 meringue on cake plate, spread ⅓ of chocolate over meringue, then ⅓ of whipped cream, and then ⅓ of sliced strawberries. Repeat in the same order with the remaining 2 meringues. This may be assembled and refrigerated up to 4 hrs. prior to serving.

Mrs. Robert Hampson

Pies That Say More

NOTES

DUTCH APPLE PIE

6 servings

9" pastry shell, unbaked

Filling:

5-6 tart apples, sliced
¾ cup sugar
1 tsp. cinnamon

⅔ cup flour
½ cup brown sugar
⅓ cup margarine

Preheat oven to 425F. Combine apples, sugar and cinnamon and place in pie shell. Mix flour, brown sugar and margarine until crumbly. Sprinkle over apples and bake 15 mins. Reduce heat to 375F. and bake 35 mins. more.

Mrs. Ken Kleis

SOUR CREAM APPLE PIE DELUXE

8 servings

9" pastry shell, unbaked

Filling:

¾ cup sugar
2 T. flour
⅛ tsp. salt
1 cup sour cream

½ tsp. vanilla
1 egg, well-beaten
2 cups apples,
   chopped

Topping:

⅓ cup sugar
⅓ cup flour

1 tsp. cinnamon
¼ cup butter

Preheat oven to 425F. Combine sugar, flour and salt; add sour cream, vanilla and egg; add apples and place in pastry shell. Bake 15 mins.; reduce heat to 350F. and bake 30 mins.

Blend sugar, flour, cinnamon and butter until crumbly and sprinkle over top of apples. Return pie to oven and bake 15 mins. more. Refrigerate at once.

Mrs. David Carlos

SWISS APPLE PIE
6-8 servings

9" pastry shell, unbaked

Filling:

4 apples, thinly-sliced	*1½ cups heavy cream*
½ cup sugar	*2 T. butter, melted*
1 T. lemon juice	*¼ tsp. nutmeg*
3 eggs, lightly-beaten	*2 T. sugar*

Preheat oven to 400F. Combine apples, sugar and lemon juice; mix well. Place in pastry shell and bake 20 mins. Combine eggs, cream, butter and nutmeg; pour over apples. Bake 10 mins. more. Sprinkle sugar over top and continue baking until apples are done, about 10-15 mins. longer. Cool at least 2 hrs. before cutting.

Mrs. Henry Mass

BANANA PARADISE PIE
6-8 servings

very unusual

9" unbaked pastry shell

Filling:

4 cups sliced firm ripe bananas (5-6)	*1½ tsp. grated lemon rind*
¼ cup pineapple juice	*¼ cup sugar*
2 T. lemon juice	*½ tsp. cinnamon*
	1 tsp. cornstarch

Topping:

⅓ cup almonds, chopped	*¾ tsp. cinnamon*
¾ cup flour	*6 T. butter*
¾ cup brown sugar	

Preheat oven to 400F. Soak bananas in pineapple and lemon juice for 20 mins. Drain and save juices. Sprinkle lemon rind, sugar and cinnamon over banana slices. Toss lightly and place in pie plate. Heat left over juices and thicken with cornstarch. Add to pie.

Combine topping ingredients with pastry blender until crumbly. Sprinkle over bananas. Bake for 20 mins. or till crust is brown.

Mrs. Jack Dozeman

FRESH BLUEBERRY PIE   *6 servings*

pastry for double-crust 9" pie, unbaked

Filling:

1 cup sugar	*2 T. tapioca*
1 qt. fresh blueberries,	*1½ T. flour*
washed and drained	*2 T. butter*
juice of 1 lemon or 2 T.	*1 T. milk*
reconstituted lemon juice	*1 T. sugar*

Preheat oven to 425F. Combine sugar, berries, lemon juice, tapioca and flour; mix well. Pour into pastry shell and dot with butter. Top with crust, brush with milk and sprinkle with sugar. Bake 10 mins. Reduce heat to 350F. and bake 30 mins. more or until bubbly and edges are slightly brown.

Mrs. Jack De Roo

BLUEBERRY GLACE PIE   *6 servings*

½ cup margarine	*½ tsp. salt*
1 cup flour	*1 T. vinegar*
1 tsp. sugar	

Filling and Glace:

1½ cups sugar	*1½ cups water*
3 T. cornstarch	*sweetened whipped*
3 cups fresh blueberries,	*cream*
washed and drained	

Preheat oven to 400F. Use a 9" pie plate. Mix margarine, flour, sugar and salt. Sprinkle with vinegar and form into a ball. Press evenly in pie plate. Bake 12-15 mins. until golden brown. Cool.

Combine sugar and cornstarch; add 1½ cups blueberries and water, bring to a boil, stirring constantly. Cook until thick and clear. Cool. Pour remaining 1½ cups blueberries in pastry shell and pour thickened mixture over top. Chill thoroughly and top with whipped cream.

Mrs. Arthur Hills

BLUEBERRY SOUR CREAM PIE

6-8 servings

9" graham cracker or crunchy nut crust

Filling:

1½ cups sour cream
2 T. flour
3 T. brown sugar,
  firmly-packed
1 egg, well-beaten

2½ cups blueberries,
  washed and drained
½ cup brown sugar,
  firmly-packed

Preheat oven to 400F. Mix sour cream, flour, brown sugar and egg. Spoon half of mixture into pie shell. Mix blueberries with brown sugar and pour over top. Top with remaining sour cream mixture and bake 10-15 mins. Chill.

Mrs. Michael Doyle

GEORGE WASHINGTON CHERRY PIE

6 servings

pastry for double crust 9" pie

Filling:

2½ - 3 cups tart red cherries,
  pitted and drained
¼ cup cherry juice
⅔ cup sugar
3 T. cornstarch

¼ tsp. salt
⅛ tsp. red food coloring
¼ tsp. almond flavoring
2 T. butter

Preheat oven to 400F. Fill pastry shell with cherries. Combine juice, sugar, cornstarch and salt and cook over low heat until thickened, stirring constantly. Add food coloring and almond flavoring. Pour over cherries and dot with butter. Arrange strips of pastry lattice fashion over top and crimp edges. Cut a small hatchet from pastry trimmings. Bake pie 25-30 mins. Bake hatchet 10-12 mins.; place on pie after removing from oven.

Mrs. Michael Calahan

PEACHES 'N CREAM PIE
6-8 servings

¾ cup flour
1 tsp. baking powder
1 (3⅜ oz.) pkg. regular
  vanilla pudding

3 T. margarine
1 egg
½ cup milk

Filling:
3 cups fresh or canned
  peaches, sliced and drained,
  reserving juice
1 (8 oz.) pkg. cream cheese,
  softened
½ cup sugar

3 T. reserved juice or
  milk
1 T. sugar
¼ tsp. cinnamon

Preheat oven to 350F. Use a greased 9'' pie plate. Combine crust ingredients and pour into pie plate.

Spread peaches over crust. Mix cream cheese, sugar and juice and spoon over peaches within one inch of edge. Sprinkle with sugar and cinnamon. Bake 30-35 mins. until golden.

Mrs. Jay Freriks

JIFFY PEACH PIE
6 servings

9'' pastry shell, unbaked
Filling:
5-6 fresh peaches, sliced
3 T. flour
1 cup sugar

1 tsp. vanilla
1 cup heavy cream
½ tsp. cinnamon

Preheat oven to 450F. Place peaches in bottom of pie shell. Sprinkle flour and sugar over top and mix. Add vanilla and cream; sprinkle with cinnamon. Bake 10 mins.; reduce heat to 350F. and bake 50 mins. more.

Mrs. Lee Beyer

OLD FASHIONED PEACH PIE   *6 servings*

9" pastry shell, unbaked

Filling:

6-8 fresh peach halves,   *⅓ cup flour*
 peeled   *1 egg, beaten*
⅓ cup margarine, softened   *¼ tsp. vanilla*
1 cup sugar

Preheat oven to 325F. Place peach halves in pastry shell. Cream margarine, sugar and flour; add egg and vanilla and mix well. Spread mixture over peaches and bake 1 hr.

Mrs. Jack Dozeman

PEACH PRALINE PIE   *6-8 servings*

9" pastry shell, unbaked

Filling:

4 cups fresh peaches, sliced   *¼ cup brown sugar,*
½ cup sugar   *firmly-packed*
2 T. tapioca   *½ cup pecans, chopped*
1 tsp. lemon juice   *¼ cup butter*
½ cup flour

Preheat oven to 450F. Combine peaches, sugar, tapioca and lemon juice and let stand for 15 mins. Combine flour, brown sugar and pecans; cut in butter until crumbly. Sprinkle ⅓ pecan mixture on bottom of pie shell, then peaches, and top with remaining pecan mixture. Bake 10 mins.; reduce heat to 350F. and bake 25 mins. more.

Mrs. Donald Cochran

PECAN PIE
8 servings

9" pastry shell, unbaked

Filling:

4 eggs, beaten	*½ tsp. salt*
1 cup sugar	*3 T. butter, melted*
1 cup dark corn syrup	*1 cup pecans*
1 T. flour	*2 tsp. vanilla*

Preheat oven to 350F. Mix all ingredients and pour into pie shell. Bake for 55-65 mins.

Mrs. James Brooks

RUM PECAN PIE
8-10 servings

very rich

9" graham cracker crust or pastry shell, baked

Filling:

¾ cup margarine, softened	*1 oz. rum or rum flavoring*
3½ cups confectioners' sugar, sifted	*¼ tsp. salt*
5 egg yolks, beaten	*1¼ cups pecans, chopped*
1 tsp. vanilla	*sweetened whipped cream*

Cream margarine until light and fluffy. Add confectioners' sugar gradually, creaming thoroughly. Add egg yolks, vanilla, rum and salt, creaming after each addition. Stir in 1 cup pecans. Pour into crust and chill until firm. Prior to serving top with whipped cream and remaining pecans.

Mrs. Ken Michmerhuizen

RAISIN CRUMB PIE
8-10 servings

9 or 10" pastry shell, unbaked

Filling:

½ lb. seedless raisins	2 T. margarine
¾ cup cold water	1 egg, well-beaten
1½ cups sugar	½ cup milk
1 cup flour	1 tsp. baking powder

Preheat oven to 450F. Combine raisins, water and ¾ cup sugar; cook until raisins are tender and plump. Set aside to cool. Mix flour, remaining sugar, and cut in margarine until crumbly. Set aside ½ cup crumbs.

Add egg and milk to remaining crumb mixture and mix well; stir in baking powder. Fill pastry shell with raisins; pour batter over raisins and top with reserved crumbs. Bake 10 mins., reduce heat to 350F. and bake 35 mins. more.

Mrs. Leif Blodee

RHUBARB PIE SUPREME
8 servings

pastry for double-crust 10" pie, unbaked

Filling:

1½ cups sugar	6 cups rhubarb, chopped
⅓ cup flour	2 eggs, beaten
½ tsp. salt	½ cup heavy cream

Preheat oven to 425F. Sift sugar, flour and salt together. Add to rhubarb and mix well. Place in pie shell. Combine eggs and cream and pour over rhubarb. Top with crust and bake 35 mins.; reduce heat to 300F. and bake 15 mins. more.

Mrs. Donald Nitz

PINEAPPLE-RHUBARB PIE   *6 servings*

9" or 10" pastry shell, unbaked

Filling:

4 cups rhubarb, diced

1 cup crushed pineapple,
* drained*

1 ¼ cups brown sugar,
* firmly-packed*

1 T. tapioca

¼ tsp. salt

sweetened whipped cream

Preheat oven to 450F. Combine all ingredients and mix well. Pour into pastry shell and bake 10 mins.; reduce heat to 350F. and bake 30 mins. more. Cool, top with whipped cream.

Mrs. Michael Calahan

STRAWBERRY-RHUBARB PIE   *8 servings*

pastry for double-crust 9" or 10" pie, unbaked

Filling:

3 cups fresh rhubarb, diced

1 cup fresh strawberries,
* sliced*

1 cup sugar

2 eggs, beaten

2 T. cornstarch
* or tapioca*

Preheat oven to 450F. Combine all ingredients and mix well. Pour into pastry shell. Arrange strips of pastry lattice fashion over top and crimp edges. Bake 10 mins.; reduce heat to 350F. and bake 30-40 mins. more.

Mrs. Richard Oudersluys

AARDBEIEN PIE
Dutch Strawberry Pie

6-8 servings

9" pastry shell, baked

Filling:

1 qt. strawberries	½ - ¾ cup sugar
½ cup confectioners' sugar	2 T. cornstarch
1 cup water	

Combine berries and confectioners' sugar and mix well. Remove 1 cup small berries, crush, and cook with water for 2 mins. Mix sugar with cornstarch, stir into mixture and cook until clear and thickened. Fill pastry shell with whole berries and pour hot mixture over top. Cool in refrigerator.

Mrs. Fred DeWilde

JIFFY FRESH STRAWBERRY PIE

8 servings

9" or 10" pastry shell, baked

Filling:

1 qt. strawberries, halved	3 T. cornstarch
1 cup sugar	⅛ tsp. salt
1 cup water	2 T. strawberry
2 T. white corn syrup	flavor gelatin

Combine all ingredients and bring to a boil, stirring constantly, until thickened. Cool mixture and pour into pie shell. Top with a few fresh berries.

Mrs. Paul Northuis

DREAMY BANANA PIE
8 servings

1 cup vanilla wafer crumbs

½ cup pecans, chopped

¼ cup margarine, melted

Filling:

2 medium ripe bananas

½ cup light rum

1 T. fresh lemon juice

¼ cup sugar

1 envelope gelatin

3 eggs, separated, room
   temperature

2 T. banana liqueur

¼ tsp. cream of tartar

¼ cup sugar

1 cup heavy cream, whipped

mint sprigs

banana slices

Preheat oven to 350F. Use a lightly buttered 9'' pie plate. Mix crust ingredients, press firmly into pie plate and bake 10 mins. Cool.

Place bananas, rum and lemon juice in blender, process at low speed until smooth. In small saucepan, mix ¼ cup sugar and gelatin. Beat in egg yolks. Stir in ½ cup rum mixture; heat, stirring until thickened. Stir in liqueur and remaining rum mixture. Refrigerate until mixture mounds when dropped from a spoon.

Beat egg whites and cream of tartar till foamy. Add ¼ cup sugar, 1 T. at a time until stiff and glossy. Thoroughly fold in ⅓ of meringue into banana mixture, fold in remaining meringue, and then whipped cream.

Pile into pie shell and refrigerate. Garnish with banana slices and mint sprigs.

Variation: for 10'' pie. Before filling pie shell, line bottom and sides with banana slices.

Mrs. Herbert Eldean

BLACK BOTTOM PIE
8 servings

10" pastry shell, baked or graham cracker crust

Filling:

1 cup sugar
1½ T. cornstarch
⅛ tsp. salt
2 cups milk, scalded
3 eggs, separated, room
 temperature

1 (1 oz.) square unsweetened
 chocolate, melted
2 tsp. vanilla or rum extract
1 T. unflavored gelatin
¼ cup cold water
½ tsp. cream of tartar

Topping:

1 cup heavy cream, whipped
1 T. confectioners' sugar

2 T. chocolate shot

Combine ¾ cup sugar, cornstarch and salt. Add to scalded milk, cooking until slightly thickened. Add slightly beaten egg yolks, stirring constantly until mixture coats spoon, about 2 mins. Remove from heat. Measure out 1 cup of the custard and to it add chocolate and 1 tsp. vanilla. Spoon into crust, cool. Soften gelatin in water and add to remaining custard, stir until dissolved. Cool, add 1 tsp. vanilla. Beat egg whites until foamy, add cream of tartar, continue beating and gradually add ¼ cup sugar, beating until stiff. Fold into gelatin custard mixture. Spread over chocolate mixture, chill.

Before serving, whip cream until stiff, stir in sugar; spread cream on pie, sprinkle with chocolate shot.

Mrs. Kenneth De Pree

BUTTERSCOTCH PIE
6 servings

9" pastry shell, baked

Filling:

3 eggs, separated, room
 temperature
1 cup brown sugar
¼ tsp. salt

⅓ cup flour
2 cups milk
3 T. butter
1 tsp. vanilla

continued

516

Beat egg yolks; add sugar, salt, flour and milk. Cook over low heat, stirring constantly, until thick and smooth. Add butter and vanilla. Pour into pie shell and cool. Beat egg whites until stiff. Spread over filling and brown in oven.

Mrs. Paul Elzinga

SNOW CAPPED CHOCOLATE PIE
(1st Place Bake-Off)

8 servings

3 egg whites, room
  temperature
1 tsp. vanilla
¾ cup sugar
1 tsp. baking powder
1 (4 oz.) bar German Sweet
  Chocolate, grated (reserve
  2 T. for topping)

1 cup Ritz Crackers,
  crushed
½ cup nuts,
  chopped
sweetened whipped cream

Preheat oven to 350F. Grease a 9" pie plate. Beat egg whites and vanilla to soft peaks. Gradually add sugar and baking powder·and beat until stiff peaks are formed. Fold in chocolate, crackers and nuts. Spread in pie plate and bake for 25 mins. Cool and chill for 6 hrs. Prior to serving top with whipped cream and grated chocolate.

Mrs. P. Martin Smallegan

FRENCH CHOCOLATE PIE

10-12 servings

10" pastry shell, baked

Filling:
1 (12 oz.) pkg. semi-sweet
  chocolate chips
1 cup margarine
½ cup butter
2 cups confectioners' sugar,
  sifted

¼ tsp. salt
4 tsp. vanilla
6 eggs
sweetened whipped cream
chocolate curls

Melt chocolate chips and cool. Cream margarine, butter, sugar, salt and vanilla until light and fluffy. Add eggs, one at a time, beating very well after each addition. Blend in melted chocolate. Pour into pie shell and refrigerate at least 8 hrs. Prior to serving top with whipped cream and chocolate curls.

Mrs. Ray Lieffers

517

COCONUT CRUST CHOCOLATE PIE   6-8 servings

2 T. butter, softened   1½ cups shredded coconut

Filling:
1 (6 oz.) pkg. semi-sweet   4 eggs, separated,
   chocolate chips   room temperature
3 T. milk   1 tsp. vanilla
2 T. sugar   1 cup heavy cream, whipped

Preheat oven to 325F. Spread a 9" pie plate with butter. Press coconut firmly into butter. Bake 12 mins. Cool. Melt chocolate chips, milk and sugar; cool thoroughly. Beat in egg yolks and vanilla. Beat egg whites until stiff; fold into chocolate mixture. Pour into pie shell and top with whipped cream.

Mrs. Chester Nykerk

MARBLED CHOCOLATE RUM PIE   8 servings

10" pie shell, baked

Filling:
1 envelope unflavored gelatin   ¼ cup rum
¾ cup sugar   1 (12 oz.) pkg. semisweet
⅛ tsp. salt   chocolate chips
2 eggs, separated, room   1 cup heavy cream
   temperature   1 tsp. vanilla
1 cup milk

In a double boiler mix gelatin, ¼ cup sugar, and salt. Beat in egg yolks, milk and rum. Cook stirring constantly, until slightly thickened. Remove from heat and stir in chocolate until well blended. Chill until thickened but not set. Beat egg whites until foamy; gradually add ¼ cup sugar and beat until very stiff. Fold into chocolate mixture. Whip cream with remaining sugar and vanilla until stiff. Alternate two mixtures into pie shell and marble with a spoon. Chill until firm.

Mrs. Donald G. Miller

CHOCOLATE MINT TOPPER PIE

12 servings

2 - 9" chocolate or vanilla wafer pie shells
Filling:

⅔ cup butter
2 cups confectioners' sugar
2 eggs, separated, room
  temperature
2 (1 oz. each) squares
  unsweetened chocolate,
  melted

1 tsp. vanilla
¼ tsp. salt
½ gallon peppermint
  ice cream,
  softened

Cream butter and sugar, add egg yolks and beat well. Blend in chocolate, vanilla and salt. Beat egg whites and fold into chocolate mixture. Pour mixture into pie shells and freeze 1 hr. Remove from freezer and spread ice cream over top. Sprinkle top with wafer crumbs, return to freezer and remove 15 mins. before serving.

Mrs. Eugene Emerson

COFFEE SUNDAE PIE

8 servings

very rich

2 cups chocolate cream filled
  cookies, crushed (about 18)

⅓ cup margarine, melted

Filling:

1 qt. coffee ice cream,
  softened
2 (1 oz. each) squares
  unsweetened chocolate

1 T. butter
½ cup sugar
1 (5⅓ oz.) can evaporated
  milk

Combine cookies and margarine and press into a 9" pie plate. Chill. Spread ice cream over crust and freeze.

Melt chocolate and butter; add sugar and milk and cook until mixture thickens; stirring constantly. Cool thoroughly. Spread chocolate mixture over ice cream and refreeze. Remove from freezer 15 mins. before serving.

Mrs. Andrew Dalman

FUDGE SUNDAE PIE   *8 servings*
   9" vanilla wafer pie shell

   Filling:
   1 qt. vanilla ice cream,   *1 cup miniature*
   *   softened*   *   marshmallows*
   1 cup evaporated milk   *¼ tsp. salt*
   1 (6 oz.) pkg. semi-sweet   *pecans*
   *   chocolate chips*

Spread ½ of ice cream over crust and freeze. Heat milk, chocolate chips, marshmallows and salt until mixture thickens. When cool, spread ½ over ice cream. Repeat ice cream and sauce layer. Place large pecans on top and freeze. Remove 15 mins. before serving.

Mrs. Kenneth Etterbeek

COCONUT CREAM PIE   *6 servings*
   9" pastry shell, baked

   Filling:
   1 envelope unflavored gelatin   *½ tsp. vanilla*
   ¼ cup water   *½ tsp. almond extract*
   2 eggs, separated, room   *¾ cup coconut*
   *   temperature*   *¾ cup heavy cream, whipped*
   ½ cup sugar   *¼ cup toasted coconut*
   ¼ tsp. salt   *½ cup slivered almonds*
   1 cup milk

Combine gelatin and water; set aside. In a double boiler beat egg yolks with ¼ cup sugar and salt. Gradually blend in milk. Cook until thickened; add gelatin and stir until dissolved. Remove from heat and chill until partially set.

Beat egg whites until soft peaks form; slowly add ¼ cup sugar; beating until stiff and glossy. To chilled gelatin mixture add vanilla, almond extract, and coconut. Gently fold in egg whites and whipped cream. Spoon into pie shell and sprinkle with toasted coconut and almonds. Serve well chilled.

Mrs. Del Van Dyke

520

COCONUT CHESS PIE

6 servings

9" pastry shell, unbaked

Filling:
3 eggs	1 cup milk
1½ cups sugar	1 tsp. vanilla
2 T. flour	1½ cups flaked coconut
1½ T. margarine	

Preheat oven to 325F. Combine eggs, sugar, flour and margarine and beat well. Blend in milk and vanilla. Sprinkle coconut over pie shell and pour mixture over top. Bake 50 mins. or until golden brown.

Mrs. Sheldon Wettack

CHRISTMAS EGG NOG PIE

6-8 servings

9" pastry shell, baked

Filling:
1 envelope unflavored gelatin	½ tsp. salt
¼ cup cold water	½ cup hot water
4 eggs, separated, room temperature	¼ cup sugar
	3 T. rum
½ cup sugar	sweetened whipped cream
	¼ tsp. nutmeg

Soften gelatin in water. In a double boiler beat egg yolks with ½ cup sugar and ½ tsp. salt until mixture is smooth. Add hot water and cook, stirring constantly, until thick enough to coat a spoon. Stir in gelatin and cool. Beat egg whites and gradually add ¼ cup sugar until meringue holds a definite shape. Fold into custard; add rum, and pour into pastry shell. Chill until firm. Prior to serving top with whipped cream and sprinkle with nutmeg.

Mrs. Michael Calahan

GRASSHOPPER PIE   6-8 servings

15 chocolate cream filled   ⅓ cup butter, melted
   cookies, crushed

Filling:
½ cup milk   1 oz. green Creme de Menthe
20 regular marshmallows   1 oz. white Creme de Cacao
1 cup heavy cream, whipped

Combine cookies and butter, press into a 9" pie plate and chill.
Melt marshmallows with milk in a double boiler; cool slightly.
Fold in whipped cream and liqueurs, blend well. Pour into pie
shell, sprinkle with cookie crumbs and refrigerate overnight.

Mrs. Phil Fredrickson

HOLIDAY NESSELRODE PIE   8 servings

1 T. butter   ¾ cup Brazil nuts, ground
3 T. sugar   ¾ cup walnuts, ground

Filling:
1 envelope unflavored gelatin   ⅓ cup candied fruit, diced
¼ cup water   2 T. candied cherries,
2 cups light cream   slivered
½ cup sugar   ¼ cup light rum or brandy
2 eggs, separated, room   1 cup heavy cream, whipped
   temperature   shaved chocolate

Preheat oven to 400F. Spread butter over bottom and sides of a 9"
pie plate. Combine sugar and nuts and press into pie plate. Bake
10 mins. and chill.

Soften gelatin in water. Heat cream until hot in the top of a double
boiler. Add ¼ cup sugar and softened gelatin. Stir until dissolved.
Beat egg yolks slightly. Stir a little of the hot cream into the egg
yolks, then stir rapidly into the cream mixture in the double
boiler. Cook over simmering water until mixture coats a spoon.
Chill until thickened, stirring often. Beat egg whites until frothy;
gradually add ¼ cup sugar and continue beating until stiff peaks
form. Fold into cooled custard along with fruits and rum. Mix and
chill until it mounds when dropped from a spoon. Heap into shell.
Chill. Garnish with whipped cream and shaved chocolate.

Mrs. John Lomen

BLENDER LEMON MERINGUE PIE   *6 servings*

8" pie shell, baked

Filling:

3 T. cornstarch
1 cup plus 2 T. sugar
¼ cup fresh lemon juice
1 T. grated lemon rind

1 T. butter, heaping
3 egg yolks
1½ cups light cream

Meringue:

3 egg whites, room
    temperature

6 T. sugar
1 tsp. lemon juice

Combine all filling ingredients in a blender. Mix on high speed until well blended. Pour into a double boiler and cook until thick and smooth, stirring constantly. Place in crust and cool.

Preheat oven to 300F. Beat egg whites until soft peaks form; gradually add sugar and lemon juice. Beat until stiff; spread over filling and bake 30 mins.

Mrs. William Lalley

LEMON STRIP PIE   *12 servings*

2 - 8" pie shells, unbaked

Filling:

2 T. butter
1 cup sugar
juice and grated rind
    of 2 lemons
2 eggs, beaten

3 T. flour
1 cup less 2 T. light
    corn syrup
1 cup water

Stripping:

½ cup brown sugar, packed
½ cup shortening
1 egg, beaten

1 cup flour
1 tsp. baking powder
1-2 T. milk

Preheat oven to 350F. Cream butter and sugar; blend in juice and rind, add eggs and flour. Gradually beat in syrup and water; mix thoroughly and pour into pie shells.

continued

Cream together sugar and shortening; add egg and mix. Blend in flour, baking powder and milk. Separate mixture in half and roll out on floured surface. Cut in 1" strips; place over pies. Do not criss cross. Bake 30 mins.

Mrs. Jacob Van Hoff

SOUTHERN LEMON CHEESE PIE   *8 servings*

2 T. butter, softened   1½ cups shredded coconut

Filling:
12 ozs. cream cheese   rind of 1 lemon, grated
3 eggs   ¼ cup fresh lemon juice
¾ cup sugar   sweetened whipped cream
¼ tsp. salt

Preheat oven to 350F. Spread a 9" pie plate with the butter. Press coconut firmly into the butter. Beat cheese until light. Add eggs one at a time, beating thoroughly after each addition. Gradually beat in sugar; blend in salt, lemon rind, and juice. Pour into pie shell. Bake 30 mins. or until firm. Cool and chill. Prior to serving top with whipped cream.

Mrs. Dennis Brewer

LIME CHIFFON PIE   *8-10 servings*

10" pastry shell, baked or coconut crust

Filling:
1 envelope unflavored gelatin   ¼ cup water
½ cup sugar   1 tsp. lime peel, finely—
¼ tsp. salt   grated
4 eggs, separated,   green food coloring
    room temperature   ½ cup sugar
½ cup fresh lime juice   1 cup heavy cream

continued

Combine gelatin, sugar and salt. Beat together egg yolks, lime juice and water. Stir in gelatin mixture. Cook over medium heat, stirring until mixture comes to a boil. Remove from heat; add lime peel and food coloring. Chill until mixture mounds. Beat egg whites to soft peaks; gradually add sugar and beat until stiff. Beat cream until stiff and fold half of whipped cream into beaten egg whites. Fold this mixture into lime custard mixture and spoon into pie shell. Chill. Garnish with remaining whipped cream.

Mrs. Roger Prins

FLORIDA LIME PIE
8-10 servings

1 ½ cups chocolate wafer
   crumbs
1 T. sugar

¼ cup margarine

Filling:
5 egg yolks
1 (14 oz.) can sweetened
   condensed milk
½ - ¾ cup fresh lime juice

3 egg whites, room
   temperature
few drops green food coloring
sweetened whipped cream

Preheat oven to 375F. Grease a 10" pie plate. Combine chocolate crumbs, sugar and margarine until well blended. Press firmly into pie plate and bake 8 mins. Cool.

Lower oven to 325F. Beat egg yolks until thick. Slowly blend in milk and lime juice. Blend in a few drops of food coloring. Set aside. Beat egg whites until soft peaks form and waver gently on the beater. Do not overbeat. Fold egg whites gently, but thoroughly into egg yolk mixture. Spoon into cooled pie shell. Bake 20-25 mins. or until filling is firm. Cool and chill. Top with whipped cream prior to serving. A coconut crust may be used in place of the chocolate crust.

Mrs. Lee Kimzey

CALIFORNIA ORANGE CHIFFON PIE   *6 servings*

9" pastry shell, baked

Filling:

1 envelope unflavored gelatin
¼ cup cold water
4 eggs, separated, room
   temperature
1 cup sugar
½ cup fresh orange juice

1 T. lemon juice
½ tsp. salt
2 T. orange rind, grated
sweetened whipped cream
orange segments
coconut

Soften gelatin in water 5 minutes. Beat egg yolks; add ½ cup sugar, orange juice, lemon juice and salt. Cook in a double-boiler until thick. Add rind and softened gelatin and stir thoroughly. Cool. Beat egg whites until soft peaks form, gradually add remaining ½ cup sugar and continue beating. Fold whites into yolk mixture. Fill pastry shell and chill. Prior to serving spread whipped cream over filling and garnish with orange segments and sprinkle with coconut if desired.

Mrs. Michael Calahan

PINEAPPLE CHIFFON PIE   *6-8 servings*

9" pastry shell, baked

Filling:

1 envelope unflavored gelatin
¼ cup water
4 eggs separated,
   room temperature
½ cup sugar
½ tsp. salt

½ cup juice (add lemon juice
   to reserved pineapple juice)
¼ cup sugar
1 cup crushed pineapple,
   drained, reserving juice

Soften gelatin in water; set aside. Beat egg yolks; add sugar, salt and juices. Cook in double boiler until thickened, stirring constantly. Stir in gelatin until dissolved; chill until slightly thickened. Beat egg whites until soft peaks form; slowly beat in sugar, beating until stiff and glossy. Fold in pineapple. Fold egg white mixture into cooled custard. Spoon into pie shell and refrigerate.

Mrs. Tom Vander Kuy

PINEAPPLE PARTY PIE

8 servings

4 egg whites, room
    temperature
⅛ tsp. salt

½ tsp. cream of tartar
½ tsp. vanilla
1 cup sugar

Filling:
4 egg yolks
2 T. lemon juice
½ cup sugar
½ cup crushed pineapple,
    drained

⅛ tsp. salt
1 cup heavy cream,
    whipped

Preheat oven to 275F. Generously butter a 9" or 10" pie plate.
Combine egg whites, salt, cream of tartar and vanilla; beat until
stiff, add sugar gradually and continue beating until very stiff.
Spread in pie plate and bake 1 hr. Cool.

Combine egg yolks, lemon juice, sugar, pineapple and salt; cook to
boiling. Spread filling over crust. Top with cream, chill.

Mrs. Ken Etterbeek

PUMPKIN CHIFFON PIE

8 servings

9" pastry shell, baked

Filling:
1 envelope unflavored gelatin
¼ cup cold water
3 eggs, separated
    room temperature
½ cup sugar
1¼ cups pumpkin

½ cup milk
½ tsp. each: salt, ginger,
    cinnamon and nutmeg
½ cup sugar
sweetened whipped cream

Dissolve gelatin in water; set aside. Beat yolks with sugar and heat
in a double boiler. Add gelatin, stirring until dissolved; cool. Stir
in pumpkin, milk and spices. Beat egg whites, adding sugar
gradually, until stiff. Fold into pumpkin mixture. Pour into crust,
chill. Prior to serving top with cream.

Mrs. Garrell Adler

PUMPKIN ICE CREAM PIE   *8 servings*

9" pastry shell, baked or graham cracker crust

Filling:

¼ cup honey or brown sugar	*¼ tsp. salt*
¾ cup pumpkin	*1 qt. vanilla ice cream, softened*
½ tsp. cinnamon	*⅓ cup pecans, chopped*
¼ tsp. ginger	*1 cup heavy cream, whipped*
dash nutmeg and cloves	

Combine honey, pumpkin, cinnamon, ginger, nutmeg, cloves and salt; bring just to a boil, stirring constantly. Cool. Beat in ice cream; add pecans and pour into crust. Freeze until ready to serve. Garnish with whipped cream.

Mrs. Kenneth Louis

SPICY PUMPKIN PIE   *serves 8*

9" pastry shell, unbaked

Filling:

1 cup pumpkin	*½ tsp. each: salt, cloves,*
1 cup brown sugar,	*allspice*
packed	*¼ tsp. ginger*
1 tsp. cinnamon	*2 eggs, beaten*
	1 cup milk

Preheat oven to 425 F. Combine all ingredients and mix well. Pour into pie shell and bake for 10 mins. Reduce heat to 350F. and bake for 45 mins. longer.

Mrs. John Marquis

RASPBERRY SUPREME PIE

6-8 servings

8" graham cracker or crunchy nut crust

Filling:

1 (3 oz.) pkg. raspberry gelatin
¼ cup sugar
1 cup boiling water
1 (10 oz.) pkg. frozen raspberries
1 T. lemon juice
1 (3 oz.) pkg. cream cheese, softened

⅓ cup confectioners' sugar, sifted
1 tsp. vanilla
⅛ tsp. salt
1 cup heavy cream, whipped

Dissolve gelatin and sugar in boiling water. Add frozen raspberries and lemon juice. Refrigerate until slightly thickened. Blend cream cheese with confectioners' sugar, add vanilla and salt. Fold in whipped cream. Spread a layer of cream mixture over crust, then a layer of gelatin. Repeat, ending with gelatin mixture. Top with additional sweetened whipped cream, if desired.

Mrs. Marie Saunders

STRAWBERRY MILE HIGH PIE

8-10 servings

10" pastry shell, baked

Filling:

1 (10 oz.) pkg. frozen strawberries
1 cup sugar
2 egg whites
1 T. lemon juice

⅛ tsp. salt
1 cup heavy cream
1 tsp. vanilla

Beat strawberries, sugar, egg whites, lemon juice and salt in a large bowl for 15 mins., or until very stiff. Whip cream and add vanilla. Gently fold into strawberry mixture. Pour into shell and freeze. Remove 15 mins. before serving.

Mrs. Jack Miller

VIRGIN ISLAND DAIQUIRI PIE

6-8 servings

9" pastry shell, baked

Filling:

1 cup sugar	¼ cup lime juice
¼ cup cornstarch	¼ cup light rum
⅛ tsp. salt	4 egg yolks, lightly-beaten
1 cup water	green food coloring

Topping:

4 egg whites, room temperature	¼ tsp. salt
	½ cup sugar

Combine sugar, cornstarch and salt; gradually add water, lime juice, rum and egg yolks. Cook over boiling water, stirring constantly until thickened and smooth, about 8-10 mins. Tint a delicate green with food coloring. Cool thoroughly and spoon into pie shell.

Preheat oven to 350F. Beat egg whites until soft peaks form; gradually add salt and sugar. Beat until stiff; spread meringue on filling and bake 15 mins.

Mrs. Michael Calahan

530

ZUIDER ZEE PIE

6 servings

1 (5¼ oz.) pkg. rusk,
   finely-crushed
½ cup margarine, softened

¼ cup sugar
1 tsp. cinnamon

Filling:
¼ cup sugar
2 T. cornstarch
¼ tsp. salt
2 cups milk

2 eggs, separated, room
   temperature
½ tsp. vanilla
¼ cup sugar

Preheat oven to 375F. Use a buttered 9" pie plate. Combine all ingredients, press firmly into pie plate saving a small amount for the top. Bake for 8 mins. Cool.

Combine sugar, cornstarch and salt in sauce pan. Gradually stir in milk. Cook over moderate heat, stirring constantly, until mixture thickens. Boil 1 min. and remove from heat. Beat egg yolks and stir in ½ of cooked mixture. Return this to mixture in pan and boil 1 min. more; stirring constantly. Add vanilla and pour into crust. Beat egg whites until soft peaks form, gradually add ¼ cup sugar and continue beating until stiff. Spread meringue on filling and sprinkle with remaining topping. Bake at 425F. for 5 mins. Serve warm or chilled.

Mrs. William G. Winter

NOTES

Kitchen Pantry

NOTES

APPLE MINT JELLY

4 lbs. tart green apples,
  quartered
1 cup mint leaves, crushed,
  tightly packed

3 cups sugar
few drops green food
  coloring

Place apples in pan with enough water to just cover. Boil until soft. Mash apples well and pour into a jelly bag (4 layers of cheese cloth). Let the juice drip overnight. DO NOT SQUEEZE. Measure 4 cups apple juice and pour into large pan. Tie mint leaves in 2 thicknesses of cheese cloth, add to juice. Add food coloring. Boil juice for 10 mins. Add sugar and continue to boil until syrup thickens (when 2 or 3 drops run together at the edge of spoon, hang a second and fall off). Remove mint bag, skim jelly and pour into hot, sterile glasses. Cover at once with a thin layer of paraffin. Cover jars with lids or foil.

Mrs. John Shepherd

APRICOT AND PINEAPPLE JAM   2 pints

2 cups apricots, peeled
  and chopped
3 cups sugar

2 cups crushed pineapple,
  partially drained
juice of ½ lemon

Mix apricots and sugar. Boil until partially thickened (20 mins.) Add pineapple and lemon juice; bring to a slow boil. Pour into hot sterile jars and seal.

Mrs. R. L. Doolittle

BLUEBERRY-PEACH JAM
7½ pints

2 cups blueberries, mashed
2 cups peaches, peeled and
finely-chopped

2 T. lemon juice
1 box powdered fruit pectin
5 cups sugar

Combine fruit and lemon juice in a large saucepan. Add pectin, mix well. Place over high heat and stir until mixture comes to hard boil. Add sugar at once. Bring to a full boil that cannot be stirred down. Boil hard 1 min. stirring constantly. Remove from heat, skim off foam. Ladle into clean jars. Adjust lids, screwing band on tightly. Invert jars. When sealed shake jar to keep fruit from floating.

Mrs. Jay Freriks

RHUBARB CONSERVE

3 lbs. rhubarb, cut
in pieces
7 cups sugar

1 lb. raisins
½ lb. walnuts, chopped

Cook rhubarb in a very small amount of water, to prevent sticking. Add sugar and raisins. Cook until thickened, stirring constantly. Add nuts. Pour immediately into hot, sterile jars and seal.

Mrs. Fred DeWilde

DILL PICKLES

cucumbers
cold water
fresh dill weed
1 tsp. mustard seed per jar
⅛ tsp. alum per jar

3 garlic buds per jar, if desired
1 qt. vinegar
3 qts. water
1 cup salt

Scrub cucumbers, soak in cold water overnight. Place 3 heads of dill in bottom of jar. Fill jar with cucumbers, add 3 more heads of dill. Add mustard seed, alum and garlic. Combine vinegar, water and salt; bring to a boil. Pour over cucumbers. Seal.

Mrs. Dave Lamar

DILL PICKLES

cucumbers, washed
fresh dill weed
garlic cloves
celery seed
mustard seed

alum
horseradish leaf, cut up
2 qts. cider vinegar
2 cups salt
3 qts. water

Put cucumbers into sterile quart jars. To each jar add 2 heads of dill, 1 clove garlic, ½ tsp. each of celery seed, mustard seed, alum and horseradish leaf. Heat together vinegar, salt and water; boil 5 mins. Pour over pickles and seal.

Mrs. E. J. Bacheller

SWEET GARLIC DILLS   4 qts.

12 heads dill weed
cucumbers, sliced
   lengthwise
garlic buds

3 cups vinegar
1 cup water
2½ cups sugar
3 T. salt

In each of 4 (1 qt. each) jars put 3 heads of dill weed, sliced pickles and 2-3 tiny buds of garlic. Combine vinegar, water, sugar and salt. Bring to a boil and immediately pour over pickles in jars. Seal.

Mrs. Lyle Sprik

BREAD AND BUTTER PICKLES
7 pints

4 qts. cucumbers, thinly-sliced
8 med. onions, thinly-sliced
2 green peppers,
    finely-chopped
2 red sweet peppers,
    finely-chopped

3 T. salt
3 cups sugar
1 tsp. tumeric
1 T. celery seed
1 T. mustard seed
3 cups vinegar
1 cup water

Combine cucumbers, onions and peppers with the salt; let stand 3 hrs. Drain. Place cucumbers in large kettle; add the remaining ingredients, mixing well. Bring to a boil and quickly remove from heat. (Do not boil or pickles will not be crisp.) Immediately ladle into sterile jars and seal.

Mrs. Walter Baron

CINNAMON CUCUMBER RINGS
9 pints

Nice addition to holiday relish trays.

large cucumbers
2 cups salt
8½ qts. water
1 cup vinegar
1 T. powdered alum

1 tsp. food color (red or green)
6 cups vinegar
12 cups sugar
2 cups water
4 sticks cinnamon

Peel cucumbers. Cut in thirds crosswise; remove seeds. Slice in ½" ring. (Should be 2 gals.) Add salt and 8½ qts. water; let stand 5 days and drain.

In large kettle combine cucumbers, 1 cup vinegar, alum, food color and enough water to cover. Simmer 2 hrs. Drain.

Combine 6 cups vinegar, sugar, 2 cups water and stick cinnamon. Bring to a boil and pour over rings; let stand overnight. Drain; reheat syrup and pour over rings. Repeat for 3 days. On 3rd day pack rings into hot, sterile jars. Pour in boiling syrup and seal.

Mrs. Jay Freriks

MUSTARD PICKLES

4 qts. cucumbers, thinly-sliced	2 tsp. celery seed
2 qts. onions, chopped	2 T. tumeric
3 T. salt	1 qt. vinegar
water	3 cups sugar
	flour

Combine cucumbers, onions and salt; add enough water to cover and let stand overnight. The next day combine the remaining ingredients and bring to a boil. Drain the pickles and add to the syrup. Boil for 30 mins. Add enough flour to thicken. Immediately pour into hot sterile jars and seal.

Mrs. Richard Johnson

NO-GARLIC DILLS   1 quart

2 cups vinegar	1 T. mixed pickling spices
2 cups water	5 cups sugar
1 stick cinnamon	1 qt. cucumbers, quartered

Boil first 4 ingredients for 15 mins. Add sugar. Boil 5 more mins. Cool. Add cucumbers to juice. Let set for several days.

Mrs. David Paulson

SWEET ONION PICKLES
1 quart

1 qt. dill pickles
cold water
¾ cup cider vinegar

2 cups sugar
1 T. pickling spice
1 small onion, thinly-sliced

Drain pickles; cover with cold water and let stand 30 mins. Drain pickles and cut into chunks. Combine remaining ingredients and stir until sugar dissolves. Pour over pickles. Refrigerate 2 days or longer.

Mrs. Jack I. Dykstra

VIRGINIA CHUNK SWEET PICKLES

2 cups salt
water
75 5" pickles
alum
water

6 cups vinegar
8 cups sugar
⅓ cup pickling spice
1 tsp. celery seed

Boil salt in 1 gal. water; immediately pour over pickles in a large crock. Let stand 1 week. (Skim daily in hot weather.) Drain and cut into chunks. Make a boiling solution of 1 gal. water and 1 T. alum and pour over pickles. For the next 2 days, pour off this solution, make a fresh supply and pour over pickles. On the 4th day, drain. Heat vinegar, 5 cups sugar, pickling spices and celery seed to boiling and pour over the pickles. On the 5th day drain the syrup and reserve. Add 2 cups sugar to reserved syrup and bring to a boil. Pour over pickles. On the 6th day, drain and save syrup. Add 1 cup of sugar to syrup and bring to a boil. Pack pickles in hot, sterile jars and cover with boiling syrup.

Mrs. E. J. Bacheller

AUNT MAGGIE'S WATERMELON RIND PICKLES

5 lbs watermelon rind, peeled
   and cut into small chunks
½ tsp. alum
2 T. salt
water

5 lbs. sugar
1 pt. white vinegar
1 T. whole cloves
1 T. cassia buds
1 stick cinnamon

Combine rind, alum and salt in a pan with enough water to cover. Boil until tender. Blanch in cold water and drain very well. Combine remaining ingredients. Boil 15 mins. Add rind and cook until transparent. Let mixture stand overnight; reheat and pour into hot sterile jars. Seal.

Mrs. Lewis Vande Bunte

PICKLED ONIONS

4 qts. tiny onions
water
1 cup salt
2 qts. white vinegar

2 cups sugar
¼ cup pickling spice (tied in
   a cheesecloth bag)

Cover onions with boiling water; let stand 2 mins. Drain. Cover with cold water, add salt and let stand overnight. Drain. Rinse thoroughly with cold water. Combine vinegar, sugar and spice bag; boil several mins. Remove spice bag and add onions. Bring to a full boil. Immediately pack into hot, sterile jars. Seal.

Mrs. Jay Freriks

SPICED PEACHES

½ bushel small uniform
  size peaches
6 lbs. sugar

1 qt. vinegar
3-4 sticks cinnamon
2-3 cloves per peach

Peel peaches. Combine sugar and vinegar; heat to dissolve sugar. Add stick cinnamon. Tie cloves in a cheesecloth bag; add to syrup. Heat syrup thoroughly and drop peaches in syrup. Cook until peaches become slightly transparent but not mushy. Pack in hot, sterile jars and fill with syrup. Seal.

Mrs. Donald Wassink

PICKLED PEARS
3-4 pints

3½ lbs. ripe pears
1 qt. water
1 T. vinegar
2½ cups sugar
1¼ cups vinegar

1 cup water
2 tsp. whole ginger
2 T. whole cloves
7 sticks cinnamon

Peel and core pears. Place immediately in 1 qt. water with 1 T. vinegar added. Combine sugar, vinegar and water; bring to a boil. Tie spices in a cloth bag and add to syrup. Cover; boil 5 mins. Remove spices. Add pears, simmer 2 mins. Pack pears in hot pint jars. Add syrup to within ½" of top. Seal. Process in boiling water bath for 30 mins.

Mrs. Jay Freriks

CRANBERRY-ORANGE RELISH

1 large orange
1 lb. cranberries
1 cup raisins

½ cup honey
⅔ cup sugar
1½ tsp. ginger

Cut orange in quarters, remove seeds and put through food chopper along with the cranberries. Add remaining ingredients; mixing well. Chill.

Mrs. Ronald Dalman

542

CORN RELISH

18 ears of corn	4 cups sugar
4 green peppers	1/3 cup salt
3 red peppers	1 qt. vinegar
1 qt. cucumbers	2 T. mustard seed
2 qts. tomatoes	1 T. tumeric
1 qt. onions	2 T. celery seed

Cut corn from cob. Grind remaining vegetables. Mix all ingredients together. Boil until corn is tender and mixture thickens. Immediately pour into hot sterile jars and seal.

Mrs. Harold Vander Bie

HARVEST CORN RELISH 12 pints

24 ears corn	4 cups sugar
2 green peppers, chopped	1 tsp. celery seeds
2 red sweet peppers, chopped	1 qt. vinegar
4 medium onions, chopped	1/2 cup flour
1 lg. cabbage, finely-chopped	1 tsp. tumeric
1/3 cup salt	3 T. dry mustard

Cut corn from ears. Combine vegetables, salt, sugar, celery seed and vinegar together in a large kettle. Boil 15-20 mins. To thicken mixture add flour, tumeric and dry mustard. Immediately pour into hot, sterile jars and seal.

Mrs. Lee Van Aelst

GREEN TOMATO PICKLE 16 pints

1 peck green tomatoes, sliced	5 lbs. onions, chopped
1 cup salt	3 green peppers, chopped
3 lbs. brown sugar	3 T. pickling spice,
2 qts. vinegar	tied in cheese cloth bag

Combine tomatoes and salt. Let stand overnight. Drain. Dissolve brown sugar in vinegar, add to tomatoes along with remaining ingredients. Bring to a boil and simmer slowly 2½ hrs. Remove spice bag. Pour into hot, sterile jars and seal.

Mrs. Jay Freriks

GREEN TOMATO RELISH 16 pints

1 peck green tomatoes,
   finely-chopped
½ cup salt
water
1 med. cabbage, chopped
24 onions, chopped
1 qt. vinegar

1 qt. water
6 cups sugar
1 tsp. cinnamon
1 tsp. ground cloves
1 tsp. pepper
1 tsp. allspice

Combine tomatoes with salt and enough water to just cover. Let stand overnight. Drain. Mix all vegetables together, add remaining ingredients and bring to a full boil. Immediately pour into hot sterile jars and seal.

Mrs. Lee Van Aelst

PENNSYLVANIA DUTCH PICKLED BEETS AND EGGS
Pretty addition to relish tray.

2 (14 oz. each) cans beets
vinegar
sugar

12 eggs, hard-boiled, peeled
water

Drain beets, reserve juice. Measure juice and add to it equal amounts of sugar and vinegar. Heat to dissolve sugar. Place eggs in bottom of jar or covered container; add juice and beets. If necessary add water to cover. Refrigerate several days for best taste and color.

Mrs. Dean Gladfelter

RAW TOMATO RELISH

1 peck tomatoes
4 hot peppers or
  3 green and 3 sweet red
6 onions
1 cup salt

1 qt. vinegar
5 cups sugar
1 bunch celery, chopped
  or ground

Grind tomatoes, peppers and onions. Add salt, mix well. Let drain in a bag overnight. Boil vinegar and sugar together. Let cool and pour over vegetable mixture. Add celery. Pour into hot, sterile jars and seal.

Mrs. Ida Washburn

SWEET RELISH

2 qts. cucumbers,
  coarsely-ground
1 qt. green tomatoes,
  coarsely-ground
1 qt. onions, ground
1 T. salt

1 cup water
1 qt. vinegar
3 cups sugar
1 T. mustard seed
1 T. celery seed

Boil ground vegetables with salt and water for 5 mins., drain well. Add remaining ingredients; simmer 30 mins. Pour into hot sterile jars and seal.

Mrs. E. J. Bacheller

CHILI SAUCE
8-9 pints

36 tomatoes, peeled and
  chopped
4-6 large sour apples, peeled
  and chopped
6 onions, chopped
2 sweet red peppers, chopped
3 green peppers, chopped

6-7 stalks, celery, chopped
2 sticks cinnamon
2 T. salt
1 T. celery seed
1¾ cups sugar
1 cup brown sugar
1 qt. vinegar

Combine all ingredients. Cook slowly over low heat at least 6 hrs., stirring often. Test thickness of sauce by putting 1 T. in a saucer. If very little water is present it is ready to can. Pour hot sauce into hot, sterile jars. Seal.

Mrs. Don Judd

CHILI SAUCE

20 lg. tomatoes	1 cup vinegar
5 lg. onions	2 cups sugar
2 bunches celery	1 tsp. cinnamon
3 green peppers	1 tsp. pepper
1 red bell pepper	1 tsp. ground cloves
2 T. salt	1 tsp. allspice

Put vegetables through a food grinder. Place in a large kettle; add remaining ingredients. Cook all day over low heat until thickened, stirring occasionally. Immediately pour into hot, sterile pint jars. Seal.

Mrs. Donald Wassink

KETCHUP   5 pints

48 medium tomatoes (8 lbs.)	3 T. salt
2 sweet red peppers, cut in strips	3 tsp. dry mustard
2 green peppers, cut in strips	½ tsp. ground red pepper
4 onions, quartered	1½ tsp. whole allspice
3 cups vinegar	1½ tsp. whole cloves
3 cups sugar	1½ tsp. broken stick cinnamon

Quarter tomatoes; remove stem end. Add peppers and onions. Put vegetables in blender. Blend at high speed. To blended vegetables add vinegar, sugar, salt, dry mustard, pepper and remaining spices tied in a cloth bag. Simmer uncovered several hours until volume is reduced ½; stir occasionally. Remove spices. Immediately pour into hot, sterile jars. Seal.

Mrs. Jay Freriks

TACO SAUCE   3 pints

5-6 stalks celery,
    coarsely-chopped
1 green pepper,
    coarsely-chopped
1 (16 oz.) jar hot cherry
    peppers, undrained

2 tomatoes
1 T. oil
¼ cup catsup
salt and pepper to
    taste

Combine all ingredients in blender; blend until vegetables are finely-chopped.

Sauce can be frozen. Keeps several weeks in refrigerator.

Mrs. Laverne Brummel

TOMATO-ZUCCHINI SAUCE   3 pints
Delicious with all meats.

¼ cup margarine
1 medium onion, chopped
1 clove garlic, minced
2 stalks celery, sliced
1 medium green pepper,
    chopped
2 medium zucchini, sliced

6 medium tomatoes, peeled
    and chopped
2 tsp. thyme
2 tsp. salt
1 tsp. sugar
½ tsp. pepper
1 bay leaf

Melt margarine in 4 qt. saucepan. Add onion, garlic, celery and green pepper. Cook until tender. Add remaining ingredients. Simmer, covered 45 mins. Remove bay leaf.

Freezes well.

Mrs. Hal Thornhill

TOMATO JUICE

1 peck tomatoes
2 medium onions, sliced

2 T. salt
4 T. brown sugar

Wash tomatoes. Remove stem end and cut in pieces. Add onions. Cook until soft. Press through a sieve to remove seeds and skins. Add salt and sugar to juice. Heat to boiling. Immediately pour into hot, sterile jars. Seal.

Mrs. Merle Berens

SNIJBOONTJES
Green Beans

The Dutch use a long flat green bean grown for this purpose, but regular green beans can be used.

green beans   **salt**

Slice beans diagonally into very thin slices. Place a 3" layer of beans into a jar, add 1 T. salt and stamp down. Continue adding beans and salt and stamp until it is covered with its own juice and jar is full. Seal jars. This will keep throughout the winter.

When ready to serve, soak overnight in cold water; drain. Cook until tender; drain. Add bacon drippings and serve.

Mrs. Chris Sas

CANNED PEACHES

½ cup sugar, per quart   **peach pits**
peaches, peeled and halved   **hot water**

Place sugar in bottom of each qt. jar. Fill jars with peach halves and one peach pit. Cover peaches with very hot water, leaving 1½" head space. Adjust lids. Process in boiling water bath for 20 mins.

Aileen Goddard

SEASONED SALT

1 cup salt   **1½ tsp. oregano**
2½-3 tsp. paprika   **1 tsp. garlic powder**
2 tsp. dry mustard   **½ tsp. onion salt**

Combine all ingredients. Pour into salt shaker.

Use as you would commercial seasoned salt. Much more economical!

Mrs. Lawrence Schmidt

Celebrity and Restaurant Fare

NOTES

RUBY-RED GRAPEFRUIT CHICKEN   *4 servings*

2 ruby-red grapefruit
½ cup whole cranberry sauce
1 T. honey
¼ tsp. cloves
¼ tsp. salt
1 (2½-3 lb.) fryer, disjointed
3 T. butter

Peel and section grapefruit, squeezing all juices from membranes into saucepan. Add cranberry sauce, honey, cloves and salt, mixing well; then bring to a boil. Stir in grapefruit sections. Preheat oven to 350F. Brown chicken in butter, then place in shallow baking dish. Baste with grapefruit sauce. Bake 45 mins., basting frequently. Serve chicken with remaining sauce.

Mrs. Betty Ford,
First Lady

PARTY CHICKEN   *8 servings*

4 whole chicken breasts,
  skinned, boned and split
¼ cup butter
salt and pepper
2 (1 lb. each) cans small
  potatoes, drained
1 cup cooked ham, cubed
1 (4 oz.) can button
  mushrooms, drained
2 T. flour
2 cups heavy cream
½ cup white wine
1 (1 lb.) can white grapes,
  drained

Sauté chicken breasts in butter. Season with salt and pepper. Transfer to a buttered 9" x 13" casserole. Brown potatoes in chicken drippings. Place potatoes, ham and mushrooms around the chicken breasts. Preheat oven to 350F. Make a cream sauce; using drippings in the skillet, blend in the flour, and slowly stir in the cream and wine. Cook until smooth and thickened. Pour the sauce over the ingredients in the casserole. Cover and bake 45 mins. Add grapes the last 10 mins. of cooking.

This is especially good served with a grapefruit and orange salad.

Helen Milliken, wife of
Governor William G. Milliken

CRAB A LA MARTIN
4 servings

1 (7½ oz.) can crab meat, drained
3 T. butter
3 T. flour
1½ cups tomato juice
1 T. onion, grated
¼ cup green pepper, chopped
1 tsp. salt
1½ cups cooked rice
pepper to taste
⅔ cup mayonnaise
buttered bread crumbs

Preheat oven to 400F. Melt butter, add flour and gradually add tomato juice. Cook until thickened, stirring constantly. Remove from heat. Add onion, green pepper, crab, salt, pepper and rice. Fold in mayonnaise. Place in 1½ qt. casserole or individual shells. Sprinkle with bread crumbs. Bake uncovered 20-30 mins. May be prepared and stored in refrigerator day before using.

Dollie Cole
wife of Edward Cole,
retired President, General
Motors Corporation

ESCABECHE DE POISSON
8 servings

2 lbs. fish filets
1 tsp. salt
juice of 2 lemons
¼ cup flour
¼ cup olive oil
1 onion, thinly sliced
1 carrot, sliced
1 pimento, sliced
8 green olives, thinly sliced
2 garlic cloves, minced
3 T. wine vinegar
lemon wedges and chopped parsley, for garnish

Cut filets in small pieces about the size of smelts. Sprinkle with salt and let stand for 30 mins. Dip pieces in lemon juice; dust lightly with flour and sauté well on all sides in oil, then remove cooked fish. To drippings add onion, carrot, pimento, olive slices and garlic. Sauté until onions turn golden. Then add vinegar and pour hot mixture over fish. Let stand covered in refrigerator for 24 hrs. Serve hot or cold as a first course. Garnish with lemon wedges and chopped parsley.

Cristina Ford
Wife of Henry Ford II, Board
Chairman, Ford Motor Company

COUNTRY PIE

8 servings

½ cup tomato sauce
½ cup bread crumbs
1 lb. ground round
¼ cup onions, chopped

¼ cup green pepper, chopped
1½ tsp. salt
⅛ tsp. pepper
⅛ tsp. oregano

Filling:
1⅓ cups raw Minute Rice
1½ cups tomato sauce
½ tsp. salt

1 cup water
1 cup grated cheese

Preheat oven to 350F. Use an ungreased 9" pie plate. Combine first 8 ingredients and mix well. Pat into pie plate to form crust.

Combine filling ingredients, saving ½ of cheese, and place in meat shell. Cover with foil. Bake 30 mins. Uncover, top with rest of cheese and bake uncovered 15 mins.

Robert P. Griffin
U.S. Senator

SALMON CASSEROLE

4 servings

1 lb. can red salmon
½ cup mayonnaise
2 T. chili sauce

¾ cup seedless dark raisins
cracker crumbs

Preheat oven to 300F. Use a well greased 1½ qt. casserole. Remove bones and skin from salmon. Break into large chunks. Cover the bottom of the casserole with half the salmon. Combine mayonnaise, chili sauce and raisins. Pour one half over the salmon in the casserole; add another layer of salmon, followed by the rest of the sauce. Cover with cracker crumbs. Bake until hot and bubbly.

Martha W. Griffiths
retired U.S. Congresswoman

CUCUMBER SOUP
4 servings

2 large cucumbers
1 tsp. cinnamon
1 tsp. salt

1 qt. buttermilk
fresh chopped mint

Peel cucumbers, cut in lengths, and dice (removing seeds). Add salt and cinnamon and stir well. Add buttermilk and refrigerate until very cold. Serve with mint sprinkled on top.

Jane Hart
wife of Senator Philip Hart

BAKED CHICKEN BREASTS SUPREME
6 servings

6 whole chicken breasts,
  halved and boned
2 cups sour cream
¼ cup lemon juice
4 tsp. celery salt
2 tsp. paprika
4 garlic cloves, minced

4 tsp. salt
½ tsp. pepper
1¾ cups dry bread crumbs
½ cup butter
½ cup shortening
4 tsp. Worcestershire sauce

Rinse breasts and wipe well with paper towels. In a large bowl, combine sour cream with lemon juice, celery salt, paprika, garlic cloves, salt and pepper. Add chicken to sour cream mixture, coating each piece well. Marinate in refrigerator overnight.

Preheat oven to 350F. Remove chicken from sour cream mixture and roll in crumbs, coating well. Arrange in a large shallow baking pan. Melt butter and shortening; spoon half over chicken. Bake, uncovered, 45 mins. Spoon remaining butter over chicken, and bake 10-15 mins. longer or until chicken is tender and nicely browned.

Louise Kaline,
Wife of Al Kaline,
retired Tiger baseball star

RAISIN BREAD

4 loaves

¼ cup warm water
2 pkgs. dry yeast
1 quart milk, scalded
½ cup butter
1 cup sugar

1 tsp. salt
3 eggs, slightly beaten
11½ - 12½ cups flour
1½ lbs. raisins

Sprinkle yeast over warm water. In a large bowl, mix together milk, butter, sugar, salt and eggs. Cool to just about lukewarm; add dissolved yeast. Add flour gradually until it can be mixed with hands without sticking. Knead 8-10 mins. Place in a greased bowl, cover and let rise in a warm place until double, about 2 hrs. Punch down dough and knead in raisins. Divide into 4 parts and let rest 10 mins. Roll each part into a 9" x 14" rectangle, roll into loaf. Place in greased 9½" x 5½" loaf pan. Repeat. Bake in preheated 400F. oven for 30 mins. Remove from pan and brush top with butter. Extra loaves may be frozen.

Dorothy Kresge,
Wife of S.S. Kresge,
founder of Kresge Foundation

TIGER BOBS

beef and pork cubes
2 eggs, beaten
1½ cups corn flake crumbs

dash of onion salt, garlic
salt and salt
2 T. Parmesan cheese
butter

Preheat oven to 350F. Dip meat cubes in eggs then in a mixture of crumbs, seasonings and cheese. Coat each cube well. Alternate beef and pork cubes on skewers. Place in shallow, greased baking dish and dot with butter. Bake 25 mins., turn and bake 20 mins. longer.

Joyce Lolich
wife of Tiger pitcher,
Mickey Lolich

BUCK'S BREAD PUDDING

4-6 servings

3 eggs
1 qt. milk
½ cup sugar

2 tsp. vanilla
4-6 slices broken, stale bread
nutmeg

Preheat oven to 400F. Use a 1½ qt. casserole. Beat eggs; add milk, sugar, and vanilla. Mix thoroughly. Stir in bread. Pour into casserole and sprinkle with nutmeg. Bake uncovered for 50-60 mins. Delicious hot or cold.

Buck Matthews,
Grand Rapids Television
Personality, WOTV

LENORE'S COFFEE CAKE

9 servings

½ cup butter
¾ cup sugar
2 eggs
1 ⅔ cup flour
1½ tsp. baking powder
½ tsp. soda

1 cup sour cream
1 tsp. vanilla
½ cup brown sugar
½ cup pecans, chopped
½ cup raisins, optional
2 tsp. cinnamon

Preheat oven to 350F. Use a greased 9" x 9" baking dish. Cream butter and sugar together. Add eggs, one at a time, beating well after each. Sift together flour, baking powder and soda. Add to creamed mixture alternately with sour cream. Stir in vanilla. Pour half into baking dish. Combine brown sugar, pecans, raisins and cinnamon. Sprinkle over batter in baking dish and cover with the rest of the batter. Bake 35 mins.

Lenore Romney
wife of former State Governor,
George Romney

FROZEN PUNCH

1 (6 oz.) can frozen
  Hawaiian Punch
1 (6 oz.) can frozen limeade

2 cans of water
3 cans of rum

Mix all ingredients together and allow to freeze overnight. Spoon into small glasses and serve immediately with demitasse spoons.

Ruth Townsend
wife of Lynn Townsend, retired
Board Chairman, Chrysler Corporation

FROSTBITE
10-12 servings

2 (1 oz. each) squares semi-
  sweet chocolate, grated
1 envelope unflavored gelatin
¼ cup cold water
3 eggs, separated,
  room temperature
½ cup sugar

1½ cups milk
pinch of salt
1 tsp. vanilla
2 T. sugar
1 cup heavy cream,
  whipped

Grease an 8" x 12" oblong dish. Sprinkle bottom with grated chocolate (reserve some for top). Dissolve gelatin in cold water. Set aside. Beat egg yolks and sugar until thick; add milk. Cook over double boiler pan until mixture coats a spoon. Add gelatin and stir until dissolved. Thoroughly cool. Add vanilla and salt. Beat egg whites until frothy; gradually beat in 2 T. sugar. Beat until stiff. Fold into cooled custard. Fold whipped cream into mixture and pour into dish. Sprinkle remaining chocolate over top. Cover, and refrigerate overnight.

Betty Van Andel,
Wife of Jay Van Andel,
Board Chairman, Amway Corporation

OVERNIGHT SALAD
12 servings

1 head of lettuce,
shredded, dry well
1 large Bermuda onion,
thinly sliced
1 lb. bacon, fried and
crumbled

1 head cauliflower, broken up
¼ cup sugar
⅓ cup Parmesan cheese
salt and pepper to taste
2 cups top-quality mayonnaise

In a large bowl layer first 4 ingredients in order given. Sprinkle over top sugar, cheese, and seasonings. Spread mayonnaise over all. Cover and refrigerate overnight. Just before serving toss well.

Carol Vander Jagt,
Wife of U.S. Congressman
Guy Vander Jagt

CELERY CRISP
8 servings

5½ cups celery, cut
diagonally into slices
1 (10¾ oz.) can cream of
celery soup

½ cup light cream
½ cup pecans, chopped
2 cups Ritz crackers, crushed
½ cup butter, melted

Preheat oven to 375F. Use an ungreased 9" x 9" baking dish. Cook celery in salt water 6-8 mins. Drain. Combine with soup, milk and nuts. Pour into baking dish. Combine cracker crumbs and butter, sprinkle over top of celery mixture. Bake uncovered for 30 mins.

Nancy Williams
wife of G. Mennen Williams,
former State Governor

FRANKENMUTH BEAN SALAD   10-12 servings

1 lb. Michigan small navy
   beans
1¼ cups celery, diced
½ cup onions, chopped
½ cup green pepper, chopped
½ cup garlic dressing (or
   any vinegar and oil dressing)
½ cup vinegar

½ cup sugar
1 tsp. dry mustard
½ tsp. garlic salt
¼ tsp. paprika
¾ tsp. M.S.G.
½ tsp. salt
several pimentos

Soak beans overnight. Cover beans with water and simmer on top of stove until tender. Drain, then add remaining ingredients. Let stand 4 hrs. in refrigerator before serving.

Bavarian Inn
Frankenmuth, Michigan

BROILED SHRIMP BROCHETTE   4-6 servings

2 lbs. frozen shrimp, peel
   leaving tail on and devein
1 cup olive oil
1 pinch oregano, rubbed
dash Worcestershire sauce

2 T. lemon juice
½ T. salt
½ tsp. M.S.G.
pinch of black pepper

Sauce Bercy:
2 cloves garlic, chopped fine
4 shallots, chopped fine
½ cup dry white wine
2 T. rich fish or chicken broth

2 T. cold butter
squeeze of lemon juice
pinch of chopped parsley

Place shrimp in a bowl; combine remaining ingredients and pour over shrimp. Marinate 12 hrs., covered in refrigerator. After marinating, place on skewers, dust lightly with paprika and broil till firm and white inside. Do not overcook.

Prepare sauce by combining garlic, shallots, and wine; bring to a boil and boil until reduced to half. Add broth; remove from heat and whip in butter, lemon juice and parsley. Pour over shrimp. Serve with a rice pilaf.

The Caucus Club
Detroit, Michigan

GREEN GODDESS DRESSING   2 cups

1 garlic clove, minced
2 T. green onion tops,
  chopped
1 T. anchovy paste
½ cup sour cream

1 cup mayonnaise
2 T. tarragon vinegar
½ tsp. pepper
½ tsp. lemon juice
1 drop green food coloring

Make a fine paste with the garlic, green onion, and anchovy paste. Add to sour cream. Combine with remaining ingredients. Mix well, and refrigerate at least 2 hrs. before using. Serve with green salads, shrimp, or crabmeat.

The Dearborn Inn
Dearborn, Michigan

VEAL A LA GOLDEN MUSHROOM   4 servings

4 (4 oz. each) veal cutlets
salt
freshly ground pepper
¼ cup butter
¼ cup onions, chopped

2 cups fresh mushrooms,
  sliced
1 cup white wine
1 cup sour cream

Pound veal thin with meat hammer. Sprinkle both sides with salt and pepper. In a skillet, brown both sides in butter over moderate heat. Add onions, and cook until transparent. Add mushrooms and wine; cook for 3 mins.

Transfer the veal to a hot platter. Add the sour cream to the drippings; stir and pour over the veal.

Golden Mushroom
Southfield, Michigan

560

SWISS ONION SOUP

12 servings

½ cup butter
2 lbs. onions, thinly sliced
1½ tsp. paprika
¾ cup flour
½ cup oil
¾ tsp. celery salt
salt and pepper to taste

6 cups beef stock
1 cup dark beer
12 slices bread, buttered
 and sprinkled with
 Parmesan cheese and
 paprika, then toasted
½ cup Parmesan cheese

Melt butter; add onions and cook until onions are soft. Add paprika. Make roux (thickening for sauce) by browning flour and oil, being certain it is evenly browned. Add to onion mixture the roux, celery salt, salt, pepper and beef stock; stir until it boils. Simmer, covered for 2 hrs. Prior to serving, add beer to soup. Bring to serving temperature. Pour into soup bowls. Add slice of toast to each bowl and sprinkle soup with Parmesan cheese.

Jim's Garage
Detroit, Michigan

CHOCOLATE FUDGE NUT BARS

1½ lb. sugar (3¼ cups)
1½ cups shortening
pinch of salt
1½ cups flour
6 eggs
1 cup pecans, chopped

7 T. cocoa
6 T. water
vanilla to taste
chocolate fondant icing
chopped pecans

Preheat oven to 400F. Grease a 17" x 12½" baking pan. Combine first 9 ingredients in mixing bowl and mix slowly until all ingredients are thoroughly blended. Do not over mix. Spread batter evenly in pan. Bake 20 mins., or until firm to the touch. Cool, turn out of pan and cover reverse side of bar with fondant icing and sprinkle with nuts. Cut into desired size pieces.

Grand Hotel
Mackinac Island, Michigan

HUDSON'S FIESTA SALAD

4 servings

Ambrosia Salad:

2 cups pineapple chunks,
   drained

2 cups oranges, diced

2 cups peaches, diced
   and drained

1 cup sweetened whipped
   cream

Blend above ingredients together and refrigerate.

Arrange on 4 lettuce-lined plates the following.

A mound of ambrosia salad, garnished with a rosette of whipped cream and shredded coconut sprinkled over the whipped cream.

Next to the salad, place a canned peach half filled with cottage cheese and garnished with a maraschino cherry.

Place on the same plate a pear half filled with lime sherbet.

Garnish plate with strawberries or your choice of fresh fruit and berries.

Fill your favorite breads with your favorite sandwich mixtures and cut into small triangles. Serve tea sandwiches on same plate or place on separate platter.

The J. L. Hudson Company
Detroit, Michigan

SAUERBRATEN WITH SOUR-CREAM GRAVY

8-10 servings

4-5 lb. pot roast
   or rump roast

1 T. salt

pepper

1 large onion, chopped

10 peppercorns

6 whole cloves

3 bay leaves

1 cup vinegar

1 cup water

1 cup Burgundy wine

2 T. cooking oil

2 T. sugar

¼ cup flour

1 cup sour cream

continued

562

Rub meat with salt; sprinkle with pepper. Place in large glass bowl. Combine onion, peppercorns, cloves, bay leaves, vinegar, water, and Burgundy wine. Bring to a boil. Cool. Pour over meat, cover and refrigerate for 36-48 hrs., turning meat several times a day. Remove meat from marinade, reserving marinade. Heat oil and brown meat on all sides. Add marinade and simmer over low heat for 1½ - 2 hrs., or until tender. Remove meat from pan; strain marinade and add water to marinade to make 4 cups. Return marinade to pan. Whisk in flour and sugar and cook until smooth and thickened. Add sour cream to gravy, heat through but do not boil. Slice meat and add to gravy.

The Little Cafe
Detroit, Michigan

SALMON FILET WITH SAUCE WILLIAM   4 servings

**4 (12 oz. each) filets of
fresh salmon**

**1½ cups clarified butter
½ cup dry sherry**

Sauce William:
2 cups mayonnaise
2 egg yolks
juice of 1 lemon

2 tsp. paprika
½ tsp. white pepper
1 tsp. chives, diced fine

Preheat oven to 350F. Place filets, skin down, on a buttered sheet pan. Pour butter over filets, then sprinkle sherry over filets. Bake for 25 mins.

Combine sauce ingredients with a wire whip for 2 mins. Refrigerate for 3 hrs. to achieve best results.

After baking filets, place on individual oven-proof platters. Ladle sauce over each filet. Immediately put under broiler until brown. Serve immediately or sauce may curdle. Serve with a lemon and parsley garnish. Wine: Vouvrey.

The Mariner's Inn
South Haven, Michigan

CHICKEN CACCIATORE
6-8 servings

3 (2½ lb. each) sectioned
  chickens

Cacciatore Sauce:
1 cup corn oil
2 lbs. onions
½ lb. fresh mushrooms,
  sliced
1 T. parsley, chopped
6 cloves of garlic, chopped

2 green peppers, sliced
1 cup dry sauterne wine
3 lbs. peeled tomatoes
1 cup water
salt and pepper

Prepare and fry chicken using your favorite method. Remove to a platter and keep warm. Place oil in a heavy casserole. Add onions. Saute until golden; add mushrooms and simmer 5 mins. Add parsley, garlic, and green peppers. Simmer 5 mins. longer; add wine and simmer 5 mins. Add tomatoes, water and salt and pepper to taste. Simmer 2½ hrs., stirring frequently. Add chicken to finished sauce and simmer 15 mins. Serve with spaghetti.

Mario's
Detroit, Michigan

MEDALLIONS OF BEEF TENDERLOIN WITH MUSHROOMS
4 servings

12 (2 oz. each) slices of
  beef tenderloin
salt and pepper
½ cup clarified butter
¾ lb. fresh mushrooms, sliced

6 shallots, finely chopped
⅓ cup medium-dry sherry
½ cup heavy cream
1 T. brandy
chopped parsley

Heat a skillet (large enough to hold meat without crowding) until smoking hot. Season meat with salt and pepper. Put half of the butter in and then the meat. Brown over high heat on one side, turn, brown on other side and transfer to a warm platter.

Add rest of butter, mushrooms and shallots; cook, stirring constantly, until mushrooms turn grey. Add sherry and cook rapidly till almost all moisture evaporates. Add cream and cook until sauce becomes syrupy. Add brandy and parsley and pour over meat.

London Chop House
Detroit, Michigan

POINT WEST FRENCH CHOCOLATE PIE   8 servings

9" baked pastry shell or
graham cracker crust

Filling:

¾ cup butter	*3 eggs*
1 cup sugar	*1 T. vanilla*
2 (1 oz. each) squares	*sweetened whipped cream*
unsweetened chocolate,	
melted and cooled	

Cream butter. Add sugar slowly and whip till smooth. Blend in chocolate. Add eggs one at a time, whipping 5 mins. after each (very important). Add vanilla. Pour into pie shell. Chill several hrs. Top with whipped cream.

Point West
Macatawa, Michigan

SHRIMP DE JONGHE   *8 appetizer servings*

24 raw shrimp	*16 tsp. Dry Sack sherry*
flour	*paprika*
8 tsp. Italian style	*butter*
bread crumbs	*parsley and lemon wedges*
½ cup Casino Butter	
(see below)	

Remove shells from shrimps, leaving tail on; butterfly and season lightly with salt. Drench shrimp in flour. Use 8 small ramekins or sea shells. Place in each the following in the order as given. Sprinkle 1 tsp. bread crumbs over the bottom; place 3 shrimp on the crumbs. Cover with 1 T. casino butter, add 2 tsp. sherry and sprinkle with paprika. Dot with butter. Place under broiler until golden. Serve with a sprig of parsley and a lemon wedge. These may be assembled early in the day and refrigerated.

River Crab
St. Clair, Michigan

CASINO BUTTER

1 lb. butter, softened
2 garlic cloves, crushed
pinch of salt and white
   pepper
1 tsp. fresh parsley, chopped

6 T. sauterne wine
1 tsp. each pimento and
   green pepper, chopped
1 anchovy strip,
   crushed

Mix all ingredients together using a mixer as the wine must be well mixed. It is very important in using as soft butter-like consistency.

Note: If using fresh green pepper instead of canned, boil for 5 mins. Chop fine and mix with other ingredients.

River Crab
St. Clair, Michigan

VEAL SCALLOPINE A LA TOSCA   2 servings

8 pieces veal cutlet
salt and pepper
2 eggs
½ cup half and half

2 T. Parmesan cheese
1 garlic clove, minced
1 tsp. parsley, chopped
flour
olive oil or corn oil

Pound meat to medallion size. Salt and pepper each side. Beat eggs; add cream, cheese, garlic and parsley. Pat meat in flour, then dip in egg mixture. Saute in oil until meat is brown on both sides (approximately 5 mins. total for both sides)

Roma Cafe
Detroit, Michigan

CARAMEL ICE CREAM PIE
8 servings

1 egg white
¼ tsp. salt
¼ cup sugar
1½ cups walnuts, chopped

2 T. margarine, softened
1 pt. coffee ice cream
1 pt. vanilla ice cream

Caramel Sauce:
3 T. butter
1 cup brown sugar, firmly
  packed

½ cup light cream
⅓ cup walnuts, chopped
1 tsp. vanilla

Preheat oven to 400F. Beat egg white with salt until stiff but not dry; gradually beat in sugar. Fold in walnuts. Turn into a very well buttered 9" pie plate. Spread evenly on bottom and sides, but not rim. Bake 10-12 mins. Cool, then chill. Fill with layers of coffee and vanilla ice cream. Serve with caramel sauce. (Pie shell may be filled with ice cream and stored in freezer until serving time.)

For sauce, melt butter in small sauce pan, add brown sugar. Remove from heat. Slowly stir in cream. Heat for 1 min. longer. Remove from heat; stir in walnuts and vanilla. Serve warm or cold over pie.

Win Schuler's
Marshall, Michigan

CHICKEN LIVERS SOMERSET
4 servings

1 lb. chicken livers
salt
1 medium onion, thinly
  sliced
2 T. butter
¼ cup chicken broth

¼ cup white wine
1 large tart apple, peeled,
  cored and thickly sliced
1 T. sugar
1 T. parsley, chopped

Sprinkle livers with salt. Sauté onions in butter until translucent; add livers and continue cooking until browned. Add broth and wine and cook to desired degree of doneness.

At last min. add apple slices, which have been sprinkled with sugar, and cook only until they begin to soften. Top with parsley.

Somerset Inn
Troy, Michigan

BLACK FOREST TORTE

8-10 servings

1 ¾ cups flour
1 ¾ cups sugar
1 ¼ tsp. soda
1 tsp. salt
¼ tsp. baking powder
1 tsp. vanilla

⅔ cup tub type margarine
   (a must)
4 oz. unsweetened chocolate,
   melted and cooled
1 ¼ cups water
3 eggs

Fillings:
6 oz. German sweet
   chocolate, melted and cooled
¾ cup tub type margarine
½ cup toasted almonds, chopped

2 cups heavy cream
1 T. sugar
1 tsp. vanilla

Preheat oven to 350F. Grease bottoms and sides of four 9" round cake pans and line bottom with wax paper and grease well. In a large mixing bowl combine flour, sugar, soda, salt, baking powder, vanilla, margarine, chocolate and water. Beat together 4-5 mins. Add eggs and beat 2 mins. longer. Pour evenly into prepared pans. Bake 15-18 mins. Cool before filling.

Prepare chocolate filling by blending cooled chocolate into margarine. When thoroughly blended and smooth, stir in nuts. Set aside. Prepare cream filling by whipping cream with sugar and vanilla; beat stiff.

Place 1 cake layer on plate, spread with ½ chocolate filling, next layer with ½ cream filling. Repeat, having cream on top. Chill.

Shield's
Traverse City, Michigan

GRAN FETTUCINE EMILIO
6 servings

2 T. butter
2 T. olive oil
1 medium onion, finely
  chopped
1 large carrot, finely
  chopped
1 large celery stalk,
  finely chopped
¾ lb. ground round

¼ lb. Italian sausage
¼ tsp. freshly ground pepper
salt to taste
1 cup tomato sauce
1½ cups dry white wine
1¼ cups beef broth
6 oz. prosciutto, sliced
  ⅛" thick
½ lb. fresh mushrooms, sliced

Bechamel Sauce:
½ cup butter
½ cup flour
1 quart milk

½ tsp. freshly ground pepper
½ tsp. ground nutmeg

Pasta:
1 lb. fettucine or other
  broad egg noodles

¾ cup freshly grated
  Parmesan cheese
¼ tsp. freshly ground
  black pepper

Heat butter and oil in a 4 quart Dutch oven. Add onion, carrot and celery; cook until tender. Add meats and cook until brown. Drain off fat. Stir in pepper, salt, tomato sauce, ½ cup wine and beef broth; simmer, covered, 1 hr. Trim fat from prosciutto and place fat in a 10" skillet. Cook over low heat until fat is rendered. Remove and discard any brown pieces. Add mushrooms to fat in skillet; cook until just colored, adding a little butter if necessary. Cut prosciutto into julienne strips. Add prosciutto and remaining wine to skillet; simmer 5 mins. Stir prosciutto mixture into meat sauce.

Prepare sauce. Melt butter over low heat in a 2 quart saucepan. Blend in flour with a wire whisk; cook 1 min. Add milk gradually, stirring constantly until mixture thickens and comes to a boil. Remove from heat and add seasonings.

Blend bechamel sauce into meat sauce with a wire whisk. Cook fettucine according to pkg. directions; drain. Reheat sauce. Toss fettucine and sauce in a large bowl or tureen to coat well. Sprinkle with cheese and freshly ground pepper.

Tosi's
Stevensville, Michigan

PORK ROAST WITH SWEET AND SOUR SAUCE

4 generous servings

4 (1 lb. each) center cut
rib (not loin) pork roasts

baked apples, garnish

Sauce:

2 cups sugar
1 cup distilled vinegar
2 T. green pepper, chopped
1 tsp. salt
1 cup water

4 tsp. cornstarch
2 T. water
2 tsp. paprika
parsley, finely chopped

Preheat oven to 450F. Place pork roasts in pan bone side down and brown in oven for 30 mins. Remove from oven when well browned and transfer to a deep baking dish with bone side up. Pour sauce over pork and bake 2½ hrs. at 300F., or until pork is tender. Baste occasionally. To serve, place on platter with sauce spooned over pork. Garnish with baked apples.

Prepare sauce while pork is browning. Mix sugar, vinegar, green pepper and salt with water. Simmer 5 mins. Combine cornstarch in 2 T. water and add to first mixture. Cook and stir until sauce thickens. Cool. Strain out green pepper. Add paprika and a bit of parsley.

The Vineyards
Southfield, Michigan

TABLE OF EQUIVALENTS

FOOD	AMOUNT	EQUIVALENT
Apples	1 lb. (3 medium)	3½ cups pared and sliced
Apricots	1 lb.	3 cups dried, 6 cups cooked
Bananas	1 lb. (3 medium)	2 - 2½ cups sliced
Beans, lima or navy, dried	1 lb. (2⅓ cups)	6 cups cooked
Bread	1 slice	¼ - ⅓ cup dry crumbs
Bread	1 slice	¾ - 1 cup soft crumbs
Cabbage	1 lb.	5 cups shredded
Cheese, hard	1 lb.	4 cups, grated
Chicken	3½ lbs.	2 cups cooked and diced
Crackers, graham	15	1 cup fine crumbs
Crackers, soda	22	1 cup fine crumbs
Cream, heavy	1 cup	2 cups whipped
Egg Whites	8-11	1 cup
Egg Yolks	12-16	1 cup
Garlic	1 medium clove	¼ tsp. chopped
Lemon or Lime	1 medium	3 - 4 T. juice
Lemon, rind	1 medium	1½ - 2 tsp. grated
Lettuce	1 lb.	6¼ cups torn
Mushrooms, fresh	½ lb.	2½ cups sliced
Noodles	1 cup uncooked	1¾ - 2 cups cooked
Onions	1 medium	½ cup chopped
Orange	1 medium	⅓ cup juice
Orange, rind	1 medium	2 T. grated
Peaches	4 medium	2 cups sliced
Pears	4 medium	2 cups sliced
Potatoes	1 lb. (3 medium)	2½ cups, sliced/diced, 2 cups mashed
Spaghetti	1 lb. uncooked	7 cups cooked
Strawberries	1 qt.	4 cups sliced
Tomatoes	1 lb. (3 medium)	1 cup juiced, chopped pulp
Vanilla Wafers	22	1 cup fine crumbs
Zwieback	6 oz.	2 cups fine crumbs

TABLE OF SUBSTITUTIONS

IF YOU DON'T HAVE	YOU CAN SUBSTITUTE
1 tsp. beef extract	1 beef bouillon cube
1 tsp. baking powder	⅓ tsp. baking soda plus ½ tsp. cream of tartar
1 oz. chocolate	¼ cup cocoa plus ½ T. fat
1 cup cake flour	1 cup minus 2 T. all-purpose flour
1 cup sour cream	1 cup evaporated milk plus 1 T. vinegar or lemon juice
1 cup sour milk or buttermilk	1 T. lemon juice or vinegar plus sweet milk to make 1 cup
1T. cornstarch (for thickening)	2 T. flour
1 cup whole milk	1 cup reconstituted dry milk plus 2 tsp. butter or margarine
1 cake compressed yeast	1 pkg. active dry yeast
1 T. fresh herbs, chopped	1 tsp. dried herbs
1 tsp. dry mustard	1 T. prepared mustard
1 garlic clove	⅛ tsp. garlic powder
1 cup tomato juice	½ cup tomato sauce plus ½ cup water
1 cup ketchup or chili sauce	1 cup tomato sauce plus ½ cup sugar and 2 T. vinegar
¾ cup honey	1 cup sugar (add to liquids)
1 tsp. lemon rind	1 tsp. lemon extract
¾ cup evaporated milk	1 cup whipping cream
1 cup molasses	1 cup honey
1 T. arrowroot	2½ T. flour for every cup of liquid
⅞ cup lard	1 cup butter
1 tsp. lemon juice	½ tsp. vinegar
1 lb. fresh mushrooms	6 oz. canned
1 cup yogurt	1 cup buttermilk
1 cup sugar (in baking)	1 cup molasses, plus ¼ to ½ tsp. soda. Omit baking powder

INDEX

574

579

587

Order Form

Holland Junior Welfare League
P.O. Box 1633
Holland, Michigan 49422
www.hjwl.org

Book Title	Quantity	Price Per Book*	Total
Eet Smakelijk		$17.50	$
Dawn to Dusk		22.50	
Dutch Treat *(one book each of the above titles)*		35.00	
		Grand Total	$

Name _____

Address _____

City_____ State _____ Zip _____

*Price includes shipping and handling charge.

The proceeds from the sales of these cookbooks will be disbursed to qualifying applicants who share in our passion for the welfare of our community's youth.

Holland Junior Welfare League
P.O. Box 1633
Holland, Michigan 49422
www.hjwl.org

Book Title	Quantity	Price Per Book*	Total
Eet Smakelijk		$17.50	$
Dawn to Dusk		22.50	
Dutch Treat *(one book each of the above titles)*		35.00	
		Grand Total	$

Name _____

Address _____

City_____ State _____ Zip _____

*Price includes shipping and handling charge.

The proceeds from the sales of these cookbooks will be disbursed to qualifying applicants who share in our passion for the welfare of our community's youth.